The Death of the Internet

The Death of the Internet

Edited by

Markus Jakobsson

IEEE PRESS

A JOHN WILEY & SONS, INC., PUBLICATION

HIGHER EDUCATION PRESS

Published by John Wiley & Sons, Inc., Hoboken, New Jersey.
Published simultaneously in Canada.

No part of this publication may be reproduced, stored in a retrieval system, or transmitted in any form or by any means, electronic, mechanical, photocopying, recording, scanning, or otherwise, except as permitted under Section 107 or 108 of the 1976 United States Copyright Act, without either the prior written permission of the Publisher, or authorization through payment of the appropriate per-copy fee to the Copyright Clearance Center, Inc., 222 Rosewood Drive, Danvers, MA 01923, (978) 750-8400, fax (978) 750-4470, or on the web at www.copyright.com. Requests to the Publisher for permission should be addressed to the Permissions Department, John Wiley & Sons, Inc., 111 River Street, Hoboken, NJ 07030, (201) 748-6011, fax (201) 748-6008, or online at http://www.wiley.com/go/permission.

Limit of Liability/Disclaimer of Warranty: While the publisher and author have used their best efforts in preparing this book, they make no representations or warranties with respect to the accuracy or completeness of the contents of this book and specifically disclaim any implied warranties of merchantability or fitness for a particular purpose. No warranty may be created or extended by sales representatives or written sales materials. The advice and strategies contained herein may not be suitable for your situation. You should consult with a professional where appropriate. Neither the publisher nor author shall be liable for any loss of profit or any other commercial damages, including but not limited to special, incidental, consequential, or other damages.

For general information on our other products and services or for technical support, please contact our Customer Care Department within the United States at (800) 762-2974, outside the United States at (317) 572-3993 or fax (317) 572-4002.

Wiley also publishes its books in a variety of electronic formats. Some content that appears in print may not be available in electronic formats. For more information about Wiley products, visit our web site at www.wiley.com.

Library of Congress Cataloging-in-Publication Data:

Jakobsson, Markus.
    The death of the Internet / by Markus Jakobsson.
        pages cm
    Includes bibliographical references.
    ISBN 978-1-118-06241-8 (pbk.)
    1. Internet–Security measures.   2. Electronic commerce–Security measures.
3. Data protection.   4. Computer crimes.   I. Title.
    TK5105.875.I57.J34 2012
    005.8–dc23
                                                    2011047198

Printed in the United States of America.
10 9 8 7 6 5 4 3 2 1

For A and Art.

Contents

Foreword

It is tempting to believe that Internet security is somebody else's problem, or that it is a problem that eventually will vanish, as technology improves. This is a dangerous belief; burglary has not vanished because of improvements in door and window locks, and Internet security is similarly unlikely to change as technology gets better. In considering the recent past, I think it is easy to say that increased awareness of Internet security has not had much impact on the rate of victimization of consumers. Given how many Internet users there now are—significantly over 1 billion people, and as high as 2 billion by some counts—consciously improving the rate of awareness of populations at this scale is incredibly difficult and time consuming. And technology leaps often make things worse, quite as much as they make things better.

This is not a Chicken Little situation of "the sky is falling, the sky is falling," but we will find ourselves in an increasingly difficult situation soon, unless we start to pay more attention to Internet problems than we have done in the last few years. To begin with, we need to ensure that we not only understand the problem—and not just its manifestation—but also its underlying reasons for being. Then, we need to start designing new technology to save ourselves—and our users—from greed and crime, from the very things that have made the Internet so successful: how efforts scale, how everybody can participate, and from the low costs of entry. We also need to consider possible regulation, as it is unlikely that the technology industry's call for self-regulation will be heeded any more than that of the road or aviation industries in the 1910s and 1920s.

Let me tell you a little bit about myself first, to give you some perspective on my viewpoint. I have been a technology strategist for nearly three decades, honing my craft first within the confines of a corporate environment, but in recent years increasingly looking outside that mothership. In the early 2000s, I spent quite a bit of time in the identity space—I was President of the Liberty Alliance, which was an open standards consortium that developed the first meaningful identity federation protocol, SAML 2.0. Since 2006, I have been CISO at PayPal. Given PayPal's global reach, the size of our user base (in mid-2011, over 100 million active customers) and the nature of our systems, which move money from any arbitrary point A to point B on the planet, we tend to find ourselves at the leading edge of new classes of criminal attacks. Willy nilly, we find ourselves having to craft solutions to problems that the rest of the industry barely recognizes as problems, let alone admits there are solutions for.

Here is what I believe we must do. We must begin by understanding our vulnerabilities, whether they are social or technical. We must then instrument our systems, both technical and societal, to collect metrics about everything relevant. After all, how can we argue about reality objectively without having hard data about it? And then we must take the next step, and measure what is not yet reality—trying to predict behaviors and vulnerabilities, in other words. With these hard won insights, we must then create plans for the future. You cannot design a system—especially not a security system—without understanding what affects security and *everything* that affects security.

That is what this book is about. It describes the Internet, and the mobile Internet, in a crisp and convincing manner. It is infused with the anticipation of trends and describes how these will affect us, for good and bad. And it gives examples of novel approaches that we can take to change the course of the future, and avoid what otherwise may become what the title of the book states—The Death of the Internet.

I encourage anyone with an interest in the Internet; in technology; in online commerce, or indeed in a fair and open society to read this book. These are important topics and this book does an excellent job in provoking alternative ways of thinking about them.

MICHAEL BARRETT

San Jose, CA
May 2012
Chief Information Security Officer, Paypal

Preface

Imagine life without electricity. Although most of humankind has managed just well without electricity, its loss would certainly impact society most profoundly. Now imagine that hundreds of thousands of criminals all over the world could make a quick profit by doing something that—little by little—killed the electric infrastructure. And that politically adversarial individuals and governments could speed up this looming catastrophe if they wanted to. It is terrible to imagine. And yet, it is a very real threat—although to the *Internet*.

Criminals have an array of ways to abuse the Internet. Most commonly in order to make money: Internet crime is both profitable and safe for criminals to engage in. Online crime scales exceptionally well, and is fast to perpetrate. It is often difficult to identify abuse, and almost always difficult to track down the criminals. And most of the time, offenders who are detected and blocked simply vanish, only to resurface with a new pseudonym shortly thereafter. While financial abuses are difficult to block and track, *politically* motivated abuse is yet harder to control. This is since politically motivated attacks do not involve taking money out of the system—which is often the hardest and riskiest part of online crime.

Any disruptions to the Internet would send shock waves through society. It would affect telephony; banking; how corporations do business; how the energy grid is controlled; and how many of us make a living. It would disrupt government, media, and military. It would impact our entire infrastructure—including our *trust* infrastructure.

Like a bridge that may tolerate increasing strains until it comes crashing down, the Internet may hold up well until the tipping point is reached. We must not wait for that moment. We must understand the problems, and defend against them—before they develop, if possible. We must understand how things can go wrong, and how we can engineer things better.

This book describes the problems the Internet is facing, and gives examples of some possible solutions. You do not need a deep technical background to understand the *general nature* of these. At the same time, each chapter has in-depth material for readers who do not want to stop at understanding the general concepts, but who want to know *exactly* how things work.

I hope that the insights that you will gain by reading this book will help you make decisions or designs—depending on who you are—that will help rescuing the Internet from the assault it is under.

Markus Jakobsson, PhD

Mountain View, CA
May 2012
Principal Scientist of Consumer Security, PayPal

Is the Title of this Book a Joke?

Maybe you thought the title of this book was simply chosen to demand attention, or a silly joke, and that the Internet cannot realistically be killed. If that is so, I want to start off by convincing you that it just is not so. *Killed* sounds drastic. Let us for a moment say "rendered useless" or "more or less abandoned." Is *that* possible?

You may ask: What would render the Internet useless? And what would make people abandon it? Let me start off my explanation with an analogy.

> Think about traveling by air. We all know that some flights get delayed. But most are not, and those that are delayed are only *reasonably* delayed. A few hours at most, but most often, they are delayed much less than that. We also know that people die in airplane accidents most every year. But most travelers arrive safe.
>
> Imagine that most flights arrived late, and often quite drastically delayed. Maybe a week, maybe two. And imagine further that airplane accidents became dramatically more common. Maybe half of all flights would not arrive *at all*, but everybody on the flight would end up on the bottom of the ocean.
>
> Nobody in their right mind would fly if this were so. It would render air travel useless from a practical perspective, and people would abandon it and take the train, or even walk rather than setting foot in an airplane. In other words, these increases of inconveniences and risks would *kill* aviation.

Now, let us talk about the Internet. The first commercial spam message was sent on March 5, 1994 by an Arizona-based law firm. In the years to follow, spam became more and more prevalent. Still, it shocked a lot of people when the amount of spam overtook that of legitimate emails. Many did not think that it could *ever* become that bad. In spite of impressive advancements in spam blocking technologies, *less than 5%* of email is legitimate at the time of writing, and most of us receive one or two spam messages every day. But a spam message that manages to sneak by the filters typically only wastes a few seconds of our time, with no further consequences to the typical recipient. Things *could* be worse.

> What would happen if, in spite of our best efforts to keep the Internet secure, less than 5% of websites were secure, and the rest were hosting malware? Defenses may improve, but what if our normal activities still resulted in malware slipping through once or twice a day? What would be the consequences to online commerce if only 5% of advertisements were honest, and the rest attempted to defraud buyers? Looking from the other side, what would advertisers do if 95% of users had infected computers that constantly were committing clickfraud? How would we be affected if less than 5% of the information we find was correct?
>
> The likely answer is that there would be a *drastic* change in how we use the Internet, and what we *dare* to use it for. Following our aviation analogy, these increases of inconveniences and risks could and *would* kill the Internet.

That is what this book is about. This book explains what might kill the Internet by making it useless and dangerous. And how we are inching toward a tipping point where the result would be the death of the Internet. Where is that point? Nobody knows.

This book also investigates what can be done to stop that from happening, given a thorough understanding of what the problem is. It does not contain an exhaustive list of all the dangers, and certainly not a complete list of meaningful solutions. But it *does* explain how to think about the problems and the solutions in a way that helps you—and others like you—start thinking about how we can prevent the death of the Internet. We depend too much on it to let it go.

So, no, the title of the book is not a cheap attention grabber or a joke. *I* am serious when I say that the *situation* is too serious.

Acknowledgments

Internet security—and *in*security—is both a compelling and terrifying topic to write about. Even more than other aspects of the Internet, it is amorphous and under constant evolution—fueled by both the introduction of new features and services and the criminal realization that these offer new opportunities. It is a vast topic. It is technical, legal, and social. It requires an understanding of the markets, computing, and psychology. You may feel that reading this book is much like drinking from a fire hose. This is also how writing it has been.

We would like to thank BITS and the BITS Security Steering Committee for permitting the reuse of portions of the BITS Malware Risks and Remediation Report. The full report, developed by members of the BITS Security Working Group, is publicly available at http://www.bits.org. BITS addresses issues at the intersection of financial services, technology, and public policy, where industry cooperation serves the public good, such as critical infrastructure protection, fraud prevention, and the safety of financial services. BITS is the technology policy division of the Financial Services Roundtable, which represents 100 of the largest integrated financial services companies providing banking, insurance, and investment products and services to the American consumer.

I could not have pulled this off on my own, and I am indebted to my many contributors, all of whom have invested their time and passion in making this book fantastic. In particular, I want to thank Ruj Akavipat, Adam Barth, Dan Boneh, Garth Bruen, Igor Bulavko, Elie Bursztein, Juan Caballero, Richard Chow, Michael Conover, Mayank Dhiman, Ori Eisen, Bruno Gonçalves, Baptiste Gourdin, Mark Grandcolas, Jeff Hodges, Mohammad Hossein Manshaei, Jean-Pierre Hubaux, Nathaniel Husted, Hampus Jakobsson, William Leddy, Debin Liu, Filippo Menczer, Steven Myers, Dimitar Nikolov, Yuan Niu, Adrienne Porter Felt, Ariel Rabkin, Emilee Rader, Gustav Rydstedt, Elaine Shi, Christopher Soghoian, Dawn Song, Sid Stamm, Andy Steingruebl, Nevena Vratonjic, David Wagner, Rick Wash, Ruilin Zhu, and Members of the BITS Security Working Group and staff leads Greg Rattray and Andrew Kennedy.

I know few people as hardworking and dedicated as Liu Yang, and I owe my sanity to him for helping me with all practical issues surrounding conversions to LaTeX, hacking the template to make things look nice, and ensuring that everything was complete.

I am also thankful for the administrative help I have received from Wiley and HEP. Finally, thanks to all my wonderful colleagues, many of whom also contributed to this book.

Contributors

Ruj Akavipat, Department of Computer Engineering, Mahidol University, Bangkok, Thailand

Adam Barth, IMDEA Software Institute, Google, Inc., University of California, Berkeley, San Francisco, CA, USA

Dan Boneh, Department of Computer Science and Electrical Engineering, Stanford University, Stanford, CA, USA

Garth Bruen, KnujOn.com LLC, Brookline, MA, USA

Igor Bulavko, PayPal, Inc., San Jose, CA, USA

Elie Bursztein, Security Laboratory, Computer Science Department, Stanford University, Stanford, CA, USA

Juan Caballero, IMDEA Software Institute, Madrid, Spain

Richard Chow, Palo Alto Research Center (PARC), Palo Alto, CA, USA

Michael Conover, School of Informatics and Computing, Indiana University, Bloomington, IN, USA

Mayank Dhiman, PEC University of Technology, Ambala, Chandigarh, India

Ori Eisen, The 41st Parameter, Inc., Scottsdale, AZ, USA

Adrienne Porter Felt, Computer Science Division, University of California, Berkeley, CA, USA

Aurélien Francillon, EURECOM, Sophia Antipolis, France

Philippe Golle, Google, Inc., Mountain View, CA, USA

Bruno Gonçalves, Northeastern University, Boston, MA, USA

Nathan Good, Principal Good Research LLC, Berkeley, CA USA

Baptiste Gourdin, LSV, INRIA & ENS-Cachan, Paris, France

Mark Grandcolas, FatSkunk, Inc., Mountain View, CA, USA

Jeff Hodges, PayPal, Inc., San Jose, CA, USA

Jean-Pierre Hubaux, School of Computer and Communication Sciences, EPFL, Lausanne, Switzerland

Nathaniel Husted, School of Informatics and Computing, Indiana University, Bloomington, IN, USA

Hampus Jakobsson, Independent Researcher, Limhamn, Sweden

Markus Jakobsson, PayPal, Inc., San Jose, CA, USA

Andrew Kennedy, BITS/The Financial Services Roundtable, Washington, DC, USA

William Leddy, PayPal, Inc., Georgetown, Washington, DC, USA

Debin Liu, Information Risk Management, PayPal, Inc., Austin, TX, USA

Mohammad Hossein Manshaei, Department of Electrical and Computer Engineering, Isfahan University of Technology, Isfahan, Iran

Ryusuke Masuoka, Fujitsu, Sunnyvale, CA, USA

Filippo Menczer, School of Informatics and Computing, Indiana University, Bloomington, IN, USA

Jesus Molina, Fujitsu, Sunnyvale, CA, USA

Steven Myers, School of Informatics and Computing, Indiana University, Bloomington, IN, USA

Dimitar Nikolov, School of Informatics and Computing, Indiana University, Bloomington, IN, USA

Yuan Niu, Yahoo!, Sunnyvale; University of California, Davis, CA, USA

Adrian Perrig, Cybersecurity Laboratory (CyLab), Department of Electrical and Computer Engineering, Department of Engineering and Public Policy, and School of Computer Science, Carnegie Mellon University, Pittsburgh, PA, USA

Ariel Rabkin, Electrical Engineering and Computer Science Department, University of California, Berkeley, CA, USA

Emilee Rader, Department of Telecommunication, Information Studies and Media, College of Communication Arts and Sciences, Michigan State University, East Lansing, MI, USA

Greg Rattray, Delta Risk LLC, Washington, DC, USA

Gustav Rydstedt, Blizzard Entertainment, Huntington Beach, CA, USA

Elaine Shi, Palo Alto Research Center (PARC), University of California, Berkeley, CA, USA

Christopher Soghoian, Center for Applied Cybersecurity Research, Indiana University, Bloomington, IN, USA

Dawn Song, IMDEA Software Institute, Google, Inc., Computer Science Department, University of California, Berkeley, CA, USA

Jeff Song, Fujitsu, Sunnyvale, CA, USA

Sid Stamm, Independent Security and Privacy Researcher, Santa Clara, CA, USA

Andy Steingruebl, Information Risk Management, PayPal, Inc., San Jose, CA, USA

Dahn Tamir, Entropy Management Services, Techlist, Las Vegas, NV, USA

Nevena Vratonjic, School of Computer and Communication Sciences, EPFL, Lausanne, Switzerland

David Wagner, Computer Science Division, University of California, Berkeley, CA, USA

Rick Wash, School of Journalism, and Department of Telecommunication, Information Studies and Media, Michigan State University, East Lansing, MI, USA

Ruilin Zhu, Peking University, Beijing, China

Part I

The Problem

If you only know half the rules of a game, do you *think* you can win?

We need to understand what is wrong before we can fix it. But the problem is not always simple. When we deal with the Internet, it almost *never* is. We need to understand the *technical* aspects of the problem. What is computed, what is stored, how can what we want to do go wrong? And the *social*—how people think, how do they make mistakes? These people—that includes *both* the potential victims and their attackers—why *do* they do what they do? Then we need to understand the *structural* aspects of the problem. Who knows what? Who can detect abuse? Who can stop it?

We will begin the book by describing the *problem*. We will explain some commonly exploited vulnerabilities—and some that are just emerging. We will talk about how taking advantage of these will enable attacker to reach his goals. That, of course, forces us to also have to understand exactly what motivates the adversary. And, of course, we have to try to understand the capabilities and limitations of the attacker. *Then* we can start thinking about how to address the problems we perceive.

This book is not about the particular vulnerabilities or solutions we will describe. It is about connecting the dots. The Internet is changing, and so are the threats that are posed to it. Once we recognize this, it becomes natural that we also need to be able to anticipate trends. Security trends are driven by both *markets* (such as an increase of vulnerable devices) and *opportunities* (such as the ability to easily monetize stolen information).We will look at existing problems through the lens of what caused them. This will give us practice to anticipate what comes next, and be proactive.

The Death of the Internet, First Edition. Edited by Markus Jakobsson.
© 2012 John Wiley & Sons, Inc. Published 2012 by John Wiley & Sons, Inc.

Chapter 1

What Could Kill the Internet?
And so What?

Anything that makes the Internet either *dangerous* or *meaningless* could kill it.

The dangers may be to your machine, to proprietary information, to your financial situation, or even to *you*.

Malware can corrupt your machine. It can destroy data and software. It can even destroy hardware—for example, by rewriting your computer's EEPROM or flash memories so many times that they burn out. That takes only a few seconds per block, and if strategically chosen blocks are damaged, the hardware is rendered useless. Malware can also affect external equipment or processes as the em Stuxnet worm gave an example in 2010. It can be used to turn on the microphone of your phone, turning you into a walking eavesdropping bot—and you would not even know it! Malware is believed to commonly be used to be used to steal corporate and national secrets.

Most of the time, though, malware will only attempt to steal your money. That is the same goal as phishers have. And it is the same goal as scam artists have, attempting to convince their victims to send them money or merchandise. Often referred to as Nigerian scammers, these are certainly not all in Nigeria, although a surprisingly high number is.

The Internet—as well as wireless networks—can also be used to spy on people, to determine their location, for example. This can have direct physical consequences, whether the attack is mounted by a crazed expartner, political enemies, or common criminals. While this type of tracking is not commonly heard about today, it does not mean that it does not happen. And it certainly does not mean that it *cannot* happen. In fact, and as we describe in Section 6.1, it can be done on a grand scale without any significant investment.

Those are just a few examples of dangers that did not exist just a few years ago, and which soon may take up first-page newspaper space. There are also plenty of ways in which the Internet may become *meaningless*.

When we speak of spam, almost everybody thinks of unwanted email. A similar type of spam affects mobile communications—SMS spam. Voice spam is closely related to telemarketing. Instant messaging and online game messaging are also vulnerable to spam. But not all spam is about selling counterfeit Viagra or Rolexes. The term is also used to refer to other junk material, whether it is intended to fool search engines to rank particular pages higher than they otherwise would have. It can be used to manipulate reputations of

The Death of the Internet, First Edition. Edited by Markus Jakobsson.
© 2012 John Wiley & Sons, Inc. Published 2012 by John Wiley & Sons, Inc.

sites and services—typically to make them look more attractive than they are, but sometimes used the other way to stab competitors. Spam is used to mean polluted peer-to-peer material—material that claims to be things it is not.

Spam is not the only source of pollution of information, though. Criminals can deceive news organizations to broadcast untruthful information. Given the increased competition to be first in online media, it is sometimes hard for journalists to balance the need to validate information—and to be first. Malware and spoofing can be used to make information appear to have originated with trusted sources. Criminals may benefit from the pollution of information in many ways. Politically, by sowing doubts and causing fear and confusion. Financially, by manipulating the markets.

The Internet could also become meaningless by becoming so dangerous that typical users restrain their activities and only dare to engage in a minimal manner.

But "meaningless" is in the eye of the beholder. Typical users would have one view of what could make the Internet meaningless. Service providers have a very different view. To online merchants, the Internet would be meaningless if nobody buys their products using it, or if it cannot be used to advertise products that are sold off-line. If this were to happen, advertising would plummet. Since many free services depend of advertisements, that type of development would affect them, and they would scale back or vanish. A lot of services we have come to take for granted fall into this category, starting with search engines, but also including online news services, many content distribution sites, email service providers (do you remember—we used to pay for email...) and other services, such as translation services, recommendation services, navigation services, consumer advice services...you name it, it is probably on the list.

So what happens if people do not dare to watch advertisements? Or if click-fraud runs rampant? It is the same end result. No advertisements...no services.

> Severe attacks on the Internet will send shockwaves through society.

If your livelihood depends on the Internet—like mine does—then you are surely aware of what the impact would be to you of any severe problems with it. You know that you would not be happy if the Internet were crippled by fraud. But if that does not describe you, you might shrug, thinking that this is not such a big deal. After all, you may think, you can live just fine without reading the news online, and you can drive to the store instead of shopping online. Right? Wrong.

- "My phone will still work." Well, maybe not. *You* may not use VoIP services, but most phone calls are still routed over the Internet. If the Internet goes down, your phone goes dead. And so will the phone of your local 911 dispatcher.

- "My lights and heat will still work." Maybe. Maybe not. Our electricity infrastructure is almost as complex as the Internet. Power is routed to where it is needed. The production is ramped up and down to meet the demand. The failure of one part of the system can cause failures in other parts of the system. And since the coordination of this complex system is done using the Internet, even electricity delivery may suffer from severe attacks on the Internet.

- "I can still walk down to the grocery store and get what I need." Yes, you can. But what if their ordering system or delivery system depends on the Internet, or on companies who depend on the Internet? Will the shelves still be full? Maybe not.

- "I still have money in the bank." You may not lose your password to phishing or malware, but what if your bank clerk loses it—or accidentally leaks your mothers maiden name? It may take a while for you to get your money back. And what if the financial system is hampered by a lack of trust; by invalid trades; by general abuse?

Even if the Internet is not taken down by attacks, we may all be affected by rising levels of fraud.

You and I may have bulletproof antivirus software on our computers —and phones—and still be affected. For example, if people passing you on town have infected phones, these phones may render your phone useless simply by making phone calls or web accesses in dramatic quantities. It would be hard for you to get a connection when you want one.

If you use a Bluetooth enabled headset and let your phone be discoverable, then your phone can be tracked by infected phones in your neighborhood. In fact, it may not matter whether your phone is discoverable or not if nearby devices can eavesdrop on signals: your phone will send its Bluetooth device identifier in the clear.

But it is not all about phones. Do you use social networking? Many services will detect if you are online or not. You online/offline patterns may say a lot about you. Who you are, what you do.

Internet terrorism is easy, and we are weak.

So far, I have argued that online attacks may result in problems in society. In lack of trust, degradation of our infrastructure, increases of costs to do business. *But the consequences of online attacks could also be what invites abuse.* If a hostile country or organization wants to hurt us, they may find that the easiest way of doing it is by attacking the Internet. Our dependence on the Internet will *invite* attacks. We have already seen instances of massive cyber attacks, such as those on Estonia in 2007. We are not safe from such attacks. If anything, we may be more vulnerable to them, as our dependence on the Internet is greater—and increasing by the day.

Since 2001, we are all aware of terrorism. What makes it terrifying is not only its arbitrariness, but its asymmetric nature. A small number of dedicated aggressors can inflict massive damage and suffering to large numbers of victims. The terrorists, of course, do not attack us because it is *fun*—they do it to further their political agendas. From their point of view, what they do is justified by the needs.

Of course, every society does what they think is justified by their needs—if they think they can get away with it, at least. Now, imagine that you belonged to an organization that needed to send a strong signal to a society or organization you disagree with. You may not have a powerful army to engage to pressure your enemy with. But you have other, and simpler, ways. You can degrade their infrastructure—with the click of a mouse. You can cause severe interruptions, degrade their economy, spread fear and confusion. Would you be tempted to click? *Of course you would.* And if you would not, then somebody else in your organization surely would.

That is also what we are up against. It is not *only* about fraudsters trying to make a profit.

Chapter 2

It is About People

This chapter aims to give a quick overview of the problem as it relates to *people*—users, victims, fraudsters. What makes them do what they do?

We start with an overview of some typical *human and social* issues that contribute to the problem (Section 2.1.) It is a very common misconception that Internet security—or *computer security* for that matter—is solely about machines, their software, and its potential flaws and vulnerabilities. Both Internet security and computer security is also about how the Internet—and the computers touching it—are used. By humans, that is. The human and social issues of the Internet is what gives rise to phishing, Nigerian scams, various forms of online fraud, and—not to be forgotten—a large portion of malware. These types of abuses take advantage of *human* vulnerabilities, not vulnerabilities in software. They are based on deceit, spoofing, and social engineering, and they benefit from the economies of scale and opportunities for anonymity that the Internet affords criminals. (In Section 4.8, we will offer a more in-depth treatment on what typical Internet users think—and how they think.)

We end this short chapter with a look at the typical criminal (Section 2.2)—because to fully understand the problem, we need to understand the actors, too. Who is the criminal? What motivates him? What does he fear?

2.1 HUMAN AND SOCIAL ISSUES

Markus Jakobsson[1]

Abstract. Computer scientists often mistakenly believe that computer security is all about computers. It is *not*. It is often also about computers being used – and misused—by humans. If we do not understand the true nature of a problem—or ignore the human aspect of it—then we are unlikely to be able to develop meaningful countermeasures. Recognizing that a particular type of problem has a social component is therefore a vital step toward addressing the problem. However, identifying that a certain type of security problem has a social component does not mean that we must look for a social *solution*—such as improved user education or better user interfaces. Although it may appear counterintuitive, social problems sometimes have technical fixes. This section introduces and discusses a collection of such security problems.

---

[1] Also known as advance fee fraud and 419 scams—419 is a section under the Nigerian Criminal Code Act that prohibits obtaining goods by false pretenses.

2.1.1   Nigerian Scams

In 2010, I worked at Palo Alto Research Center and hosted a visitor, Kim-Kwang Raymond Choo, for a few months. Ray and I were talking about Nigerian scam, and wished we knew more about them. Unlike phishing attacks and malware attacks, almost nothing is known about Nigerian scams. This makes it harder to defend against this increasingly common type of fraud, and almost impossible to predict the extent to which it may become worse onward. We decided that we needed to learn more.

We designed and performed an experiment that allows us to take the pulse on Nigerian scammers. Are the scammers really from Nigeria, you may ask? What do they want, and how do they get it? What are their strengths, what are their weaknesses? Are they at the peak of their success, or should we fear that they can become dramatically better at what they are doing? What can organizations do to secure themselves and their users?

> Here is the experiment in a nutshell. Imagine a camera that sells for $750 new, and I offer one for sale on Craigslist for $250. Only used for a few weeks, in perfect condition. Good deal, right? But what if I instead were to ask $750 (or more) for it used? Not so hot, you might say. It makes more sense for you to buy it in the store. You would not bother contacting me. *But fraudsters would.* We used the technique of offering too expensive merchandise to find fraudsters without bothering honest people. In fact, we used it to make the fraudsters find us, while avoiding everybody else. Once we have identified the fraudsters, we acted as innocent victims to see what they wanted.

Fraudsters would contact us and ask to buy our overpriced item—even at a premium. They will tell me where to ship it, and they will send me a payment. Or rather: something that *looks like* a payment to a would-be victim, who would not realize that it really was not a payment until after the item was shipped.

Here are some of our findings:

- Nigerian scams are aptly named. Indeed, almost all of the fraudsters we interacted with wanted us to ship our merchandise to an address in Nigeria. Knowing this may help a little in designing countermeasures, whether legal or technical.

- Most Nigerian scammers "pay" using PayPal. Then they send an email that looks a lot like a PayPal payment notification. But, interestingly, they do *not* spoof emails. If they were, which would be very easy, they would no doubt increase their yield. Somehow, they do not, though. Maybe it is not worth it? Maybe they do not know how to do it?

- Some Nigerian scammers "pay" using Western Union. Then they send a confirmation code that lets the seller pick up the money—but with some digits starred out. "When you send me the tracking number, I will send you the missing part, and you can pick up the payment." The fact that they do this means that people fall for it.

- Some Nigerian scammers "pay" using Credit Cards. They request the victim's credit card details so that they can "transfer" the money to his or her account. Just another way of stealing credit card numbers, of course.

- Nigerian scammers are bullies. As a would-be victim has agreed to sell, but then expresses second thoughts, the scammer becomes mean and threatening. He sends angry emails in all-caps; tells the would-be victim that he or she will be blacklisted or reported; he even sends a notification from a payment provider, stating that the would-be victim's account has been revoked. (This can only be undone by responding to the notification with your password, we were instructed . . .)

- Nigerian scammers know what they want. They want fancy cameras, but do not care as much for laptops, and do not give a darn about refrigerators and other bulky electronic appliances. It makes sense: The merchandise needs to be shipped to them, and then be resold in Nigeria.

Knowing that the scammers remain in business, we can infer that they are reasonably successful. In fact, we see more and more Nigerian scams. So we can conclude that there are enough people who are not very careful, and that bullying them pays off. This is not about people lacking technological skills, it is about them not thinking critically. User awareness and education campaigns could change that.

Of course, Nigerian scams are not limited to Craigslist, nor to frauds in which they try to obtain people's cameras for free. Our experiment only gives us a glimpse at one particular type of scam at one particular point in time. But it gives us hope that it is possible to create a taxonomy of scams and scammers, and develop tools and campaigns that hurt their bottom line.

2.1.2 Password Reuse

People cannot manage as many passwords as they have accounts at various service providers, and therefore, they reuse passwords. Password reuse —or more generally, *credential reuse*—is rampant. It hurts organizations when their end users' credentials are stolen elsewhere—whether on less secure sites, or by phishers or malware attacks—and then used to access the users' accounts. This is surprisingly common, and a very frustrating problem to service providers, as this problem prevents them from protecting their own security, and that of their users.

Analysis of equality (or substantial similarity) of passwords between different domains indicate that password reuse is a tremendous problem, and that between one third to one half of all users reuse passwords between sites [119]. While this analysis is specific to a small number of sites, and people may behave differently for other sites, the numbers are sobering. Other results indicate that between 12% [191] and 20% [207] of passwords are reused.

Password reuse looks like a true social problem—it is certainly not a problem that is rooted in flawed code or cryptographic vulnerabilities. However, that does not mean that there are not technical ways of addressing it, too.

How to Discourage Credential Reuse.

There are at least five principal ways in which we can discourage credential reuse:

1. **Educate users** It is not easy to change people's practices, but it is *possible*. It is commonly understood that passwords are necessary, and even though many people use poor passwords, there are also many who use reasonable passwords. It may reduce password reuse if organizations were to explain to their users both the *risks* of password reuse, and—in a very hands-on manner—*what to do* to manage many passwords without resorting to reuse. Educational efforts need to explain both the need for change, and how to practically achieve the desired goals.

2. **Avoid compatibility with others**   A site that wants to reduce credential reuse can make impose different credential requirements on their users than other sites and services do. As an extreme example, a site can demand that their users create passwords that has an odd number of vowels, and where the digits in the password add up to a number that is divisible by six. Of course, and as is probably obvious from this example, this is very likely to annoy users to no end. And while it may prevent that credentials from other sites are reused on the "protected" site, there are no guarantees that people do not reuse in the opposite direction. In a less extreme example, a password can be associated with a user-selected image that he or she has to select from a list of candidate images both at the time of creating the credential and upon using it. Whereas this does not guarantee a dramatically different credential from other credentials, it does add an opportunity to detect almost correct login attempts—which may be indicative of credential theft.

3. **Reduce the *need* to reuse**   People reuse credentials because they cannot easily remember many. If we make it easier to remember credentials, we also reduce the need to reuse them. One way to make credentials easier to remember is to rely on mnemonics. We have to be cautious when relying on mnemonics, however, as this has been shown to cause security drawbacks when done carelessly [312]. A mnemonic-based authentication scheme is described in Section 7.2. Schemes like that are likely to—at least to some extent—reduce the need to reuse credentials.

4. **Identify vulnerable accounts**   Service providers can share data about leaks and compromises and monitor dropboxes and forums in which password leaks are discussed. They can then attempt to identify whether any of the accounts they maintain are affected by such leaks. Sometimes, it may not be clear whether two user names for two different services correspond to one and the same user. However, it is possible to test whether a given account uses a leaked credential, and if it does, flag the account in order to observe any suspicious activity on it more carefully onward.

5. **Restrict the user's freedom to choose credentials**   Traditional passwords are chosen by users. However, other forms of credentials restrict users' freedom—examples are the image-based authentication method described in Section 7.4. In that particular scheme, the user selects a credential by identifying a collection of things he *likes* and another collection of things he does *not* like from a large collection of topics. During authentication, users are shown only the things they identified as liking and those they identified as disliking (and *not* all the items they did not classify either way), and asked to identify all they like from these. Users cannot choose any images they want during account registration, but only among the topics that they are shown. A random collection of all available images are shown, in a random order. This makes cloning of credentials highly unlikely. Another example of how one can restrict user choices is given next.

For concreteness, let us look more in detail at how to prevent password reuse by restricting the user's freedom to choose credentials.

Consider an authentication scheme where the setup (or registration) phase shows the user a four lists, and asks the user to select one word from each list to make a memorable sentence. These lists contain words that are drawn at random from large lists of suitable words. The sentence structure may also be selected at random from a collection of meaningful sentence structures. (For four words, there are at least two sentence structures in English language.) In one case, a user may see the following selections:

List 1	List 2	List 3	List 4
I	ate	the	rat
You	saw	my	bill
Jesus	licked	his	frog
Mom	took	your	car
We	tossed	a	pen

One particular user may select the words "You," "licked," "'my," "rat," making the credential "You licked my rat." That is what the user has to input when he or she authenticates. Or he might select "I took the bill." For another account setup, he will be given a different collection of words, and maybe a different sentence structure. He might select "The cow drove home." Therefore, if the user sets up two or more accounts—whether on the same or on different sites—he will not be able to select one and the same credential.

It is easier to remember something that means something to you—or something colorful—then something that is just some words. So providing the user with some ability to select a credential, it becomes easier to remember. It may still be difficult for a user to remember what crazy sentence he used at what site—even if he *were* to remember all the sentences. But that can be addressed as follows: During authentication, the system would present a large collection of words—maybe 24 of them—among which the "correct" four words can be found. (These would always be the same 24 words for all login attempts for a given account, to avoid attacks looking at intersections between subsequent collections.)

The user is asked to click on these four words in the right order. An adversary would neither know what the sentence structure is nor what four words the account owner selected. If there are, say, two possible sentence structures, and there are six words of each type, there would be $(6^4)^2 \approx 2^{21}$ ways of selecting these words. Of course, some of these may not make much sense from a semantic point of view—but it is a relatively small portion, and an automated script is unlikely to know which ones.

Since both setup and authentication can be completed without any typing—clicking is sufficient—this is practical for handsets.

2.1.3 Phishing

Look at these three URLs: www.accountonline.com, www.democratic-party.us, www.wachovia.pin-update.com. Can you tell which (if any) correspond to legitimate service providers? Do you think the average Internet user can tell, too?

In fact, most people have no idea how to tell a good URL from a bad one. A study I coauthored with Jacob Ratkiewicz [279] showed that Internet users are not the least suspicious of so-called cousin-name domains. A cousin-name domain is a URL, like www.democratic-party.us, that is "semantically correct"—in this case it makes it look like it should belong to the Democratic Party. (At the time of writing, it belonged to *me*—and for a full year, nobody had demanded that I transfer it to them!)

Jacob's and my study also showed that most people do not identify subdomain attacks in which the *subdomain* is used to semantically defraud—like www.wachovia.pin-update.com has nothing to do with Wachovia.

Part of the problem is that people are people, not string matching machines. We are just not very good at remembering things verbatim, but we are pretty good at making sense of cues—which is what gets us into trouble. But that's not all. The problem is made worse by companies that register and use domains that have nothing in particular to do with their brand. Like www.accountonline.com, which belongs to CitiBank and is used to access credit card accounts. Why not use the regular citibank.com domain? Or at least citicards.com? Now, CitiBank is not the only financial institution that uses weird domains . . . unfortunately, this is the *rule* rather than the exception.

What should we conclude from this? First of all, phishers and crimeware authors will make increasing use of deceptive domain names. This means that blacklisting will become less and less meaningful and that we will have to rely on whitelisting, heuristics, and our own ability to be careful. Not a happy thought.

Of course, phishing does not end at URLs. In fact, many phishers use meaningless URLs that have nothing at all to do with the brands and Web sites they are trying to impersonate. Since this apparently is sustainable, we know that many users do not notice the URL. They simply fall for the *message*.

Do you think logos matter? Phishers know they do.

Some time ago, my colleague Ruj Akavipat and I performed a study in which I asked large number of subjects to rate a given Web site, where a purchase checkout was shown. We were intentionally vague about just what we wanted them to rate. Some subjects surely thought that I wanted to know whether the merchandise was nice. Some might have looked at whether the price was good. Or the vendor reputable. Still others may have looked for whether the site seemed secure. By giving no instructions we made people act naturally. If we had told them that they were participating in a phishing study, they would not have acted naturally at all.

All of the supposed purchases were for the same item, and at the same price, and for the same vendor. Some of the sites screen shots showed sites that were SSL secured—others not. Some showed clearly phishy URLs—others legitimate URLs. And the different sites showed different payment preferences, and the logos associated with these organizations.

Each subject only saw one of these screen shots, and gave us one rating. But with hundreds of subjects for each category, we could compare the averages of the ratings for different payment providers. Here is the amazing thing: People noticed the absence of SSL and the use of phishy URLs much more when the payment provider was less established.

What does this mean? It means that the subjects were pacified by the presence of the known logos, and less suspicious as a result. And, in contrast, they were more suspicious of the site when the logo did not provide them with this sense of security.

This is at the heart of what makes phishing work. It works because people—normal people, typical users—are not good at judging whether something is secure or not. We are lulled into peace by logos and professional design, and we fail to notice technical indicators of risk.

Is There a Way to Stop Phishing?

Before we talk about how to address the problem, we need to understand it. We need to establish what it is that makes phishing work.

Let's begin by clarifying what exactly we mean by phishing: In a phishing attack, an adversary—the phisher—sends out messages to would-be victims, posing as a trustworthy entity and requesting the message recipients to provide the phisher with valuable information that people would not want to give to nontrustworthy people and organizations.

Now, let's focus on what makes an attack successful:

1. The *phisher impersonates* a trustworthy organization in a plausible manner.

2. The *victim reacts* in a way that benefits the phisher, that is, responds to requests for information.

In particular, we know that if the phisher would fail to impersonate a trustworthy information to an intended victim, then they would not be successful—that is as if you were to receive an email from a bank that you do not have a relation with, asking for your password, or receiving an email that is an evident spoof. But is not enough that victims believe that they have received information from trustworthy and relevant organizations. In order for the phisher to be successful, he also needs to collect credentials or other valuable information.

Now, we are ready to think about countermeasures.

To defend against phishing, we need to make one of the two steps fail: either the phisher should not be able to impersonate organizations or the victim should not be able to react in a way that benefits the phisher. Most counterphishing focus on the former step, for example, by highlighting what URLs are safe, or by warning the user of unsafe webpages. Browser extensions such as *PwdHash* focus on the latter step by performing site-specific transformations of user-provided passwords: if the "right" password is provided to the "wrong" site, then it is modified in a different way than the right password would be to the right site. In Section 7.6, we describe another approach that prevents phishing by making the second step fail. The method is based on the following principle:

If the action to *proceed* with a transaction on a *good* site is identical to the action to *abort* a transaction on a *bad* site, then bad sites posing as good will fail.

2.2 WHO ARE THE CRIMINALS?

Igor Bulavko

Abstract. This chapter explores the main characteristics of cybercriminals and describes who they are.

Like the Internet itself, cybercrime has been woven into the fabric of modern life. Along with cybercrime came the notion of a cybercriminal, also known as fraudster, miscreant, or "hacker"—which seems to be the name of choice for most folks. Perhaps by association with the common offline thug, the public opinion often holds cybercriminals to be either drug addicts, or terrorists, or, more generally, lazy lowlifes without conscience, or some other sort of antisocial element. That comparison is about as accurate as comparing email server admins to USPS mailmen. The actual image of today's cybercriminal is different.

As Steve Carell's Maxwell Smart puts it in *Get Smart*, "[...] until we understand that our enemies are also human beings we will never defeat them. Yes, they are bad guys, but that is *what they do*, not *who they are*." (Emphasis added.)

2.2.1 Who are they?

The cybercriminals are white collar criminals. They are the Bernard Madoffs and Raj Rajaratnams of the world, if only on a slightly smaller scale. In fact, many of the criminals may very well think of themselves as modern Robin Hoods. Their parents may be proud of them for helping their extended families, and for outsmarting foreigners who are rolling in money anyway. They are not unshaven drug dealers or a collection of Dr. Strangeloves. They are well educated; they make lots of money deceiving others, and are really good about covering up their illicit activity. You would never think they were cybercriminals if you met them on the street. Many of them have day jobs, although some of them don't need one anymore.

2.2.2 Where are they?

They are all over the world. Cybercrime is often believed to be committed by people in Eastern Europe, China, Vietnam, and Nigeria, but in reality there are plenty of cybercriminals in Western Europe and all over every other continent except Antarctica. They have simply been eclipsed by the others' notoriety. Adding to this perception is the fact that the language spoken by cybercriminals is often mistaken for their location. Russian, for example, is widely used on the criminal scene, but it would be inaccurate to assume that all of the scene actors are from Russia. Researchers estimate that in 2010 the gross income of Russian-speaking fraudsters living outside of Russia was twice the income of the Russian-speaking fraudsters living in the Russian Federation ($2.5 billion vs. $1.3 billion) [232].

2.2.3 Deep-Dive: Taking a Look at Ex-Soviet Hackers

The common view that most criminals are from Russia is probably founded in the fact that a relatively large portion are. How do they think, and what shapes their actions? Let's take a look at their past for a better chance of understanding their present and future actions.

Many of them grew up in the nineties, and in a nutshell, here's what life in the ex-Soviet states was like back then:

- **Anarchy** The Soviet Union had just collapsed. The ensuing confusion and lack of proper government turned the former republics into a "Wild West" territory. In the race for money and power no holds were barred, bribes were commonplace, corruption rampant. Personal connections and your own cunning were the only things that kept you safe on the way to your fortune. Early retail businesses thrived (open borders let in a flood of imported goods), and so did criminal gangs. The state apparatus that had been built for 70 years became a mere shell of its former self. Law enforcement could be bribed, legal documents – purchased. This state of events had a profound influence on the young people of that age. They saw for themselves the vulnerability of the political and economic systems, and opportunities it created.

- **Poverty** Money was scarce. The people were not starving by any means, but salaries were low, and saving for high-value items like cars, let alone houses, took many years. Today, it is not uncommon for an Eastern European family to have a monthly income corresponding to $200 or less. In the nineties, the number was closer to $75. On the other hand, the few people who were considered rich enjoyed the higher quality of life, public attention, and many other benefits.

- **"West is rich" myth** Developed Western countries like the United States were viewed as extremely rich nations where everyone was affluent. This perception was formed by a variety of factors:
  - Income levels in the developed countries were indeed much higher.
  - Media reports, Hollywood movies and books often supported this perception.
  - Foreign visitors reinforced the belief that "the West" was rich with their behavior. In particular, this can be said about American immigrants visiting their native country. They spent large (often unthinkable in local terms) amounts of money on goods and services, brought expensive gifts for their relatives, and always told stories of how good life was in the United States and how every American was awash in money, with a house and several cars per family and regular exotic

vacations. These stories were later recounted many times, becoming part of the folklore. United States of America was considered a legendary country, a wonderland.

- **"Us versus them"** The Soviet-era ideology delivered through the public education system had made sure that the entire population of the country, starting from a very early age, viewed the West as their natural opponent in everything. Everyone was motivated to be better, smarter, faster, and stronger than anyone in the West. The only thing they could not beat the West in was its famed financial well-being, but this well-being too was perceived as a negative trend, as some sort of detrimental decadence.

- **Free information** Intellectual property rights were either nonexistent or very loosely enforced. Information, and, by extension, anything intangible, was free.

- **Money = cash** The only kind of money was cash. It was a tangible currency that one could physically handle and protect. The understanding of any kind of noncash transaction, like checks and credit cards, was poor and was mostly based on Hollywood movies of the time ("Blank Check," etc.).

- **Computers = toys** There were absolutely no laws around Internet, or even computer-based, activity. Computers were perceived mostly as toys, educational machines, or advanced typewriters; they had very little impact on the country's economy.

Naturally, when some people realized they could use the Internet to steal money, the West, and the United States as its primary representative, was a natural choice of a cash cow. Consider the irony of this situation: By using what was essentially considered toys, these young "hackers" made real money out of thin air (they weren't stealing cash, right?), thus living up to their ideals of (a) enriching themselves, (b) boosting their reputation among peers, and (c) outsmarting the foreigners, both individuals and entire companies. This was an archetypical "rags to riches" discovery that could only be compared to striking gold in the times of the Gold Rush.

So, why do cybercriminals from the Eastern Europe choose to commit these crimes, cross over to the dark side, become "the bad guys"? That's not the right question to ask. For them, the notions of Good and Bad, Right and Wrong often mean "Good for YOU versus YOU can get Caught." Their societies reflect this belief. The notion of "Bad for somebody else" is dependent on the individual's principles and honor, and is often treated as a very loose guideline. Just because something may be considered bad/illegal/immoral by somebody else, doesn't mean you shouldn't do it. You shouldn't do something only if you can get caught and punished for it or if it's against your principles.

Of course, that only describes the state of mind of Eastern European Internet criminals. The story will be different for each country, but one thing is common: we are talking about regular people, who take a very small risk earning a lot of money by committing what they can easily argue is not a serious crime, and in a way that does not hurt, and even helps, their local communities.

In February 2008, for example, FoxNews reported [441] on how hundreds of residents of a small Romanian town of Drăgăşani had gotten rich over the years by conning eBay users with fake auctions. And 3 years later, in February 2011, the Wired magazine ran an article in the same vein [116] on a neighboring (30 miles away) town of Râmnicu Vâlcea, where Starbucks coffeehouses, Western Union stores, and luxury car dealerships have been springing up all over town in the last decade, thanks in a large part to the revenues from Internet crimes committed by some of its residents. The local communities appear to be fully aware of the source of this wealth, but not at all serious about putting an end to cybercrime, with only four police officers assigned to investigating digital offenses.

From this point of view, you can see why there will always be people looking for and finding ways to enrich themselves at the cost of others.

2.2.4   Let's try to Find Parallels in the World we Live in

Think of an activity that requires a certain degree of moral flexibility. Here are some examples:

- Using a technicality in tax law to keep a bit more money for yourself. That's a loophole, it's not illegal. It's your money, after all. Aren't you robbing the government of that $100/$1,000,000? Ah, the government has more than enough money already. You will find a better use for it.

- Passing transaction processing fees to consumers. Is it illegal? No. Against the Terms of Service? Maybe. Do you care? No. Let's call it 'Handling and Processing fee' and pass it to the customers. More money in your pocket.

- How about borrowing a song from a friend (in MP3 format). Did you ever erase it after you were done borrowing it? How about downloading those MP3s and AVIs from P2P sharing networks? Is it illegal to deprive the artist of the rightfully earned $0.99? Yes. Did you get caught? No. At best, you got one of those hand-slapping emails from your ISP.

- Aggressive telemarketing sales. It is most certainly not illegal to impose on other people, peddling a product that they don't need and probably will never use. Does the dissatisfied buyer feel bad about caving in? Yes. Do you care? No. You care about your sale commission. You care about paying your mortgage and feeding your family.

Such moral trade-offs are common. We are desensitized to the point of not noticing them or treating them as completely legitimate and acceptable behaviors. Now, how about cybercriminals?

Cybercriminals hailing from Eastern Europe are commonly desensitized to the fact that using credit card of someone from the other side of the Globe to buy a laptop is actually stealing. To them, the victim is a faceless source of funds who is going to get their money back anyway through chargeback. They know that it is the bank, the merchant, or the insurance company that is going to sustain the loss, but for the bank, the merchant, and the insurance company this is the risk of doing business.

2.2.5   Crime and Punishment?

The criminals understand that their chances of getting caught are very low: There have been very few arrests over the recent years. And even those arrests, which are supposed to set the example and deter the fraudsters from committing more fraud, are not harsh enough.

Just a couple of examples:

- Dmitry Golubov, who is believed to have been one of the top dogs of the carderplanet.com underground forum, was first arrested for allegedly stealing over $10 million from US banks and then released after 6 months, when the prosecution failed to collect enough evidence to try him. Mr Golubov is now a politician: he leads the Internet Party of Ukraine.

- Vlad "Vladuz" Duiculescu, a Romanian fraudster who had spent years victimizing eBay users, was arrested in 2008 and released in January 2010, awaiting trial. In February 2011, in one of the most important criminal cases in the history of eBay Inc, he was convicted on multiple charges, including the development of the first wide spread phishing kit used against eBay and a number of other scams.

The court sentenced Vladuz to a total of 3 years in prison with credit for the 22 months he had already served. The remainder of his sentence was suspended, and Mr. Duiculescu was released under supervision for a period of 8 years.

Were those prison terms commensurate with the amount of damage inflicted by their activities, and, more importantly, harsh enough to deter others? That is unlikely. Why is the justice system not harder on them? Why are their crimes not considered worse?

Considering all of the above, it would be naïve to the point of foolishness to expect cybercrime to come to an end of its own accord. We should not expect the people behind these crimes to "grow out of it," "settle down," or "get a real job": they are not misguided youths who are going through a rebellious period of their life, or looking to assert themselves among their peers. Online crime is a new type of crime, more pervasive and virulent than similar real-world crimes like theft, robbery, extortion, and espionage. Cybercriminals feel justified in their activity, are well incentivized to keep at it, and are intelligent enough to adapt to countermeasures and hide their traces. Our reaction to it, therefore, should be as serious, if not more so, as our reaction to offline crimes. However, more often than not the community tends to write off cybercrime incidents as obnoxious and inconvenient pranks. We should start by changing our own view of the world of cybercrime, and then focus on helping others see it for what it is—a real threat that has far greater implications than minor financial losses and isolated data breaches.

So where does that leave us?

We believe it is important to track and help prosecute criminals. But we argue that this is hard to do well. It is even better to block crime from even taking place. That requires better security protocols, better risk-based detection engines to identify and block abnormal activities, and better user education. We just cannot continue to blame the criminals and the governments of the countries in which they live.

Chapter 3

How Criminals Profit

This chapter explains and gives examples of just how criminals profit. In the end, the criminals do not actually care about stealing your password or infecting your machine. They do not have any interest in your data, nor in making it appear to others that you are interested in some peculiar product. What they care about— no surprise here—is *money*. They want to make money.

Of course, sometimes, the wish of the criminals to make money makes them steal passwords, infecting machines, access private data, and clicking on advertisements. But to see how, we need to understand the process of monetization. How, in other words, can criminals make money by subverting machines and deceiving end users?

We start in Section 3.1 by a description of advertisement fraud. Many end users are blissfully unaware of this type of fraud, simply because they are not the ones losing money— in spite of the fact that it is their machines that are corrupted. Interestingly, ad fraud is not always a crime—just a breach of the terms of service. We then briefly describe *another* type of scam—which, like ad fraud, is *also* not necessarily a crime. Section 3.2 describes a new class of scams that are really offers for services that nobody who understands the offers would want—but that are designed to deceive. Interestingly, this is also a category of scams that relies on the Internet for collection of data—but not for delivery of the scam. These scams are on the rise, as the criminal's profit margins are sufficiently high to pay postage instead of simply relying on spamming potential victims.

In Section 3.3, we describe the problem of phishing by overviewing some common variants from a structural point of view. Common for all of these is the criminal goal of collecting access credentials (such as passwords), or other financial information (such as credit card numbers). Passwords can be used to access the associated accounts and transfer funds from them, while stolen credit card information is used to *create* accounts and transfer funds from them.

We then turn to malware in Section 3.4. Malware is an enabler of many of the vices we see. Ad fraud, for example, is often committed from infected machines. Phishers use infected machines to spam victims, and to host their spoofed webpages. And malware—in itself—boxes a threat by stealing credentials, data, and resources; and by infiltrating organizations and the infrastructure. (We also discuss malware later on in the book – both from the angle of its potential for tracking people, and from the angle of what can be done to better address the problem.)

Finally, we review monetization in Section 3.5. There we review how criminals translate various types of fraud into real money. After all, that is the *real* goal of their pursuits.

The Death of the Internet, First Edition. Edited by Markus Jakobsson.
© 2012 John Wiley & Sons, Inc. Published 2012 by John Wiley & Sons, Inc.

3.1 ONLINE ADVERTISING FRAUD

Nevena Vratonjic, Mohammad Hossein Manshaei, and Jean-Pierre Hubaux

Abstract. Over the last decade, online advertising has become a major component of the web, leading to large annual revenues (e.g., $26.04 billion in United States in 2010 [65]). Internet advertising is a very successful form of advertising as it provides an easy and effective way for advertisements to be targeted to individual users' interests. Unfortunately, fraudsters were able to exploit several vulnerabilities of the online advertising model and started abusing the system in order to make a profit out of it. These attacks are illegal only in a few countries and states (e.g., click fraud is a felony covered by Penal Code 502 in California and the computer misuse act in the United Kingdom). In most of the cases, the fraudsters instead violate terms of service of online advertising networks (e.g., in Nigeria where there is no law against this type of cybercrime and in India, where companies even advertised in national newspapers looking for people willing to use computers to click on ads, with no repercussions from authorities). In this section, we aim to provide a better understanding of vulnerabilities of online advertising systems, the well-known attacks, and possible countermeasures. We first address the online advertising system model and discuss different revenue models for it. We explain vulnerabilities of these models and classify the identified attacks into four main types: click fraud, malvertising, inflight modification of ad traffic, and adware. For each type of attack, we address how fraudsters can make profit from the existing advertising system. We discuss in more detail some of the attacks reported in practice. Finally, we address the possible countermeasures to each of the attacks. In Section 4.1, we take a step back and discuss the principles behind online advertising, and who knows what. Read that for a big-picture view of what the problem is, and what can and cannot be done.

3.1.1 Advertising on the Internet

Online advertising is a form of marketing that relies on the Internet to deliver marketing messages to the targeted users. Internet advertisement typically comprises a short text, an image, or an animation embedded into a webpage. The purpose of an ad is generally to capture a user's attention and persuade him to purchase or to consume a particular product or a service and, consequently, to increase the revenue of the advertiser. Advertisers pay for their ads to appear online, thus online advertising has become the major business model for monetizing online content. In contrast to other types of media (e.g., television or radio), online advertisements are not limited to an audience at a given time or a geographic location. An additional benefit is that online advertising allows for the customization of advertisements, thus increasing the probability that a user is interested in the advertised products and services. Hence, many advertisers, realizing the opportunities of online advertising, invest significant budgets into this form of advertising. Consequently, for many of the websites that users visit, a number of advertisements appear together with the content of a webpage.

Now let us look at how online advertisements are embedded into the content of webpages, which techniques are used to tailor ads to users' interests and the main revenue models in online advertising.

3.1.1.1 Ad serving architecture

Ads are embedded into webpages either through an ad serving system, or by websites themselves. Although it might be a straightforward task for major publishers with marketing units to sell the advertising space on their webpages to advertisers, this is not the case for a large number of small publishers for which the

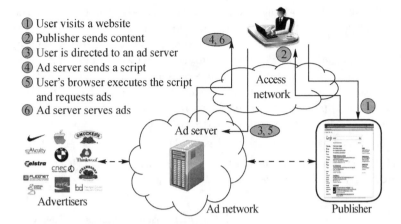

① User visits a website
② Publisher sends content
③ User is directed to an ad server
④ Ad server sends a script
⑤ User's browser executes the script
   and requests ads
⑥ Ad server serves ads

Figure 3.1   The ad serving architecture. *Advertisers* subscribe to an *Ad Network* whose role is to automatically embed ads into related webpages. *Publishers* and ad networks have a contractual agreement (dashed arrow) that lets ad servers add advertisement to publishers' webpages. Ads are stored at *Ad Servers*, which belong to the ad network. When a *User* visits a website of a publisher that hosts ads (step 1), the user's browser starts downloading the content of the webpage (step 2), and is then directed to one of the ad servers belonging to the ad network (step 3). During the first communication with the ad server, a script is served to the user (step 4) that executes on the user's machine and requests ads from the ad server (step 5). The ad server chooses and serves ads that match users' interest (step 6) in order to maximize the potential ad revenue.

overhead of doing so may surpass the benefits. Ad networks emerged as a solution to increase the reach of online advertising campaigns across these small publishers as well. Publishers offer their advertising space to ad networks that deal with advertisers and sell the advertising space on behalf of publishers.

The prevalent model of the Internet advertisement serving architecture is depicted in Figure 3.1. In this model, an ad network plays the role of intermediary between advertisers and publishers, and its job is to automatically include ads into the appropriate online content. For this purpose, the ad network provides publishers with the HTML code that publishers should include (i.e., copy – paste) into the HTML code of their webpages. When users browse these webpages, relevant ads appear together with the publishers' content.

The protocol, illustrated in Figure 3.1, can be represented as follows:

1. A user's browser issues a request for the webpage corresponding to the *URL* the user types into browser's address bar.

2. The downloaded webpage contains the publisher's content and the block of the HTML code provided by the ad network. The HTML code redirects the browser to communicate with an ad server and download the ads that should accompany the publisher's content. This approach makes the ad serving system scalable, as the workload is distributed across users, rather than having a website communicate with an ad network on behalf of each user and deliver the ads together with the content. In addition, it allows ad servers and advertisers to keep the control, as ads are stored and maintained at their servers.

3. Typically, the user's browser first requests a script (e.g., JavaScript) from the ad server.

4. When the script is fetched, it executes locally on the user's machine and collects certain parameters that influence the selection of ads by the ad server, including the HTTP cookies if they were deposited

by the ad server during previous interactions. Cookies uniquely identify users and enable the profiling of their browsing preferences. This enables ad servers to track users across multiple websites. Besides collecting relevant information about the user before actually serving the ads, an additional benefit of having the HTML code that directs users to first download the script is that it is simple and easy to maintain, as only a few lines of a generic code (a reference to the JavaScript) are added in the code of webpages. Thus, if the ad network wants to modify the way ads are included in online content, it can simply modify the script that is hosted on their servers, rather than requesting each of the associated publishers to implement the corresponding modifications.

5. Information collected by the script is communicated back to the ad server with the request for ads.

6. The ad server chooses and serves the most appropriate ads for the given user. The browser merges the ads with previously downloaded elements of the webpage.

Due to its many advantages, this approach is widely used in practice. However, there are several drawbacks as well. Because users fetch ads from third-party servers (i.e., servers different from publishers' servers), the ad serving technology slows down the display of webpages, consumes extra bandwidth, can be used as an attack vector to compromise the security of users' machines and affects the privacy of users [308].

In an alternative online advertisement serving architecture, a website can embed advertisements locally and serve them to users, together with the content of a webpage. This ad serving technique is not very popular because it puts more workload on the web servers compared to the previous approach, thus it does not scale as well. Some of the ad networks deploy this model when serving mobile advertisements, that is, advertisements that are displayed on users' mobile devices. In this particular case it might be justified to put the overhead on web servers rather than on users, because with mobile devices the available bandwidth and computational power is limited, the latencies are higher and the communication is more expensive for the user. The previous approach is also preferred by ad networks because direct communication of users to ad servers allows for better profiling of users' online behavior, thus better matching of ads to users interests and consequently higher potential revenues.

3.1.1.2 Targeted advertising

A notable difference between online and traditional advertising (e.g., television, radio) is that online ads can be *targeted* to individual user's interests. To maximize the potential revenue, ad networks use *ad targeting techniques* to serve the ads that match users' interests. The most popular ad targeting techniques are *contextual*, *behavioral*, and *location-based* targeting. With contextual targeting, ads are related to the content the user is currently viewing. Behavioral targeting customizes ads based on users' *digital footprints*, that is, information about the observed behavior of the users in the digital world, including usage of the Internet, mobile phone, and so on. With location-based targeting, users receive location-specific ads on their mobile devices.

Targeted advertising aims at providing each user with the ads that best suit his interests. At ad servers, users' interests can be expressed with *keywords*. The ad server associates ads with each keyword and runs auction algorithms to select the most relevant ads and the order in which they appear on the webpage, with the goal of maximizing the profit of both advertisers and websites hosting the ads. In particular, small businesses find that online advertising offers maximum exposure for a minimal cost.

3.1.1.3 *Revenue models*

There are three main revenue models: Advertisers may pay the ad network on a per *impression*, per *click* or per *action* basis.

In the per impression model, advertisers pay the ad network for the exposure of their ads to end users, that is, there is a *cost-per-mille* (CPM) (cost to expose one ad to 1000 users). This model is widely used for *brand advertising*, that is, increasing customers' awareness and ability to recall and recognize the brand, typically by displaying banner ads. Brand awareness is of critical importance as customers will not consider a brand if they are not aware of it. The impression-based model is an online counterpart to the traditional mediums for conveying a brand image to customers, such as print (where impressions are created by the placement of ads in subway cars, billboards, etc.) and television (where impressions are created by the emission of commercials). Thus, many advertisers are choosing impression-based online advertising as a way to establish their brand as a trustworthy friend to the consumer.

In the pay-per-click (PPC) model, advertisers pay the ad network a *cost-per-click* (CPC) for each user-generated click on an ad that directs the user's browser to the advertised website. From an advertiser's point of view, a click on an ad represents a user's choice. The benefit of the PPC model is that it offers instant feedback and the opportunity to measure the effectiveness of an advertising campaign. The success of an advertising campaign can be expressed with *clickthrough rate* (CTR). A CTR is obtained by dividing the "number of users who clicked on an ad" on a webpage by the "number of times the ad was delivered" (impressions). As of 2006, PPC started gaining prevalence over other revenue models. The trend continued over the years to reach approximately 62% of the advertising revenues that are priced based on this model in 2010, according to the Interactive Advertising Bureau [65].

If a click on an ad is followed by a predefined action on the advertiser's website (e.g., online purchase or registration for a newsletter), advertisers pay a *cost-per-action* (CPA) to the ad network. This model is widely used by many organizations primarily in service based businesses, rather than by companies who sell tangible "mail order" types of products online. These service-based businesses (e.g., insurance companies, mortgage companies, real estate brokerage, etc.) are aware that customers generally do not buy these kind of services on a first impression. Therefore, these organizations using CPA media are instead generally far more interested in collecting initial, focused, targeted leads (i.e., potential sales contacts) from their advertising. As these markets are very competitive, businesses know and appreciate the fact that if they can get someone to join their email list or find some other method of encouraging people to complete their online form, they would instantly have a significant head start on their competition. Therefore, they are willing to pay for CPA ads knowing that they are paying only for leads that are focused, refined and targeted for their business.

The ad network gives a fraction of the ad-generated revenue to the publisher who hosted the ad that resulted in an impression, a click or an action. These models provide incentive to participate in the ad serving system: advertisers earn the revenue created by ads, ad networks earn money for storing the ads and finding proper publishers to display ads, and the publishers earn money for hosting ads and directing users toward advertised websites. Users benefit from obtaining advertisements that are tailored to their interests.

3.1.2 Exploits of Online Advertising Systems

Surprisingly, online advertising and web browsing still rely on the HTTP protocol, which does not provide any guarantees on the integrity or the authenticity of online content. Given the lack of security protocols, an adversary may perform ad fraud attacks to exploit the online ad serving system for its own benefit. Considering the amount of money at stake, the security of online advertising is becoming a pressing concern for advertisers, ad networks, and publishers. As online advertising has emerged as the main source of revenues for most online activities, the attacks on online advertising systems could undermine the business model of the participating stakeholders and thus may represent a concern for the future of the Internet.

3.1.2.1 *Adversary*

An adversary launching an attack on an advertising system can take various forms in practice. We consider a *selfish* adversary intending to take advantage of the ad serving system: A selfish adversary exploits the system with the goal of diverting part of the ad revenue for itself. In contrast, a *malicious* adversary may perform any types of attack on the ad system, typically for nefarious purposes (e.g., launching a Denial-of-Service Attack, spreading a malicious software or hurting a competitor).

The adversary can be part of the ad serving architecture or part of the access network that provides Internet connectivity to end users (Figure 3.1). As discussed, all entities of the ad serving architecture benefit from the delivery of ads to end users, however there are various ways in which they may try to increase their revenue. In contrast, the access network that carries all users' traffic does not receive any ad revenue. Thus, the access network may also be tempted to tamper with the transiting data to generate benefits for itself.

Depending on the amount of resources and know-how available to the adversary, it can either attempt simple attacks from a single computer or it may deploy automated mechanisms to perpetrate large-scale attacks from a number of machines worldwide. Today, botnets are a very popular tool for perpetrating distributed attacks on the Internet and are used very often to commit ad fraud. A botnet is a collection of software robots, or bots, that run autonomously and automatically. Bots are typically compromised computers running software, usually installed via drive-by downloads (i.e., downloads that happen without users' knowledge or consent) exploiting web browser vulnerabilities, worms, Trojan horses, or backdoors, under a common command-and-control infrastructure. A bot master controls the botnet remotely, usually through a covert channel (e.g., Internet Relay Chat) for the botnet to be stealth and to protect against detection or intrusion into the botnet network. An adversary wanting to use a botnet for ad fraud may build its own or rent an existing botnet from another botnet master.

Although botnets typically enslave PCs to act like zombies in a botnet, a (believed to be the first) botnet of compromised wireless routers was detected in 2009 [16]. The botnet was used to launch a Distributed Denial-of-Service attack on DroneBL, a distributed DNS Blacklist service. It was estimated that the botnet gained control of approximately one hundred thousand routers, targeting home routers that have web interface and an SSH port directly accessible without requiring a password or with a weak username and password combinations. This problem was later solved with a firmware update. Once it gained access to the system, the botnet loaded a file that turned routers into bots. This example demonstrates that the botnet problem is not something that only affects PCs. An adversary may use *warkitting attacks* to subvert home wireless routers [469]. Warkitting refers to a drive-by subversion of wireless home routers through unauthorized access by mobile WiFi clients. It is shown that in practice an adversary can perform warkitting with low-cost equipment and that a large number of routers are susceptible to such attacks.

A botnet of wireless routers can perpetrate powerful man-in-the-middle (MITM) attacks, as routers are in a position to *eavesdrop*, *alter*, *inject*, and *delete* communications. It also has the advantage of having the bots almost always connected to the Internet (compared to the typical end user machine that is connected to the Internet only from time to time). In addition, it is more difficult to detect that a device has been compromised, due to the lack of security software for such devices (e.g., no antivirus software).

3.1.2.2 Ad Fraud

An online advertising system can be abused in many ways. We will focus on the ad fraud attacks that have been the most prevalent in practice and that yield monetary benefits for the adversary: click fraud, malvertising, inflight modification of ad traffic and adware. We also address possible countermeasures to these attacks.

3.1.3 Click Fraud

In each of the revenue models (i.e., impression-based, click-based, and action-based), an advertiser who pays for his ads to be included in online content has a positive return on investment (ROI) only when genuine impressions, clicks, and actions are generated by legitimate users. ROI is used to express the actual or perceived future value of a marketing campaign and is calculated as the ratio of the revenue gained or lost, relative to the initial investment. An adversary can simulate interest in ads (by creating illegitimate ad impressions, clicks, or conversions in the corresponding revenue models) that provides advertisers with little or no ROI, because they are not a result of legitimate users being exposed to ads. We refer to this type of ad fraud as *click fraud*.

The two most occurring types of click fraud are *publisher click inflation* and *advertiser competitor clicking*.

With a *publisher click inflation attack*, a publisher tries to over-report its contribution in exposing users to ads. As publishers are rewarded by ad networks proportionally to the number of impressions or user-generated clicks and actions on the ads included in the publisher's webpages, they sometimes inflate the numbers in order to obtain more revenue from ad networks. To do so, they generate fraudulent impressions, clicks and actions for which advertisers are charged by ad networks, and the fraudulent publishers receive a share of that revenue.

With an *advertiser competitor clicking attack*, an advertiser tries to undermine the advertising campaigns of its competitors. In order to increase the visibility of its own advertisements, an advertiser may create artificial impressions, clicks, or actions on advertisements of its competitors. If its competitor advertisers are charged for these, their daily budgets may be exhausted rapidly and the fraudulent advertiser's ads would have the advantage of being selected and served to legitimate users.

Depending on the revenue model, an adversary generates artificial interest in ads as follows:

- In the *impression-based model*, an adversary generates fraudulent ad impressions by issuing HTTP requests for webpages containing ads that users never see.
- In the *pay-per-click model*, an adversary generates fraudulent clicks on ads by issuing HTTP requests for ad impression URLs, that were not generated by legitimate users.
- In the *conversion-based model*, an adversary can produce fraudulent conversions by issuing HTTP requests that represent an advertiser-defined action, such as a subscription, in order to simulate the action of a legitimate user.

Fraudsters may generate ad fraud themselves and deploy a third-party or automated programs to do so. Automated ad fraud attacks very often rely on botnets. An example of a botnet click fraud in the PPC model is Clickbot.A, the botnet that executed a low-noise click fraud attack against syndicated search engines and was investigated in detail by Google [167]. The botnet consisted of over one hundred thousand compromised machines and it perpetrated a publisher click inflation ad fraud. The bot operator acted as a publisher and created several websites that contained links that eventually led to ads on which the clickbot would click.

Automated ad fraud attacks can also be executed without compromising the end users' machines. For example, in the PPC model an attacker can launch a stealthy, automated click-fraud attack called "badvertisement" where fraudulent clicks are generated on ads hosted by the attacker [201]. The goal is accomplished by corrupting the JavaScript required to properly include ads into webpages and does not depend on any client-side vulnerability. The script causes an ad to be automatically clicked and processed by a client's web browser. Consequently, the click is accounted for by the ad network, the advertiser is charged and part of the revenue is transferred to the fraudulent publisher. Badvertisement attack is also an example of a publisher click inflation ad fraud.

An attacker can also generate fraudulent clicks by tricking users with "clickjacking" attacks to click on ads. Clickjacking happens when the attacker uses multiple transparent layers of webpages to trick a user into clicking on a button or a link on a hidden page when they were intending to click on the bottom visible page [414]. Therefore, the attacker can trick users into performing actions that the users never intended and thus "hijack" their clicks. The clicks can then be turned into fraudulent clicks on CPC ads. Figure 3.2 shows an example of a clickjacking attack where a victim surfs the bottom page (a fraudulent site that launches the clickjacking attack, e.g., *myphotos.com*), while actually affecting the site in the top frame (e.g., Google search result page) that the victim does not see. In the example, we have made the top page partially transparent

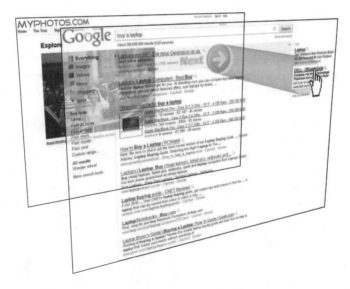

Figure 3.2   Clickjacking attack. In a clickjacking attack, a victim browses a webpage (in this example *myphotos.com* in the bottom frame) that loads an invisible top frame (in this case a Google search result page) and tricks the victim into clicking on the bottom frame while actually affecting the site in the top frame. We have made the top frame partially transparent for the purpose of illustration, whereas in the actual attack the top page is invisible to users. When the victim clicks on the button "Next" to proceed to the following photo on the *myphotos.com* page, the click is hijacked and turned into a click on a CPC ad on the invisible Google search result page.

for the purpose of illustration, whereas in the actual attack the top page is invisible to the victim. When the victim clicks on the button "Next" to proceed to the following photo on the webpage of *myphotos.com*, the click is hijacked and turned into a click on one of the CPC ads positioned on the right side of the Google search result page. In order to generate profit from clickjacking attacks, the fraudster may load his own website in the top frame (instead of Google search results as in the example) and turn hijacked clicks into clicks on CPC ads that appear on the fraudster's webpages (i.e., perform a publisher click inflation attack). Alternatively, the fraudster may load webpages on which its competitors' ads appear and generate fraudulent clicks on these (i.e., perform an advertiser competitor clicking attack). Clickjacking is possible because of web browser vulnerabilities and an interested reader can find details about countermeasures in Ref. [414]. Also, see Section 5.3 for more details on so-called tapjacking.

Fraudulent clicks have a negative effect on advertisers' returns on investment and ideally, the ad network would detect all of the fraudulent clicks, mark them as *invalid* and not charge advertisers for those clicks. To avoid the detection and ensure the revenue, the fraudulent clicks should be indistinguishable from the legitimate ones generated by users such that ad networks charge advertisers and share the revenue with publishers. That is why the fraudsters try to generate behavior patterns that resemble the behavior of legitimate users. Consequently, it is not possible to know with an absolute certainty whether a click is fraudulent or legitimate. Therefore, in order to preserve a good user experience even when a click is marked invalid, the user agent is still redirected to advertiser's website.

Estimates of the extent of the click fraud vary widely, and this is a subject of much discussion among advertisers and PPC search engines. According to Adometry (formerly, Click Forensics, Inc.), a company that performs ad traffic quality control, the click fraud rate declined in the fourth quarter of 2010 to 19.1% of the clicks being fraudulent, compared with 22.3% in the third quarter of 2010 [85]. Although this is an improvement, overall click fraud levels are still higher than the rate of 15.3% seen in 2009. However, Adometry's CEO says that this trend might not last: "While the overall click fraud rate dropped last quarter for PPC advertising, we saw the emergence of new schemes focused on display advertisements" [85].

We next present a case study of an ad fraud scheme that targets websites with display advertisements.

3.1.3.1   *Case study: advertisers scammed by porn sites*

A case of click fraud reported in 2011 is a very good example of how a fraudster may orchestrate a large scale automated attack in a way that is difficult for ad networks to distinguish fraudulent clicks from legitimate clicks, thus producing high revenue for the fraudster.

The overview of the scheme is presented in Figure 3.3. The fraudster hosts a website accessible at *www.mainsite.com* that contains links to pornographic video websites. In order to attract visitors to its website, the fraudster participates in the traffic exchange with a popular pornographic website (e.g., *www.pornsite.com*). In this traffic exchange, *www.pornsite.com* sends traffic of its legitimate visitors to *www.mainsite.com* for monetary remuneration. The traffic exchange is made possible by a man-in-the-middle website (*TrafficHolder.com*) that provides a catalog of the traffic and corresponding prices that one can buy. The scheme then executes as follows:

1. To implement the traffic exchange, when legitimate users visit *www.pornsite.com*, the site opens a pop-under window and loads the fraudster's website *www.main-site.com*, which generates traffic at the fraudster's site. According to the agreement, *www.pornsite.com* in return receives money from the fraudster. By cooperating in this way with popular websites, the fraudster is able to obtain millions of unique visitors for its own website.

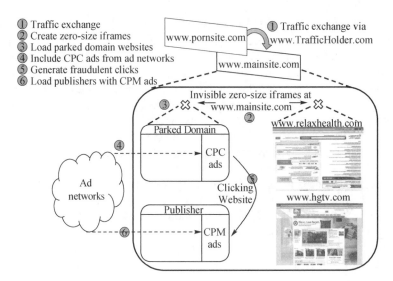

Figure 3.3   Schema of a click fraud attack. A fraudster buys legitimate traffic from a pornographic website in order to generate traffic at its own website (step 1) and produce legitimate-looking click traffic on ads. The fraudster's website creates a number of invisible iframes (step 2) that load parked domain websites (step 3) owned by the fraudster and hosting CPC ads (step 4). In collaboration with clicking websites, the parked domain websites produce fraudulent clicks on their CPC ads (step 5). Fraudulent clicks result in loading of legitimate big-name-brand publishers with their own CPM ads (step 6). Reputable advertisers that pay for their ads to appear on quality publishers' websites have their ads appear within pornographic websites, which enables AdSafe to detect the fraud.

2. When *www.mainsite.com* loads in the pop-under window, it generates a number of invisible zero-sized (i.e., 0×0 pixel) iframes.

3. Each of the iframes will load one of the *parked domain* websites registered by the fraudster. Parked domain websites are single page websites that typically do not have any content. These domains may be reserved for future development or to protect against the possibility of cybersquatting, that is, registration of Internet domain names that contain trademarks with no intention of creating a legitimate website, but instead of selling the domain name to the trademark owner. Domain parked websites typically display advertisements and thus generate revenue for the registrant. In this scheme, the parked domains loaded in invisible iframes are all registered by the fraudster and they all include advertisements. The domain names do not seem suspicious and are not related to pornographic websites (e.g., *www.relaxhealth.com* or *styleandmore.net*). This is important as most of the ad networks are not likely to include ads in pornographic websites.

4. Parked domain sites with corresponding advertisements are loaded in invisible iframes.

5. A number of clicks on ads occur. To generate the clicks, the fraudster can simply deploy one of the "clicking websites" that already have such techniques.

6. The fraudulent clicks on the ads in the parked domains will eventually result in loading one of the big-brand-name publishers (e.g., HGTV) with its own CPM advertisements.

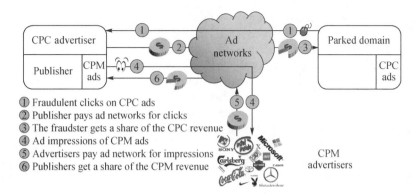

Figure 3.4   Monetization of the attack. The fraudster generates fraudulent clicks on CPC ads on his parked domain websites (step 1), for which the ad network charges the big-brand-name publishers (step 2) and shares part of the profit with the fraudster (step 3). The publishers are willing to pay as these clicks result in traffic on their websites that creates ad impressions (step 4) for which ad networks charge CPM advertisers (step 5) and share the profit with the publishers (step 6). In this scheme, the fraudster, the publishers and the ad networks make profit whereas the CPM advertisers lose revenue.

It is important to note that the big-brand-name publishers have a dual role, acting as (i) *CPC advertisers*, paying ad networks to include CPC ads with links to their websites into online content and (ii) *publishers*, collaborating with ad networks to host ads of CPM advertisers.

How does this scheme actually generate money for the fraudster? The monetization scheme is represented in Figure 3.4 and can be summarized as follows:

1. The fraudster generates fraudulent clicks on CPC ads of big-brand-name publishers that appear on his parked domain websites.

2. Ad networks charge the big-brand-name publishers (now playing a role of CPC advertisers) for the corresponding fraudulent clicks.

3. Ad networks pay a percentage of the CPC revenue to the registrant of the parked domains where the fraudulent clicks occur, that is, to the fraudster.

4. By receiving traffic from the parked domains, ad impressions on big-brand-name publishers' webpages are generated. For these ad impressions the publishers (now acting indeed as publishers hosting the ads) will obtain the revenue themselves. For this reason the fraudster cleverly targets only big-brand-name publishers that sell pay-per-impression and video ads and do not measure conversions, because for them only impressions count and any traffic is good. If the fraudster tries to load an e-commerce site that actually checks the quality of the traffic, this scheme would be detected. In addition, one more reason not to be suspicious is that the traffic toward publishers originates from legitimately sounding domain names.

5. Ad networks charge the CPM advertisers for the impressions generated on big-brand-name publishers' websites.

6. Ad networks share the CPM revenue with the big-brand-name publishers.

The ones that are hurt the most by this scheme are big-brand advertisers whose ads normally appear on reputable publishers' websites. The publishers and ad networks earn revenue by serving and displaying

CPM ads, thus they are not concerned with the scheme. Therefore, big-brand advertisers are the ones who should fight the fraud. However, they do not want their reputation to be damaged by being associated with the fraud and in addition, the scheme does not target a single party, it rather distributes the damage across a number of advertisers such that each individual does not have much incentive to fight the fraud itself.

This type of fraud has been detected by AdSafe, a company that ensures that brand advertisements appear with an appropriate content. Loading big-brand-name publishers' content and ads within the iframes of the fraudster's *www.mainsite.com* has triggered an alarm at AdSafe as advertisements of reputable brands have appeared within frames of the pornographic website. As the fraud is based on the traffic of the legitimate users who visit *www.pornsite.com*, the click patterns appear as genuine (having different IP addresses, different web browsers and at different times of the day) and are difficult to distinguish from legitimate clicks. Ad networks have a hard time detecting these clicks as fraudulent, because these clicks do not follow typical bot-generated click patterns.

A back-of-the-envelope calculation [263] shows that the fraudster may have earned between $50K to $700K per month with this scheme. Given that the scheme has been running for 8 months, in total the fraudster may have earned $400K to $5M. This proves that a moderately sophisticated ad fraud scheme can result in substantial monetary gain. In addition, the fraudster does not violate law in most of the cases, but only terms of service of online advertising networks. Therefore, legal repercussions may not be sufficient to deter the fraudster from committing ad fraud, given the revenue at stake.

3.1.3.2 *Countermeasures to fight click fraud*

As ad networks charge advertisers based on a number of impressions or clicks on advertisements, it might be counterintuitive for ad networks to have incentive to fight click fraud. In the short term, ad networks indeed earn more revenue by not filtering out fraudulent clicks. However, in the long run, the bad quality of the ad traffic may affect the reputation of the ad networks and result in poor performance of advertising campaigns, thus advertisers may stop investing in this form of advertising and publishers may not want to host the ad networks' ads within their content. Also, users may perceive ads as useless. Basically, if fraudulent clicks are not filtered out, an entire system may be ruined. An economic analysis [360], based on a game-theoretic model of the online advertising market, shows that ad networks that deploy effective countermeasures against click fraud gain a significant competitive advantage, as both publishers and advertisers will choose ad networks that offer the best return on investment.

The goal of the countermeasures deployed by ad networks is to make a successful attack more difficult or more costly for an attacker, rather than to absolutely eliminate click fraud. Most of the ad networks' techniques are kept confidential, otherwise it would be easy for the attacker to avoid detection. Typically, ad networks look for signals that indicate fraudulent click activity. Those signals may be different characteristics of HTTP traffic, anomalies in the ad click and conversion traffic, browser and user behavior that deviates from the expected behavior. Some techniques can be deployed to prevent click fraud as well, such as setting up a trust boundary between a publisher's content and ad slots on the publisher's webpages. For example, assume that a publisher embeds a script into the content of his webpages with a purpose of generating fraudulent clicks on ads that appear on these pages. If an ad network includes ads dynamically in the content in a way that the browser does not allow any script on other parts of the webpage to access the ads (e.g., by including ads in an iframe), it may prevent a potential publisher click inflation attack.

In the case suspicious activities are noticed, ad networks may set an ad traffic monitoring team to investigate and potentially terminate collaboration with publishers on whose pages a lot of fraudulent clicks occur. Trusted third-party companies are employed to verify the practices of ad networks in examining ad traffic. Such companies are independent from ad networks and advertisers, and their job is to make sure that the clicks are properly labeled as legitimate or invalid, thus assuring advertisers that they are justifiably charged for the clicks.

3.1.4 Malvertising: Spreading Malware via Ads

Malvertising, one of the fastest growing security threats on the web, is a class of online ads that attempt to infect an ad viewer's computer. It is particularly scary, because any site hosting ads and any operating system could be a potential target. Moreover, users do not even have to click on ads to trigger malware. For example, according to the report published by *Blue Coat's* research lab [316], an ad server can serve a JavaScript that, instead of fetching the legitimate ads, injects a hidden iframe tag into the original webpage. The iframe instructs the victim's browser to silently communicate with a malware server in the background, eventually resulting in the download of a PDF exploit file.

An advertiser can launch a malvertising attack, by adding its ad to a legitimate ad network. The ad network embeds the ad in publishers' websites and users click on it eventually. Publishers can also embed malvertisements into the content of their webpages to direct a user to the malicious website and install malwares.

Most of malvertisements are hosted by so-called *remnant advertising networks*. These networks sell empty advertising slots at the last opportunity. They aggregate advertisements and charge low rates. Consequently, there is less revenue and possibly less caution over the quality of advertisements.

Malvertisements can even appear at well-known websites, such as *New York Times* (reported on September 14, 2009 [284]), *Facebook* (reported on April 12, 2010 [448]), and *London Stock Exchange* (reported on March 1, 2011 [255]). For example, visitors of the London Stock Exchange's website were exposed to malicious ads, that were designed to popup fake security messages on their computers in order to sell antivirus software.

Figure 3.5 shows a malvertisement that was embedded in Microsoft's search engine Bing (reported on July 3, 2010 by *StopMalvertising.com* [458]). The ad appears among the sponsored results and it refers to Macromedia Flash, while it points to *Flash.Player-Pro-Download.com* that does not belong to Adobe. Users who click on the ad go through *rc12.overture.com* and from there browsers are redirected to *player-pro-download.com*. This looks like a clear and nice website, but no mention of Adobe anymore. Instead there are promotions for online Flash games and professional Flash tutorials. If a user tries to download such software, browsers may issue security warnings because the content is not signed with a valid security certificate.

According to Dasient (an Internet security company that protects businesses from losses of traffic, reputation, and revenue caused by web-based malware attacks) in the last 3 months of 2010 attackers managed to serve three million malvertisement impressions every day. In another study, Niels Provos (a researcher from *Google*) identified that about 2% of malicious websites were distributing malware through advertisements, based on an analysis of about 2000 known advertising networks [391].

3.1.4.1 Countermeasures to fight malvertising

Appropriate and regular checks of advertisements are the best way to avoid malvertising. The publishers and ad networks should perform regular checks to verify the advertising content providers for any kind of active or malicious code. If they detect any unexpected or unwanted behavior such as automated redirections,

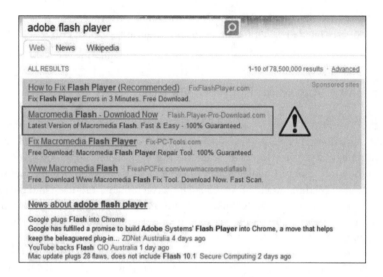

Figure 3.5   Malvertisement promoting the latest version of Adobe Flash Player was embedded in Microsoft's search engine Bing. Bing included the malvertisement as one of the sponsored search results for the keyword search "Adobe Flash Player." The malvertisement thus appeared in a colored box that marks sponsored links on the top of the results page. We single out the malvertisement with the rectangle and a danger symbol. Web browsers cannot distinguish malvertisements from legitimate links and warn the users.

they should not publish the ads to the end users. In June 2009, *Google* launched a new search engine called *investigative research engine*, publicly available at *www.Anti-Malvertising.com*. This is to help ad network partners, identify potential providers of malvertising. The Internet users should also install and update appropriate antimalware softwares on their machines to minimize the risk.

3.1.5   Inflight Modification of Ad Traffic

A novel type of ad fraud has appeared, consisting in the inflight modification of the ad traffic itself. A prominent example is the *Bahama botnet*, in which malware causes infected systems to display to end users altered ads, as well as altered search results (e.g., Google) [3]. The difference, compared to the traditional click fraud where ad networks may even earn revenue from fraudulent clicks, is that the traffic and the revenue is diverted from ad networks.

In the case of the Bahama botnet, compromised machines take their users to a fake page that looks just like the real Google search page and even returns results for queries entered into its search box. The attacker redirect users' traffic to a fake website by corrupting the DNS translation method on the infected machines. As a result, the domain name "Google.com" is translated to an IP address that is not owned by Google, but by an attacker. When a user enters a query into the search box on what they believe is a Google server, the traffic actually goes to the fraudulent server that pulls the search results for the given query from Google, meddles with them (notably, it turns organic search results into paid links) and sends the results back to the user. Consequently, the results displayed are different from what they would otherwise be. A click on an "organic" link (in this case is actually a masked CPC ad) will result in a paid click through several ad networks or parked domains. Advertisers will be charged and the click fraud has occurred. Essentially, the

Bahama botnet diverts the traffic and the revenue from major ad networks (e.g., Google) and redirects it to smaller ad networks and publishers.

Instead of compromising the users' machines, an attacker may also rely on botnets of compromised wireless routers [16]. Once a wireless router is infected with a malware and turned into a bot, the botnet master can instruct the bot to perform inflight modifications of the traffic that passes through the router. Many public hotspots rely on a similar business model: providing free Internet access to users and in return generate revenue by embedding ads into the users' traffic.

There are reports of similar behavior of some ISPs [403,506]. TrendWatch, the malware research team of web security company TrendMicro, has investigated the practices of an Estonian ISP that was replacing ads included in the webpages users were browsing [405]. The ISP was in charge of a number of DNS servers and was redirecting ad traffic from legitimate ad servers (e.g., Google ad network) to the servers of its choice. Consequently, users received ads that websites did not intend to show to its visitors. The investigation shows that thousands of ads were replaced per day, which implies that a significant ad revenue was diverted from legitimate victim ad networks.

The consequence of inflight modification of the ad traffic is that when users click on altered ads they generate revenue for the attacker instead of the legitimate ad network. Thus, the modification of the ads undermines the business model of ad networks. In addition, such attacks may also negatively affect the security of end users (malvertisement may be included instead of legitimate ads), the reputation of websites and the revenue of legitimate advertisers.

3.1.5.1 *Countermeasures to fight inflight modification of ad traffic*

In order to prevent inflight modifications (or in general, man-in-the-middle attacks) well-known solutions consist in deploying authentication and data integrity mechanisms to help guarantee the end-to-end security of communications, as done with HTTPS [404]. Nevertheless, such mechanisms have various drawbacks that hinder their large-scale deployment. First, the protection of the web content relies on cryptographic operations that induce a large computation cost on servers [404]. Second, these authentication mechanisms make use of digital certificates to enable the authentication of web servers. Digital certificates are inherently expensive because trusted certification authorities must manually verify and vouch for the identity of web servers. If a website owns a certificate issued by a trusted certification authority, then a chain of trust can be established and web browsers can authenticate the website. Alternatively, in order to avoid such costs, website administrators often choose to use self-signed certificates. This allows website administrators to produce certificates themselves instead of relying on third-party certification authorities. However, self-signed certificates could be tampered with and may not protect against man-in-the-middle attacks. A web browser cannot trust the identity of a website based on a self-signed certificate and it requires users to make a decision whether they trust the corresponding server or not. However, it is hard for end users to understand how certificates work and to validate a given certificate, which often results in users communicating with a malicious server. In order to help users properly verify self-signed certificates, the system of network notaries is built to monitor consistency of web servers' public keys over time [485]. However, this solution also has several drawbacks [485].

For these reasons, various alternative approaches are proposed to protect web content in an efficient fashion [314,403,477]. Previous work suggests encrypting all web communications using opportunistic encryption [314]: a secure channel is set up without verifying the identity of the other host. This provides a method to detect tampering with webpages, but only for expert users who know how to check certificates. But, it does not defeat man-in-the-middle attacks because an adversary can still replace the certificates used for authentication to impersonate websites. Another approach focuses on the protection of web content integrity by detecting inflight changes to webpages using a web-based measurement tool called web tripwire [403]. The web tripwire hides JavaScript code into webpages, which detects changes to an HTTP webpage and reports them to the user and to the web server. Web tripwire offers a less expensive form of a page integrity check than HTTPS but, as acknowledged by the authors, is noncryptographically secure. A secure scheme that relies on cooperation between web servers and ad networks is also proposed as a solution to thwart inflight modification of ad traffic [477]. This solution relies on the fact that most of online advertising networks own digital authentication certificates and can become a source of trust, needed to provide authenticity and integrity of the traffic.

Implementing the proposed solutions to protect against inflight modification of ad traffic incur a cost for ad networks and publishers. However, an economic analysis [478] that uses a game-theoretic model to analyze the interactions of an ad network and an ISP that performs inflight modification of ad traffic shows that, under certain conditions, investing into security of advertising systems is the best strategy for ad networks.

3.1.6   Adware: Unsolicited Software Ads

The term adware refers to any software that displays advertisements without users' permission [147,436]. They are often designed to present advertisements according to the websites users visit. Adwares are produced by advertisers or by publishers of free software. Accordingly, adwares can broadly be divided into two main groups.

The first group of adwares are published for users who do not wish to pay for certain software. Many programs, games, or utilities are ad supported and distributed as adware (or freeware). If users purchase a registration key, they can disable displays of ads. The ads should also disappear as soon as the user uninstalls the software. In this case, adware is usually seen by the developer as a way to recover development costs, and in some cases it may allow for the software to be provided to users free of charge or at a reduced price. The income derived from presenting advertisements to users may allow or motivate the developer to continue to develop, maintain, and upgrade the software product. As an example, the *Eudora* mail client displays advertisements as an alternative to shareware registration fees.

The second group of adware can be described as a form of *spyware* that collects information about users in order to display advertisements in the web browser. In other words, it displays advertisements related to the data it collects by spying on users. When adware becomes intrusive like this, it can be categorized as *spyware* and users should avoid it for privacy and security reasons. In this case, adware can intercept all information that users enter via the web, add unauthorized sites to desktops and Internet favorites, track and monitor browser activity or attach the unwanted toolbars and searchbars to browsers without users' knowledge or approval. Moreover, the personal information can be sold to other parties without users' knowledge or consent. Finally, adware can hijack the default homepage and settings so the user cannot change them.

As an example, *YapBrowser* is an adware (spyware) that served unsolicited, aggressive advertisements, redirected users to undesirable websites, and modified essential system settings. This product was designed to be illegally installed on users' computers in order to make profit for spyware and adware creators. It must be noted that YapBrowser was bundled with the *Zango* software, a software company that provided users access to its partners' videos, games, tools, and utilities in exchange for viewing targeted advertisements on their computers. In June 2006, YapBrowser was acquired by UK's *SearchWebMe*. *SearchWebMe* assures that the new *YapBrowser* download does not contain any adware or harmful applications. *Gator Software* from *Claria* Corporation and *Exact Advertising's BargainBuddy* are two other famous adwares in this category.

3.1.6.1 Countermeasures to fight adware

Users should avoid visiting untrusted websites because they are mainly delivering adware and spyware to unsuspecting users. Moreover, they can also install and update regularly antiadware softwares. Finally, they should carefully read the terms of use for free software as they potentially install the adware as well. Note that it is required by law to state whether or not software has adware bundled with it.

3.1.7 Conclusion

Internet economy relies on online advertising as the main business model for monetizing online content. Given the ad revenue at stake and the lack of legislation against ad fraud in many countries, fraudsters have economic incentive to engage in fraudulent activities and exploit online advertising systems.

This section provides a detailed description of existing online advertising systems and their vulnerabilities. We explained how fraudsters can exploit these vulnerabilities and launch ad fraud attacks that we broadly divide into four main categories: *click fraud*, *malvertising*, *inflight modification of ad traffic*, and *adware*. For each type of attack, we presented techniques that fraudsters deploy to make profit from the advertising systems. In particular, we presented a case study of a click fraud attack that made substantial amount of money (up to $5M) for the fraudster while stealthily running for 8 months. We discussed challenges of ad fraud detection and mitigation as well as several deployed countermeasures. However, much research is still needed in order to design more robust countermeasures and protect the Internet business model.

3.2 TOEING THE LINE: LEGAL BUT DECEPTIVE SERVICE OFFERS

Markus Jakobsson and Ruilin Zhu

Abstract. Phishing is illegal in most jurisdictions. However, as described in Section 3.1, advertisement fraud is commonly only a breach of terms of service. This section describes another type of activity that—while unwanted and deceptive—may not be illegal. We describe a particular instance of this type of abuse, and estimate the size of the profit for the perpetrator.

Given the lack of risk and the quite substantial profits, we expect that this type of abuse will substantially increase in commonality.

The nature of the abuse is for perpetrators to send deceptively phrased service offers to unsuspecting users, where a large portion of the users will believe that the service offers are invoices they have to pay. This is not illegal, since the perpetrators in fact are service providers, and the users sign up for their services by paying. However, the services are not of any value to the users, and no users would have paid if they had understood the true nature of what they are paying for.

This is not a new type of abuse, but it is one that we expect could increase in commonality quite dramatically given the ease with which the perpetrators can collect the contextual information needed to target users in a convincing way. All it takes is a search engine, or access to public databases—at least for the particular instance that we describe.

We describe a deceptive offer in which perpetrators identify recently filed patents and trademarks, and send official-looking invoices to inventors and their organizations. These invoices are, if read carefully, simply offers to list the patent or trademark application in a web-facing database. This is not at all a valuable service to the inventor or person registering the trademark, as it does not positively affect their ability to obtain the patent or trademark. (However, the publication is very helpful for us to estimate the profit of the perpetrators.)

3.2.1 How Does it Work?

1. Imagine that you file an international patent or trademark application. It is messy and confusing, and there is lots of paperwork and fees. But you do it anyway.

2. As your application is received, this fact is *published*. Anybody who cares to see what patents and trademarks have been filed internationally can go through the database, and they will see your name, address, and the name and number of the application. That is what the perpetrator does.

3. The perpetrator then sends you an invoice—asking you to pay around $2500 to register the patent or trademark application in some country. And then another invoice for about the same amount, to register it in another country. And maybe a third one as well—you get the point. All of these invoices look like they relate to your application. They have your name, address, the name and number of the application. If you read the find print, though, you will see that registering the patent or trademark really means to postinformation about it—the information the perpetrator has already obtained about your application!—on a website that the perpetrator controls. That is the service you are paying for—not to have the patent or trademark application *processed* in that country.

4. Say you send them the money, and later realize what happened and complain. Will they refund the money? Not so likely. What if you report them to the police? No problem for them—they have not done anything illegal! They *did* follow their part of the agreement: to publish the information about your application on their website.

The invoices are sent by regular mail. This is probably for two reasons. The first one is that it makes it very realistic, and it is worth their investment of a stamp. Second, they have your address, but not your email address, so itâŁ™s really the *only* way to do it.

3.2.2 What do they Earn?

We have found more than 30 sites performing this "legal scam." All these websites have seemingly formal names and layouts that—while simple—keep their side of the bargain: to publish the information of the "victims."

Reviewing some of these databases, we see that several of them have a substantial number of entries, each of which indicates a successful deceptive offer. We can use that to estimate the profit of the perpetrators.

The scam yields big profits for the perpetrators due to the huge difference between the high income and the low expenses to obtain the contextual information, send the mails and to operate the databases. Take WPTI (World Patent and Trademark Index) for example, which has the smallest number of entries in our example. Rough estimates indicate that the gross income from 2008 to 2011 amounted to more than $7.7 million, given that 3085 entries were added and each entry corresponds to an income of approximately

Table 3.1   Type and Number of Entries Per Year for Two Databases

Database	Type	Number of entries (per year)	Year
WPTI	Patent	74	2008
(World Patent and		138	2009
Trademark Index)		63	2010
		2,810	2011
RIPT	Patent	48,955	2010
(Register of		16,779	2011
International Patents	Trademark	18,699	2010
and Trademarks)		4,365	2011

For each entry, somebody regretted paying around $2500 for no particular reason.

$2500. Looking now at the cost of retrieving information and maintaining the database, we estimate that this should not have cost more than $5000. The cost of sending out letters is estimated at $2 a piece. With an estimated yield of 1%—which we believe is a vast underestimate—and 3085 victims, that suggests a mailing cost of $610,000. This provides a profit of $1.8 million *a year*, since this database runs from 2008 to 2011. Seen another way, the profit per letter sent out is $23 according to these estimates. This is for *one* of the databases alone. The profit corresponding to the other databases in Table 3.1 exceeds $100 million per year, or $160 million all in all if we assume that other databases *only* have the same profits as WPTI. No wonder this is an increasingly common scam!

It is apparent from Figure 3.6 that after some fluctuations in the number of entries for WPTI from 2008 to 2010, there is a dramatic jump in 2011. This trend is echoed by the number of entries in RIPT, which was very large in 2010 and 2011. The slight decline in 2011 may be due to fierce competition for the attention and money by many more sites launched recently.

In response, many official organizations and agencies issue warnings and alerts to make potential victims aware of this scam. People are told to be careful when receiving an invoice asking for payment of

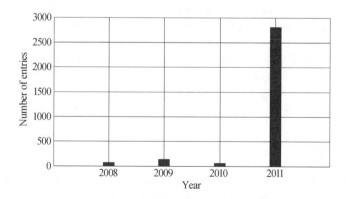

Figure 3.6   Number of entries for the database called WPTI (World Patent and Trademark Index) between 2008 and 2011, with an accumulated profit of approximately $7.1 million. WPTI is only one of the many operations that have sprung up to separate the careless inventor from his or her money.

fees. However, inventors are not well aware of the scam at all—this is evident from the number of entries in the databases, as seen in Table 3.1 and Figure 3.6.

3.3   PHISHING AND SOME RELATED ATTACKS

Markus Jakobsson and William Leddy

Abstract. This section summarizes a variety of attacks that try to capture a user's account and password information, including a potential new attack that could target mobile users. In this new attack, which we call the man-in-the screen attack, a fraudster can simulate the appearance of a mobile device reboot through a webpage and then attempt to collect user information.

3.3.1   The Problem is the User

First, let's look at the problems and attacks that cause exposure of personal user information like account IDs, passwords, credit card numbers, and more.

Typical users will

- click on any link in their browser or email attachments,
- install anything they find on the Internet onto their system without vetting the source.

Users are the biggest security weakness in the system.
At the same time, these same users expect to be completely protected so when there is a lapse they feel that their confidence has been betrayed.

Fraudsters will continue to victimize these users as long as it is an easy path for them to make money. Fraudsters have a variety of attack scenarios to capture user account IDs, passwords, and financial information or to trick the user into performing transactions for them. These include phishing, man-in-the-middle, key-logging, man-in-the-browser (MITB), mobile malware, and a new potential attack that we describe and that we call the "man-in-the-screen" attack.

The rapid rise of mobile phone applications and the ability to make easy payments within the applications is a great convenience to users. The range of services and payment options should explode over the next few years but security concerns are likely to be ignored in favor of ease of use. This will make mobile devices a new favorite target for attackers.

3.3.2   Phishing

Phishing email and phishing sites continue to be a simple low-cost and low-risk tool for attackers to gather user information. The user receives an urgent email to login into their account to check, update their information, or participate in a survey. The email contains a link to a fake site that collects account information. Once the phisher has the user's account information, he can log in into the user's account and start making transactions. For example, a phisher can make payments to other accounts he controls to get the funds out of the system.

Or, if the phisher captures a credit/debit card or bank number, he can create a new online account at multiple merchants. For example, a phisher can make online purchases of goods that are sent to drop addresses where no one is home during the day so he can pick them up from the porch or sent to unwitting helpers that forward goods overseas. The phisher gets goods or funds while the victim gets the bill.

The sophistication of phishing sites has increased substantially in the past few years. It is no longer sufficient to look for poor wording or formatting to detect a suspect site. Phishers have become better at disguising the true URL in their email. For example, most phishing email contains web links like www.name_of_a_bank.com that appears to be correct when viewed as rich text or html in Outlook, but the actual link destination does not match the appearance. This is a feature of HTML that is intended to make the text message readable while hiding the complexity of the link, but fraudsters exploit it to hide the true destination. The URLs at phish sites have become more complex to obscure their true destination. Links like name_of_a_bank.myphishsite.com intend to confuse users. Here, instead of something obvious like www.myphishsite.com there would be a web domain that the phisher created and registered with some name that appears safe, like customersupport.z345x.com. Or the phisher could have taken over a subdomain of a legitimate website like *support*.legitwebsite.com by creating more pages on a legitimate website, or manipulating DNS servers that resolve names to websites. In these cases the administrators of legitwebsite do not even know that a subdomain has been created.

Phishers come up with novel bait every year, like an order confirmation notice for a bogus item with the request that you immediately log in at the linked address "if you did not place the order." Another example is the "Nationwide Survey" targeting Chase customers with an offer to "credit your account with $50" if you complete the survey. The worst phishing examples exploit human tragedies like the earthquake in Haiti or Japan to ask users for donations. As long as users continue to click on the phishing email links, phishers will continue to make money. This gives them means and motivation to continue the evolution of their approach.

Spear phishing uses targeted email containing user specific information. This could include the user's full name, address, or bank name. Using only a small amount of user information like first name, last name, and bank name, the phisher can send the victim a customized email. The phish email can be personalized for the user to include first and last name or some other personal information like the victim's address. Since the user sees their correct first and last names in the greeting, they are more likely to click on the link in the email. The phisher can further obscure themselves by hiding the true source of the email by making it look like it came from the user's bank like donotreply@name_of_a_bank.com. The user is requested to immediately log in to their account to confirm recent suspicious transactions by clicking the link.

With a little more user information due to lax security by firms and a small bit of additional work by fraudsters, phishing continues to remain a profitable approach by evolving. Just a few details add greatly to the credibility of the scams and yield higher profits for the fraudsters.

Mobile phishing is more dangerous than phishing, because users are "always on" with mobile technologies, and so, will be able to react to phishing messages much faster. That makes takedown efforts less helpful.

3.3.3 Man-in-the-Middle

Let's start by reviewing the well-known man-in-the-middle and man-in-the-browser attacks, and then look at a new style attack, not yet seen in the wild. For a MITM attack, the fraudster tricks the user into connecting to a fraudulent system that forward all traffic to and from the legitimate web server. The user cannot easily detect the man-in-the-middle attack because it comes from the legitimate server the entire experience is authentic. The user appears to have the expected interaction with the web server, but the fraudulent system collects the user's account ID and password for future use or inserts additional actions. Once a user has logged into a web service the fraudulent system could create additional transactions to send goods or funds to the fraudsters. So if you buy flowers for $60 for that special someone, the middleman "Transaction Generator" can insert another transaction to send $50 to markus@bad_guy.com without being challenged for additional authentication. The user will not see the transaction because it is silently inserted and it is unlikely that an additional authentication challenge would be triggered because a larger transaction was already allowed. The user won't find out about the additional transactions until he gets the bill or reviews his account some time later.

The web server may be able to detect a man-in-the-middle attack by analyzing the IP addresses and traffic rates, but this has been made more difficult because the fraudsters control large networks of hijacked systems so-called botnets. By routing the traffic through the botnets, the fraudsters can diffuse the traffic across many machines. Since the fraudster can use a different machine in their network for each new victim, the legitimate service cannot identify many accounts accessing the site from the single IP. By using only a small botnet the attack is likely to go undetected.

Even if the legitimate web site suspects that a man-in-the-middle attack is happening, additional authentication does not help. Challenges like Security Questions or receiving an Out-of-Band SMS message are useless to detect or block the attack since the challenge is passed to the legitimate user to answer. For example, if the user is challenged by sending an SMS one time password to the user's legitimate phone number, the user will receive the SMS and enter the value into the webpage. When the user submits the value it goes to the middleman server that forward it to the legitimate server. The bad server in the middle is not detected or blocked since it just forward everything.

The device ID (see Section 7.7) is based on browser cookies, flash objects or a hardware identifier can provide only limited help to address the man-in-the-middle attack. Since many good users clear or block these identifiers with the intention of protecting their identity, they are indistinguishable from the fraudsters who are even more likely to block these identifiers. Good users are also constantly buying new devices and logging in from new IP addresses, so new machines accessing an account are not a strong indicator of fraudsters.

3.3.4   Man-in-the-Browser

A man-in-the-browser attack is similar to a man-in-the-middle attack, but the fraudster's software is running on the user's machine instead of a separate server. The user is tricked into installing malware onto their system that targets the browser. It may be part of some browser plugin the user thought he needed. It may be completely transparent to the user. For example, the user may have been asked to install some special video plugin to watch a funny video, but the plugin contained more than the user knows about. Man-in-the-browser attacks typically result from user actions and vulnerable browsers or operating systems, or other software vulnerabilities permitting infection of the client machine.

The man-in-the-browser malware can invisibly modify transactions information like the amount or destination. It can also create additional transactions without the user knowing. Because the requests appear to come from the user's legitimate machine, it is very difficult for the web service to detect that the requests are not legitimate. Because the device information (see Section 7.7) appears to correctly match the user's past account activity, the receiving website receiving the traffic will not be suspicious.

3.3.5 New Attack: Man-in-the-Screen

A man-in-the-screen attack can be performed in a variety of ways. In one version, the attack starts by getting the victim to open a malicious webpage in their mobile device browser. This could be initiated by simply clicking on a link in a phishing email. It could also be an enticing web ad link. The attacker's webpage is intended to be displayed on a mobile browser. He makes the webpage look like the screen of a typical such device (Figure 3.7), including a collection of common icons that may be available on the device as it is purchased, but the webpage is longer than the screen. A command (see Section 5.3.2) to scroll the view down can be issued to make the webpage hide its address bar, which is commonly allowed on handsets in order to conserve important screen real estate.

As a result, the user can be tricked into believing that his phone has crashed and reverted to an earlier state. After a few seconds or after some end user action is observed, the bogus webpage can show what looks like a popup that explains to the user that the phone has crashed. The webpage can then request that the user input some password (such as the iTunes password) to complete the crash recovery.

The user enters their password into what he believes is a local application but is really a just a clever and malicious webpage. The use has now given his account and password to the attacker, who could then automatically log in to the user's account (iTunes or other marketplace account) and determine what applications are installed, such as financial applications. Then, the attacker can display apparent popups to the user asking the user to input passwords for these applications, and collect the passwords that the user enters. Many versions of this attack are possible, and it is not easy to detect these using traditional means. The mobile web browser has no way to recognize an ill-behaved website that attempts this attack. That is because it is hard for the browser to determine how a webpage would be rendered and understood by an end

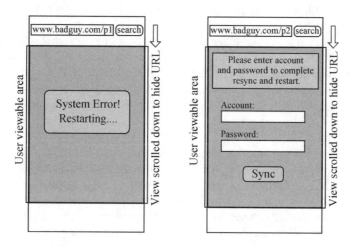

Figure 3.7 The fraudster's web address is hidden by scrolling the display: The user is tricked into viewing a page on his mobile device without the address bar. A command (see Section 5.3) makes the browser URL field at the top of the page scroll out of view so the user does not realize he is still viewing a webpage. The fraudster can then simulate a restart of the mobile device. During the fake restart, the webpage can request a variety of user information. The user will likely provide the information since he believes that it is only a local interaction with his device. The fraud webpage captures the user's information and redirects the user to another page. The user may never realize that he gave his information to a fraud site. Later the fraudster sells or uses the account information to steal funds and goods while the user gets the bill.

user, and to determine whether this is abusive or intends to defraud. Since the browser controls the entire context there is no other application to monitor this behavior, even if there was a clear pattern to identify. The window scrolling behavior that lets a fraudster and legitimate app to hide the true URL effectively enables this attack, but is a feature that is needed for legitimate use due to the limited mobile screen size. At the time of the writing, man-in-the-screen attacks have not been identified in the wild.

In Section 5.1, we take a look at the particular problem of *mobile* phishing, and in Section 7.6 we look at what can be done to mitigate the phishing threat—on mobiles and elsewhere.

3.4 MALWARE: CURRENT OUTLOOK

Members of the BITS Security Working Group and staff leads Greg Rattray and Andrew Kennedy

Abstract. We describe the malware situation at the time of writing, with a focus on historical trends and an outlook on the likely future.

3.4.1 Malware Evolution

Software-enabled crime is not a new concept [304]. Computer-enabled fraud and service theft evolved in parallel with the information technology that enabled it. Since the advent of mainframe-based automated bank account systems, FIs have been victims of malware-based cyber attacks. Criminals altered software to transfer other people's money to accounts they controlled, and emptied the accounts anonymously. As computers were shared on networks, these services experienced service theft, wherein criminals altered system software to hide reconnaissance activities that enabled theft of both valuable services and valuable information [456].

This coevolution of technology services and cybercrime may have created some confusion in the general population, for whom attacks on technology do not seem to be as significant as attacks on physical assets. Those not familiar with the emerging technology itself find it difficult to understand the implications of software compromise. General confusion over cybercrime objectives is exacerbated by the element of opportunism in some types of cybercrime, wherein attackers do not select specific victims, but simply let rogue software loose to find its own targets. This type of cybercrime appears to some segments of the public as bad luck for the victim rather than as a direct result of adversarial intent.

Nevertheless, even opportunistic cybercriminals select their targets, if only by selecting the operating system platform on which malware may be processed. Where the platform is the latest version of an emerging technology, the selected victim class may be assumed to be those financially able to afford that new technology. Another selection made by cybercriminals is the specification of data that malware processes. Where data concerning credit card numbers is sought, the target victim class includes all credit card holders and associated institutions. Where the data sought is bank account numbers, all financial firms are targets. The attraction of cybercrime lies in the high return on investment, low-to-no-risk operating environments, and proliferation of vulnerable computing resources. The ubiquitous connectedness provided by the Internet has allowed for multiple elements of the criminal community to operate in tandem to pursue profit-driven crime as well as other malicious activities, using malware.

To the casual observer, headlines about cyber attacks may seem unrelated. Attacks are scattered across geography and technology. They involve different companies and nationalities. As recently as 5 years ago, security standards publications identified malware and phishing attacks as separate threats [349]. However, today security analysts agree that various types of malware are used in conjunction [32]. Cooperation and collaboration among cybercriminals have created crime patterns that evolve in concert with emerging technology, and all users of emerging technology are victims. There is also evidence that cybercriminals operate in geopolitically identifiable groups. As one analyst put it, "the phrase 'campaign' is more appropriate than 'adversary' [155]."

Malware is typically used to steal information that can be readily monetized, such as login credentials, credit card and bank account numbers, and intellectual property such as computer software, financial algorithms, and trade secrets. Although many cybercriminal groups are trafficking in commodities shared by multiple industry sectors, such as credit card numbers, there are some situations wherein a single company is obviously the target of a single adversary, whether it be an organized crime syndicate, nation-state, or a single operative. For example, the work of a single nation-state adversary was evident to Google upon analysis of its 2009 cyber attack [266]. The extent to which any given attack lands on one set of companies or customers rather than another depends on a variety of factors.

Just as information technology software tools and techniques have become more proficient, more effective, and more economical over time, malware crime patterns have become more finely tuned.

3.4.1.1 *Malware categories*

Malware may take as many forms as software. It may be deployed on desktops, servers, mobile phones, printers, and programmable electronic circuits. Sophisticated attacks have confirmed data can be stolen through well written malware residing only in system memory without leaving any footprint in the form of persistent data. Malware has been known to disable information security protection mechanisms such as desktop firewalls and antivirus programs. Some even have the ability to subvert authentication, authorization, and audit functions. It has configured initialization files to maintain persistence even after an infected system is rebooted. Upon execution, sophisticated malware may self-replicate and/or lie dormant until summoned via its command features to extract data or erase files.

A single piece of malware is generally described by four attributes of its operation [109]:

- **Propagation** The mechanism that enables malware to be distributed to multiple systems.
- **Infection** The installation routine used by the malware, as well as its ability to remain installed despite disinfection attempts.
- **Self-defense** The method used to conceal its presence and resist analysis, these techniques may also be called antireversing capabilities.
- **Capabilities** Software functionality available to malware operator.

Note that Table 3.2 refers only to single pieces of software and that there is no hierarchy in malware classification. However, alluded to in the description of a bot is the fact that a typical cybercrime will require multiple different types of software acting in coordination in order to achieve the full crime capability. For example, a criminal may use email spamming software (a form of flaw exploit) to trick a user into downloading a keylogger from an infected website. The criminal would then have to host a site for the keylogger to deliver the stolen credentials. The criminal would presumably use software to read and analyze the credentials, and then perhaps use vulnerability scanning software to see which websites identified by them have flawed software. The criminal may then use the user name and password to execute flaw exploits against the website. The steps a criminal must follow in order to accomplish a typical cybercrime are outlined in Figure 3.8 [155]. Activities included in each step are as follows:

Table 3.2   This Table Lists Some Examples of Malware in the Context of this Taxonomy

	Propagation	Infection	Self-defense	Capabilities
Keylogger	Infected websites and/or USB or other media	Vulnerable browsers or unpatched OS or application	Replace IO device drivers or APIs	Collect user keystrokes including credentials
Rootkit	Infected websites and/or installs on servers by hackers or insiders	Exploited trusted admin access, vulnerable browsers, or unpatched OS or application	Replacing OS kernel-level API routines	Collect data and impersonate user activity for entire machine and its interfaces
Flaw exploits	Execution of unexpected commands to flawed software by remote hackers	Vulnerable software-to-database and command execution interfaces	Impersonation of authorized users	Download or upload data from data repositories between target and malware operator site
Bot (the same bot on multiple machines from the same malware operator is called a botnet)	Bots are generally delivered via infected websites, or links to malicious websites embedded in phishing email.	User may voluntarily install individual bots based on deceptive messages in email or web instruction, or via browser/OS vulnerabilities	Bot updates security patches and antivirus on machine to ensure stable operation and keep other bots out. Lays dormant until activated	When activated by botnet operator, the operator may direct bot to execute a variety of standard or custom functions
Denial of service (host or network)	IP packet delivery	Internet protocols that automate packet processing	Simultaneously attack from multiple sources	Consume computing resources on targets

It is not meant to be complete, but to provide an appreciation for the variety of software types and capabilities that fall into the general category of malware.

- **Reconnaissance**   Criminal surveys the target to identify points of vulnerability, an attack-planning phase.
- **Assembly**   Criminal creates, customizes, or otherwise obtains malware to satisfy attack requirements.
- **Delivery**   Malware propagation occurs.
- **Compromise**   Malware infection occurs.
- **Command**   Malware capabilities are unleashed.
- **Execution**   Malware delivers data to malware operator (exfiltration) or otherwise accomplishes attack objective.

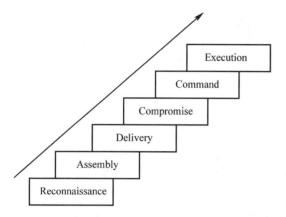

Figure 3.8 The life cycle of a sophisticated cyberattack.

Although there are a wide variety of words and phrases that the media uses to refer to malware, they all have their roots in the execution paths illustrated in Table 3.2 and Figure 3.8. The specialized terminology tends to refer to the type of crime perpetrated using the software rather than the technical description of the attack. For example

- **Malvertising** The practice of paying for web advertisements and using them to cause malware propagation.
- **Ransomware** The use of malware to block access to computers or data until a payment is made, also continues to be used for extortion purposes.
- **Rogueware** Malware that is written to look and act like legitimate packages, in order to trick victims into downloading and installing it.
- **Scareware** Malware that is written to look and act like legitimate security antivirus packages, in order to trick victims into buying worthless software to fix nonexistent virus or spyware problems, scareware may be a form of rogueware.
- **Spearphishing** Phishing attacks directed at wealthy or otherwise singularly attractive targets with specific knowledge, capability, or expertise.
- **Spyware** The use of malware to observe any user activity, including keystrokes and screenshots, and network connections, typically used to transfer passwords and credit card numbers to the malware operator.

3.4.1.2 Malware example

As described in Section 3.4.1, malware usage is enabled by emerging technology, and evolves with it. For example, the advent of iframe technology in web services has enabled a specific brand of malware. The technology allows a URL to be placed in a webpage hosted on server A that displays content from server B. The user accessing server A does not see the call to server B, as server B's content appears displayed in the page rendered by server A. There are a variety of legitimate reasons why a legitimate website may want to display content from multiple servers simultaneously. There may be complex specialized algorithms required to display numerical data that is generated in real time, and so, beyond the CPU capacity of a single web server. There may be business relationships that require display of partner logos or advertisements from

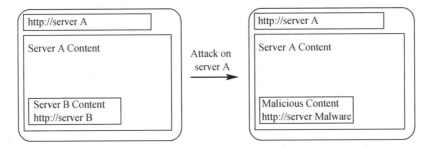

Figure 3.9   Following the compromise of server A, the attacker, unbeknownst to the web client, replaces the legitimate third party iframe source to one with a malicious payload.

business partner servers. For whatever reason, the legitimate iframe feature exists. The iframe feature by itself does not enable malware. Criminals take advantage of the feature by exploiting web server vulnerabilities and inserting their own servers in replacement, or in addition to a legitimately placed server B (for a full explanation of this vulnerability, see [33]). Figure 3.9 illustrates how the server is modified to set up for a subsequent attack on a web server user. There also are vulnerabilities in browsers with which users visit sites that have iframes. The combination of server and browser vulnerabilities enable malware criminals to use iframes for malware propagation and infection. The iframe-enabled web server, the code it links to on the malware host site, and the code that is downloaded to the user when the user accesses the iframe are different pieces of malware. They are used in combination to infect the user. Only after the infection takes place for the last of these pieces, the malware on the end user target, is it fully enabled with self-defense and functional capabilities required to harvest data.

As described, successful crime execution using malware is a multistep process. Figure 3.10 illustrates these steps using the iframe attack as an example.

The actual malware installed by a propagation and infection process, such as that illustrated in Figure 3.10, will vary. An archetypal example is Zeus [52]. On an infected system, Zeus' self-defense mechanisms include evasion of system-monitoring tools by modifying system Application Programming Interfaces (APIs). This enables it to hide Zeus' configuration files on disk and inspect incoming and outgoing network traffic. Zeus also disables the Windows firewall. Postinfection, Zeus capabilities include, but are not limited to

- exporting private key certificates
- exporting protected storage passwords
- monitoring for file transfer and email passwords (FTP and POP3)
- logging keystrokes
- taking screenshots
- HTML injection
- form grabbing for transaction authentication numbers (TAN)
- automatic transaction hijacking (ATH)
- transfer of encrypted stolen credentials to malware operators in near real time (using Jabber)
- routing connections through the infected machine
- attacking other systems on the local network

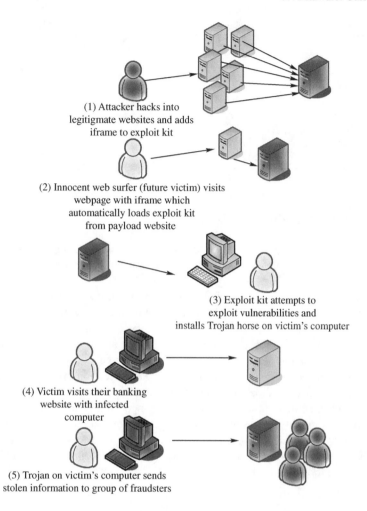

(1) Attacker hacks into
legitigmate websites and adds
iframe to exploit kit

(2) Innocent web surfer (future victim) visits
webpage with iframe which
automatically loads exploit kit
from payload website

(3) Exploit kit attempts to
exploit vulnerabilities and
installs Trojan horse on victim's computer

(4) Victim visits their banking
website with infected
computer

(5) Trojan on victim's computer sends
stolen information to group of fraudsters

Figure 3.10   Notice how once the attack is set up, the process for stealing sensitive information is highly automated and scalable with little interaction by the fraudster.

3.4.1.3 *Polymorphic malware*

Remediation of modern malware is becoming increasingly more difficult due to several factors. There are significantly more varieties of malware being found in the wild that exploit zero-day vulnerabilities. "Zero-day" modifies the word vulnerability to mean that the vulnerability is not known to potential victims, and so victims have had no days to prepare for it. Malware has also now been designed with polymorphic capabilities. Polymorphic malware changes certain characteristics of itself upon each instance or infection. This change can be in the form of a nonfunctional code change. This technique circumvents signature-based detection mechanisms because these typically use a hash algorithm to produce a unique signature from a file containing malware, so any change to the file will change its signature. Polymorphic malware can also change its own filename on each infection, and this also makes detection more difficult by traditional means.

Table 3.3 Example Prices for Stolen Information

Type of stolen information	**Price**
CCV	$3.25
OS administrative login	$2.50
FTP exploit	$6.00
Full identity information	$5.00
Rich bank account credentials	$750.00
US passport information	$800.00
Router credentials	$12.50

3.4.2 Malware Supply and Demand

The root cause of malware is the black market for stolen information. Data thieves can sell their spoils in a variety of forums [350]. Examples of prices obtained for various types of stolen information are listed in Table 3.3 [208].

In any dynamic marketplace, the prices claimed for a commodity will fluctuate with supply and demand. In any technology marketplace, prices will also fluctuate with the utility of the commodity, given changes in technology landscape. The dollars commanded for stolen commodities listed in Table 3.3 motivated the creation of secondary malware markets that produce software tools that make malware increasingly effective at enabling information theft. Individuals use software generally to automate tasks that are both tedious and resource intensive, and malware perpetrators are no exception. Automating malware delivery and data harvesting tasks reduces operating costs and allows malicious perpetrators to obscure their activities. Malware delivery and operations systems have become increasingly modular, and these modules have themselves become a commodity. Prices obtained for modular software information theft enablers are listed in Table 3.4. The prices were observed in the same timeframe as the prices that were commanded for stolen information in Table 3.3. It is obvious that information on financial accounts may be sold for multiples above the cost to purchase the tools that enable the theft.

Table 3.4 Example Prices for Malware and Crimeware [208]

Theft enabling commodity	Price
Keystroke logger	$25 on average
Botnets	$100 to $200 per 1000 infections, depending on location
Spamming email service	$.01 per 1000 emails, reliability of more than 85% delivered
Shop admins (credit card databases)	$100 to $300
Credit card numbers without CCV2	$1 to $3
Credit card numbers with CCV2	$1.50 to $10.00, depending on the country
Socks accounts	$5 to $40/month
Sniffer dumps	$50 to $100/month
Western Union exploits	$300 to $1000
Remote desktops	$5 to $8
Scam letters	$3 to $5

When such malware software support systems are discovered to exist, the software is referred to as crimeware [277]. Continuing the Zeus malware example from Section 3.4.1, a good example of crimeware is the Zeus toolkit. Zeus malware was introduced in 2006, and its corresponding crimeware followed in 2007. Zeus' crimeware takes advantage of its modular design, so attackers can configure and deploy new functionality very quickly. A user-friendly graphical interface allows an attacker to select the capabilities to be incorporated in a "release" as well as to select a personal encryption key for harvested data. Over 5000 releases of the Zeus software have been created using Zeus crimeware [301]. Although several Zeus users have been identified and charged with cybercrimes, the Zeus crimeware authors remain at large.

3.4.2.1 The malware industry

Malware development and distribution is highly organized and controlled by criminal groups that have formalized and implemented business models to automate cybercrime. Just as the software industry has spawned a business model in reselling, installing, and maintaining legitimate code, the malware industry has spawned distribution and support networks to assist criminals in successful malware usage. Developers of crimeware profit from the sale or lease of the malware to third parties who then use it to perpetrate identity theft and account fraud. Figure 3.11 illustrates the interaction between components in a typical crimeware business model. Individual groups of criminals coordinate their efforts, and the product is crimeware as a service (CAAS).

The process depicted in Figure 3.11 leads with software vulnerabilities being sought by criminals in a systematic way. The figure begins with "zero-day" vulnerabilities, because these are more valuable to malware creators because potential victims are unsuspecting. These vulnerabilities are sold to criminals who engineer malware to exploit the vulnerability, and aggregate multiple malware vulnerability exploits into kits whose components can be systematically installed as in the iframe example in Section 3.4.1.3. Because many vulnerabilities exist in unpatched systems long after they have been announced, exploit

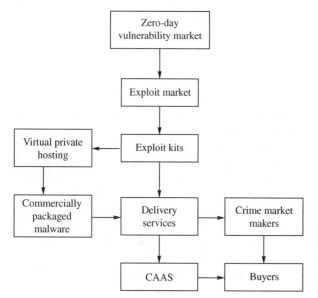

Figure 3.11 Zero-day vulnerabilities are highly sought commodities and once integrated into preexisting exploitation delivery and data exfiltration middleware or services require little technical expertise to operate by the cybercriminal.

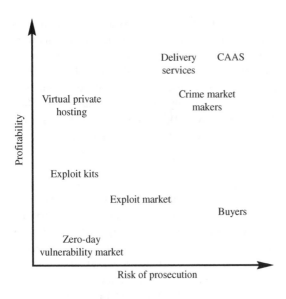

Figure 3.12 Note how a hacker who discovers and disseminates a zero-day exploit bares the least exposure but also reaps less reward than the middleware producers who package the exploit and the actors who operationalize the criminal activity.

kits may include combinations of zero-day and older attacks. The kits are configured to send harvested data to private hosting services, and this configuration may be customized for a given buyer. Crimeware market makers contact potential customers via email and chat, agree on prices and sell not just software, but crimeware services. They engage malware delivery services to operate the malware on behalf of buyers, who pay the market makers via anonymous e-commerce payment systems. Crimeware operation is blatantly illegal, yet individual risk of criminal prosecution is minimized by the overall business model. Each malware profit center has a level of exposure corresponding only to its role in the overall marketplace. For example, in academic circles, the study of vulnerabilities is common. Academics write papers on engineering and reverse engineering of exploits, and this is not considered criminal activity. The relative prosecution risk to profit ratio for each activity in Figure 3.11 is estimated in Figure 3.12.

3.4.2.2 Malware supply chain

Earnings for malware development are time sensitive but are very low risk. During the life cycle of malware, protections are developed to mitigate the risk. To remain competitive and profitable new malware must be released frequently. Security analysts are seeing dramatic increases in the number of malware specimens created and distributed. One report claims that a full third of all viruses that exist were created in 2010 [50]. The profit incentive driving these activities creates a persistent risk for financial institutions. The supply chain in the malware industry encompasses more than just software. It is an elaborate collection of organizations, people, technologies, processes, services, and products. Financial services such as moneygrams, virtual credit cards, and online money transfer services allow anonymity between buyers and sellers. However, not all of the players in this black market are criminals. The marketing of malware, crimeware, and associated services and products can be found on both black market forums and legitimate sales channels. Crimeware operators will use legitimate online payment services to process purchases and then the payment details are used to facilitate fraudulent transactions. They will also use legitimate Internet service providers (ISP) to host databases of stolen data. Hence, another way to view the malware industry depicted in Figure 3.11 is

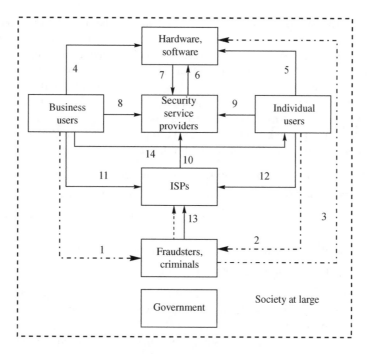

Figure 3.13 The inclusion of legitimate business interests in the ecosystem of malware-enabled cybercrime sometimes makes crimeware and malware operators difficult to distinguish from Internet entrepreneurs.

to follow the money. Figure 3.13 demonstrates the interaction between legal and illegal transaction flow in the malware market.

In Figure 3.13, solid lines show legal financial flows and dotted lines show illegal financial flows. The lines are numbered with types of transactions included, and these are described as follows [32]:

1: Extortion payments, click fraud, compensated costs of ID theft, and phishing.

2: Uncompensated costs of ID theft and phishing, click through, stock price pump and dump schemes, email scams, and other forms of consumer fraud.

3, 4, 5, 6: Hardware purchases by criminals, corporate, and individual users.

7, 8, 9, 10: Security service purchases by hardware manufacturers, corporate and individual users, ISPs.

11, 12, 13: ISP services purchased by corporate and individual users, criminals.

14: Payments to compensate consumers for damages from ID theft.

In addition to its use for criminal purposes, malware also enables other malicious actors that pose risks for the financial services sector. The term advanced persistent threat (APT) is now increasingly used to describe a category of malicious activities facing a growing number of government institutions and commercial organizations. As described in a recent Financial Services Information Sharing and Analysis Center (FS-ISAC) report, "APT refers to an advanced, clandestine means to gain continuous, persistent intelligence on an individual, company or foreign nation-state government or military [77]." The report shows there has been a history of APT attacks since 1986. Key risks posed by APT actors generally include efforts to access and exfiltrate data that contains sensitive and/or classified information. The information may be related to technology and operations, intellectual property, proprietary business processes, business strategy, and/or personal data pertaining to executives. APT activities include network mapping and software modification to gain and maintain remote access to a variety of systems within the target domain. Such sustained access, knowledge of networks and business processes allows perpetrators to lay groundwork for future disruptive activities. Increasingly, APT discussions also include the use of tools specifically designed to achieve disruptive effects such as Stuxnet, which is malware designed to attack Iran's nuclear power plants [306]. The possibility of attacks focused on data corruption in the future has also been identified. Key characteristics of APT activities include, but are not limited to

- threat actors with clearly identified long-term objectives guiding their attacks;
- structured, sustained intrusive activities to deploy, support and maintain exfiltration operations;
- ability to conduct intelligence on individuals, organizations, and processes that will prove to be valuable targets;
- use of sophisticated software tools and techniques to conduct activities;
- flexible and adaptable operations to avoid detection.

Public recognition of these activities has risen dramatically. Numerous reports exist related to ongoing activities against governments and defense industries worldwide, specific activities focused on the US energy industry and the highly publicized attacks against Google, as part of Operation Aurora [154,168,494]. With regard to financial services, limited open source information exists regarding specific activities but the financial services sector is often identified in discussions and doctrinal writings about cyber warfare between nations [200].

The conduct of APT activities relies fundamentally on the use of malware to establish access, to maintain footholds within organizations and to exfiltrate sensitive data and/or conduct disruption of IT systems or networks. Directed efforts using spearphishing have been a principal approach of many of the operations against governments and the defense industry. Often, the payloads of spearphishing attacks include a range of malware targeted at the most common types of applications for enterprise users, particularly those in Microsoft Office and Adobe products. Often this malware uses well-known code exploiting well-known vulnerabilities, but APT activities also employ new and custom code not detectable by enterprise intrusion detection and antivirus systems. APT actors are generally highly aware of the state of enterprise information security practices. They employ code and techniques not only to avoid detection but also frequently use malware to disable antivirus, intrusion detection systems, and other security software on exploited computers, and even across broader portions of the enterprise. More significantly, APT actors may have a portfolio of capabilities at hand to ensure the ability to continue activities even when discovered. Malware more unique to APT activities often includes redundant and diverse tools to conduct exfiltration of user credentials and sensitive data.

FIs must be cognizant of the growing risks posed by malware specifically designed to disrupt operations, particularly the operation of industrial control systems (ICS). The emergence of the Stuxnet worm in 2010 targeted at the Siemens ICS provides concrete evidence that cyberspace can have devastating effects on physical resources such as data center environment and power systems, electric grids, gas pipelines, water delivery systems, and manufacturing equipment [306]. While the original purpose of this malware appears to be targeted at the Siemens ICS utilized in nuclear programs in Iran, key features of the worm pose much larger concerns that should inform the financial services sector. The possibility of another actor capturing the code and repurposing it for other purposes such as disrupting power grids is a significant possibility. As a Department of Homeland Security official testified before a Senate committee, "What makes Stuxnet unique is that it uses a variety of previously seen individual cyber attack techniques, tactics, and procedures, automates them, and hides its presence so that the operator and the system have no reason to suspect that any malicious activity is occurring. The concern for the future of Stuxnet is that the underlying code could be adapted to target a broader range of control systems in any number of critical infrastructure sectors [347]." More generally, the financial services sector could be targeted by disruptive ICS malware specifically designed to exploit vulnerabilities in ICS applications used in this sector, specifically heating, ventilating, air-conditioning (HVAC), and power supply equipment used to monitor and control data centers.

The FS-ISAC has conducted a more detailed analysis of APT threats, risks and mitigations available to FS-ISAC members.

3.5 MONETIZATION

Markus Jakobsson

Abstract. Monetization is the word that describes "taking the money out of the system." It is not enough for a phisher or a malware author to steal passwords. They need to convert these passwords into money. To the uninitiated, that might seem like plain: just transfer the money out of the account. But that is not how it is—monetization is as complex as the rest of the fraud scheme. Understanding monetization is a very important step in the direction of limiting fraud. Here, we provide a brief overview of the complexity of monetization.

3.5.1 There is Money Everywhere

It is obvious that money might be lost—and gained, depending on the perspective—if a fraudster gains access to a bank account or other financial account. The fraudster could then transfer money to an account he controls, *quickly* withdraw it, and vanish. But what else is there to know?

To some extent, monetization to fraudsters is a game of triumphing over security measures, such as temporary holds on funds and efforts to quickly detect irregularities. And to the defenders, it is a corresponding game of detecting abnormal or undesirable patterns, and putting holds on funds that appear to be at risk. But there is much more. To understand monetization, it will help you to stop thinking of it as transferring money, and instead thing in more general terms: converting access to accounts and machines into abilities, where these abilities have a value in the real, physical world. We will provide a few examples to highlight this.

Let's start by asking ourselves how attackers can monetize accounts that on the surface have nothing to do with keeping and transferring money. What can the fraudster, for example, gain by accessing Blizzard (online gaming) accounts, Facebook accounts, or Skype accounts?

A fraudster with access to an online gaming account can purchase virtual merchandise—such as shields, weaponry, and other in-game items—and then sell these on external marketplaces. For example, the fraudster can offer such an item on an auction site, collect payment (to an account not associated with the game), and then transfer the item in the game—for example, by setting a rendezvous with the buyer in the game's virtual world, and handing over the item. The fraudster can also simply sell off preexisting virtual belongings of the avatars associated with the accounts he has taken over.

Therefore, it is clear that it does not have to be *money* that the attacker transfers out. It can be anything that has a value to somebody else. Even virtual resources, you conclude. Yes, *in particular* virtual resources. They are so much easier—and less expensive—to transfer than physical merchandize.

A fraudster who has taken control over a Facebook account can hope that this is connected to a bank or credit card account, for example, for the account owner to purchase Facebook credits and later use these for games and other applications. If there is no financial account connected, fraudsters commonly attempt to social engineer the owner into revealing information that allows the attacker to connect the victim's bank or credit card account. Once there is an account connected, the fraudster may use this to pay for things that he can then monetize. He can, for example, buy advertisements on Facebook on behalf of a company that does not ask many questions, or sell the Facebook credits on an underground marketplace, and somebody else will use the credits.

This provides us with a second example of how an attacker can translate access to an account into access to a valuable resource, and then translate this to real money. What about if the attacker fails to connect a financial account to the corrupted Facebook account? No problem—to the attacker, that is.

If a fraudster has gained access to a Facebook account that is not connected to any funding source, that is *still* a potential source of income for him. To begin with, and as is discussed in Section 6.2, the fraudster can use the corrupted account to send out spam (which has an advertisement value), or to use spam to distribute malware. He can also impersonate the user of the corrupted account, contacting all the contacts of this person and explaining that he (the account owner, that is) is in a troublesome situation, and needs the financial assistance of the friend. Typically, the account owner was robbed in London, and needs the friend to send money for his hotel charges and ticket back. The fraudster asks the friend of the owner of the corrupted account to send money using Western Union or moneygram, since both of these services makes tracking difficult, and reversing transactions is not possible.

How about a setting, like Skype, where there is only one payee (Skype), and there is only one purpose for payments (i.e., paying for phone calls)? If an attacker gains access to your Skype account, he can place phone calls anywhere he wants, right? Big deal, you think, he will be able to call his mom, but just how long can they be on the phone. But wait, there is more.

A fraudster with access to one or more Skype accounts—or accounts for other phone services—can place calls to toll numbers. In particular, he can place calls to toll numbers he owns, and maybe to some he does not own, for the sake of good appearance. He will receive less than 50 cents for every dollar he spends—the phone companies keep the rest, for hosting the service—but that is not really a problem. Why be thrifty when it is somebody else's money you spend?

This shows us that account access means money. It is evident, then, that access to a machine—for example, planting malware on a victim machine—can also mean money, because the fraudster can install a keylogger, giving him passwords . . . and account access. But with access to a machine, there are other things he can do. This machine could act as a bot in a bot network. Bot networks can be used to mount Distributed Denial of Service (DDoS) attacks, which is commonly done to demand money. Off-shore gambling sites often are threatened with DDoS attacks in order to stay up, and many pay.

What other types of information can an attacker monetize? Here is one very common crime:

A fraudster has stolen—or purchased—a collection of credit cards. He then sets up accounts with online service providers— Blizzard, Facebook, Skype—and extracts money as described above. Or he sets up PayPal or Amazon accounts, and funds these from the stolen cards, purchasing items, and paying for them with his victim's credit cards. Typically, he sends the loot to mules—people hired to reship the merchandize in exchange for a payment—in order to make it harder to track him down or block him in the first place. The fraudster has several weeks to shop until he gets discovered, and by then he has moved on to new accounts and maybe also a new address.

I do not want to give too many examples or too much detail, but I am sure you are starting to see the complexity of monetization. If we think "money" every time we hear "access," then we know what the fraudster thinks. It is not enough for us to work on ways to reduce the theft of credentials, but it is also important to understand monetization—and make it difficult and costly to perform.

Now, knowing that there is an opportunity for monetization in essentially every direction we look, it is time to think of Willie Sutton for a moment. Willie Sutton, an infamous bank robber of the twentieth century, is famous for answering the question why he robbed banks with by saying that "because that's where the money is." With this in mind, it is clear why Internet fraud is becoming almost as big as the Internet itself.

Chapter 4

How Things Work and Fail

There is a dizzying number of ways in which things can fail, where any such failure opens up the Internet to abuse. This chapter describes a collection of ways things can break, to bring justice Internet's complexity—and to Internet security.

The chapter starts in a conceptual manner, by reviewing the principles behind online advertising (Section 4.1). Here, we ask and answer the questions: "What is a click?" "Why is it secret what clicks are billed?" "What does the criminal know about how things work?" Knowing this is relevant to understanding exactly how the security behind online advertising works—and fails.

We then make a big leap and describe a common vulnerability—cross-site scripting (or XSS)—and how it is exploited by fraudsters. We begin by a general overview of XSS for those who are not familiar with it (Section 4.2). We then show how XSS is much more complex than most of us realized, by looking at one particular type of XSS attack in depth (Section 4.3.)

We move to email spam, then, and make efforts to defend against it (Section 4.4), followed by a description of *other* types of spam (Section 4.5). Spam is crucial to understand as it is a delivery vector for many of the attacks we see on the Internet.

Taking a big step toward application-layer vulnerabilities, we review CAPTCHAs and their vulnerabilities (Section 4.6). CAPTCHAs are lightweight security measures implemented to complicate automatization of attacks, but they are constantly under assault. Another step toward the user takes us to a review of the problems associated with password reset (Section 4.7). Password reset is commonly the weakest link of user authentication, and is increasingly targeted by fraudsters.

Clearly, technology is important to security, but so is human use of technology. We take a look at typical consumer behavior, and the underlying beliefs (Section 4.8), in an attempt to better understand the human aspect of security—and insecurity, of course.

Internet *in*security is often attributed to the computers and handsets of end users, and the gullibility of these same users. We end the chapter by describing how that is not necessarily the case (Section 4.9). In particular, it could be the *infrastructure*: All it takes is the corruption of a Certification Authority (CA)—and there are many of these, not all, that are being security conscious.

Of course, this chapter is not even describing a tenth of all the ways in which things can break, but is intended to give a meaningful overview of common problems of various types.

The Death of the Internet, First Edition. Edited by Markus Jakobsson.
© 2012 John Wiley & Sons, Inc. Published 2012 by John Wiley & Sons, Inc.

4.1   ONLINE ADVERTISING: WITH SECRET SECURITY

Markus Jakobsson

Abstract. Online advertising is what generates revenue for many online service providers—from Google and Facebook to *New York Times* and *Pandora*. Put differently, without online advertising, these companies would not subsist—or they would have to find alternative ways of supporting the services they offer.

Since advertising is central to the Internet, and the services offered on the Internet, it is important to understand its structure—especially aspects that relate to potential abuses. There are three principal types of charging—per impression, per click, and per action. An impression is simply the display of an advertisement—much like a highway billboard in the sense that one cannot tell whether the consumer pays attention or not. For click-based advertising, the revenue event is when the consumer clicks on a banner advertisement (or similar) and is taken to a page where more information is provided. In action-based billing, the revenue event is a specified action—a purchase, for example.

In this section, we will focus on click-based billing ("pay per click" (PPC)) for purposes of concreteness. However, the principles we describe also apply to other types of billing structures.

We will focus on how filtering of clicks works, since that is central to understand in order to later understand how fraudsters abuse the system. We also explain why, in contrast to many other types of security mechanisms, the security of click filtering is based on keeping the exact construction secret. Finally, we discuss how to evaluate how well filtering works, and what we may assume that fraudsters know.

This section is conceptual. Make sure also to read the much more hands-on section on ad fraud—Section 3.1.

4.1.1   What is a Click?

First of all, we need to understand what a click is—or at least what a *valid* click is. Surprisingly, that is not as straightforward as it may seem, since not all clicks are equal.

A click corresponds to the request to retrieve a document associated with a hyperlink displayed on a webpage. Typically, clicks correspond to a human action of clicking on a hyperlink, but they could also correspond to programmatically initiated retrieval requests. Advertisers expect to pay for "human" clicks, but not for automated clicks, since there is no chance of conversion for those. Here, conversion is defined as the desired user action associated with accessing an advertisement; for example, buying a product, registering for a newsletter, or "liking" a merchant.

At the core of online advertising is therefore the question of what clicks are *valid* clicks. These are the clicks that should be billed, whereas invalid clicks should not. Independent of whether a click is billed or not, the material is displayed to the user—this is both to provide a meaningful user experience when the click is misclassified and for the network to avoid tipping off fraudsters about how their filtering algorithms work.

Although the majority of clicks are legitimate and intentional, some clicks are performed due to mistakes and some are initiated solely to manipulate the system. Examples of invalid clicks are duplicate clicks of regular users (e.g., a person double-clicking on a banner, thinking that this is how to access the associated advertisement); clicks generated by software (e.g., a toolbar that prefetches all material to reduce the latency between a click and the rendering of the associated page); and clicks that were initiated with the sole goal of causing the advertiser to be charged.

Since it is understood that only *valid* clicks should be billed, the importance of a good definition of what constitutes a valid click is evident. A definition is in place.

It is natural to say that a valid click is one where there is an *intent* to view the associated advertisement, with a nonzero probability of a conversion. This intuitive view is taken by Jansen:

> Jansen [282] defines a valid click as *the intentional click on a sponsored link by a visitor where there is a realistic probability of generating value once the visitor arrives at the Website.*

However, *intent* can be difficult to operationalize, as it requires an understanding of the psychological processes of the people initiating the clicks. In other words, it may not be helpful to define valid clicks as those where there was user intent, since we cannot know what the user's intent was. Alexander Tuzhilin [471] describes this difficulty. Tuzhilin explains, "Unfortunately, in several cases it is hard or even impossible to determine the true intent of a click using any technological means." He continues to say, "Therefore, in some cases the true intent of a click can be identified only after examining deep psychological processes, subtle nuances of human behavior and other considerations in the mind of the clicking person."

This, he argues, makes it difficult to use the notion on intent for click filtering purposes: "Moreover, to mark such clicks as valid or invalid, these deep psychological processes and subtle nuances of human behavior need to be operationalized and identified through various technological means, including software filters. Therefore, it is simply impossible to identify true clicking intent for certain types of clicking activities and, therefore, classify these clicks as valid or invalid."

Tuzhilin concludes that "In summary, between the obviously clear cases of valid and invalid clicks, lies the whole spectrum of highly complicated cases when the clicking intent is far from clear and depends on a whole range of complicated factors, including the parameter values of the click. Therefore, this intent (and thus the validity of a click based on the above definitions) cannot be operationalized and detected by technological means with any reasonable measure of certainty."

While it is not trivial to create an operational definition of what a valid click is based on the intent of the user initiating the click, we also see that from a pragmatic point of view, the notion of intent is very valuable. This is since this is how we, as a community, typically and intuitively relate to what clicks are valid. This chasm can be bridged by talking about *predicting* intent. This means that a valid click is one where the system *predicts* that there is user intent to view the advertisement—based on past observations and accumulated knowledge about users. Then we transfer the problem from determining whether there was intent to the very closely related problem of building good predictors of intent. Instead of asking "was there intent?", we ask "is this a good predictor?" That is a lot easier to operationalize.

Predicting intent is typically done by identifying known *in*valid clicks and then assuming that the remaining clicks are valid. For example, traffic from known bots and spiders would be considered invalid. Repeat clicks from otherwise well-behaving users would also be considered invalid. Similarly, anomalous clicking—such as clicking a remarkably large number of times within a short period of time—would also be considered invalid. This is the general approach for filtering clicks that is typically taken by ad networks.

As the network learns more about what traffic is bad, they improve their filters to avoid billing for such traffic onward. This way, the resulting predictor of intent (consisting of all the filtering rules in unison) improves over time. However, since intent is very complex and not well understood at all, it should not be surprising that *predictors of intent* are also complex and poorly understood. Therefore, the filters are not perfect, and it is clear that they cause both false positives and false negatives. The best we may hope for may really be a filter that takes into consideration everything that is known about intent, and predicting intent, and does as good job as it is possible to translate this knowledge into a classification of clicks.

We might call a predictor a *best effort predictor* if and only if

1. it conforms to best practices, and there are no known material improvements that could be made to it;

2. its design and maintenance were given proper attention, resources, and dedication;

3. the engineers and scientists designing and maintaining it were well suited for the task they were given; and their focus was the minimization of error rates of the predictor, along with the practical achievability of the predictor, given the available resources.

Of course, it is very hard to know whether a predictor satisfies these requirements. In particular, how can one tell if there are ways to substantially improve a filter? It is hard to know how good is "good enough." What makes it even harder is the fact that no network will disclose exactly how their filtering works. Why is that?

Since valid clicks are money—somebody's money—it is dangerous for ad networks to disclose what makes clicks valid. That would make it much easier to game a system that is already vulnerable to abuse.

In spite of the secrecy surrounding filter design, ad networks are believed to use similar general techniques to filter their clicks. This is since some general principles are commonly known—such as not to bill for traffic that comes from known bots or spiders—and since any ad network with substantially worse filters would get to know this (without necessarily knowing, however what makes their filters weak). Namely, ad networks commonly have their clicks scored by third-party providers that provide feedback on the anticipated click quality and validity. This helps the networks to identify clicks that are believed to have been misclassified by their filters. As part of the service, they are also told how they are doing relative to other networks—in an aggregate sense. And even if the networks did not use the services of third-party providers, they would still receive feedback from advertisers and publishers who have their click streams scored. As a result, networks learn what clicks they do not filter correctly—according to the third-party providers, that is, which in turn is helpful information for them to have when they tweak their filters.

4.1.2 How Secret Filters are Evaluated

Since the exact design of the filters is secret and their design determines who pays and who gets paid, it is natural for those involved to want to know how accurate the filters are. Advertisers want to know what they pay for and why. They want to be able to customize what traffic they receive onward—for example, by requesting traffic from certain geographic regions only—and they want to be able to file complaints if they think they were overcharged. Publishers, of course, want to know that they get paid for all good traffic. And the networks want to maximize their short-term profit while curbing abuse to maintain their business and remain attractive to both advertisers and publishers. At the same time, fraudsters want to know how to maximize their profit or maximize the damage they cause to their competitors, all while remaining undetected. This makes it difficult for the networks to be open about their filtering strategy.

This begs the question: How can the quality of secret filters be evaluated? There are several ways to assess the accuracy of click filters. Advertisers and publishers are limited to third-party solutions that score clicks and identify likely invalid clicks. Networks can also compare their *current* filters with their *past* filters—on the same inputs—to see how they compare. Let us take a look at how such approaches work.

4.1.2.1 Third-party click scoring

There are third-party companies that score clicks. These companies identify the likelihood of clicks they are fed to convert, based on click predicates such as where they come from (clicks from different geographic areas are not equally likely to convert and they exhibit very different rates of fraud) and on historical behavior of the IP address from where the click originated. These services also identify likely fraud. This can be done by identifying the origin of a click as a known malware-infected computer or by identifying clusters of computers or accounts with similar—and unusual—behavior. The latter is likely a sign of collusion.

Advertisers and publishers typically rely on the reports of services of this kind not only to request refunds from ad networks but also to determine what traffic is most valuable to them. Since many ad networks allow advertisers to specify what areas they are interested in targeting—and sometimes much more specific traffic predicates—this is a helpful service to them.

4.1.2.2 Ad network check: new filter, old clicks

Ad networks typically test all parameter changes to their filters before deploying these. This is done by computing the output of the updated filters and comparing this with the output of the active filters. However, since ad networks store all their clicks in click logs, it is also possible for them to retroactively classify old clicks using new filters. This answers the question: "How much better is the updated filter than the old one?" It quantifies what portion of historic clicks that were billed using the old filters would have been filtered out had the new filters been used instead.

There is one catch, however: *This is not always possible to do.* Imagine a new filter that uses the browser agent to classify a click. The browser agent contains information about the operating system, the browser type and version, and much more. (We refer to Section 7.7 for a more thorough description of the browser agent.) However, if this new filter is the first filter the ad network has produced to use the browser agent, then it is unlikely that the historical logs contain information about the browser agent. Similarly, if no old filter uses HTML cookies, then these data may not have been logged. And yet again, if the IP address of the visitor was not used for historical filters, then this might also not have been logged.

This is a problem, of course. If the data needed to compute the filter output are not available for historical clicks, how could one compare the efficacy of the old and new filters? It is possible to do—we will just have to turn things around.

4.1.2.3 Ad network check: old filter, new clicks

Instead of determining how much better a new filter does on old clicks, one can also determine how much *worse* the old filter does on new clicks. This is surprisingly easy! Since more and more data are typically logged, the new logs are likely to contain all types of data that the old logs did—and more. This makes it possible to run old filters on more recent clicks. By looking at the click logs and identifying what "new" clicks were considered invalid (by the new filters) but which would have been billed by the old filters, we identify the differences between the old and the new filters.

However, there is no free lunch. The "new filter, old clicks" approach—to the extent that it works—would produce a list of clicks that should be refunded. On the other hand, the "old filter, new clicks" approach instead produces a list of clicks that were invalid, but which would have been mistakenly billed if the filters had not been updated. This is clearly of less practical value.

There may be a way for ad networks to identify whom to refund—if that is the goal of determining the difference between the old and new filters. They can determine how much better new filters work than the old ones by first measuring how much *worse* the old filters worked—an instance of "old filter, new clicks." They can *then* develop and run algorithms to attribute what clicks should be refunded. While the way in which this is best done differs between situations, a general approach is to determine how the "reclassified" clicks differ from the average click and then use this to identify what historical clicks may deserve a refund.

Whatever method is used, we can see that it is possible to determine how well a collection of filters are doing. This is of interest to everybody, not least the ad networks, who know that the prices they can charge depend on the quality they are seen to deliver.

4.1.3   What do Fraudsters Know?

As mentioned, ad networks do not disclose how their filters work. To begin with, the user cannot tell whether their click was billed for or not, because independent of whether it was filtered out for billing purposes, the user sees the same information—the advertisement that is shown if one clicks on the banner ad. For the same reason, the ad networks do not tell publishers and advertisers what clicks were billed—they only see a bill or check with the total amount on it. This begs the question: What do fraudsters know?

To begin with, competent fraudsters know all public information. They know what the industry standards are—as outlined by the Interactive Advertising Bureau [65]. They also know the basic structure of the filtering mechanism from published reports, such as expert reports in class action suits [282,471]. Reading Tuzhilin's report [471], for example, the fraudsters know that Google detects whether publishers manually click on the ads they display. This suggests that Google pays attention to IP addresses (including those of privacy proxies, most likely). For the same reason, it is clear that Google must pay attention to HTML cookies, and it is likely that they also use the user agent and other device identifiers. The Tuzhilin report also mentions click farms (i.e., sweatshops with workers paid to click). To detect these, it is likely that Google identifies IP addresses with abnormal number of clicks, and that they associate reputations with IP addresses and IP address ranges.

Knowledge of what abuse the ad networks are aware of guides the understanding of the attacker of how the countermeasures might possibly work. The rest is a matter of learning the parameters. For example, if an ad network filters out clicks if too many clicks§ originate from some IP address for a given time, the only question is: what is the limit? This can be found out by the fraudster with some experimentation. For example, the fraudster can initiate some number of clicks on a victim advertisement and determine whether these clicks appear to have been billed—this is possible to tell for advertisers with low budget caps, as the clicks may push the advertiser over the daily limit. (Of course, this may not occur, and if it occurs, it may be for natural reasons—but with a reasonable number of experiments, the fraudster will know.)

If the fraudster is a publisher—or collaborates with one—then it is even easier for him to tell. Was there a surge in revenue for a time period when a given strategy was used? Then the strategy probably worked.

Once a fraudster knows how one ad network filters clicks, he may assume that another may do the same. Maybe not using the same parameters, and maybe the filters work somewhat differently, but it is a fair guess that they will be similar. It is not implausible that this knowledge is bought and sold by fraudsters and, therefore, it is fair to assume that fraudsters in general have a reasonable understanding of just what they can get away with.

4.2 WEB SECURITY REMEDIATION EFFORTS

Jeff Hodges and Andy Steingruebl

Abstract. We begin this section by presenting a brief overview of the various seemingly piece-wise approaches being taken to mitigate the arrayed threats to web applications. First, we discuss web browser-based "built-in" security mechanisms. These, such as the Same Origin Policy, are more or less uniformly implemented by major web browsers. Next, we look at selectively invocable browser-based security mechanisms. These are mechanisms that a web application may invoke by signaling web browsers. They include things such as Secure-flagged cookies, "framing" restrictions, and strict transport security declaration. We note the lack of uniformity of web browser implementation and behavior with respect to these various security mechanisms. We assert that the time is right for the various stakeholders to work together to create a set of robust standards for coherent web security policy framework(s).

4.2.1 Introduction

As vulnerabilities and attacks are discovered, and in some cases exploited, industry introduces new web security indicators, techniques, and policy communication mechanisms in order to attempt to mitigate the downside risks to both web applications and users. Historically, such mechanisms have been sprinkled throughout the various layers of the Web and HTTP unfortunately yielding a haphazard collage that is not uniformly implemented across web browsers. For example, all the selectively invocable browser-based security mechanisms we discuss below were initially supported by only a subset of web browsers. Some are now supported more or less uniformly, but some not.

Not to be overlooked is that there is a plethora of "standard" browser security features, for example, the *Same Origin Policy* (SOP), network-related restrictions, rules for third-party cookies, content-handling mechanisms, and so on. However, they are also *not* implemented uniformly in today's popular web browsers. For example, the Same Origin Policy, which generally restricts a webpage to only be able to load data from its own server, is not implemented uniformly across browsers in terms of the policy's detailed effects. Unfortunately, the same is true for all the other web browser security mechanisms we discuss below, as is documented in the Browser Security Handbook [504]. This makes life even harder for website administrators. They must make allowances in their approaches to site security mechanisms in consideration of which web browser a visitor may be using at any particular time.

This section first provides an overview of various web browser security mechanisms. It then describes desired characteristics for a site security policy framework, briefly analyzes these characteristics, suggests priorities for designing such features, and concludes with a discussion of the industry forums in which these issues are being addressed.

4.2.2   The Multitude of Web Browser Security Mechanisms

There is an incoherent multitude of web browser security mechanisms. This section introduces a variety of them. First, we discuss the web browser security mechanisms that apply to any web application's loaded webpages. Then, we introduce various other security mechanisms that are selectively invocable by web applications and enforced by the web browser. We then note a case of one security mechanism interfering with another and conclude by describing some advanced security mechanisms.

4.2.2.1   Web browser-based built-in security mechanisms

The below typical, "built-in" web browser security mechanisms are ostensibly present in all major web browsers. These mechanisms are largely *de facto* standards in the sense that many of them are not formally specified anywhere but in the running code of various web browsers. In many cases, they began in the development shops of a web browser vendor and may have been documented in only a blog post (as opposed to a proper specification). Other web browser vendors then tend to follow along with their own implementations if the new security feature seems to be a good idea. This process, however, contributes to the spotty and noncoherent implementation of these security features across the various web browsers [452,504].

The Same Origin Policy   Brendan Eich originally defined the notions of both *origin* and the *Same Origin Policy* as part of inventing JavaScript [370], which appeared in Netscape Navigator 2.0 [179]. A web resource's origin has three key components: scheme, host, and port. A web application's origin is determined by extracting the those components from the *web address* or URI,[1] from which the web application is initially loaded. For example, if we load the web address https://www.example.com:443/application.html, then the resulting webpage's origin consists of the set of these three items: https (the scheme), www.example.com (the host), and 443 (the port).

Given the foregoing definition of origin, the Same Origin Policy builds upon it by generally preventing a given webpage from a given origin from accessing or manipulating any other loaded webpages from different origins. A webpage's JavaScript can manipulate the web browser's in-memory Document Object Model (DOM) representation of the page [250]. Without the restrictions of the Same Origin Policy, the JavaScript contained within one page could arbitrarily modify the DOM representation of other loaded webpages.

The above describes what is presently variously referred to as the Same Origin Policy for *JavaScript* or for *DOM access*. In the next section, we will describe the Same Origin Policy for network access, among other network-related restrictions.

Network-related restrictions   Web browsers impose a varied collection of network-related restrictions upon web applications' loaded pages. Among them are the restrictions on the XMLHttpRequest JavaScript object [475]. This object facilitates the JavaScript in a loaded webpage in making arbitrary HTTP requests back to its server. The network-related restriction in this case is that by default, these requests may be made only to web addresses of the same origin. This is known as the *Same Origin Policy for network access*.

---

[1] Web addresses themselves are today formally known as *Uniform Resource Identifiers* (URI) [114], but are still sometimes referred to as *Uniform Resource Locators* (URL), which is their former formal name.

```
<HTML>
 <BODY>
   <P>This is a paragraph in a simple HTML document.</P>
   <P> Here is a cool picture:
   <IMG SRC="http://www.example.com/picture.jpg"/>
   </P>
 </BODY>
</HTML>
```

Figure 4.1   A simple HTML document containing an example of an <IMG> element with a SRC attribute specifying from where to retrieve image data.

There are several other arcane network-related restrictions built into web browsers by default—impacting the capabilities of loaded webpages. We discuss three relevant network-related restrictions (further restrictions and details are thoroughly discussed in Ref. [504]):

- **Web Address Scheme Access Rules**   Many different web address *schemes* exist, representing many different data access mechanisms and data types. There is the file scheme, for example, signifying that the URI refers to a file in the local (to the web browser) file system. There is also the ftp scheme, indicating that the browser must use the *File Transfer Protocol* (FTP) to fetch the data. Another one is the JavaScript scheme, indicating that the remainder of the URI is JavaScript code that the web browser may execute.

  First we need to briefly introduce HTML, the *HyperText Markup Language* [395]. HTML supplies the "skeleton" for webpages, and thus web applications. A HTML document is constructed using *elements* (sometimes elements are also referred to as *tags*), such as <HTML>, <BODY>, and <P>. The elements are arranged in a hierarchical manner—an element may contain another element. Refer to Figure 4.1 and note how the <P> (paragraph) elements are contained within the <BODY> element's "content." Also note that the second <P> element contains an <IMG> element. The <IMG> element has an *attribute* named SRC.

  Many HTML elements have a SRC attribute. When the web browser, while processing a webpage's HTML skeleton, comes across an element with a SRC attribute, it will process the SRC attribute if it is present and fetch the data it refers to. In case of the <IMG> element shown in Figure 4.1, the web browser would retrieve the image data and display it as a part of the rendering of the "page" represented by the HTML document.

  We term this behavior of automatically following web addresses obtained from HTML element attribute values as *element-driven web address following*. It is referred to as *Web Address Scheme Access* in the Browser Security Handbook [504].

  However, allowing such elements to cause the web browser to follow just any web address served by just any webpage one runs across is a poor idea security-wise. For example, if the web address's scheme is javascript, then the browser will be executing JavaScript code whose provenance may be suspect, as shown in Figure 4.2.

  Therefore, some web browsers disallow the element-driven web address following of file and JavaScript URI schemes, as further discussed in Ref. [504].

- **Redirection Restrictions**   The HTTP protocol [188] has a notion of *redirection*. This is where a special HTTP *redirect response* from a web address directs the web browser to immediately send a

```
<IMG SRC="javascript:doSomething()">...</IMG>
```

Figure 4.2   An example of an <IMG> element with a SRC attribute containing a URI with a JavaScript scheme. This would cause a browser processing this HTML to automatically execute the JavaScript embedded in the SRC attribute's value, which could cause the web browser to be exploited if the JavaScript code is malicious.

request to a redirect web address included in the redirect response. Of interest is the URI scheme specified in the redirect web address. Some web browsers place restrictions on this and disallow the scheme from being one or more of data, JavaScript, or file.

For example, a user can be tricked into invoking (also referred to as "visiting" or "loading") a malicious web application in various ways, such as through receiving an email message with an embedded URI, which the user is enticed to click. The malicious web application can then begin to attack the web browser or other web applications that may be loaded, by sending it a redirect response containing a JavaScript URI. See Figure 4.3.

- **Port Access Restrictions**   A *port* is an artifact of web addresses and other means of denoting Internet addresses. Its significance is *per host*. For example, a given Internet host may provide varying services and applications on different ports. Indeed, a web application that answers when contacted at http://www.example.com/ (here the port is implicitly 80 because that is the standard port for HTTP) could be *completely* different from one at http://www.example.com:7777/. Similarly, a totally different service, such as a File Transfer Protocol server, may be available on yet another port on the host.

    Over the years, various security vulnerabilities have been discovered that relate to allowing web browsers to connect to certain ports [466]. For example, before port access restrictions were put into place, an attacker could craft a simple malicious webpage featuring a HTML form, which when loaded by the web browser, filled-in by the user, and submitted caused the web browser to send email to a victim host. This was done by causing the web browser to contact port 25 (the email submission port) on the victim host. In some cases this may be benign, but it could also be used to send email (e.g., spam email) that the server would not otherwise allow—the victim user could be authorized (e.g., by IP address) to send email via that server, but the perpetrator of the malicious web application may not be.

    Thus, there is a smattering of ports that are disallowed. Unfortunately, this varies on a browser-to-browser basis and even among web browser versions (see Ref. [504] for further details).

Content-handling mechanisms   Any HTTP request a web browser makes to a web server can return almost any type of data, for example, HTML, JSON, JavaScript, executable machine code, other binary data

```
HTTP/1.0 301 Moved Permanently
Location: javascript:doSomethingNasty()
Cache-Control: no-cache
Pragma: no-cache
Connection: close
Content-Length: 0
```

Figure 4.3   An example of HTTP redirect response message containing a Location URI with a JavaScript scheme.

(e.g., video), ASCII text, and others. These returned data are often simply referred to as *content*. HTTP has a means for servers to declare the type of content returned, but sometimes this declaration is missing from responses. And sometimes it is incorrectly specified. As a result, web browsers have all evolved various baroque means of *sniffing*, or otherwise looking within, returned data and tried to determine its type, and thus how to process it.

What is important to note here is that the approaches to *content sniffing*, the subsequent behaviors, and the resulting vulnerabilities vary across web browsers. For example, a browser might fetch what it believes are image data. Then, in the act of sniffing the data, it begins executing the data as Java code. This can be the basis for an attack [106]—a variation of *cross-site scripting*—and is a case of *privilege escalation*, as explained in Section 4.3.1.

Third-party cookie rules   *Cookies* are separable bundles of data that a web server can send to a web browser along with any HTTP response message. Doing so is called *setting a cookie*. Web browsers are obliged to accept and store these cookies. Subsequently, the cookies are returned to their server of origin along with any future requests the web browser makes to that server. Thus, cookies are a means by which HTTP servers can scalably maintain relatively small amounts of per-client data—that is, they simply store it on the web browser, and the web browser returns it automatically with future requests. This process, formally known as a *HTTP State Management Mechanism*, is now specified in detail in Ref. [104], but was originally specified in a document [369] by Netscape from September 1994 [311].

Most web applications use cookies to maintain some amount of user-specific data. For example, often *session tokens* denoting that the user has logged in, as well as other sensitive information, are stored in cookies by web applications. Therefore, cookies often have security implications, and some cookie-specific security properties and mechanisms have evolved. Here, we discuss one that is inherently implemented in web browsers: *Third-party Cookie Rules*.

As we described above in Web Address Scheme Access Rules, loading a webpage will cause the web browser to fetch various webpage components by resolving URIs associated with elements such as <IMG> via their SRC attribute. The resulting network requests can be directed to origins other than the present webpage's origin. Web browsers place restrictions on whether these other, so-called *third-party* origins may successfully set cookies at this time. That is, when they are not the *first-party* server, the browser will not remember any cookies they attempt to set. One reason for this restriction is to prevent *tracking* of users across unrelated web applications, as could be done if these web applications all relied on some of the same third-party web applications, such as web advertising networks [311,504].

4.2.2.2   Selectively invocable browser-based security mechanisms

Now that we have introduced you to some of the built-in web browser security mechanisms, we will discuss mechanisms that web applications can selectively invoke by signaling the web browsers. We begin by discussing some *cookie flags*. Second, we discuss approaches to managing *framing*, which is how one web application can load another web application. Third, we look at antisniffing measures, which are ways for content to declare that the web browser must not try to look inside response messages and determine the content's data type on its own. We follow by introducing HTTP Strict Transport Security (HSTS) which is a means for a web application to declare that it must be accessed only over Transport Layer Security (TLS)/Secure Socket Layer (SSL). Fourth is an introduction to Content Security Policy (CSP), by which a web application can declare from where the browser is allowed to load the web application's components.

```
<HTML>
  <BODY>
    <P>This is a paragraph in a simple HTML document.</P>
  </BODY>
</HTML>
```

Figure 4.4   A simple HTML document.

We finish by looking at Cross-Origin Resource Sharing (CORS), which is a means for a web application to selectively share its resources with other origins.

Cookie flags: Secure and HttpOnly   The original de jure cookie specification [369] defined the *secure flag*—simply the string "secure" properly appearing in a cookie—denoting that any cookie it appears in is to be returned to the web server only over a secure channel, rather than over either secure or insecure channels. In practice, this means that so-called *secure cookies* are to be returned to the web server only over TLS/SSL channels [172]. This protects the secure cookies from passive eavesdroppers. This is important because, as we discussed above in Third-party Cookie Rules, compromise of session token cookies can lead to the attacker being able to actively impersonate a victim user.

The other cookie flag we will discuss is HttpOnly. It originally appeared in Microsoft Internet Explorer 6 SP1 [352] in 2002. Since then, almost all other web browsers have implemented this feature. The HttpOnly flag is a signal to the web browser internals to disallow manipulation of the cookie by all client-side scripts. Thus, the cookie can only be manipulated by the web server—that is, created, updated, read—using HTTP. Neither the server nor any other server can instantiate script in the web browser and have that script manipulate the cookie. This is to protect against XSS attacks (see Section 4.3).

Preventing framing   HTML supplies the "skeleton" for webpages and thus web applications. HTML has a hierarchical structure, an element's content may be another element. Refer to Figure 4.4 and note how the <P> (paragraph) element is contained within the <BODY> element's "content."

HTML features the <IFRAME> element that allows one web application's webpages to *frame* another web application's webpages,[2] as illustrated in Figure 4.5. The content fetched from http://example.com/foo.html will be displayed in an area of the parent webpage when loaded into a web browser. This is quite useful for constructing complex web applications. It is used, for example, to include advertisements on webpages.

Unfortunately, if one web application (the *parent*) simplistically frames another web application's pages (the *child*), as shown in Section 4.5, then scripts running in the parent's context will be able to manipulate the child web application's pages in various ways. This includes being able to obscure the child's rendered information and potentially mislead users into performing actions they would not otherwise authorize. This is colloquially known as *clickjacking* or *user interface* (UI) *redressing*, and is discussed in detail in Ref. [231].

To counter such threats, Microsoft introduced the X-Frame-Options HTTP response header [318] in Internet Explorer 8 in early 2009, and updated its specification in early 2010 [319]. This HTTP header provides a means for a web application to signal to the web browser:

---

[2]There are actually several means for "framing" content, which vary depending on the flavor and version of HTML being used.

```
<HTML>
  <BODY>
    <P>This is a paragraph in a simple HTML web application.</P>
    <IFRAME SRC="http://example.com/foo.html"/>
  </BODY>
</HTML>
```

Figure 4.5   A simple HTML document "framing" another HTML document.

- That the browser must not allow other web applications to frame this web application's pages.
- That the browser can allow this web application's pages to be framed by pages emitted by the same origin.
- That the browser can allow this web application's pages to be framed by pages emitted by an explicitly specified different origin.

Initially, only Internet Explorer 8 implemented this, but almost all web browsers now support it. You can find in-depth details on who supports it in Ref. [504].

Antisniffing   Earlier during the Internet Explorer 8 development cycle in 2008, Microsoft developed the X-Content-Type-Options HTTP response header [317]. This response header provides a means for a web application to declare that the web browser must not attempt to determine, by content sniffing, the content type of the conveyed message body. This is important to some web applications because web browsers, as we noted above in content-handling mechanisms, will attempt to "sniff content" by default, and they sometimes get it wrong, which can lead to vulnerabilities.

So far, it appears that X-Content-Type-Options is only implemented by Microsoft Internet Explorer 8 and later.

HTTP Strict Transport Security   Although TLS/SSL [172] provides very secure communication channels, there are some issues. These have to do mostly with how it is utilized by web browsers and web servers. There are also issues with how certain user interface aspects have traditionally been implemented by browsers.

When a user browses the web on a local wireless network, at a coffee shop, for example, an attacker on the same local network can possibly eavesdrop on the user's unencrypted web interactions, regardless of whether or not the local wireless network itself is secured [110]. Freely available wireless sniffing toolkits, "Aircrack-NG" [176], for example, enable such passive eavesdropping attacks of secured local wireless networks. Also, if the network is unsecured, tools such as Firesheep [134] make it trivially easy to capture credentials for popular web applications from your fellow patrons. A passive attacker using such tools can steal session identifiers and hijack the user's web session(s) by obtaining, for example, the cookies containing authentication credentials [264].

To mitigate such threats, some web applications support access using secure transport, typically TLS/SSL [172]. However, they often do not force *all* connections to be secure. These web applications sometimes store session credentials in non-Secure cookies to permit interoperability with versions of the web application offered over insecure connections ("Secure cookies" are those cookies that contain the "Secure" attribute; see Section "Cookie flags: Secure and HttpOnly"). For example, if the session credential for a web application is stored in a cookie, it permits a passive eavesdropper to hijack the user's session if the user's web browser makes *a single insecure* HTTP request to the application.

```
Strict-Transport-Security: max-age=86400
```

Figure 4.6   An example of HTTP Strict Transport Security header field. "max-age" is declaring that this expression of HSTS policy must be cached for 1 day by the web browser.

Even if a web application does redirect all incoming insecure http connections to secure https ones, there are various windows of opportunity for an attack if at least one HTTP connection is made insecurely. Among them are the non-Secure cookie stealing attack mentioned above, as well as impersonating a user's Domain Name System (DNS) server in order to direct the user's insecure HTTP connections to a malicious attacker-controlled web application. This malicious web application could impersonate the user's target web application. In the latter case, no warning dialogs will pop up if the malicious web application is not TLS/SSL enabled. Users will often not notice the absence of the "lock icon," nor that the connection is being made over insecure http. Even if a malicious web application supports https and a victim uses it to connect, she is apt to *click-through* the resulting certificate warning dialogs in order to continue with her task [460].

Users often invoke, or *visit*, web applications either by clicking on links in some webpage or email message or by entering a fragment of the web application's web address in their web browser's *location bar*, or by using bookmarks they have established earlier. If these initial connections are made over insecure http, then the user is open to the attacks described above.

ForceHTTPS was invented to combat this scenario [264]. It later was refined with input from commercial web application service providers, as well as web browser vendors, yielding the draft *HTTP Strict Transport Security* (HSTS) [248] specification. HSTS defines an HTTP response header that signals the web browser to remember—for a specified amount of time—to only establish connections with the web application's host over a secure channel (see Figure 4.6).

Further key aspects of the HSTS policy are as follows:

- The web browser will close the connection if there are any TLS/SSL warnings or errors. This mitigates *click-through insecurity*, especially if done without user recourse.

- The web browser will transform all insecure http web addresses, referring to that host, to secure https ones before resolving them.

- HSTS policy is applied per-host, rather than per-origin. This means the policy holds for all ports on a host.

Thus, the attack scenarios described above are mitigated, except for the very first time one connects to a HSTS-protected web application, or if the time period for remembering this policy has lapsed. Some web browsers are addressing the first case, known as *Trust on First Use* (TOFU), by having a vendor-loaded HSTS site list [315], and the second case is mitigated by web applications setting a long remembrance time for the policy, for example, months or more.

The draft HSTS specification is presently implemented in Google Chrome 4.0. 211.0 and later as well as Mozilla Firefox 4 and later.

Content Security Policy   *Content Security Policy* [453], originating from Mozilla, is a draft set of security directives that web applications may selectively declare to web browsers regarding the sources and types of *content* that the web application's web pages may include. Recall that content can mean HTML, JavaScript, style sheets, images, and so on—that is, objects that the web browser will process.

```
X-Content-Security-Policy: default-src 'self'
```

Figure 4.7 An example of Content-Security-Policy header containing a single directive, default-src, with a value of "self."

Content injection is the act of inserting components into a web application's webpages that the web application is not otherwise prepared for or anticipating. This is the fundamental basis of Cross-Site Scripting attacks.

CSP gives web applications a multifaceted tool for declaring specifically which web application components are to be loaded by webpages and from where. Thus, CSP is a means for foiling XSS through control of content inclusion.

CSP policies are declared by web applications and conveyed from web servers to web browsers in the X-Content-Security-Policy HTTP response header,[3] which we refer to as the *CSP header*. The web browser interprets the policy conveyed by the CSP header and applies it to *the specific loaded webpage instance that the policy was conveyed with*. Different webpage instances loaded from the same origin *may* be returned with varying CSP policies.

For example, let us say a web application returns a HTML-based webpage in response to a web browser's request. Let us further suppose the HTTP response message includes a CSP header containing the default-src directive, with a value of "self," as illustrated in Figure 4.7. Then the web page, instantiated by the web browser as a result of receiving that particular HTTP message, will only be able to fetch content from its own origin. As before, "content" refers to images, scripts, video or audio media, objects, framed pages, fonts, and so on.

To continue this example in more detail, let us say that a web browser implementing CSP was to resolve the web address of https://example.org/page.html—which has an origin of https, example.org, 443—and subsequently receives the HTTP message, as shown in Figure 4.8. Note that the message includes a X-Content-Security-Policy response header with a declared policy of default-src "self."

A web browser implementing CSP will not be able to resolve and load the style sheet pointed to from within the message, as shown in Figure 4.8 (by the <LINK> element), because the directive returned in the X-Content-Security-Policy HTTP response header declares that this webpage may only make requests to example.org—by virtue of the default-src "self" directive—but the <LINK> element is pointing to a style sheet at foo.example.org. In this case, the web browser will likely render the message's HTML content, but without the benefit of any formatting specified in the style sheet.

The draft CSP specification is presently implemented in Mozilla Firefox as of version 4, and in Chrome as of version 13.

Cross-Origin Resource Sharing   *Cross-Origin Resource Sharing* [474] is a draft specification defining a means for a web application to explicitly authorize or deny access to its functions and data by other web applications. We will define the following terms in order to describe how CORS works:

- **Web application server**   A web application server is the server-side component of a web application. It is the network entity that answers the requests made by web browsers when a web address is resolved. A web application server typically has a distinct origin (see Section "The Same Origin Policy"), or even a distinct host.

---

[3] Since CSP is presently a draft specification, the HTTP response header name is subject to change.

```
HTTP/1.1 200 OK
Date: Mon, 27 Jul 2009 12:28:53 GMT
Server: Apache
Last-Modified: Wed, 22 Jul 2009 19:15:56 GMT
Accept-Ranges: bytes
Content-Length: 14
Vary: Accept-Encoding
Content-Type: text/plain
X-Content-Security-Policy: default-src 'self'

<!DOCTYPE html> <HTML LANG="en-US">
  <HEAD>
    <TITLE>CSP example</title>
    <LINK REL="stylesheet"
          TYPE="text/css"
          HREF="https://foo.example.org/style.css" />
  </HEAD>
  <BODY>
    <P>
      A CSP example.
    </P>
  </BODY>
</HTML>
```

Figure 4.8 An example of HTTP response message protected by the CSP policy declared in the X-Content-Security-Policy response header.

- **Web application client** Fundamentally, a web application client is a webpage loaded in a browser. That is, it is a client-side piece returned by a web application server when the browser resolved a web address. Two distinct characteristics of web application clients are that they typically inherit the origin from where the web browser loaded them, and they typically contain JavaScript that uses the XMLHttpRequest object in order to make requests of its web application server component or perhaps other web application servers with origins different than its own.

In web browsers that do not implement CORS, web application clients are limited to making requests via XMLHttpRequest only to web application servers of the same origin as their own. Conversely, requests made to different-origin web application servers fail. This is known as the Same Origin Policy for network access, as we discussed in section "Network-Related Restrictions." With CORS, web application clients may make requests to web application servers of differing origins. The origin of a web application client is conveyed in a Origin HTTP request header (defined in Ref. [105]) to the different-origin web application server. For example, a webpage from example.com could make a request of the web application at example.net. In its reply, the web application server informs the web browser whether or not to release the response message data to the calling web application client. This authorization is conveyed in HTTP response headers, which are defined in the CORS specification [474].

For example, if a web application client whose origin is example.com makes a request to a different origin via the XMLHttpRequest object, the request message will contain an Origin request header, as illustrated in Figure 4.9.

```
Origin: http://example.com
```

Figure 4.9   An example of Origin HTTP Request Header issued in XMLHttpRequest requests made by the example.com web application client.

Upon receiving the response to the request, the web browser examines the CORS HTTP response headers and decides whether to make the response message data available to the requesting web application client.

The key CORS response header is Access-Control-Allow-Origin. For example, in Figure 4.10, we show this header declaring that the requesting web application whose origin is http://example.com should be granted access to the data contained in the response message.

If CORS is not used, a web application server's data and functions are available by default to only those web application clients loaded from the same origin as that of the web application server. This restriction is the built-in SOP implemented by web browsers, as we described in Section "The Same Origin Policy."

The draft CORS specification is presently implemented by most major web browsers.

Adobe Cross Domain Policy File   Adobe Flash Player [493] and Adobe Acrobat Reader [492] are popular web browser plugins. Adobe Flash Player processes files in the SWF format, which conveys multi-media content, such as animations and videos. Adobe Acrobat Reader processes files in PDF format, which conveys document content and layout information. Both SWF and PDF files may contain references to arbitrary network resources, in much the same manner as HTML. This means you can create a PDF or SWF file that causes the plugin processing to make requests to arbitrary origins. A loaded SWF file can also upload data back to its server. Since web browser plugins are isolated subsystems, the web security mechanisms in web browsers do not generally apply to them.

As with JavaScript-based web application clients, which we discussed in section "Cross-Origin Resource Sharing," allowing any other web application to obtain another application's data and then convey it elsewhere presents security risks.

Adobe addressed this for SWF and PDF with the Adobe Cross Domain Policy File facility [84]. Such a policy file is known as a *crossdomain.xml* file. A web application server administrator may compose a crossdomain.xml file that stipulates various policies regarding which domains are authorized to make requests and receive information from the administrator's web application.

The Cross Domain Policy file is based upon XML and has a defined format consisting of a set of policy declarations. For example, you can declare which domains to allow access to, allowing access to requesters with certain specific credentials, which HTTP request headers to allow, and the location of subordinate policy files.

The crossdomain.xml file is made available by the web application server administrator at the web application's domain *root*. For example, if the web application is www.example.com, then the Cross Domain Policy file for that web application may be obtained at www.example.com/crossdomain.xml.

When a browser loads SWF or PDF files with references to www.example.com, the plugin handling the file requests the Cross Domain Policy file for www.example.com. If the requesting SWF or PDF files were loaded from http://www.example.net/, and the crossdomain.xml file contains the policy directives illustrated

```
Access-Control-Allow-Origin: http://example.com
```

Figure 4.10   An example of Access-Control-Allow-Origin HTTP Response header indicating that the requesting web application whose origin is http://example.com should be granted access to data of the response message.

```
<?xml version="1.0"?>
<!DOCTYPE cross-domain-policy SYSTEM
"http://www.adobe.com/xml/dtds/cross-domain-policy.dtd">

<cross-domain-policy>
  <site-control permitted-cross-domain-policies="master-only"/>
  <allow-access-from domain="*.example.net"/>
</cross-domain-policy>
```

Figure 4.11 A simple crossdomain.xml file allowing example.net and any of its immediate subdomains to make requests to the web application hosting this policy file.

in Figure 4.11, then the requests would be successful. Conversely, if the requesting SWF or PDF files were loaded from http://some.other.place/, then they would not be successful.

Application Boundaries Enforcer   There's also the Application Boundaries Enforcer (ABE) [332], included as a part of NoScript [331], a popular Mozilla Firefox security extension. ABE monitors the requests web application clients make and evaluates them against a *rule set*, which is supplied by the web browser user or the web application site administrator. In the latter case, the web application administrator can place her ABE rule set at a well-known web address for downloading by individual clients [333], similar to Flash's crossdomain.xml, discussed in Section "Adobe Cross Domain Policy File." Figure 4.12 illustrates a simple ABE rule set.

However, an important distinction is that ABE policies apply to distinct HTTP protocol operations initiated by conventional (HTML and JavaScript) web application clients, such as GET and POST. In contrast, crossdomain.xml policies are applied to requests initiated by Adobe-specific content. It is processed and managed only by the requisite plugins.

4.2.2.3 Advanced browser-based web security mechanisms

Researchers are constantly working on new approaches to improve web security in general and web browser security features in particular. Among the ongoing work are various proposals aimed at addressing other facets of inherent web vulnerabilities, for example, JavaScript postMessage-based mashup communications such as PostMash [107], hypertext isolation techniques [327], and service security policies advertised via the Domain Name System [381]. Going even further, there are efforts to redesign web browser architectures [402], of which Google Chrome and IE 8 are deployed examples.

```
Site *.example.com
Accept POST SUB from SELF https://www.example.com
Accept GET
Deny
```

Figure 4.12 A simple ABE rule allowing only example.com, via a secure https channel, to make POST and SUB (submit) requests to itself. GET requests are accepted from anywhere, all other interactions not already specified are denied.

4.2.3   Where do we go from Here?

As we noted throughout the above sections, these various built-in and selectively invocable security mechanisms are *not* implemented uniformly in today's various popular browsers and web application development frameworks. This makes life hard for web application administrators in that allowances must be made in web application security posture, and approaches, in consideration of which browser a user may be wielding at any particular time.

Although industry and researchers collectively are aware of all the above issues, our responses to the various classes of security vulnerabilities have, to date, been issue specific and uncoordinated. What we are ending up with looks perhaps similar to Frankenstein's monster—a design with noble intents, but whose final execution is an almost random amalgamation of parts that do not work well together. It can even cause destruction on its own: witness the problems Internet Explorer 8 had with the X-XSS-Protection response header that disabled its anti-XSS features [351].

We believe that it is desirable for industry—both web application deployers and web browser vendors—to work together with the goal of deploying web browsers featuring more coherent security properties than are present today. Cooperatively working together to address specific subsets of the overall problem space will yield measurable results for web application deployers, browser vendors, and users.

The time appears to be right for a concerted effort by various stakeholders to create a set of robust standards for coherent web security policy framework(s). The continued ad hoc creation of new security mechanisms as inevitable, but with coordination and well-specified framework, industry can maximize the benefit and reduce the risk of introducing such new security mechanisms. We believe that a generalized web security policy framework is within reach and is achievable in the near-to-intermediate term, if we can work together to achieve this goal.

4.3   CONTENT-SNIFFING XSS ATTACKS: XSS WITH NON-HTML CONTENT

Juan Caballero, Adam Barth, and Dawn Song

Abstract. Cross-site scripting (XSS) attacks are a prevalent class of attacks that occur when some content escalates its privilege. Cross-site scripting defenses often focus on HTML documents, neglecting attacks involving the browser's *content-sniffing* algorithm, which can treat non-HTML content as HTML. This section introduces the reader to content-sniffing XSS attacks, a poorly understood class of XSS attacks that leverages the browser's content-sniffing algorithm. This section details what content-sniffing XSS attacks are, how they come to happen, how to find instances of such attacks, and how to protect against them.

4.3.1   Introduction

Cross-site scripting is a prevalent vulnerability type that affects web applications. In 2005 it became the most prevalent vulnerability type [152]. Five years later it was still the most widespread and dangerous vulnerability type [151].

Cross-site scripting vulnerabilities are routinely used by attackers to launch attacks on the users of vulnerable websites. Due to its prevalence and impact, XSS attacks need to be understood not only by security practitioners but also by anyone involved in the design and operation of web applications. Understanding XSS attacks is also important for any user of web applications, since users are the target of such attacks. Most descriptions of cross-site scripting explain that in an XSS attack, the attacker injects JavaScript code into a web application. This section provides the reader with a different, broader, view on cross-site scripting. It presents a new kind of cross-site scripting attack that most readers will not be familiar with. It also explains why you should view an XSS attack to be a privilege escalation attack. Most readers, even if familiar with cross-site scripting attacks, should benefit from this material.

Before delving into details, a couple of important facts need to be explained. These may be new to people not familiar with XSS attacks and should serve as a quick review for other readers. First, in an XSS attack, there are typically three parties involved: an attacker, an honest web application that accepts external content, and some users who are the victims of the attack. In a nutshell, the attacker uploads some malicious content into the honest web application. When a user visits the honest website (possibly induced by the attacker), the user's browser downloads the malicious content uploaded by the attacker and corruption happens in the user's browser. Thus, XSS attacks only affect websites that accept external content. However, in today's Internet, most webpages are dynamically generated using external content from different sources. Static content stored in the web server is often only a fraction of the page served by a web application to the user's browser. Other content included in the webpage may come from data in the HTTP request sent by the user's browser to the web application, for example, URL parameters, form fields, and cookies; from content uploaded by other users, for example, pictures in a photo sharing application and user comments in a web forum; and from third parties such as advertisers. An attacker may be able to upload malicious content into an honest web application if the web application does not sufficiently vet the external content it accepts.

Second, it is important to understand that different types of content in a webpage are handled differently by a web browser and can perform different actions. Some types of content like text or HTML are directly handled by the web browser, while others like images or PDF documents are handled by external programs such as the image viewer or the PDF plugin. More importantly, some types of content such as text and images are passive and simply displayed to the user, while others such as HTML are interpreted and can possibly contain active content (JavaScript, Visual Basic scripts, Flash, ActiveX) that is executed by the browser. Active content can perform a variety of actions that passive content cannot, such as accessing session cookies and sending data back to the website that it was downloaded from. We say that the more the actions a type of content can perform, the higher its *privilege*. Content like HTML has higher privilege than the other content like text or figures, because HTML can contain active content. The fact that different kinds of content have different privileges lies at the core of cross-site scripting attacks.

Think about the following scenario. A user asks how to implement certain functionality using HTML in a programming web forum. Another user posts a reply that simply contains some HTML code that implements the requested functionality. It is important to realize that the reply comment is both text and HTML code and we already know these two types of content are handled very differently by a web browser. In this case, the web forum correctly treats the comment as text and includes it into the webpage served to another visitor. When that visitor's web browser receives the page that includes the reply comment, it does not have any contextual information about that comment (e.g., that it was written by a user of a web forum), so it could potentially decide that the reply comment is not text that should be displayed to the visitor, but rather it is HTML code that should be interpreted. This is problematic because the user that posted the comment may not be trustworthy and because HTML can contain active code that can perform actions such as posting in the web forum on behalf of the user.

The problem in this scenario is that the same content is considered as being of different type by the web application and by the web browser. Furthermore, the web application believes the content is low-privilege text, while the web browser believes it is high-privilege HTML. This escalation in the privilege level of the content is fundamental because if the web forum thought the comment was HTML it may have filtered it. Such *privilege escalation*, caused by the different views of the same content by the web application and the browser, is at the root of any XSS attack.

Using this fact we can formulate XSS attacks in a new light, as privilege escalation attacks where the web application delivers some content that it considers low-privilege (e.g., passive) to the user's browser, but where the browser considers the same content as having higher privilege (e.g., being active code or possibly containing active code).

A key implication is that XSS attacks not only happen with text that is interpreted as HTML containing JavaScript code (as typically described in the literature) but may also occur with any content, for example, images or documents, that is considered low-privilege by the web application. Furthermore, an XSS attack happens if low-privilege content is interpreted as any other content type with higher privilege. Here, HTML is often the target because it has the highest privilege in a web browser, that is, it can execute scripts, but attacks may exist with other content types with intermediate privilege like Adobe Flash. In addition, it becomes evident that XSS attacks are independent of the type of active content embedded in the HTML, regardless of JavaScript, Visual Basic scripts, or ActiveX.

At this point, we hope you understand cross-site scripting attacks as privilege escalation attacks. The rest of this section deals with a particular class of XSS attacks called *content-sniffing XSS attacks* where low-privilege, non-HTML content is interpreted as high-privilege HTML by the web browser. Content-sniffing XSS attacks take their name from *content-sniffing*, a functionality implemented by every web browser. Although content-sniffing XSS attacks have been known for some time [6,12,23], they are poorly understood. The rest of this section details content-sniffing, content-sniffing XSS attacks, as well as the defenses to protect against them.

4.3.2 Content-Sniffing XSS Attacks

Content-sniffing XSS attacks are best illustrated with an example. HotCRP [7] is a conference management web application used by many research conferences that lets authors upload their papers in PDF or PostScript format so that they can be downloaded by the reviewers that evaluate them. Suppose a malicious author uploads a paper to HotCRP in PostScript format. By carefully crafting the paper, the author can create a *chameleon* document that is valid PostScript and contains HTML (see Figure 4.13). HotCRP accepts the chameleon document as PostScript, but when a reviewer attempts to read the paper using Internet Explorer 7, the browser treats the chameleon as HTML, letting the attacker run a malicious script in HotCRP's security

```
%!PS-Adobe-2.0
%%Creator: <script> ... </script>
%%Title: attack.dvi
```

Figure 4.13 A chameleon PostScript document that Internet Explorer 7 treats as HTML. This chameleon document can be used by an attacker to launch a content-sniffing XSS attack against users of a website that accepts PostScript documents since it is valid PostScript, but Internet Explorer 7 treats this file as HTML, executing the JavaScript code contained between the script tags.

origin. The attacker's script can perform actions on behalf of the reviewer, such as giving the paper a glowing review and a high score.

At this point, you may wonder why the browser treats the above file as HTML. The reason lies in a piece of code in the browser called the *content-sniffing algorithm*, from which this class of attacks take their name and which we explain next.

4.3.2.1   Content-sniffing

Every web browser employs a *content-sniffing algorithm* that inspects the contents of HTTP responses to determine what type of content is being delivered by the server. A savvy reader may wonder why this is needed since HTTP identifies the type of content in uploads or downloads using the Content-Type header, which carries a *MIME type* such as text/plain or application/postscript. For readers who are not familiar with Multipurpose Internet Mail Extensions (MIME) types, it is an Internet standard [195,196,358] originally developed to let email include nontext attachments, text using non-ASCII encodings, and multiple pieces of content in the same message. The MIME standard defines MIME types, standardized names for some types of content (e.g., application/postscript for PostScript files). MIME types are used by a number of protocols, including HTTP. The browser uses this MIME type to determine how to present the content to the user or to select an appropriate plugin.

Content-sniffing algorithms are needed by browsers for compatibility, to render approximately 1% of HTTP responses that either lack a Content-Type HTTP header or have an incorrect value in that header. For example, a server might send a GIF image with a Content-Type of text/html or text/plain. Other HTTP responses lack a Content-Type header entirely or contain an invalid MIME type, such as */* or unknown/unknown. To render these webpages correctly, browsers use content-sniffing algorithms that guess the "correct" MIME type by inspecting the contents of HTTP responses. In a competitive browser market, a browser that guesses the "correct" MIME type and correctly displays those webpages is more appealing to users than a browser that fails to display them. Once one browser vendor implements content sniffing, the other browser vendors are forced to follow suit or risk losing market share.

If not carefully designed for security, a content-sniffing algorithm can be leveraged by an attacker to launch cross-site scripting attacks.

4.3.2.2   A detailed view of content-sniffing XSS attacks

In a content-sniffing XSS attack, the attacker uploads a seemingly benign file to an honest web application. Many web applications accept user uploads. For example, photograph sharing sites accept user-uploaded images and conference management sites accept user-uploaded research papers. After the attacker uploads a malicious file, the attacker directs the user to view the file. Instead of treating the file as a low-privilege image or a research paper, the browser's content-sniffing algorithm treats the file as high-privilege HTML (possibly overriding the MIME type provided by the server). The browser then renders the attacker's HTML in the honest site's security origin, letting the attacker steal the user's password or transact on behalf of the user.

Web applications that accept user uploads employ different policies to restrict those uploads. For example, some web applications (e.g., file storage services) might let users upload arbitrary content, whereas other might restrict the type of uploaded content (e.g., photograph sharing services) and perform different amounts of validation on the uploaded content before serving it to other users.

Based on our experience, we believe that most web applications restrict user uploads by limiting the *type* of content users can upload. For example, a photo sharing site might verify that uploaded files actually appear to be images and a conference management web application might check that uploaded documents actually appear to be in PDF or PostScript format. For this, web applications typically use an *upload filter* that returns "yes" if the content is accepted or "no" if the content is rejected. The upload filter typically classifies uploaded content into different MIME types and then checks whether that MIME type belongs to the application's list of allowed MIME types. The list of allowed MIME types comprises only low-privilege MIME types, since high-privilege MIME types such as HTML are typically considered dangerous and not accepted. The upload filter of websites has three options for assigning a MIME type to the uploaded content. It can (1) use the MIME type received in the Content-Type header, (2) infer the MIME type from the file's extension, (3) and infer the MIME type from the file's contents. In practice, if the user uploading the content is untrusted, neither option (1) nor option (2) is reliable because the Content-Type header and the file extension can be spoofed and may not represent the real type of the content. For these reasons, many sites choose option (3). Thus, we consider that an uploaded file will be accepted by the web application's upload filter if the MIME type that it infers from the file's contents matches one of the allowed (low-privilege) MIME types defined by the application's administrators.

Now that we have introduced the website's upload filter and the browser's content-sniffing algorithm, we can detail the conditions under which content-sniffing XSS attacks exist. An attacker can mount a content-sniffing XSS attack when (1) the uploaded content is accepted by the upload filter, the assigned MIME type is in the list of low-privilege MIME types accepted by the web application, and (2) the browser's content-sniffing algorithm assigns a higher privilege MIME type (most often text/html) to the same content when downloaded by the user.

To mount a content-sniffing XSS attack, the attacker creates a chameleon document that exploits a mismatch between the MIME type inferred by the website's upload filter and the one inferred by the browser's content-sniffing algorithm. For example, the upload filter of the HotCRP conference management web application will infer a MIME type of application/postscript for the chameleon document in Figure 4.13, while the content-sniffing algorithm in Internet Explorer 7 will infer a MIME type of text/html for the same document. Since application/postscript is a low-privilege MIME type, but text/html is a high-privilege MIME type, the chameleon document escalates its privilege, enabling the attacker to run any JavaScript embedded in the chameleon file in the user's browser. Similar to other XSS attacks, you can view content-sniffing XSS attacks as privilege escalation attacks.

4.3.2.3 Why do mismatches happen?

Now that you know that content-sniffing XSS attacks happen due to mismatches between the MIME type inferred by the *upload filter* and the MIME type inferred by the *content-sniffing algorithm*, you may be wondering why these mismatches happen. The main reason is that the upload filter needs to mimic the behavior of the browser's content-sniffing algorithm, but the developers of the web application often do not understand the inner workings of the browser's content-sniffing algorithm.

This happens for several reasons. Content-sniffing is a rather obscure topic, so some web developers do not even know about it. For the ones that do know, the problem is that content-sniffing has not been standardized. Each browser implements its own algorithm, which is often poorly (if at all) documented. To further complicate the problem, the content-sniffing algorithm in some popular browsers such as Internet Explorer and Safari is proprietary (a large portion of Safari is open-source as part of the webKit project [484], however, Safari's content-sniffing algorithm is not part of the webKit project), so web developers who are aware of content-sniffing XSS attacks and want to protect their applications cannot even refer to the algorithms' source code to understand how they work.

To examine the extent of this problem, we analyze the content-sniffing algorithms used by four browsers: Internet Explorer 7, Firefox 3, Safari 3.1, and Google Chrome. Note that an upload filter that wants to protect users against content-sniffing XSS attacks, regardless of which of those four browsers they use, needs to account for the *union behavior* of all four browsers, that is, it needs to protect the user regardless of the differences in implementation of the content-sniffing algorithm across the browsers. Our analysis uncovers that the algorithms follow roughly the same design, but that subtle differences exist on several key points, which have dramatic consequences for security.

For example, we find that each browser limits content sniffing to the initial bytes of each HTTP response, but that the number of bytes they consider varies by browser. Internet Explorer 7 uses 256 bytes, Google Chrome uses 512 bytes, and Firefox 3 and Safari 3.1 use 1024 bytes. Knowledge about the size of the content-sniffing buffer is important because to account for the union behavior of all four browsers, the upload filter needs to be applied over the largest of these sizes, that is, needs to examine at least the initial 1024 bytes of the content.

We also find that some HTTP responses trigger the content-sniffing algorithm, but that others do not. Browsers determine whether to sniff based on the Content-Type header, but the specific values that trigger content sniffing widely vary. The list of Content-Type values that trigger content sniffing is important to determine which MIME types the attacker can use to create chameleon documents, which are a critical part of content-sniffing XSS attacks.

All four content-sniffing algorithms use byte patterns to infer the MIME type of the content. We call the set of byte patterns associated with a MIME type its *signature*. For example, the signature for image/gif used by Firefox 3 is that the first 4 bytes of the content need to be the string "GIF8." The algorithm scans the content looking for a matching signature. When a match is found, it assigns the MIME type of the matching signature to the content. We find that the signature used for a MIME type widely varies across browsers. Table 4.1 shows the differences in the signatures for four popular image types. The complete list of signatures used by each algorithm is available online [14].

Table 4.1 Signatures for four popular image formats

image/jpeg	Signature		image/bmp	Signature
IE 7	DATA[0:1] == 0xffd8		IE 7	(DATA[0:1] == 0x424d) &&
Firefox 3	DATA[0:2] == 0xffd8ff			(DATA[6:9] == 0x00000000)
Safari 3.1	DATA[0:3] == 0xffd8ffe0		Firefox 3	DATA[0:1] == 0x424d
Chrome	DATA[0:2] == 0xffd8ff		Safari 3.1	N/A
			Chrome	DATA[0:1] == 0x424d
image/gif	Signature		image/png	Signature
IE 7	(strncasecmp(DATA,"GIF87",5) == 0) ||		IE 7	(DATA[0:3] == 0x89504e47) &&
	(strncasecmp(DATA,"GIF89",5) == 0)			(DATA[4:7] == 0x0d0a1a0a)
Firefox 3	strncmp(DATA,"GIF8",4) == 0		Firefox 3	DATA[0:3] == 0x89504e47
Safari 3.1	N/A		Safari 3.1	N/A
Chrome	(strncmp(DATA,"GIF87a",6) == 0) ||		Chrome	(DATA[0:3] == 0x89504e47) &&
	(strncmp(DATA,"GIF89a",6) == 0)			(DATA[4:7] == 0x0d0a1a0a)

DATA is a pointer to the content-sniffing buffer, which contains the first n bytes of the content. DATA[x:y], where $n > y \geq x \geq 0$, is the subsequence of DATA beginning at offset x and ending at offset y (both offsets inclusive). For example, Internet Explorer 7 uses the following signature for image/jpeg: DATA[0:1] == 0xffd8. To match this signature, an HTTP response must contain at least two bytes, the first byte of the response must be 0xff, and the second byte must be 0xd8. These signatures also use two C string functions: strncmp for case-sensitive comparison and strncasecmp for case-insensitive comparison.

We also find differences in the order in which the signatures are applied, which is important because chameleon documents may match signatures for two different MIME types. If the order in which signatures are matched differs between the upload filter and the content-sniffing algorithm, the same content may be assigned different MIME types even if the signatures used by the upload filter and the content-sniffing algorithm are identical.

In addition, we find the algorithm in Internet Explorer 7 has a special characteristic that also affects the order in which signatures are matched. The algorithm has two distinct behaviors. If the value in the Content-Type header corresponds to one of seven popular MIME types, it uses a *fast path* where it checks first the signature for the indicated MIME type. Otherwise, the algorithm checks the signatures in a predefined order. For example, if the conference management system sends the value application/postscript in the Content-Type header along with the document in Figure 4.13, then signatures are applied in the predefined order. However, if it instead sends image/gif in the Content-Type header along with the same document, the first signature applied is the signature for the MIME type image/gif, because this is one of the seven MIME types that trigger the fast path. Readers interested in the full description of the differences we found can refer to Ref. [106].

4.3.2.4 *Finding content-sniffing XSS attacks*

An important goal is how to automatically find chameleon documents that exhibit a mismatch between an upload filter and a content-sniffing algorithm. Armed with such chameleon documents, one can demonstrate to the filter's developer the necessity of improving the filter so that it more accurately resembles the union behavior of the content-sniffing algorithms.

To automatically identify such chameleon documents, we propose an approach that compares a model of the upload filter with a model of the content-sniffing algorithm. For our purposes, we can model the upload filter as a Boolean formula that takes as input the content and returns "yes" if the content is accepted by the web application and "no" if it is rejected. For example, the upload filter for the HotCRP conference system can be modeled as (strncasecmp(DATA, "%PDF-",5) == 0) || (strncasecmp(DATA, "%!PS-",5) == 0), where DATA is a pointer to the content. This Boolean expression is a disjunction of two terms. The first term says that if the first 5 bytes of the content are the string "%PDF-" (case insensitive), then it is a PDF file and should be accepted. The second term says that if the first 5 bytes of the content are the string "%!PS-" (case insensitive), then it is a PostScript file and should also be accepted. Otherwise, the file is rejected.

We can model the content-sniffing algorithm as another Boolean formula that takes as input the content and returns "yes" if the content is considered HTML (or other high-privilege MIME type) and "no" otherwise. For example, a naive content-sniffing algorithm could be modeled as (strstr(DATA, "<HTML",5) != 0), which says that if the content contains the string "<HTML", then the content will be assigned the MIME type text/html. In reality, content-sniffing algorithms can be rather complex and thus its Boolean models may comprise hundreds or even thousands of terms.

Given these two models, finding a chameleon document is equivalent to finding an input that makes both models return "yes." Such chameleon document is considered low-privilege by the upload filter and thus accepted, but it is considered high-privilege HTML by the content-sniffing algorithm, thus escalating its privilege. For example, given the above two models for the HotCRP upload filter and the naive content-sniffing algorithm, the input DATA="%!PS-...<HTML>" returns "yes" for both models. Such input is a chameleon document because it is considered PostScript by the upload filter and HTML by the naive content-sniffing algorithm.

There exists off-the-self tools called *solvers* that given the Boolean models can automatically find those inputs for us. STP is one such solver [202]. Since finding the inputs given the models can be automatically done using a solver, the main problem we need to address is how to extract the models of upload filters and content-sniffing algorithms.

When source code is available, we manually analyze the source code to build the model. Specifically, in our work, we manually extracted models of the content-sniffing algorithms from the source code of two browsers, Firefox 3 and Google Chrome, and the upload filter of two web applications, Wikipedia and HotCRP [7]. Extracting models from Internet Explorer 7 and Safari 3.1 is more difficult because their source code is not publicly available. We could use black-box testing to construct models by observing the outputs generated from selected inputs, without looking at the source code or the binary code. However, experience shows that models extracted by black-box testing are not very accurate. For example, the Wine project [27] uses black-box testing and documentation [15] to reimplement Internet Explorer's content-sniffing algorithm, but Wine's content-sniffing algorithm differs significantly from Internet Explorer's content-sniffing algorithm. This is problematic because if the model does not closely resemble the content-sniffing algorithm, the inputs returned by the solver may not really be chameleon documents.

To extract accurate models from the closed-source browsers, we propose a kind of white-box approach where we have access to the binary code of the application, but not to its source code. Our approach is called *string-enhanced white-box exploration*. While a detailed description of our approach is beyond the scope of this section, for the curious reader we next briefly introduce our approach. String-enhanced white-box exploration is similar in spirit to previous white-box exploration techniques used for automatic testing [136,215,216]. Unlike previous work, our technique builds a model from all the explored paths incrementally. Our technique also reasons directly about string operations rather than the individual byte-level operations that comprise these string operations, and we apply our technique to building models rather than generating test cases. By reasoning directly about string operations, we can explore paths more efficiently, increasing the coverage achieved by the exploration per unit of time and improving the fidelity of our models. An interested reader can find a detailed description of string-enhanced white-box exploration in Refs [106,135].

4.3.2.5   Example 1: Under the hood of the HotCRP attack

Now that you understand how mismatches open the door for content-sniffing XSS attacks, we can revisit the attack on HotCRP in Figure 4.13, which we reproduce next for convenience:

```
%!PS-Adobe-2.0
%%Creator: <script> ... </script>
%%Title: attack.dvi
```

Even though we have reported this attack to the HotCRP author and the underlying problem has been fixed in the latest version, describing the details of the attack is still useful to understand how content-sniffing XSS vulnerabilities manifest in real applications.

Before accepting a file, the upload filter in HotCRP checks whether the file appears to be a valid PostScript or PDF file. For PDFs, it checks that the first 5 bytes of the file are %PDF- (case insensitive), and for PostScript, it checks that the first 5 bytes of the file are %!PS- (case insensitive). The above chameleon document satisfies the PostScript signature and is accepted by HotCRP. The problem is that the above chameleon document satisfies both the PostScript and the HTML signatures used by the content-sniffing algorithm of Internet Explorer 7. The PostScript signature checks that the first 2 bytes of the file are %!, while the HTML searches in the content for a number of HTML tags including <script (case insensitive). It happens that the content-sniffing algorithm in Internet Explorer 7 checks the HTML signature before the PostScript one. The HTML signature matches the tag in the second line. Thus, Internet Explorer 7 treats the document as HTML and runs the attacker's JavaScript as if the JavaScript were part of HotCRP, which lets the attacker give the paper a high score and recommend the paper for acceptance.

4.3.2.6 *Example 2: An attack on wikipedia*

Wikipedia is a popular encyclopedia that lets users upload content in several formats, including SVG, PNG, GIF, JPEG, and Ogg/Theora [26]. To check uploaded content, Wikipedia uses an upload filter that performs three checks:

1. It checks whether the file matches one of the accepted MIME types. For example, Wikipedia's GIF signature checks if the file begins with the string "GIF". For this, it uses PHP's MIME detection functions, which in turn use the signature database from the Unix file tool [5].

2. It checks the first 1024 bytes of the content for a set of blacklisted HTML tags such as "<HTML". The Wikipedia developers are aware of XSS attacks and use this step to try to prevent HTML content from being uploaded. Unfortunately, the set of HTML tags they blacklist is not complete and later we show how a nonblacklisted tag can be used to bypass this defense.

3. It uses several regular expressions to check that the file does not contain JavaScript.

   Even though Wikipedia developers are aware of content-sniffing XSS attacks and have developed an upload filter that takes the above three steps to try to prevent dangerous content to be uploaded by a malicious user, our analysis still uncovers a subtle content-sniffing XSS attack. This highlights the complexity of building a robust defense without detailed knowledge of the inner workings of content-sniffing algorithms. We construct the attack in three steps, each of which defeats one of the steps in Wikipedia's upload filter:

1. Wikipedia's upload filter requires that a valid GIF file begins with the string "GIF", while the content-sniffing algorithm in Internet Explorer 7 assigns the MIME type image/gif to a file if it begins with either string "GIF87" or "GIF89". Here, we start the file with string "GIF88", so that the file is accepted by Wikipedia's upload filter as a valid GIF file and delivered to the user's browser with a MIME type of image/gif in the Content-Type header. When received by Internet Explorer 7, the image/gif value in the Content-Type header triggers the fast path inside the content-sniffing algorithm. Since the GIF signature check fails, the content-sniffing algorithm in Internet Explorer 7 searches the file for any other matching signature.

2. Wikipedia's blacklist of HTML tags is incomplete. To circumvent the blacklist, we include the string "<a href", which is not on Wikipedia's blacklist but causes the file to match Internet Explorer 7's HTML signature and be assigned a MIME type of text/html.

3. So far we have achieved to create a chameleon file that is accepted by Wikipedia's upload filter and considered to be HTML by Internet Explorer 7. At this point any JavaScript code embedded in the file will be executed, as long as it does not match the regular expressions used by Wikipedia to detect

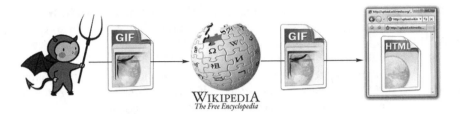

Figure 4.14 To mount a content-sniffing XSS attack, the attacker uploads a GIF/HTML chameleon to Wikipedia. When a user visits Wikipedia using Internet Explorer 7, the browser downloads the chameleon document and treats it as HTML, running any JavaScript embedded by the attacker in the chameleon document as it was coming from Wikipedia. The JavaScript code can be used by the attacker to edit Wikipedia on behalf of the user, without the user's knowledge.

JavaScript content. To bypass Wikipedia's regular expressions, JavaScript code can be embedded in the following manner:

```
<object src="about:blank"
  onerror="... JavaScript ...">
</object>
```

As illustrated in Figure 4.14, to launch the attack, the attacker uploads this file to Wikipedia and directs the user to view the file. This attack leverages a very subtle mismatch between the GIF signatures used by Wikipedia and Internet Explorer 7. Such subtle difference may escape manual analysis and demonstrate the importance of using an automated tool, which in turn requires extracting precise models of the content-sniffing algorithm and the upload filter. Variants on this attack also affect other web applications that use PHP's built-in MIME detection functions and the Unix file tool.

The production instance of Wikipedia mitigates content-sniffing XSS attacks by hosting uploaded content on a separate domain. Wikipedia hosts English language articles at en.wikipedia.org, but hosts images at upload.wikimedia.org. Since active code is only allowed to connect back to the same domain that it originated from, content-sniffing XSS attacks can compromise the upload.wikimedia.org origin but not the en.wikipedia.org origin, which contains the user's session cookie. This approach does limit the severity of this vulnerability, but the installable version of Wikipedia, mediawiki, which is used by over 750 websites in the English language alone [21], hosts uploaded user content on-domain in the default configuration and is fully vulnerable to content-sniffing XSS attacks. (After we reported this vulnerability, Wikipedia has improved its upload filter to prevent these attacks.)

4.3.3 Defenses

Now that you understand what content-sniffing XSS attacks are and how they come to happen, we can describe defenses to protect against them. We present two kinds of defenses. First, we describe server-side defenses including general defenses against XSS attacks that help to ameliorate content-sniffing XSS attacks. We show that we can use our models to construct a secure upload filter that web applications can use to protect against content-sniffing XSS attacks. Second, we propose addressing the root cause of content-sniffing XSS attacks by securing the browser's content-sniffing algorithm.

4.3.3.1 Server-side defenses

Content-sniffing XSS attacks are a class of XSS attacks. As such, defenses for XSS attacks already deployed by web applications on their servers may help ameliorate content-sniffing XSS attacks, but typically do not provide a complete defense.

The most common defense against XSS attacks is sanitizing all external inputs to the web application. Two widely used approaches for sanitization are *input validation* and *output encoding*. Input validation is the process of filtering or rewriting external input before using it inside the web application. Input validation can be implemented in three flavors: accepting only external input that is considered safe for the web application (whitelisting), blocking external inputs that are considered unsafe (blacklisting), and rewriting external inputs into a safe form (input encoding). Output encoding is the process of rewriting the output of the web application into a safe form before passing it to another application, for example, before sending it to the user's browser. The main difference between input and output encoding is where the sanitization happens: before using the input for input encoding and before sending the output for output encoding.

A detailed description of input validation and output encoding for general XSS protection is beyond the scope of this section. We refer the interested reader to the OWASP site for details [380]. The key idea is that while both input validation and output encoding are defenses that should be implemented by a web application as part of a defense-in-depth strategy, they are often not enough to protect against content-sniffing XSS attacks by themselves. There are three main problems with using sanitization as the unique defense. First, it is difficult to apply input and output encoding to nontextual content since rewriting can cause content like images to render incorrectly. Second, due to the differences in HTML parsing across browsers, input validation defenses based on blacklisting are too often incomplete and leave some dangerous inputs unfiltered. Finally, whitelisting nontextual input is difficult because each content type (PDF, PostScript, JPEG, etc.) requires a different whitelist. Thus, upload filters often implement the approach described earlier: infer the MIME type of the uploaded content and accept the content only if the inferred MIME type is in the list of whitelisted MIME types.

We have already shown that popular sites that implement sanitization, for example, Wikipedia, are still vulnerable to content-sniffing XSS attacks. Recall the attack on a Wikipedia user that we described in Section 4.3.2.6. In that attack, Wikipedia's upload filter was implementing both a whitelist of accepted MIME types and a blacklist of some HTML tags and JavaScript strings, not allowed to appear in the uploaded content. We were able to defeat these defenses by creating a chameleon document that bypassed the MIME type whitelist and by using some HTML and JavaScript strings that did not appear in the (incomplete) blacklists. This attack illustrates the shortcomings of relying uniquely on sanitization for protecting against content-sniffing XSS attacks.

We believe a defense against content-sniffing XSS attacks should not be built uniquely using sanitization. However, to help web applications that want to implement a server-side defense, we use our models of the content-sniffing algorithms of four browsers to implement an upload filter in 75 lines of Perl that protects web applications from content-sniffing XSS attacks. Our filter uses the union HTML signature in Table 4.2. If a file passes the filter, the content is guaranteed not to be interpreted as HTML by the content-sniffing algorithm in Internet Explorer 7, Firefox 3, Safari 3.1, and Google Chrome. Using our filter, web applications can block potentially malicious user-uploaded content that these browsers might treat as HTML.

There are other server-side XSS defenses that can ameliorate content-sniffing XSS attacks. One such defense is transforming the uploaded content. For example, the popular photo sharing site Flickr [189] converts user-uploaded PNG images to JPEG format. This saves on storage costs and makes it more difficult to

Table 4.2   To Identify Content That Could Be Interpreted as Being HTML by Any of the Four Browsers Analyzed, an Upload Filter Needs to Use the Union of the HTML Signatures for Each Browser

text/html signature

```
(strncmp(PTR,"<!",2) == 0) ||
(strncmp(PTR,"<?",2) == 0) ||
(strcasestr(DATA,"<HTML") != 0) ||
(strcasestr(DATA,"<SCRIPT") != 0) ||
(strcasestr(DATA,"<TITLE") != 0) ||
(strcasestr(DATA,"<BODY") != 0) ||
(strcasestr(DATA,"<HEAD") != 0) ||
(strcasestr(DATA,"<PLAINTEXT") != 0) ||
(strcasestr(DATA,"<TABLE") != 0) ||
(strcasestr(DATA,"<IMG") != 0) ||
(strcasestr(DATA,"<PRE") != 0) ||
(strcasestr(DATA,"text/html") != 0) ||
(strcasestr(DATA,"<A") != 0) ||
(strncasecmp(PTR,"<FRAMESET",9) == 0) ||
(strncasecmp(PTR,"<IFRAME",7) == 0) ||
(strncasecmp(PTR,"<LINK",5) == 0) ||
(strncasecmp(PTR,"<BASE",5) == 0) ||
(strncasecmp(PTR,"<STYLE",6) == 0) ||
(strncasecmp(PTR,"<DIV",4) == 0) ||
(strncasecmp(PTR,"<P",2) == 0) ||
(strncasecmp(PTR,"<FONT",5) == 0) ||
(strncasecmp(PTR,"<APPLET",7) == 0) ||
(strncasecmp(PTR,"<META",5) == 0) ||
(strncasecmp(PTR,"<CENTER",7) == 0) ||
(strncasecmp(PTR,"<FORM",5) == 0) ||
(strncasecmp(PTR,"<ISINDEX",8) == 0) ||
(strncasecmp(PTR,"<H1",3) == 0) ||
(strncasecmp(PTR,"<H2",3) == 0) ||
(strncasecmp(PTR,"<H3",3) == 0) ||
(strncasecmp(PTR,"<H4",3) == 0) ||
(strncasecmp(PTR,"<H5",3) == 0) ||
(strncasecmp(PTR,"<H6",3) == 0) ||
(strncasecmp(PTR,"<B",2) == 0) ||
(strncasecmp(PTR,"<BR",3) == 0)
```

In the union HTML signature shown here, DATA is a pointer to the content-sniffing buffer, and PTR is a pointer to the first nonwhitespace byte of DATA. This signature uses three C string functions: strncmp for case-sensitive comparison, strncasecmp for case-insensitive comparison, and strcasestr for case-insensitive search. For example, the entry (strncmp(PTR,"<!",2) == 0) means that the first two nonwhitespace characters in the content-sniffing buffer should be the left angle character and the exclamation character. The entry (strcasestr(DATA,"<HTML") != 0) means that the content-sniffing buffer should not include the string "HTML" (case-insensitive).

construct chameleon documents because HTML content in the PNG is often destroyed by the transformation. Another defense is to host user-supplied content on an untrusted domain, as Wikipedia does (Section 4.3.2.6). These defenses are not complete and may present compatibility issues, but are also useful as part of a defense-in-depth approach.

For web applications not concerned with compatibility, a specific server-side defense against content-sniffing XSS attacks is to disable content sniffing. For example, Gmail disables Internet Explorer's content-sniffing by padding text/plain attachments with 256 leading whitespace characters that exhaust the sniffing buffer. Internet Explorer 8 lets sites disable content sniffing for an individual HTTP response by including a proprietary X-Content-Type-Options header with the value nosniff [10].

A common limitation of all server-side defenses is that users are protected only if their favorite web applications deploy them. For example, the secure upload filter defense requires each website to adopt our filter.

4.3.3.2   *Secure content-sniffing*

Browser vendors can help protecting web applications that do not implement strong server-side defenses against content-sniffing XSS attacks by improving their content-sniffing algorithms. Content-sniffing algorithms trade off security and compatibility. To guide the design of secure content-sniffing algorithms, we propose two principles that help the algorithm maximize compatibility and achieve security.

- **Avoid privilege escalation** Browsers assign different privileges to different MIME types. A content-sniffing algorithm avoids privilege escalation if the algorithm refuses to upgrade one MIME type to another of higher privilege. For example, the algorithm should not upgrade a response with a valid Content-Type header to text/html because HTML has the highest privilege.

- **Use prefix-disjoint signatures** A content-sniffing algorithm uses prefix-disjoint signatures if its HTML signature does not share a prefix with a signature for another type commonly used on the web. More precisely, a set of signatures is prefix-disjoint if there does not exist two distinct sequences of bytes with a common prefix such that one matches the HTML signature and the other matches a signature for a non-HTML type commonly used on the web. Firefox 3 and Google Chrome adhere to this principle, but Internet Explorer 7 and Safari 3.1 do not.

Avoiding privilege escalation protects web applications that restrict the values of the Content-Type header they attach to untrusted content because the browser will not upgrade attacker-supplied content to HTML (or another dangerous type) and will not run the attacker's malicious JavaScript. For example, if HotCRP believes that the user-uploaded content is a PDF file and sets the Content-Type header to have type application/pdf when it sends the content to a user's browser, then the browser's content-sniffing algorithm would not upgrade the content to any type with higher privilege such as text/html. Unfortunately, avoiding privilege escalation is insufficient to protect all sites that filter uploads. For example, if a site serves content without a Content-Type header, then the browser might sniff the uploaded content as HTML, opening the site up to attack.

Prefix-disjoint signatures, however, protect web applications that filter uploaded content even if they use signatures that differ from the ones used by the browsers. If the site's signature is more strict than the browser's signature, then files accepted by the site will be sniffed correctly by the browser. If the site's signature is less strict (i.e., uses fewer initial bytes), then the site will be protected from content-sniffing XSS attacks in a browser that uses prefix-disjoint signatures. For example, suppose that the site acts like Wikipedia and checks only the first 4 of the initial 8 byte sequence required by the PNG standard [18]. If the browser uses prefix-disjoint signatures, no extension of this 4-byte sequence will match the HTML signature because this sequence can be extended to match the PNG signature. Even if the rest of the document consists of HTML tags, a browser that employs prefix-disjoint signatures will not treat the file as HTML and will prevent the attacker from crafting an exploit like the one in Figure 4.13.

The HTML signature used by Internet Explorer 7 and Safari 3.1 is not prefix-disjoint because the signature searches for known HTML tags ignoring the initial bytes of the content, which might contain a signature for another type. For example, the string "GIF87a<html>" matches both the GIF signature and the HTML signature. Firefox 3 and Google Chrome use a strict HTML signature that requires the first nonwhitespace characters to be a known HTML tag. This signature is prefix-disjoint and according to our experiments on Google's search database (see Section 4.3.3.3), it matches 9% more documents than requiring the initial characters of the content-sniffing buffer to be a known HTML tag. We recommend all browser vendors to adopt the Firefox 3 and Google Chrome HTML signature and to remove any other signatures that are not prefix-disjoint with the HTML signature from their content-sniffing algorithms.

4.3.3.3 Adoption

Our design principles for secure content-sniffing have been deployed in Google Chrome, have been adopted in part by Internet Explorer 8, and have been standardized by the HTML 5 working group.

Google Chrome   We implement a content-sniffing algorithm that follows both of our design principles and collaborate with Google to ship the algorithm in Google Chrome. This process involves an extensive compatibility evaluation of our design principles that comprises three steps:

1. We evaluate the compatibility of our design principles over Google's search database, which contains billions of web documents.

2. Google's quality assurance team manually tests our implementation for compatibility with the 500 most popular websites.

3. We deploy the algorithm to millions of users and instrument Google Chrome to collect metrics about the effectiveness of each signature from users who opt into sharing their anonymous statistics. We find that the six signatures in Table 4.3 are responsible for 96% of the time the content-sniffing algorithm changes the MIME type of an HTTP response. We also find that we can remove over half of the signatures used by the initial algorithm with a negligible effect in compatibility. We modify the algorithm accordingly.

The final algorithm produced in this process has been deployed to all users of Google Chrome.

Table 4.3 The Most Popular Signatures According to Statistics Collected from Opt-In Google Chrome Users

Signature	Mime type	Percentage
`DATA[0:2] == 0xffd8ff`	image/jpeg	58.50%
`strncmp(DATA,"GIF89a",6) == 0`	image/gif	13.43%
`(DATA[0:3] == 0x89504e47) &&`	image/png	5.50%
`(DATA[4:7] == 0x0d0a1a0a)`		
`strncasecmp(PTR,"<SCRIPT",7) == 0`	text/html	16.11%
`strncasecmp(PTR,"<HTML",5) == 0`	text/html	1.25%
`strncmp(PTR,"<?xml",5) == 0`	application/xml	1.10%

The nomenclature is the same used in Tables 4.1 and 4.2.

Internet Explorer 8   The content-sniffing algorithm in Internet Explorer 8 differs from the algorithm in Internet Explorer 7. The new algorithm does not sniff HTML from HTTP responses with a Content-Type header that begins with the string `"image/"` [11], partially avoiding privilege escalation. This change significantly reduces the content-sniffing XSS attack surface, but it does not mitigate attacks against sites, such as HotCRP, that accept nonimage uploads from untrusted users.

Standardization   The HTML 5 working group has adopted both of our content-sniffing principles in the draft HTML 5 specification [256]. The current draft advocates using prefix-disjoint signatures and classifies MIME types as either *safe* or *scriptable*. Content served with a safe MIME type carries no origin, but content served with a scriptable MIME type conveys the (perhaps limited) authority of its origin. The specification lets browsers sniff safe types from HTTP responses with valid Content-Types (such as text/plain), but forbids browsers from sniffing scriptable types from these responses, avoiding privilege escalation.

4.3.4   Conclusion

This section has described content-sniffing XSS attacks, a class of XSS attacks that leverages the content-sniffing algorithm in the browser and affects non-HTML content. It has explained why you should think of XSS attacks as privilege escalation attacks.

It has shown that one can automatically find chameleon documents used in content-sniffing XSS attacks by comparing models of a web application's upload filter and a browser's content-sniffing algorithm. Such models can be extracted using string-enhanced white-box exploration and source code inspection. It has detailed attacks found using these models against HotCRP and Wikipedia.

It has also described defenses against content-sniffing XSS attacks. Defenses can be deployed at the application's web server or at the user's browser. For web applications, this section provided a filter based on the extracted models that blocks content-sniffing XSS attacks. To protect sites that do not deploy the filter, it described two design principles for securing browser content-sniffing algorithms. These design principles have been implemented in a content-sniffing algorithm, which has been deployed in Google Chrome. The design principles have also been partially adopted by Internet Explorer 8 and incorporated into the draft HTML 5 specification.

After reading this section, we hope you view XSS attacks in a new light.

4.4   OUR INTERNET INFRASTRUCTURE AT RISK

Garth Bruen

4.4.1   Introduction

The Internet is more than cables, signals, servers, routers, and software, it is a political structure as well. Political, in the classical sense of the word. Beyond technical specifications, the Internet is built on organizational initiatives, consensus policies, contracts, memoranda, and international law. In network imagery, "Internet" is often depicted as a blurry cloud. Even the term "Ethernet" evokes a murky, undefined space for what is really a highly defined realm where everything has purpose and direction. The amorphous cloud images may help fuel the false perception that the Internet is a lawless, unaccountable entity that exists beyond policy. Criminals who drive policy with hidden hand exploit this common view. What is breaking the Internet is not lack of policy but lack of policy enforcement and accountability. Internet criminals appear to exist outside the policy structure when the reality is that they are embedded in it, their livelihood in fact depends on the Internet functioning regularly, quickly, and efficiently. To this end, Internet criminals have become their own service providers or have coopted other providers with loose ethics or oversight. Fraud and risk emerge from a lack of accountability as exploiters find policy failure like water finds spaces between rocks. As a political entity, the Internet has many constituencies, such as consumers, business, governments, educators, and technicians, each using their resources to shape policy for their own benefit. It must be acknowledged that criminals constitute a secret constituency whose political will is just as powerful, or stronger even, as any other group. Because of this, it is not enough to track malicious activity as a technical or criminal problem, but it is also necessary to thwart their political will.

Damage from malicious activity is frequently thought of in terms of infected computers, hijacked bandwidth, vandalized websites, and stolen databases. The exploits discussed in this section occur several layers deep and sometimes years before a problem is actually noticed. Below we examine each critical policy layer of the Internet starting with a brief overview of the political structure and an explanation of how it came to exist. This structure generated the basic unit of the Internet: the DOMAIN NAME, a human readable identifier mapped to a networked machine number called an Internet Protocol (IP) address. Each Domain must have what is called a WHOIS record that describes where the domain is located, who owns the domain, who to contact in case of a problem, and which company sponsors the name. Domain name sponsorship is handled by REGISTRARS that is authorized by the Internet Corporation of Assigned Names and Numbers (ICANN). ICANN contracts with REGISTRARS to sell DOMAINS and REGISTRIES to sponsor top-level domain (TLD) structures like .COM, .NET. ORG, and other DOMAIN extensions we are familiar with. Country code TLDs (ccTLDs) are assigned by ICANN to sovereign governments, for example, .UK for United Kingdom and .CA for Canada. ICANN also issues raw Internet Protocol Numbers (IPs) to Internet service providers (ISPs). The Internet structure is an ocean of acronyms, and many will be presented here. Each level of the Internet is established by policy and the relationships between each layer are defined by contracts and complex agreements. No portion of the Internet, in theory, is truly undefined, undocumented, or uncontrolled. Each following section explains these structures, the relationships between them, and how each is under threat from exploitation by criminals and general negligence.

4.4.2 The Political Structure

Who owns the Internet? The answer has been hotly debated and is widely unknown and misunderstood. Until October 2009 [66], the simplest and most correct answer would be US President Barrack Obama and previously Presidents George W. Bush and William J. "Bill" Clinton. The maintenance of the general functions of the Internet was a matter of contract with the US Department of Commerce (US DOC), an executive agency reporting to the President [79]. It is a fact of history that the groundwork of the early Internet occurred at US colleges, was funded by US taxpayers, and sponsored by the US military [62]. One of the first Internet "chat rooms" in 1975 included then governor Ronald Regan who commented: "neat stuff!" [59]. Clearly, since then the Internet has become global and international. In 1998, President Clinton signed the Memorandum of Understanding (MoU) that initiated the public Internet we now know.

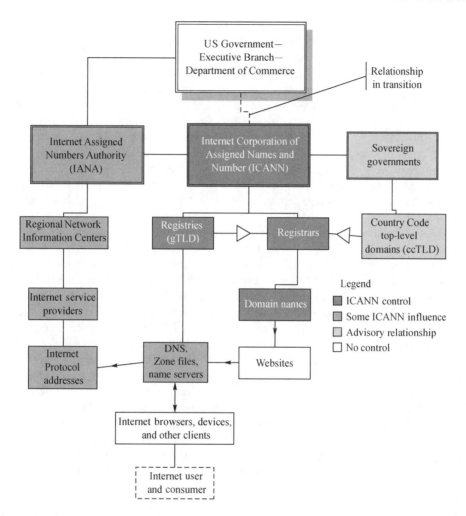

Figure 4.15   Top – down Internet policy structure. What often seems lawless and unaccountable is in fact a clearly defined hierarchy of entitles created to provide the space where Internet content is produced. Someone, somewhere is responsible for each segment of the global network.

The MoU also created the ICANN, a quasi-public, nonprofit body tasked with making the Internet truly public and universal. The MoU was replaced by the Joint Project Agreement (JPA) between ICANN and the Commerce Department that sunsetted in 2009 [71]. This was all planned as the original MoU promised to relinquish US control in 10 years while gradually privatizing the Internet. As might be expected, other nations have not been comfortable with US control; specifically, Russia, Syria, Venezuela, China, and Iran have all made multiple attempts to change this [409]. The MoU and JPA were replaced with the Affirmation of Commitments in 2009, a very loose agreement between ICANN and the US DOC but still notes US law governs the relationship even without direct sponsorship (Figure 4.15) [463]

The Internet, of course, had been expanding for 20 years before the MoU and ICANN. Previous to this, the main Internet body was the Internet Assigned Numbers Authority (IANA). IANA has been under the management of ICANN and issues IP addresses in blocks to ISPs and assigned the last Internet Protocol Version 4 (IPv4) address block in 2011 [320]. IPv4 refers to the numbering scheme for network addresses: 0.0.0.0 through 255.255.255.255. This address range allows around 4.3 billion unique locations, and while that is a big number, the addresses have been used up quickly. This is what many refer to as "the Internet running out of space," which sounds like a dire prophesy, but the size of the Internet is virtually unlimited. While all addresses have been allocated, many are still unused and each IP address can serve many websites. The problem really only refers to the numbering scheme. Internet Protocol Version 6 (IPv6) allows 340 Undecillion (a number with 36 zeroes; a million times a million 11 times) addresses [473]. Clearly, managing the Internet address space is big and complex job that may be why the Department of Commerce reopened the bidding for management of IANA 2011, a suggestion that ICANN was not living up to expectations [63].

ICANN's main functions are to maintain contracts with Registries, which sponsor top-level domain names like .COM and .NET, called "Generic" top-level domains (gTLDs); maintain contracts with Registrars who sponsor individual domain names; issue country code TLDs through agreements to sovereign governments [73], and administer IANA in its issuance of IP addresses to the five regional Network Information Centers (NICs). The five NICs represent North America (ARIN), Latin America/Caribbean (LACNIC), Europe/Central Asia/Middle East (RIPE), Africa (AfriNIC), and Asia/Pacific (APNIC). These NICs issue subblocks of IP addresses to Internet Service Providers who lease them to smaller providers and companies.

The existence of each body and their role is dictated by contract, based on policy initiatives. The individual technical pieces that make up the Internet—TCP/IP (network packet transitions), SMTP (email), FTP (file uploading and downloading, HTTP (web page access), and thousands of other data handling packages—were developed through written policies called Request for Comment documents (RFCs) [462]. The Internet Engineering Task Force (IETF) maintains these policy documents that are turned into technical tools.

The point of this structure is to provide companies and individuals with the ability to own, manage, and develop their own DOMAIN NAME. This structure chiefly exists to support the creation of domains to host web content and Internet consumables. The importance of the DOMAIN in Internet development and its use in crime cannot be understated and each layer that allows it to exist must carefully be understood.

4.4.3   The Domain

What is the point of spam or malicious webcode? To direct a user to a domain name that serves as a transaction platform. A transaction in the malicious sense could include voluntary purchase of an illicit product or service, but it also covers any situation where an Internet user willingly or unwillingly electronically provides a criminal with money, access, or credentials by visiting a domain, frequently without the knowledge of the Internet user. While malicious activity can direct users to raw IP addresses, a domain name has some advantages for the criminal. One is that the IP address can be updated if suspended by an ISP, another is that the domain name can be transferred for a fee, even if it is suspended for cause [76]. Criminally used domains suspended by one Registrar frequently appear at another fairly quickly. Domains suspended for spam, selling counterfeit goods and drugs have "clean slate" status at their new sponsor.

Domain sponsorship is one of the most fundamental relationships on the Internet as it associates a human readable string with a networked machine number or IP address where web content or scripting is actually located. The Domain Name System is in essence a "big phonebook" that links a DOMAIN NAME

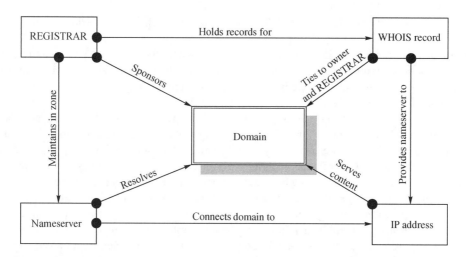

Figure 4.16   Foundation of a domain. Every domain has four critical relationships, which support its existence: an owner to register it, a Registrar to sponsor it, a Nameserver to resolve it, and an IP Address to host it. These are not one-time relationships, but are rather connections that require regular maintenance and renewal.

with a nameserver, and the nameserver with an IP address. There are several "books" that comprise the DNS called "Zone Files." Each REGISTRY that sponsors a specific top-level domain extension publishes and regularly updates a large file that maps individual domain names to nameservers. An Internet browser uses the domain extension to determine which zone file to read, the nameserver then tells the browser to where to retrieve the domain's content.

All domains have four critical relationships: (1) with its owner through a WHOIS record; (2) with a REGISTRAR through sponsorship; (3) with hosting provider for the content; and (4) with a nameserver for its resolution. These relationships can often exist as a bundle through a single party or through three different parties. The hosting and nameserver service could also be done by the owner, but the registration sponsorship must be done by a Registrar. These relationships can be seen as a four-sided pyramid, with the domain at the top point of the pyramid (see Figure 4.16). The four services are all connected to each other at the base and support the domain equally. A DOMAIN NAME does not become a "website" until it has content to server and a nameserver to resolve it.

Some common perceptions are that domain owners can "do whatever they want" with a domain name and that Registrars "have no control over domain content or usage." Both are false [35]. When domain owners enter into an agreement with a Registrar, they become a party to the Registrar Accreditation Agreement (RAA), which obligates the Registrar to follow local law and regulations and further obligates the domain owner not to use their domain for an illegal activity. Domain registrants are bound by Terms of Service (TOS), Acceptable Use Policies (AUP), and other agreements with the underlying service providers, in addition to the RAA. These policies are not optional, they are in fact required by the RAA and must be posted publicly. Domain owners who violate the TOS/AUP or the RAA may lose their domain. Compare a domain with an automobile, which is a fairly common and easily obtained resource. The automobile must function properly to be legally driven; the driver must safely share the resource of the road; and abusing this privilege will result in the loss of the driving privilege. Someone who uses an automobile in crime or steals another's automobile will face serious consequences. The only major difference is that there is no license to own a domain, no tests or qualification. While not treated as such, owning a domain name is a grave responsibility.

The low cost and barriers for domain ownership not only help the Internet's growth and openness but also create an opportunity for exploitation. Domain owners are not automatically briefed in access control or security procedures even when they are in reality "network administrators." DOMAINS now commonly come with a suite of tools, such as online databases, shopping carts, PHP (a powerful web scripting language), mail relays, and domain forwarding. Criminals can use all the added DOMAIN services as weapons and DOMAIN owners are rarely aware of this. Whether they know it or not, domain owners are responsible for securing access to their domain, otherwise they may lose their domain if an abuser hijacks the domain and violates the TOS/AUP or RAA. While criminals are adept at exploiting the resources of others and escaping, the victims have little recourse after being hijacked and may find themselves blacklisted.

There are an untold number of ways domain names can be exploited by criminal owners or criminal intruders. Thousands of domains are regularly suspended for various infringements, including spam, malware, trademark infringements, phishing, child exploitation, intrusions, unlicensed pharmacy, inaccurate WHOIS (an accurate contact record required for domain ownership), and other illicit transactions. The idea that a victim, government, or Registrar is powerless against a domain is simply false. The WHOIS record mentioned above is the critical trust link between Internet consumers and the Internet infrastructure, a link that is under constant threat.

4.4.4   WHOIS: Ownership and Technical Records

WHOIS is a loose term that can refer to several related topics: (1) An owner record associated with a domain name, (2) a system that delivers WHOIS records based on queries, or (3) the total set or database of WHOIS records. A WHOIS record should tell a queriant who owns or sponsors a domain name where it is served from and how to contact a responsible party associated with it. Because the Internet is a shared resource and data are passed from node to node on the basis of general trust, it is critical to be able to contact other node owners in case of a problem. Of course, in order to be useful, WHOIS must be publicly accessible. In theory, every domain, IP address, or "node" (a network end point or device) on the Internet must have a WHOIS record; in practice, this is not always true. As a matter of policy, WHOIS records must be accurate; in reality, this is an exception not the rule. Since ICANN launched the accuracy and accessibility of WHOIS has been under scrutiny [343], a number of studies have concluded that the WHOIS record is grossly inaccurate and persistently blocked [178]. It may surprise the reader that ICANN in fact does not maintain these records and does not even have direct access to them [64]. Truthfully, there is no single WHOIS record, rather there are hundreds of fragmented and inconsistent databases run by Registrars and REGISTRIES. There is also no standard format for a WHOIS record and a wide variety exists, making automatic auditing difficult. ICANN has attempted to centralize the information, through escrow, but this effort has been met with delay and challenge as the escrow service, Iron Mountain, has been unable to meet the demand [70].

WHOIS records provide a critical link for investigators attempting to confront criminality, trademark infringement, abuse, and technical issues. If a record is falsified or obsolete, then the sponsoring Registrar is required to address the issue. If the Registrar does not cooperate, ICANN is supposed to act and even sanction the Registrar. However, the ICANN process may be less than ideal as demonstrated in the following cases:

1. In September 2010, an intruder at Godaddy placed malicious code within PHP files of thousands of websites hosted by the Registrar [300]. This code redirected visiting browsers to a domain called

"CLOUDISTHEBESTNOW.NET" that would attempt to download fake antivirus software or "scareware" onto a victim's computer [40]. Because the redirect was pointed to a domain rather than to a raw IP address, the hosting could be easily updated if an ISP detected the malware and suspended services. An investigation showed that the WHOIS record for CLOUDISTHEBESTNOW.NET was false. Following ICANN procedure, a complaint was filed through ICANN's WHOIS Data Problem Reporting System (WDPRS). This system alerts the Registrar and domain owner to the false WHOIS record and requires that the record be updated or the domain deleted within 45 days. One and a half months would seem an extremely long time to leave a malware site active. Many Registrars would have acted quickly to fix or suspend a domain involved in this activity, but the Registrar in question, BIZCN, allowed the domain to keep infecting PCs for the full 45-day period and suspended the domain after only being contacted by ICANN. BIZCN has been cited by ICANN previously [368]. WDPRS has been criticized for its ineffectiveness, and has even completely crashed and been unavailable for months at a time [442].

2. In addition to WDPRS, ICANN has another process called the Uniform Dispute Resolution Policy (UDRP) [67], which is used for settling trademark disputes. This process, in theory, is supposed to allow brand owners to file complaints against cybersquatters and be granted ownership of the infringing domain. The initial purpose of this procedure was to transfer domains that a complainant had rights to and wanted for their own use. For example, if the domain "MICHAELJORDAN.COM" was not owned by the basketball legend and the actual owner was profiting from use of the name with no benefit to Jordan, Jordan could file a UDRP and likely obtain the domain and begin his own profitable use of it. However, Jordan has no use for "MIKEJORDAN23.COM," "MJORDANBASKETBALL.COM," or for a thousand other possibilities. Cybersquatted domains dilute brand market value and are used to deceive consumers. There are a virtually unlimited number of possible variations of any brand name that have no value to the brand holder. While UDRP functions as designed, it has been held up as a failure in practice [175] and is now regularly bypassed by brand owners who directly sue registrants and Registrars over disputed names. The problem stems from another controversial issue: Private WHOIS. Private WHOIS records, or Proxy WHOIS are used to replace a domain registrant's real WHOIS record with generic contact information, usually the Regsitrar's. While ICANN concluded that the general use of Private WHOIS is around 18% [257], a study of illicitly used domains showed much higher usage: 33% for spammed domains and 39% for illicit drug-trafficking domains [126]. This abuse harms legitimate use of privacy services by noncommercial domain owners, political dissidents, or groups with lawful needs for anonymity. For obvious reasons, criminals benefit from the secrecy provided by Private WHOIS. The UDRP requires Registrars to release the WHOIS record to the brand owner complainant, and the WHOIS record is frequently the privacy-protected WHOIS. While the Registrar has technically complied with the UDRP, they have in fact provided the complainant with nothing useful and are actually helping to obfuscate the issue [181]. Because privacy-protected cybersquatters rarely respond to UDRP proceedings, the domain name is transferred to the complainant by default. The transferred domain is mostly worthless at this point. The identity of the cybersquatter is never revealed and the Regsitrar is never sanctioned. As a result, brand owners such as Microsoft, Verizon, and Yahoo! ignored the UDRP and sued a Registrar, OnLineNIC, directly because OnLineNIC was suspected of shielding cybersquatters or possibly even being the original registrant [356]. OnLineNIC paid the plaintiffs tens of millions of dollars in an out of court settlement. Verizon has also sued another Registrar, DirectNIC, for the same reason in a case that revealed additional problem of the Registrar hiding its actual location [367].

3. Above the obligations concerning specific domain records, Registrars have a specific contract requirement to provide persistent, public access to the WHOIS record through the Registrar website and through a "Port 43" service [80]. It is through this that Registrar provided command-line WHOIS service that ICANN and many other basic network functions depend on for information about domains and many Registrars have blocked this service or have tacitly weakened it to render it useless. In all, 11 Registrars have been cited or terminated for not providing a WHOIS service.

By providing Internet consumers, technicians, and law enforcement with ready access to contact or owner information, WHOIS is intended to create a system of trust. However, as a system of trust, WHOIS is a complete failure as policies are violated on a massive scale with impunity. REGISTRARS have failed in their contractual obligation to both validate the records and allow access to them. ICANN has failed in its obligation to properly vet and monitor the Registrars. The Registrars hold the keys to accurate WHOIS and access, and the trust on which domain usage depends.

4.4.5   Registrars: Sponsors of Domain Names

Registrars are contracted parties to ICANN, with a special authority to sell and sponsor domain names to consumers. The core contract is called the Registrar Accreditation Agreement [29]. There are two active versions: the 2001 RAA and the 2009 RAA. Registrars are required to sign on to and qualify for the 2009 RAA when their older agreement expires. While ICANN prides itself on "transparency and accountability" [78], its oversight of the Registrars has been criticized as lacking and the Registrars themselves frequently act in secrecy [224]. The reason for this is likely money, as REGISTRARS provide ICANN with the bulk of its funding. The cost for becoming a REGISTRAR is US $2500 plus US $4000 per year. For each DOMAIN registered, the REGISTRAR pays US$0.18 to ICANN annually. With nearly 200 million domains in existence, ICANN receives in excess of US $30 million each year for DOMAIN purchases and renewals [503]. As a powerful financial contributor to ICANN, the REGISTRARS hold particular influence.

Registrars represent a crucial segment of the Internet that is at risk of breaking and has broken in the past with a number of REGISTRAR failures and criminal infiltration. In 2007, the Registrar named *RegisterFly* was deaccredited for failing to transfer customer domains properly. *RegisterFly* then refused to turn over its WHOIS database, so the sponsored domains could be transferred to a new Registrar [31]. This exposed the danger posed by a rogue Registrar that could potentially hold a significant portion of the Internet "hostage." Because of this, ICANN developed an escrow system to warehouse all Registrar WHOIS data in case of a similar situation in the future. While well intended, this project has been fraught with problems, including more Registrars refusing to escrow their WHOIS records [34]. The third party responsible for this escrow, Iron Mountain, was unable to complete the project and ICANN solicited new bids for this role.

Failure to escrow is just one of many reasons a Registrar could be deaccredited. Other reasons are bankruptcy, insolvency, failure to pay fees, legal or criminal issues, and failure to provide mandated services like WHOIS. Several Registrars have been terminated for all of the above reasons leading critics to question how well Registrars are vetted during the accreditation process [57]. In the above case of *RegisterFly*, the owner was never scrutinized by ICANN as he obtained the accreditation from someone else [237]. In the infamous case of Registrar *EstDomains*, the CEO was a convicted felon, unbeknownst to ICANN. The criminal history of this Registrar was more than a coincidence, as *EstDomains* was widely known to sponsor domains for criminals [252]. Although ICANN terminated EstDomains, it was only after widespread coverage in the media [305]. Other REGISTRARS have had similar legal problems, but ICANN has not acted [142]. The sponsorship of criminally used domains, especially ones dealing in illicit drugs, is a growing problem for REGISTRARS; it is also one that has gained the attention of the US government that responded by summoning ICANN and the REGISTRARS to the White House in 2010 to discuss ways of addressing the growing problem of online drug-trafficking [307]. Most REGISTRARS did not respond to the invitation and ICANN outrightly refused to attend [361]. Some of the larger Registrars have the bulk of problems because inexpensive, extended services provided by the Registrar are just as attractive to criminal groups as lawful customers [328]. It may seem the Registrar is a simple victim of the criminal groups, but some Registrars have refused to suspend illicit domains even after being contacted by regulatory bodies [140] and some speculate that sales of illicit domains contribute significantly to a Registrar's income [354]. If one of these large Registrars were to be indicted and convicted, it could cause an epic disruption to Internet commerce as they also have large portfolios of lawful domain customers who would have to be mass transferred to a new Registrar. In general, weak oversight of the contracted parties is one of the biggest threats to Internet stability.

Criminals are hiding behind the false WHOIS information held by REGISTRARS, and the REGIS-TRARS have a vested interest in maintaining the easy access to DOMAIN sales. This is made no clearer than by Godaddy's vice president Tim Ruiz: ". . . proactive measures to make data accurate would not be affordable or useful" [410]. Although REGISTRARS sell DOMAINS, they must do so under the sponsorship of specific top-level domain REGISTIRES that set different policies for each domain extension the REGISTRAR can offer.

4.4.6   Registries: Sponsors of Domain Extensions

Registries are contracted parties to ICANN, similar to Registrars, but perform a different function as they sponsor specific generic top-level domain extensions like .COM and .ORG to Registrars the way Registrars sponsor specific domain names to consumers (see Figure 4.17) [74]. Registrar failures occur frequently and are troublesome, but a registry failure could be catastrophic and the scenario is not all that farfetched [427]. For example, the viability of *Tralliance*, the company sponsoring .TRAVEL, was questioned and may have been in breach of their ICANN contract for sponsoring nontravel-related domains [258]. *Employ Media*, the company sponsoring .JOBS, was also issued a breach notice by ICANN [72]. If a Registrar fails, domains can be transferred to another existing Registrar; however, if a registry fails, there is no entity handy to quickly absorb an entire structure. Even the largest registry, *VeriSign*, which sponsors .COM and .NET, has been sued under Anti-Trust laws for being a monopoly because *VeriSign* does not simply sponsor .COM, it is the only company allowed to by ICANN [411].

Not all Registries and gTLDs are open to the general public. .GOV is reserved for US government entities, .MIL is restricted to the US military, and only accredited US institutions may register .EDU domains. Other gTLDs were originally restricted, but have opened up to expand the domain market; .ORG, for example, was intended for nonprofits and .TEL for telecommunications entities, while .MUSEUM remains closed to nonmuseum use. .COM ("company"), .INFO ("information"), and .NET ("network") have all lost their original meaning and are now publicly accessible for a variety of commercial and noncommercial uses.

Although there are few REGISTRIES at the moment, this is changing drastically with the adoption of a new gTLD policy by ICANN that would allow for "Dot-Anything." Intellectual property folks are concerned about brand names being hijacked as new gTLDs and governments are concerned about the dilution of the value of their ccTLDs. The real security concern is that new gTLDs can be used to create a completely unaccountable structure with policies that favor criminality and secrecy. This is not as far-fetched

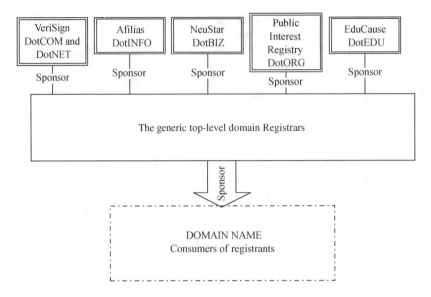

Figure 4.17   TLD Registry Mode: ensures that .COM, .ORG, and every other extension have an approved sponsor that in turn licenses Registrars to sell individual domains to consumers. Each Registry has a different set of policies and intended use. Registrants should not assume that contracts and agreements will be the same for each TLD even if purchases for different types of domains are made through the same Registrar.l

as it sounds as criminals have already hijacked some ccTLDs, become Registrars, and controlled ISPs. Two companies located in the United States, McColo and Hostfresh/Atrivo, provided a range of boutique services to Internet criminals from spam and illicit site serving to hosting child exploitation and botnets [54].

A New gTLD operator could in theory block all WHOIS access, create illegal strings (strings with certain characters that trick browsers or divert traffic), and fail to respond to abuse reports or legal inquiry. In essence, a new gTLD could become its own virtual "sovereign" nation, for example, the ccTLD for Niue, a small island nation in the South Pacific but managed by a company in the United States, which has set the policy of not supplying any WHIOS information, Registration for .NU is not restricted to citizens of Niue. This creates a complex question about who is responsible for misuse of domains in .NU and adds layers of obfuscation for investigators [428]. Although not created specifically for criminal use, the .NU situation is very attractive to criminals. Even international law enforcement has some influence over ccTLDs through diplomacy, there are none with a rogue new gTLD.

We will use a fictitious new gTLD called ".CRIME" to highlight potential issues. A criminal group could put up a straw man, with no criminal record, and a shell company outside the United States to obtain the .CRIME TLD. .CRIME could then refuse to have any public WHOIS and invite Internet criminals register domains there. It could become a bazaar for stolen goods, counterfeit merchandise, pirated media, and other illicit activity. The operators could be anonymous and unaccountable, as long as they dutifully pay their fees to ICANN on time. Although hypothetical, this is entirely plausible. In 2010, REGISTRAR of *A Technology Company* was found to be concealing its location and manipulating its WHOIS service to hide their own WHOIS record. ICANN issued a contract termination notice to *A Technology Company*, and in an unprecedented move, ICANN reversed the termination after *A Technology Company* paid a sizable amount of overdue accreditation fees [48].

The common perception is that cybercrime is generated by outsiders and "hackers," however, the ease with which criminal groups have exploited REGISTRARS and ISPs points to cybercriminals being industry insiders with a keen interest in driving policy to their ends. Issues of CCTLDs are mentioned above and make the Internet infinitely more complex with hundreds of different yet parallel policies and open concerns about authority and accountability.

4.4.7 CCTLDs: The Sovereign Domain Extensions

Country code top-level domain structures in their function are similar to Registries, with one major difference: once assigned by ICANN, they become virtually unaccountable except to their own governments. There are 256 CCTLDs and because each represents a different sovereign nation, there are 256 different sets of policies and legal systems. Many CCTLDs, in fact, have no stated policies [122]. This is complicated by the fact that many are not sponsored or hosted in within the sovereign nation, but rather outsourced to private companies in the United States and elsewhere [30]. In addition, the status of some "nations" is in question, examples being .BV (Bouvet, an inhospitable and uninhabited island) and .SU (Soviet Union, a defunct government, now a dozen independent countries). Some ccTLDs have become known havens for cybercrime, for example, .RU (Russia) is consistently ranked highest in spam-advertised domains [365]. Some ccTLDs have strict policies, but are difficult to monitor or enforce them; for example, .US (United States) requires a US nexus for registrations, either citizenship or business location. However, a review of illicitly used .US domains shows foreign registrants easily obtain domains and use them in crimes [125]. It is an open question as to whether the policies of each country and CCTLD are or even can be communicated to DOMAIN customers.

The popular URL shortening service BIT.LY uses the Libyan CCTLD. Most users would likely be unaware that use of BIT.LY could be impacted by the turmoil and civil war in Libya that started in early 2011 following uprisings in Tunisia and Egypt [392]. In the face of people being killed and nations destroyed, it may seem callous to wonder about the availability of a URL shortening service, but effective electronic communication is a critical part of our civilization. During the widespread February 2011 protests in Egypt, the government shut off Internet traffic in and out of the country because the use of social media helped coordinate and fuel the protests [389]. This backfired on the Egyptian authorities because Egypt's banks, businesses, and financial structure depended on the Internet [291].

Several ccTLDs issued to sovereign governments have been redelegated to private companies and reproposed for sale in the domain name market, and the original meaning of the ccTLD has lost. For example, the extension intended for Moldova (.MD) is managed by Max.md that handles domain registration and is in Fort Lee, NJ and is being marketed for medical professional websites [75]. For several years, Laos's ccTLD, .LA had been managed by *CentralNic USA Ltd.* in Woodland Hills, California and marketed exclusively as the "Los Angeles" TLD. There was no mention of Laos anywhere on the ccTLD website, they even posted the current weather for Los Angeles on the home page. In 2011, the government of Laos demanded their ccTLD back [363].

ICANN does have a ccTLD compliance program with very specific rules of conduct, but it is unclear how often, if at all, these conditions are monitored and what remedies are available in case of compliance failure [60].

4.4.8 ICANN: The Main Internet Policy Body

The Internet Corporation of Assigned Names and Numbers is the top-level Internet policy body. The core responsibilities of ICANN are establishing contractual relationships with REGISTRARS and REGISTRIES and executing the policies that govern the operations of REGISTRARS and REGISTRIES. Because of these, ICANN is the most important piece of the Internet infrastructure. The enforcement, or lack of enforcement, of ICANN policies impacts everyone who uses the Internet.

ICANN is an Internet institution, but it is not a permanent one. ICANN's president, Rod Beckstrom, said in 2010, "The DNS can break at any time," meaning it is under constant attack and various Internet providers are engaging in manipulative activities that redirect traffic [464]. The end of US sponsorship of ICANN is hailed as the final step in freeing the Internet and making it truly global, but ICANN itself enjoyed a certain amount of protection in this structure, as anyone attempting to take down or take over ICANN would have to deal with the US government first. A financial or organizational dilemma at ICANN could be addressed with support from the government as well, but now this is not a guarantee. Although it is believed that ICANN can truly blossom in independence, it now faces threats of capture, competition, and replacement. The function of managing IP assignment by the Internet Assigned Numbers Authority is still a matter of contract with the US Department of Commerce but was reopened for public bidding. Loss of this function would limit ICANN to the domain name function of the Internet. Since network technology has been extended and reimagined globally, the creation of separate "Internets" is a real possibility. This would be the effective end of our current open Internet, replaced with several separate closed systems. It has been suggested by some that China may split and have its own separate national network [159]. Chinese Registrars rarely participate in ICANN meetings and do not hold a seat on the Government Advisory Committee (GAC), the body of sovereign government representatives, which develop ICANN policy [55]. Internet companies seeking to do business in China have been forced to develop completely different policies [163]. Other nations or regions with resources could follow in China's footsteps and create a new Internet segment with different rules. Iran has proposed a "Halal (Arabic: Lawful)" Internet [69]. Several countries have disconnected from the Internet, including Egypt, Libya, and Algeria, because the open flow of information was seen as a threat to government [161]. Denying citizens free access to communication is antithetical to ICANN's mission statement [61], but this power is granted to governments by ICANN [260]. In fact, ICANN's role is not exclusive. There are already alternative domain structures unknown to the general public that could be enlarged and standardized; commonly called "Alternate DNS," this service provides access to dozens of domain extensions not sanctioned by ICANN [160].

One of the leading alternative services, *OpenNIC* resolves all the standard domains and others such as: .GEEK, .FREE, .BBS, .PARODY, .OSS, .INDY, .FUR, .ING, .MICRO, .DYN, and .GOPHER. One of *OpenNIC*'s home pages is at HTTP://WWW.OPENNIC.GLUE. Attempt to enter the URL "OPENNIC.GLUE" in a normal Internet browser will not resolve, regardless of it is there at 69.162.67.19 and served from nameserver NS1.OPENNIC.GLUE. The concept sounds mysterious, but is fairly simple: instead of looking in the default DNS for a website, a browser can be configured to search in a different directory for the location. This is a second Internet within the space of the existing Internet and only visible to clients with the proper software. *OpenNIC* describes itself as a group of hobbyists with the goal of providing "access to domains not administered by ICANN" [58]. However, freelance hackers are not the only ones producing an alternative DNS, the Internet corporate giant *Google* has also created "Google Public DNS"; also, the .BIZ REGISTRY, *Neustar*, offers "DNS advantage," which they claim is safer and faster than the current DNS [371]. In addition, there are at least a dozen known alternative DNS projects and an unknown number of unpublished or secret DNS structures. It is entirely possible for criminals, terrorists, or rogue governments to create a surreptitious web that can be used for transactions or used to disrupt the public Internet. For these reasons, alternative DNS has been harshly criticized [261]. There is already a .XXX extension in one alternative, DNS that conflicts with the .XXX (designated for adult/pornographic domains) authorized by ICANN in 2011 [346]. An alternative DNS could potentially redirect .COM domains and any other web traffic. In simplest terms, the existing DNS resolves yahoo.com to 98.137.149.56, an alternative DNS record could potentially direct yahoo.com to a different IP address. There are examples of these problems occurring in various cases of intentional or accidental DNS hijacking of rerouting. In 2010, the US Internet traffic was briefly rerouted through China, including US military traffic [344].

Aside from the potential for competition is the issue of capture, which means ICANN could come under the control of a specific entity or interest group. While ICANN claims to be secure against capture [259], some contend ICANN has already been captured by the Registrar constituency [198]. The REGISTRARS provide ICANN with the bulk of its income through DOMAIN registration fees and, as many claim, provide much of the influence. In addition, ICANN has been criticized as being ". . . a guild of REGISTRARs . . . with no real interest represented for registrants" [426]. Indeed, the reliance on REGISTRARS for financial support could be its undoing especially if the domain name market slows or collapses [385].

Beyond the external threats to ICANN, its most serious challenge may be internal. ICANN continuously shows signs it could collapse under its own weight in increased domain expansion. At times, ICANN seems unable to perform its basic function of overseeing the Registrars. In a simple example, ICANN appeared to be unaware of where all of its Registrars were located [127]. There is also an open question of how many Registrars exist as different ICANN reports show varying counts: icann.org lists 972, the ICANN operational site InterNIC.org has 968, and iana.org discloses that over 1500 accreditations have been issued without completely marking which have been terminated [56]. Also, nearly half of the estimated 1000 accreditations are through shell companies ultimately held by an oligopoly of five Registrars [124]. Competition among Registrars may be an illusion. These five REGISTRARS also supply ICANN with an extra US $1.9 million per year through excessive and redundant accreditation fees, *Demand Media* (AKA *eNom*) pays over half-a-million USD each year for superfluous accreditations. Why these companies voluntarily pay ICANN what amounts to 3% of its annual budget has never been fully explained [123]. Financial questions have plagued ICANN, as the self-professed, transparent organization has been slow to release budget data [193] and lost a significant amount of money in the public market [325] leaving some to wonder how this could happen in a nonprofit institution. There are also a number of terminated, defunct, or otherwise unaccredited organizations claiming to be ICANN accredited.

ICANN's ability to manage complaints about WHOIS inaccuracy through its WDPRS system is also in question as the system has failed a number of times and was offline for an extended period [502]. The system was upgraded after 7 years in 2009 [37]. In Internet time, 7 years is an eternity of obsolescence. ICANN admits that it was unable to track Registrar compliance with Port 43 availability until 2009 [9]. The Port 43 service is required of all REGISTRARS, it allows their database to be queried for WHOIS records; when a REGISTRAR fails to provide this service, Internet consumers cannot then discover who is behind a website possibly engaging in fraud. The trust between consumer and ICANN falters as domain owners become anonymously unaccountable. According to an ICANN report in 2010, one of their biggest problems is inter-Registrar domain transfers and there is no process for automatically tracking them [38]. In 2010, ICANN also lost a number of key compliance staff for unknown reasons, leaving this critical department with fewer than 10 people to handle potential disputes with nearly 1000 contracts and 100 million domain names [362]. ICANN's work to expand into new gTLDs seems at odds with its current capacity. Policy researchers, such as Professor A. Michael Froomkin of the University of Miami School of Law, have argued that the problems began with ICANN's creation, its very existence birthed in folly. Froomkin argues that

Internet control should have been administered directly through a US executive agency and expanded through trusted partners [197].

4.4.9 Conclusion

After reviewing the policy structure of the Internet, we see it does not exist in a vacuum. Each layer of the Internet is defined by policy and the relationships between each party are established in documented agreements (see Figure 4.18). Proper use and ownership of the basic Internet unit, the DOMAIN NAME, can be viewed through a chain of legitimacy starting with its Registration Agreement for sponsorship with the Registrar, then the Registrar Accreditation Agreement with the Internet Corporation of Assigned Names and Numbers defines obligations for the Registrar, and varying contracts or agreements with the US government grant authority for ICANN to deal with the parties beneath. There are many other agreements in between that clearly define additional relationships, but the crucial point is that the Internet in all its layers and functions is policy based. The obligations and expectations of each participating member exist before connections occur. Even when connecting to a public wireless hotspot, the user must agree to terms. In general, there is a policy counterpart for every malicious activity. With this in mind, it is easy to wonder why there is so much fraud, drug dealing, child exploitation, harassment, denial of free speech, and privacy intrusion. The answer is lack of policy enforcement.

Given that we just reviewed the hierarchy of the Internet with the US government as the original policy initiator, it is reasonable to ask why the United States does not enforce Internet policy. The answer is that

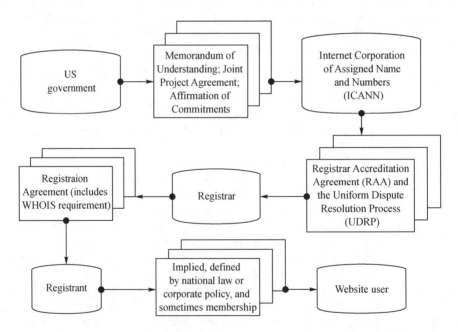

Figure 4.18   The Chain of legitimacy. The Internet is not an amorphous and unknown structure, but one built on carefully drafted policy agreements issued by authorized bodies. Some bodies may shirk their responsibilities or ignore obligations, but they can be held to them with proper oversight.

ICANN was created to this in a multistakeholder model outside the US government. Trust was placed in ICANN to fulfill these duties, but that trust may have been mistaken. Although ICANN has the mandate and authority to enforce policy, it rarely does so. One reason is a lack of critical tools. We have discussed the general failure of ICANN's WHOIS Data Problem Reporting System (WDPRS) and the shocking truth is that this is the only enforcement area ICANN has an automated tool for. According to Doug Brent, ICANN's former vice president, "contractual enforcement mechanisms which today go no further than requiring investigation of inaccuracy complaints." [342]. ICANN must keep the public trust by properly vetting Registrars and Registries, and then monitoring them once in place. The Registrars are the keeper of (WHOIS) records as a matter of contract; there should be no questions about their obligation to serve and verify the records, but this remains one of ICANN's constant failures. Although policy failures at multiple levels have been identified, ICANN has the obligation to set the tone for acceptable conduct and the tone is one of permissiveness that keeps the money flowing until the problems are too large to easily remedy.

4.5 SOCIAL SPAM

Dimitar Nikolov and Filippo Menczer

Abstract. Spam is a problem Internet users encounter on a daily basis. In addition to email spam, which has been a problem for decades, a newer kind of spam, *social spam*, has become very pervasive with the emergence of the Web 2.0. Social web applications such as YouTube, Flickr, Twitter, and Delicious have become major online destinations, as judged by the large amounts of traffic they generate. This popularity has come at the price of increased attention from spammers, who can thrive in the largely user-driven structure of the social web. In this section, we examine motivations for and common examples of social spam and also approaches for its detection. In addition, we present a case study of a spam detection system in a social bookmarking website and describe algorithms that make it possible to combat spam successfully. Finally, we offer a broader discussion of the context in which spammers thrive, what can be done to change it, and what challenges social spam researchers face.

4.5.1 Introduction

The defining characteristic of *Web 2.0* is its social nature, which encourages people to share information, collaborate, and form social links. Social web applications achieve this in several ways. First, they make their users the primary producers of content. For example, in Facebook, users create profiles representing their online personas to facilitate communication with friends and the forming of new social links. In Flickr, users post and annotate photos. In Delicious, users save their bookmarks in a platform-independent way and share them with the other users of the system. Second, social web applications allow users to easily interact with each other and share the content they have produced. Users can post comments on blogs and online message boards, annotate different online resources with tags, and exchange messages in a public way so that other users can join in their conversations.

These features of social media have the implication that they create a large network of connections between users and content that is controlled almost entirely by the users. This places great power in the hands of well-intentioned users to engage with others and express themselves, but it also provides an opportunity

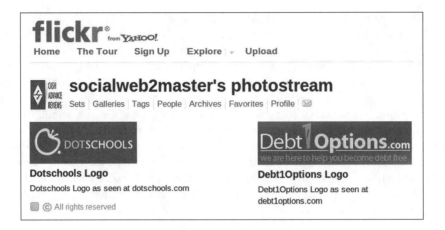

Figure 4.19   A spammer on the Flickr image sharing website posts images of the logos of a variety of websites. The logos or the captions below them display URLs of spam websites that try to sell various products or services.

for spammers to exploit the social web for their own interests. As a result, social web applications have become tempting targets for spam and other forms of Internet pollution.

Most of the spam on social websites comes in the form of posting messages or resources that try to trick users into navigating to the spammer's own website. Once there, a user can be tricked into giving away personal information, buying an illegitimate or low-quality product or service, or following advertisements. Examples of spammers who use these strategies are shown in Figures 4.19–4.21.

Social media are different from email, an application domain that is more familiar to spam researchers. Thus, while there has been great success in developing spam detection methods for email, not all of them transfer successfully to the social media domain. In addition, Web 2.0 sites offer the opportunity for developing new and unique detection methods. Consider, for example, a website like YouTube, where users can post videos and tag them with keywords, exchange messages, watch and comment on other users' videos, and subscribe to their feeds. Users who are on each other's subscriber lists or who frequently message each other, or who use the same tags can be considered similar. Likewise, videos that are annotated with the same tags

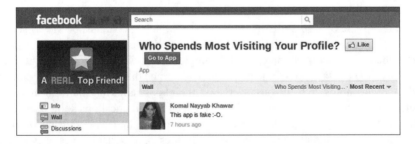

Figure 4.20   A spam Facebook application claims to allow users to see who views their profile, a feature often requested by many users of Facebook. The application does not serve its advertised purpose, but still manages to collect personal information about its users, such as name and location. Such information can be used for identity theft or phishing. In other cases, applications request even more information, such as email addresses or access to friend lists.

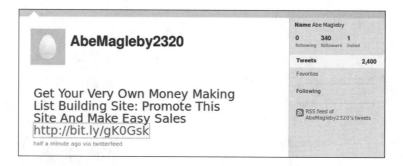

Figure 4.21   A Twitter spammer posts a variety of tweets on making money online, with links to a website that sells software and an advice handbook.

or visited and commented on by the same users will also be similar. Examining such relationships between users and content, most of them unique to social media can be informative in detecting spamming activity. In the end, the differences between email and the social web are both a challenge to existing detection methods and an opportunity to create new methods that could not be used in the email domain.

4.5.2   Motivations for Spammers

To facilitate the understanding of social spam and its detection, it is important to understand the motivations of social spammers and the particular strategies they rely on. The most common motive for spammers is financial gain [245,302,334]. With advertising platforms such as those offered by Google (google.com/adsense), Yahoo (advertising.yahoo.com), and Microsoft (adcenter.microsoft.com), it is easy for a spammer to set up a website and start generating ad income provided a large number of users can be tricked into visiting the website. A common way of doing this is through traditional email spam (see Section 4.4 for more detail). However, with improved quality of email spam filters and increasing popularity of social media, promoting ad-filled websites in online communities such as Delicious, Facebook, or Twitter has become a cheap and an effective alternative. Advertising services such as the ones mentioned above have many legitimate clients, but it is easy to abuse them and generate websites based on popular keywords or search trends that will generate income from ads in spite of a lack in real content.

There are several ways to generate *fake content*. The first is to hire freelance writers to do it cheaply. *Content farm* websites, discussed in more detail in Section 4.5.5, use this approach to generate highly derivative, redundant, and arguably low-quality content based on search query popularity (see Figure 4.22 for an example).

A second method is to generate content automatically, which can be done easily and with a trivial amount of base content. To demonstrate that revenue can be generated with this approach, we created the "Gossip Search Engine" website (carl.cs.indiana.edu/fil/cgi-bin/gossip) (see Figure 4.23) and registered it with Google's AdSense program. Although the content looks as if originating from a news source, it is generated automatically using a very simple grammar. Additional news and images on the website are generated using publicly available RSS feeds. In the end, taking only minimal effort to set up, the website is able to generate a small amount of revenue. When fully automated and applied *en masse*, simple methods like these can be used to generate revenue from hundreds or thousands of spam websites, as long as users can be tricked into visiting them.

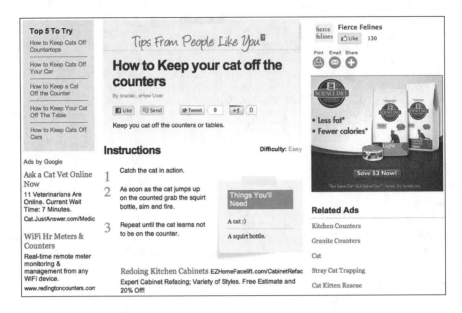

Figure 4.22   An example of ad-driven, low-quality result page on the content farm website eHow. Suppose we are interested in ways to keep a cat off the kitchen counters. Upon submitting the query "cat counters" to eHow.com, we get numerous highly derivative articles with small variations of a general theme in their titles (incidentally, one of these articles appeared on the first page of results when we submitted the query to Google). The result shown here is typical—a very short article that describes a step-by-step process for accomplishing the given goal. There is little in-depth discussion or elaboration on the steps. The rest of the page contains many ads and links to similar articles (only some of which are shown).

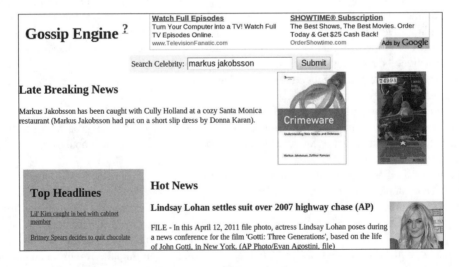

Figure 4.23   The Gossip Engine is a website that demonstrates how easy it is to automatically create fake news content that seems legitimate on a first viewing. The Late Breaking News section is generated automatically based on user queries, the Top Headlines are generated automatically from celebrity names, and the Hot News section is plagiarized. The ads, however, generate real revenue.

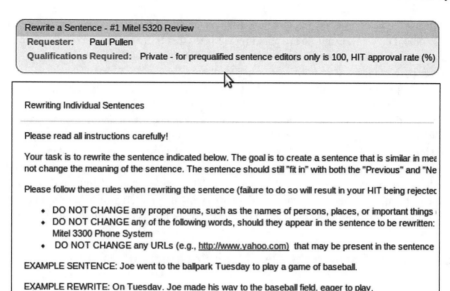

Figure 4.24 Creating fake content on Mechanical Turk. Users are paid to rewrite sentences so that their language structure is changed, but their meaning is preserved.

Third, legitimate web sources such as Wikipedia, blogs, or online media can be plagiarized and their content pieced together to produce a webpage that does not appear anywhere on the web. More sophisticated spammers may even superficially edit plagiarized content so that the plagiarism is not obvious. One ingenious way of doing this *en masse*, easily and cheaply, is through Amazon Mechanical Turk (mturk.com). The spammer offloads the rewriting of individual sentences to many different users and pays them a small amount of money per sentence (see Figure 4.24 for an example). Amazon Mechanical Turk can be exploited for many other questionable activities such as to generate product reviews or comments that give a false impression of popularity about a product, a company, or a website, to generate clicks to particular pages, or to collect email addresses. For example, in Figure 4.25, users are offered a payment to write positive comments about a healthcare company and "like" on its Facebook page. Similar problems with fake reviews have also been documented on the consumer review website Yelp [425].

In addition to promoting websites that generate income from ads, spammers on social media websites may try to trick unsuspecting users into visiting even more harmful places on the web. Websites that serve

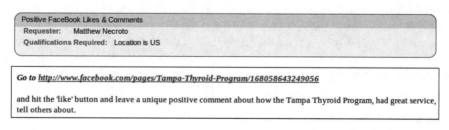

Figure 4.25 Creating fake content on Mechanical Turk. Users are paid to submit positive comments and "likes" on a company's Facebook page.

malware such as spyware or keystroke loggers that collect data from the user's machine are common examples. Another dangerous example are phishing websites that try to collect personal information such as names, addresses, account passwords, and credit card numbers by copying the user interface of well-known web services or pretending to offer legitimate services themselves.

Finally, some spammers are motivated not by personal monetary gain, but by a desire to control the flow and information content in domains where being able to do so gives them an advantage over competitors. An example of such a domain is politics, where being able to influence the online discourse has serious implications for the power that interest groups and election candidates gain. In cases where the information being disseminated is clearly false or an agent artificially tries to give the impression that an idea is shared by a large portion of online users when it is not, this issue transitions from the simple spreading of a message to a gray area that could be considered the domain of social spam. The *Truthy* project (truthy.indiana.edu) [398,400] has investigated this phenomenon and has found a variety of such patterns of behavior and signals helpful in their detection. A more detailed examination of this phenomenon is available in Section 6.3.

4.5.3 Case Study: Spam in the GiveALink Bookmarking System

To illustrate particular approaches to combat social spam, let us consider a case study, namely, the spam detection system in the *social bookmarking* site GiveALink.org. In GiveALink, users submit their bookmarks so that they can be accessed in a platform-independent way. When a bookmark is submitted, the user has the option to annotate it with one or more *free-form* tags (not from a predetermined vocabulary). For example, a user can assign the tags "news," "articles," and "currentevents" to the resource "nytimes.com." The GiveALink system was initially created as a research platform to study social search and recommendation algorithms and the tagging behavior of users [336,455]. With time, the system became a target for spammers to such an extent that most of the bookmarks in it were spam. This motivated our previous efforts in social spam detection [334] as well as the work described here.

The GiveALink spam detection system is worthy of attention in our examination of social spam for two main reasons. First, an examination of spam in GiveALink will allow us to make more concrete our assertion from Section 4.5.1 about the differences between social spam and spam in other domains such as email. Second, the structure of GiveALink is very similar to that of other popular Web 2.0 systems, to which the methods described in this section generalize well.

On the second point, GiveALink's structure is characterized by the presence of three basic entities—users, tags and resources—and the connections between them. Such a structure is commonly called a *folksonomy* and is widely used among social media websites. Twitter, YouTube, Flickr, Delicious, and other popular Web 2.0 services all use this structure. The main difference between these and other folksonomies are the types of resources they allow their users to share – photos in Flickr, videos in YouTube, links in GiveALink and Delicious, links and messages in Twitter. As we will see when we discuss spam detection features in Section 4.5.3.3, a lot of power can be harnessed by exploiting the folksonomy structure in general, without regard to the types of resources in it. This makes it possible to develop spam detection methods that are independent of the types of resources in the folksonomy and are thus applicable to different systems.

4.5.3.1 Supervised learning applied to spam detection

The difficulty in solving the spam detection task is that an algorithmic solution for it cannot be easily defined. Indeed, the very definition of spam is flexible and subjective. Spam can be defined as the unsolicited sending of messages online to a large number of recipients, possibly with commercial or malicious intent—whether a message is unsolicited and its intent are largely determined by context—the user who receives the message, the user who sends it, and the system in which the communication takes place. Thus, a good spam detection system needs to take into account both users' previous behavior and the behavior of the users in the system as a whole, to decide whether spam activity is occurring. More generally, the system needs to be able to learn from experience what kinds of activities constitute spam.

There is a large body of research in the field of machine learning [355] that solves exactly these kinds of problems with varying degrees of success. The spam detection systems in the literature typically take an approach called *supervised learning* or *classification*. The idea of supervised learning is that a program called a classifier is trained to recognize classes of objects by being given a large number of labeled examples. In this context, an example is labeled if it is known which class it belongs to. The representation of examples largely depends on the domain to which supervised learning is applied. Most commonly, an example is a vector of features, followed by a label. The features are precomputed values that characterize what is being classified in a way appropriate to the classification task.

To make this discussion more concrete, let us consider the example in Table 4.4. In this toy dataset, each example is the user of a tagging system. The features chosen reflect common intuitions about spamming activity, such as using derivative, number-filled email addresses, or trying to promote online pharmacy websites. The examples have been manually labeled by humans. In a typical website, the labeling can be done by site administrators, or other trusted persons. The regular users of a website can also be provided an interface to report spam, but in this case precautions need to be taken that the reporting system does not fall victim to spam itself. In addition to human judges, spammers can be identified automatically by social honeypot profiles [483]. These are profiles specifically created by a social media site's administrators, which can be used to lure spammers into interacting with them, but whose activity presents little interest to legitimate users. In a study on Twitter spammers, Lee et al. [321] have shown that social honeypots can discover a large number of spam profiles, which are representative of the larger population of spammers. Given the data in the table, a classifier might learn that likely spammers are users whose emails come from the "example.com" domain or who have a large number of digits in their email addresses, or who frequently use the tag "viagra."

Machine learning researchers have developed sophisticated types of classifiers, such as decision trees, instance-based classifiers, support vector machines (SVMs), or ensemble classifiers. The choice of classifier is an important part in any system, because it determines the types of data preprocessing needed to be done before the classification step and the types of data that can be used for the features. It is not our aim to discuss these topics in detail here. Interested readers are referred to Ref. [355] or to any other introductory machine

Table 4.4 A Toy Example of a Dataset for Which a Classifier Can Be Trained to Classify Spammers

Email domain	Digits in email	Mentions of tag "viagra"	Label
rocketmail.com	0	15	Spammer
indiana.edu	2	0	Nonspammer
live.com	0	1	Nonspammer
gmail.com	7	0	Spammer
example.com	0	0	Spammer

The examples in the dataset are users of a tagging system. The features chosen to represent them are in columns 1–3, and the label of each user is in the last column.

learning text. For the remainder of this section, a classifier can be viewed as a black box that given a vector of feature values, outputs the name of a class.

4.5.3.2   Unit of spam

Next to the classification approach, the other major design questions for a spam detection system are what features to use and at what granularity level to classify spam. These questions highly depend on each other.

Consider the GiveALink user in Figure 4.26. They are trying to promote a family of shopping websites by entering individual product pages into the system: clearly a case of spam. We can tell this is so by looking at the aggregated activity of the user. Were we looking at individual bookmarks in isolation, we would not have arrived at this conclusion perhaps so easily. We could decide an individual bookmark by the user is spam because it references an obscure shopping site with search engine-friendly URL. On the other hand, we could be misled by the fact that the tags describe each link well. All of these are examples of different granularity levels at which to classify spam.

The first granularity level at which we looked at the user in Figure 4.26 is the user level. Working at this granularity level requires that all of a user's activity is taken to be spam or not. It is possible, however, that a user makes a portion of good entries into the system in addition to spam. For example, a user could bookmark legitimate pages of interest to trick the spam detection algorithms or the administrators of a website. Working at the user granularity level does not allow to discriminate between these two types of posts by the same user.

The second granularity level at which we looked at in the example above is the post. In the context of a tagging system like GiveALink, a post represent a user adding a resource (URL) to the system and annotating it. That is, a post is a triple (u, r, T), where u is a user, r is a resource, and T is a set of tags. At the post level, we can discriminate spam from nonspam more precisely and legitimate bookmarks do not have to be considered spam because of the user's other activity. This does not mean that the post level is

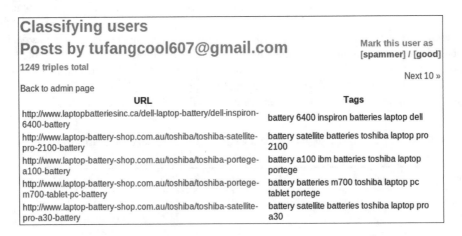

Figure 4.26   The interface used by GiveALink administrators to label users as spammers or nonspammers by hand. The interface presents the user's email address and a sample of their bookmarks. The administrator may label the user only based on that information or they may decide to investigate further by visiting the user's URLs or inspecting more of their bookmarks. The user in question is a spammer who is trying to promote a family of shopping websites by entering individual product pages into the system.

necessarily better. Each post in Figure 4.26—for example, annotating "laptopbatteriesinc.ca" with "battery," "camcoder," and so on—may appear legitimate by itself. But looking at the user's aggregated activity of bookmarking, hundreds of product pages on the same site are suspicious.

Other granularity levels at which we can classify spam include the resources by themselves or various combinations of users, resources, and tags. The granularity level of the system determines what kinds of features can be used for the detection of spam. It is not the goal here to compare these different approaches, but to make the reader aware that social spam can be attacked from different angles. The GiveALink system detects spam at the user level.

4.5.3.3 Detection features

At this point, we have built enough background knowledge about the detection process that we can look at particular features used in GiveALink. The GiveALink spam detection system leverages a number of features from the social spam literature [303,334], such as those in Table 4.5. These are immediately applicable to the user granularity level and represent various intuitions about the motivations and activity patterns of spammers. For example, spammers often create many accounts with derivative names to promote the same site. Or, they register in the system and immediately submit a large number of bookmarks, but then their activity stops.

The features above are straightforward to compute, but barely take advantage of the information available in the GiveALink system. In Section 4.5.1, we discussed how there are characteristics unique to online social systems that can be leveraged to fight spam. We make this discussion more concrete next.

Consider the network in Figure 4.27. Here, users are nodes, which can be connected to each other based on the resources they have in the system and the tags they use. A link can be added to the network if two users share the same resource or tag or if they made the same annotation ((*resource*, *tag*) pair). Based on these cooccurrences, we can compute the similarities between a target user and the well-known spammers by counting the edges formed by the edge relationships defined above or by using more sophisticated similarity measures [420]. Note that Figure 4.27 shows a single network of users, but networks based on each of the possible edge types can be constructed separately for more fine-grained analysis.

The features described so far translate well to the user granularity level. It is possible, however, to compute features that characterize other entities in the system such as resources and posts and aggregate them over all such entities that a user owns.

For example, GiveALink uses two resource-based features. One is the number of ads found on a page, which can simply be averaged over all webpages tagged by a user. This feature is motivated by our earlier discussion of how many spammers will try to serve ads on their pages to generate income.

Table 4.5   A List of User Features Used for Training a Classifier to Detect Spam

User-based detection features
Number of digits in email and nickname
Length of email and nickname
Number of users in the domain
Date difference between registration and first tagging
Average and total tags per post

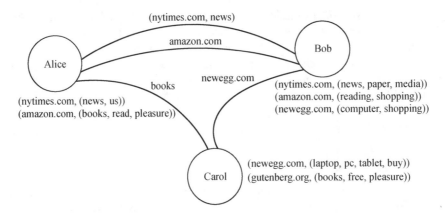

Figure 4.27 A cooccurrence graph that links users based on the content they share. In a tagging system, users can share resources (in this case URLs), tags, or annotations, that is, pairs (resource, tag).

A second resource feature is called *DomFP* and is motivated by our discussion of using automated methods to create spam webpages *en masse*. One side effect of using such automated methods is that the pages will have a very similar HTML structure; for example, they may be generated from a common template. To exploit this intuition, as a preprocessing step, DomFP downloads the source code of pages, which have been manually labeled as spam, strips them of all of their content until only HTML tags are left, and saves them into a database. This gives the system a set of page templates that it can compare against. To make these comparisons more efficient, an encoding technique can be used to compress the HTML structures into more compact *fingerprints* (the *FP* portion of the DomFP name comes from the word fingerprint; *Dom* refers to the *Document Object Model* that formally defines the rules for writing valid HTML code). We then devise a similarity measure that, given the two page fingerprints, estimates the likelihood that the two were generated from a common template. The DomFP algorithm uses this similarity measure to compare the fingerprint of a resource under examination with those of all spam pages. DomFP measures how many spam fingerprints are similar to the target, how many spam pages match the similar fingerprints, and how strong are the similarities. A high value of the DomFP feature indicates that a user posts pages with HTML structure similar to that of many known spam pages.

Finally, we give an example of a postlevel feature, *TagBlur*, which can be aggregated among all posts of a user. TagBlur is based on the observation that spammers would often annotate a resource with several popular but unrelated tags, such as "web," "sex," "apple," and so on, to promote it in most popular lists. These posts are *blurry* because the tags are not focused on any coherent topic. Blurry posts in a user's history may signal spamming activity. The challenge in formalizing this notion is to define a measure of how related a pair of tags are. In a tagging system, this can be done in a variety of ways by looking at how tags cooccur in the system. The interested reader is referred to Ref. [335] for comprehensive descriptions and comparisons of several tag similarity measures. Assuming we have a tag similarity measure at hand, we compute the similarity between each pair of tags in the same post and sum the dissimilarities (inversely proportional to similarities) across the pairs to obtain a measure of post blur. To apply this measure to a user, the blur of all posts of the user can be aggregated. High *TagBlur* values flag users who tend to apply tags unlikely to appear in a common context.

Table 4.6 Spam Detection Results in the GiveALink System Using Various Public Classifiers [235]

Classifier	Accuracy	AUC
MultiBoosting	98.89	0.989
AdaBoost	98.79	0.993
Bagging	98.08	0.994
Fast decision tree	98.08	0.972
C4.5 decision tree	97.98	0.960
Bayes network	96.57	0.988
Support vector machine	95.87	0.901
K-nearest neighbors	83.67	0.716
Naive Bayes	62.50	0.870

Accuracy is the fraction of instances (users in our case) that are correctly classified as spammers or nonspammers. AUC (Area Under ROC Curve) is another performance measure that evaluates the quality of the classifier's tradeoff between true and false positives; a value close to one means that most of the spammers can be detected while misclassifying few nonspammers.

Once the features of the system have been defined and computed, a classifier can be trained with a small set of labeled users and then used to classify the rest of the users in the system. In GiveALink, all features are recomputed for all users at weekly intervals, so the system can respond to changing spamming strategies. In addition, when a new user enters the system, their bookmarks are not immediately included in search results, most popular lists, or the output of web services provided by the GiveALink system. In other words, new users are not trusted until they are classified by the system as nonspammers.

4.5.3.4 *System evaluation*

The most important question in evaluating a spam detection system is whether it is effective. In GiveALink, we experimented with several publicly available classification algorithms [235] and present the results in Table 4.6. Classifier accuracy is quite good with a variety of classifiers, and so are AUC (Area Under ROC Curve) values. AUC is a performance measure that evaluates the quality of the classifier's tradeoff between true and false positives; a value close to one means that most of the spammers can be detected while misclassifying few nonspammers. The high AUC values imply that both the number of false positives (good users labeled as spammers) and the number of false negatives (spammers labeled as good users) are low. False positives are particularly important for spam detection systems, because their high incidence can quickly discourage people from using the system. Below we present further details on spam detection performance using the best-performing classifier from the list in Table 4.6.

In addition to measuring effectiveness, there are a few other questions that further illuminate the performance of a spam detection system. In the first place, we want to know which features have the highest discriminative power and whether a relatively simple classifier, employing a reasonably small set of features, can yield near-optimal performance. If one feature depends on another, its inclusion in the classifier may add to the computation time without a significant contribution to the accuracy. Rather than looking at the correlations between all pairs of features, which would be very time consuming, we first rank the features according to their discriminative power. Table 4.7 reports on the most discriminative features in the GiveALink

Table 4.7   The Most Effective Features for Spam Detection in the GiveALink System, Ranked by the χ^2 Discrimination Value

Feature	χ^2
Url-Tag cooccurrence	875.13
Url cooccurrence	850.35
Tag Blur	186.87
Tag cooccurrence	133.11
Number of users in the top-level domain	86.66
Total number of tags used	77.13
Average number of tags per post	63.45

system. We can evaluate the classifier by starting with the most discriminative feature and then adding the other features in order of their discriminative power. In Figure 4.28, we see the classifier's performance as new features are added one by one. Even with one feature, the classifier performs very well, and the top seven features (Table 4.7) provide a good balance between optimal performance and computational efficiency.

Finally, we can use the data from the GiveALink system to investigate how much labeled data are needed before we can say that the system is classifying new (unlabeled) users correctly with high degree of confidence. In Figure 4.29, we see that it does not take long before the system achieves a high level of accuracy.

4.5.4   Web Pollution

Having examined what social spam is and how it can be countered, let us briefly discuss the social spam phenomenon in a broader context as a motivation for future research work in the field. In the discussion so

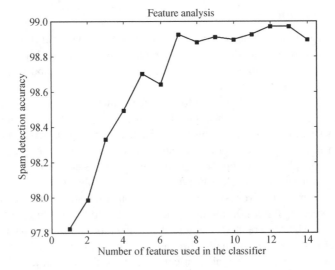

Figure 4.28   Change in spam detection accuracy as features are added to the classifier sequentially, starting with the most discriminative.

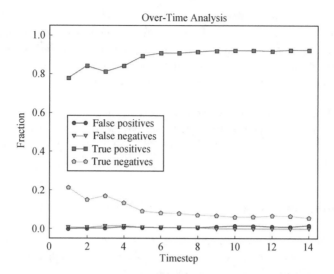

Figure 4.29 Performance of the system as more labeled examples are provided. On the *x*-axis, each time step represents 500 new users being labeled as spammers or nonspammers by human evaluators. In total, close to 7000 examples were labeled. The false positive rate was between 1% and 2%, and false negative rates were around 0.1%.

far, we have assumed that social spam activities are clearly harmful. However, it is important to examine this assumption. After all, one could make a case that no one is harmed by ad-driven spam—advertisers receive legitimate user clicks, spammers generate money from these clicks, and the users voluntarily click on the spammers' links. But this last observation is true only superficially. Similar to the cases of online fraud, most users probably do not want to be part of spammer and advertiser schemes, but end up being so because of their naiveté and inexperience.

There is also a larger issue than user gullibility. The kinds of spam we have described not only trick naive users but also make the web a less useful resource for everybody, except the small number of spammers who profit on the backs of everyone else. Importantly, spam makes quality information more difficult to find online. It introduces noise into the web and makes the job of search engines more difficult, and their results less reliable. It also makes online social systems less useful and friendly. We thus think of social spam as the online analogue of *pollution*. As we have been made painfully aware during the time when GiveALink did not have any spam detection infrastructure, spam can become so pervasive as to make a system very difficult to use.

Even though the above intuitions about the undesirability of spam are shared by many, there is value in their more rigorous study. Although spammers are a small proportion of the web population, there are additional questions that can be asked about this demographic. What kinds of systems are most vulnerable to spam? Are services with large user bases less vulnerable to spam because of the many good users who generate data that can in turn power antispam tools? Or, does the popularity of well-known services make them more desirable targets for spammers, and hence more vulnerable? Although there has been some work aimed at answering these questions using synthetic data generated from models [302], more study is needed in this area.

Regardless of their prevalence in the general web population, spammers could not function in isolation. In order for them to make money, spammers take advantage of a web advertising model whose weak points need to be examined and pointed out. For example, a case of fraud shows that advertising platforms on the web can be tricked in such a way as to give little incentive to legitimate entities to actively seek out and prosecute spammers [384]. In addition, to succeed in their activities, spammers need to make use of the infrastructure of legitimate ISPs and hosting providers and they need their own infrastructure to automate the process of generating fake content, because as we have seen, they can only profit if their activities are carried out at a large scale.

The interactions between legitimate web content providers and their content, social media, advertisers, and the flow of money that occurs in this system form an ecosystem that the spammers and other malicious users threaten with their pollution. Studying this ecosystem and quantifying its incentive and cost structure is an important direction for future research.

4.5.5 The Changing Nature of Social Spam: Content Farms

The social spam cases discussed above can be identified by a human unambiguously or, in any case, with a high degree of confidence. There are, however, instances of web pollution that are not so easily defined and that pose new challenges for social spam countermeasures.

The quantity of information available on the web and the problem of retrieving high-quality results has been the major challenge for search engines since they first appeared on the web. As search engine technology has matured, and especially with the appearance of Google and its PageRank algorithm [121], search results quality has greatly improved. With the growth of the web, however, the quantity of pages relevant to a query has increased as well, so the problem of finding good quality results has evolved from simply finding pages relevant to a query to finding the relevant pages that are most useful and informative. The need for improvement in search engine quality can be inferred from the existence of subscription web services. These websites stay in business despite the large amount of free information available online. Examples of such services include Experts Exchange (expert-exchange.com), which offers advice and step-by-step instructions on solving technical problems; Consumer Reports (consumerreports.org), an online extension of the magazine that employs experts to review consumer products and provide recommendations to its readers; and Meta Filter (metafilter.com), a community blog, message board, and chat, which charges a one-time sign-up fee to achieve higher quality of interaction and discussion among its users. These and other similar websites manage to generate a large amount of Internet traffic despite requiring a subscription fee.

A phenomenon that puts a twist on the challenge of spam detection and good quality web search is the emergence of so-called *content farm* websites. These websites can be either user-driven or employ freelancers to generate hundreds or thousands of content pieces each day. This content usually takes the form of short answers to questions or how-to articles, as seen in the example of Figure 4.22. Articles are written in style aimed to increase the chance of being ranked highly among search results and topics are driven by search demand. DemandMedia and Answers.com, both in the top 15 of most valuable web properties as of March 2011 [157], are examples of the largest companies associated with these kinds of content generation. While there is a debate as to whether content farms are spammers, Google has altered its ranking algorithm to give these websites less relevance [353]. We believe that content farms are an excellent example of web pollution.

Because content farms are not a well-defined concept, creating systems for their detection without relying on black lists and other inflexible approaches presents an interesting challenge and will be a future goal for social spam research. While research is still needed on automatic methods for evaluating the quality of websites, this area of machine learning has shown promise and has been very active. The 2010 ECML challenge [112] dealt with categorizing websites according to their quality. The winning entries of the challenge employed a variety of methods, such as sentiment analysis and link analysis [209,326,374,445]. A detailed study of the effectiveness of these methods to detect content farms is yet to come.

4.5.6 Conclusion

Similar to email spam, detecting social spam is a never-ending race between spammers and countermeasures. The detection methods described in this section are only a subset of what can be found in the spam detection literature. However, we have presented a number of issues and challenges posed by social spam and illustrated how it differs from traditional email spam. Web pollution and content farms are subtle spamlike practices that call for both awareness campaigns and new research directions. Security and machine learning researchers can do a great deal to contribute to these efforts not only by developing effective countermeasures but also by shedding light on the methods, motivations, and incentive models of online polluters.

ACKNOWLEDGMENT

This material is based upon work supported by the National Science Foundation under Grant No. 0811994.

4.6 UNDERSTANDING CAPTCHAs AND THEIR WEAKNESSES[4]

Elie Bursztein

Abstract. In his 1950 paper, "Computing Machinery and Intelligence," Alan Turing proposed what became the standard way for a human to test a computer's ability to demonstrate intelligence. In the Turing test, a human judge engages remotely in a natural language conversation with one human and one machine, each of which trying to appear human. If the judge cannot reliably tell the machine apart from the human, the machine is said to have passed the test. Sixty years later, telling humans apart from machines is a critical problem in Internet security—but the judge is a machine, not a human. These reverse Turing tests, or captchas (*Completely Automated Public Turing tests to tell Computers and Humans Apart*), form websites' first line of defense against automated abuse such as sending spam and creating fake accounts. Captchas are called reverse Turing tests, because the goal is for a computer to judge if a remote client is human or not. In this section, we will discuss the different types of captchas, their current weaknesses, and how to strengthen them.

4.6.1 What is a Captcha?

Distinguishing computers from humans has become a central issue for website security, and many services rely on this distinction to work properly. For example, Gmail must prevent abuse by automated spammers, eBay must prevent bots from flooding its site with scams, and Facebook must prevent the proliferation of fake profiles used to spam and cheat at games. Completely Automated Public Turing tests to tell Computers

---

[4]We write this acronym in lower case for readability.

and Humans Apart [366] allow websites to make this distinction automatically. Captchas usually take the form of small images or short audio files that are easy for humans to process, but hopefully difficult for computers to process. The attack surface of a captcha is broad. Most web services, such as Facebook and Google, allow users to solve either a text-based captcha or an audio one for accessibility purpose. An attacker can choose between two very distinct approaches to bypass captcha tests: the first is to create an *automated solver* using machine learning algorithms. The second approach, called a *crowd-sourcing attack*, relies on humans to solve captchas. These humans may be cheap labor hired through underground services. Or they may be unwilling workers that are either tricked or coerced into solving these captchas, either by malware or by social engineering. For example, a malicious website can pretend that the user have to solve a captcha to play a flash game to ensure fairness, while in fact it is a Google captcha that the user will solve for the attacker.

4.6.2   Types of Captchas

Current websites mainly use two types of captchas: *text-based captchas* and *audio captchas*. A *text-based captcha* consists of a sequence of characters embedded into an image. The user must correctly identify all the characters in order to pass this test. As shown in Figure 4.30, the sequence of characters is distorted using methods designed to thwart optical character recognition (OCR) techniques. A typical *audio-based captcha* consists of one or several speakers saying letters or digits at randomly spaced intervals. A user must correctly identify the letters or digits in order to pass the captcha. To make this test difficult for computers, various background noises are injected into the audio file. Alternative types of captcha exist, but they are primarily research prototypes and are not widely deployed. Most are based on analyzing picture content. It is surprisingly difficult to come up with a secure alternative approach. As discussed later, even one of the most serious attempts in this direction [180], made by Microsoft, ended up being broken [217].

4.6.3   Evaluating Captcha Attack Effectiveness

The basic method to evaluate the effectiveness of a captcha attack is to measure its *accuracy*, which is the fraction of the total captchas that were answered correctly either by the automated solver or by the human

Figure 4.30   Various text-based captcha schemes taken from popular websites in 2010. These captchas illustrate the diversity of the techniques used to prevent the attacker to build automated solvers.

solver. However, it is often more efficient for the attacker to respond to some captchas and reject others without answering them, as web services usually limit the number of attempts per IP address [131]. For example, eBay audio captchas are always six digits long, so an answer that contains more or fewer digits is clearly incorrect. A more precise way to evaluate solvers is to use the coverage and precision metrics. *Coverage* is the fraction of captchas that the tool attempts to answer. In the eBay case, it is the number of captchas that are correctly segmented into six digits as we know that they always contain 6 digits. *Precision* is the fraction of the captchas attempted that the solver guesses correctly.

Captcha security goal is that "automatic scripts should not be more successful than 1 in 10,000" attempts (i.e, a precision of 0.01%) [143]. Of course, it is next to impossible to require security against crowd-sourced human solvers, because everything that hurts them will hurt legitimate users as well. Because automated attacks exploit captchas' design weaknesses, it is important to understand captcha design and, in particular, their security and usability tradeoffs.

4.6.4 Design of Captchas

Although the high-level design of captchas is to simply find something that is easy for humans and hard for computers, their implementation has proved to be difficult. Creating a captcha is a subtle balance between usability and security. If the captcha is too hard for human, then the service it protects will not be used; if it is too easy for a computer, then it will fail at its purpose of preventing automated abuse. The Google text captchas shown in Figure 4.31 are a good illustration of the tension between making captchas hard for computers and easy for humans. This captcha is mainly hard for computers to process because the letters are collapsed, but this collapsing also makes these captchas hard for humans.

4.6.4.1 Unusable captchas

Surprisingly, until recently, most research efforts have been focused on evaluating captchas' security rather than on their usability, so we are just beginning to understand how to design captchas that are easy for humans. As a result [132,417], many current captcha schemes are very inconvenient for users, and therefore do not fully perform their role. An extreme example of unusable captchas is the old phpBB captcha (2009) illustrated in Figure 4.32, which is almost impossible for humans to decipher. It is clear that this early design

Figure 4.31 Five samples of the Google captcha scheme (2011). Having the letters collapsed not only defeats optical recognition algorithms but also makes these captchas harder for humans.

Figure 4.32   Example of an unusable captcha scheme, the old phpBB scheme (2009).

was not created with usability in mind. A more recent example (2011) of unusable captcha is the one used by the biggest Russian website *mail.ru*, depicted in Figure 4.33.

4.6.4.2 Case study: designing a text-based captcha scheme

Fortunately for the users, it is possible to design usable text captcha as, in general, humans are extremely good at processing strings that are not distorted. In one of our experiments, we asked 1000 people to transcribe random strings that became longer and longer to see how far can we go before human accuracy become problematic (<85%). Surprisingly getting below this threshold is very hard: as shown in Figure 4.35, even when the string is 30 characters long, humans can accurately transcribe these long strings 85% of the time. However, as soon as we started distorting (Figure 4.35) the string to make it difficult for computers to process, the human accuracy dropped rapidly. Figure 4.36 shows how rapidly human accuracy decreases when the string's characters are collapsed as in the Google captcha: the accuracy drops to 55% for a 30-character string. Because of the human accuracy discrepancy on undistorted and distorted text, the first step to design new captcha schemes is to understand how humans will react to the distortions that the scheme will use. For example, if the security of the captcha is based on collapsing characters, then it is essential to understand how aggressively collapsing them will affect users. Figure 4.37 summarizes how humans react when the

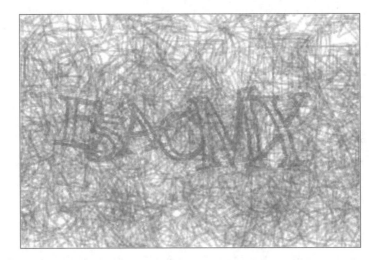

Figure 4.33   Example of an unusable captcha scheme, the mail.ru scheme (2010).

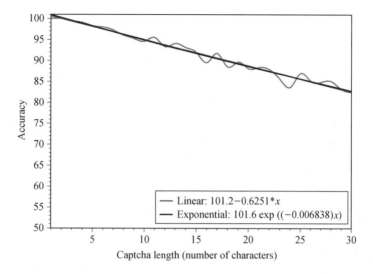

Figure 4.34 Human accuracy at solving a random string.

space between letters decreases. It is clear from this experiment that humans are still able to decipher the string when the letters are touching (space = 0) or when there is a slight overlap, but as the overlap increases, human accuracy decreases rapidly to the point where captchas become unusable.

Because humans' ability to process a given distortion is relatively stable, the security it adds boils down to how good computers are at processing this distortion. The gap between what humans can do and what computers can do can close up very quickly if someone comes up with a new algorithm. This is why, as in cryptography, it is important to think ahead and to have alternative schemes ready in case of an attack breakthrough. Figure 4.38 summarizes many parameters that designers can tweak when designing a new scheme. Some of them, like using a confusing background or a fancy text color, have no impact on automated solver, but can certainly hurt the user. For example, if the contrast between the foreground and the background is insufficient, people will have a hard time deciphering a captcha. Other distortions, such as adding lines, are fairly efficient at preventing automated attacks as long as the line is correctly placed. However, placing the line correctly is not that easy. For example, we found that each line needs to cover at least three characters; otherwise, it is very confusing for users.

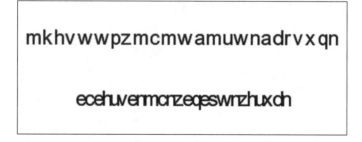

Figure 4.35 Example of a very long easy and a very long hard captcha.

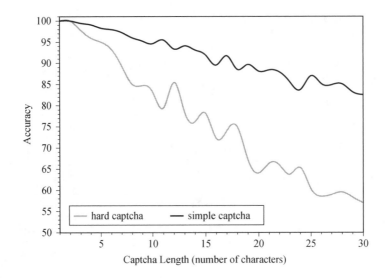

Figure 4.36   Human accuracy at solving a random string with collapsed characters.

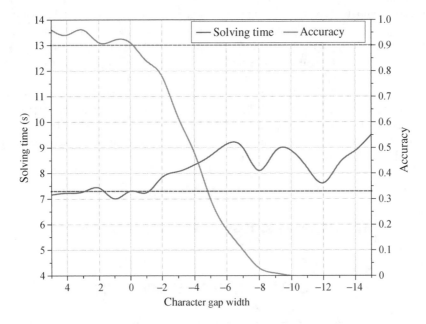

Figure 4.37   How humans perform when the gap between characters decreases. When the overlapping is too important, the captcha become undecipherable by humans.

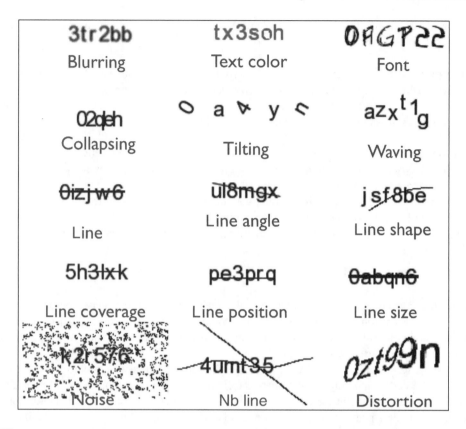

Figure 4.38 Example of features that a designer can vary in order to make captchas more secure and usable.

4.6.4.3 *Case study: designing an audio captcha scheme*

Audio captchas fall into two categories. *Noncontinuous speech captchas* present a single word or random string by pronouncing each letter or digit separately. This category is by far the most popular one and is currently used by every major company. *Continuous speech captchas*, on the other hand, use standard human diction and are much harder for human to understand, especially when the voice is distorted to prevent auto-mated attacks. Currently, the "hard" version of recaptcha [476] uses old radio records as continuous speech captchas, but the technique is not otherwise widely deployed. Besides choosing between noncontinuous and continuous speech, designers can play on three parameters to make captchas harder from computers. The first is the *type of noise* injected into the captcha to confuse the solver, the second is the *signal to noise ratio* (SNR) of the injected noise, and the last is the speaker's voice pitch and pace.

Type of noise   The three kinds of noise that a designer can use to make his captcha secure are additive noise, convolutive noise, and semantic noise. Additive noise is an extra-independent noise, such as the white noise, that is injected at random intervals on top of the voices. This is the least effective defense. Convolutive noise is the distortion that alters the voice to make recognition more difficult. Finally, semantic noise sounds like real voices, but is not simply an echo or distortion of the signal. This is the most effective defense, but unfortunately also the hardest for human. For example, the "easy" recaptcha scheme that use semantic noise extensively is almost unsolvable for humans [130].

Signal to noise ratio   The signal to noise ratio is roughly the ratio of intensity between the human voice and the noise masking it. The lower this ratio is, the harder it is for a human to hear the voice. We have demonstrated [130] that reducing the SNR does not significantly deter automated attacks. As having a very low SNR hurts users, it is not an effective defense, it should be avoided.

Pitch and pace   Finally, it is possible, in particular if the voice is generated by a computer, to alter the voice pitch and the pace in the hope to make the recognition harder. However, deviating too much from what humans are accustomed to significantly impacts the captcha's usability.

The design space for audio captchas is relatively unexplored and it is currently hard to tell what will work and what will not. Accordingly, as of 2011, computers have the upper hand in this domain. The most pressing issue is to design secure captchas that are accessible to visually impaired users.

4.6.5   Automated Attacks

The state-of-the-art approach to create an automated solver is to use a three-phase approach, consisting of *preprocessing*, *segmentation*, and *classification* [146]. Variants of this three-stage approach are used against both text-based and audio-based captchas. An example of this approach applied to Blizzard's World of Warcraft captcha scheme is shown in Figure 4.39.

In the first phase, the automated solver preprocesses the captcha to make it easier to analyze, for instance, by removing colors or by applying noise reduction techniques like spectral subtraction. In a second phase, the program attempts to segment the captcha into chunks that contain exactly one character, for example, by clustering. In the last phase, a machine learning classifier, often a support vector machine, is used to recognize which character is contained in each chunk.

It has been demonstrated several times that combinations of custom segmentation algorithms and machine learning algorithms are far more efficient at attacking captchas than off-the-shelf OCR systems or speech recognition systems. For example, Bursztein and Bethard [131] showed that for the eBay audio captcha, the accuracy of one of the best speech recognizers does not exceed 1%, whereas a custom classifier

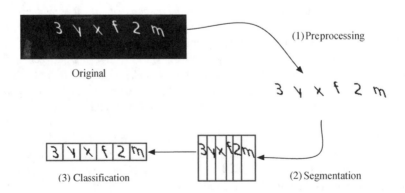

Figure 4.39   The three-phase approach applied to the current Blizzard World of Warcraft captcha.

can exceed 75%. Various experiments [144] and successful attacks [496] have demonstrated that the security of a captcha scheme mainly relies on preventing segmentation. For example, the robustness of text-based schemes depends on the difficulty of finding *where* the character is, rather than on *which* character it is [144]. Finally, it is worthwhile to note that the classifier used to recognize the chunks must be trained on labeled data before it can be effective. Accordingly, the attacker needs to manually annotate (or have annotated) several hundred captchas before the classifier model is accurate enough. The number of examples required depends greatly on the captcha scheme, and it is currently unknown how to estimate how many captchas will be needed beforehand.

Let us illustrate how automated attacks work by examining three concrete cases.

4.6.5.1 *The old Microsoft text captchas*

The old Microsoft text captcha, visible in Figure 4.40, is a good illustration of how the three-phase attack presented in the previous section is applied to break text-based captchas. It also demonstrates how a new algorithm can render a given scheme obsolete. This scheme's security was based on several distortions: rotating the characters, waving them, and most importantly using short lines (arcs) to prevent segmentation. This scheme was proposed in 2004 by Chellapilla et al. [145] as a response to the machine learning attacks they had developed previously. Using these small arcs as a way to prevent segmentation was considered safe until 2008, when this scheme was broken [496]. Figure 4.41 summarizes the attack steps. The first step is to "binarize" the captcha to black and white, so that it is easier to process. The second step is to "repair" the letters as some pixels might have been removed by the binarization operation. The segmentation phase starts with a standard segmentation that will obviously fail to some extent because of the lines, as seen in our example. To deal with these lines, the letters are clustered by grouping together contiguous black pixels. Once this is done, we end up with too many segments, as shown in step 5 of Figure 4.41. Two heuristics are used to find out which segments are the letters and to remove the "decoy" segments. The first heuristic relies on the fact that only real letters and numbers have a "loop." It uses a circle detection algorithm to detect these letters and numbers (such as the number 9 in our example) and to mark them as reliable letters. The filling algorithm works by filling the white around the letter with another color from the top-left corner. If the segment has a loop, then some white will be left, and otherwise not. A second heuristic is to use a pattern detection algorithm (step 7) to remove the remaining arcs based on their positions. If everything went well, the captcha is perfectly segmented into eight segments that contain one letter each, as in our example. Overall, the authors of Ref. [496] were able to achieve a 91% segmentation accuracy.

The first version of the attack fail when a line touches two characters, as shown in Figure 4.42. Although this was rare in the Microsoft scheme, one can wonder if adding more of these arcs can be used to fix this scheme. The answer is no: as demonstrated in Ref. [254], using the well-known technique called projective segmentation, these arcs can be removed easily as visible in Figure 4.42. The projective segmentation works by projecting pixels to the X-axis and then removing the dips and is also being used successfully by the same authors to attack the old Yahoo captcha.

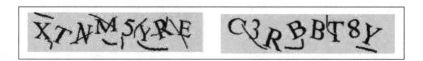

Figure 4.40   Samples from the old Microsoft text-based captcha scheme.

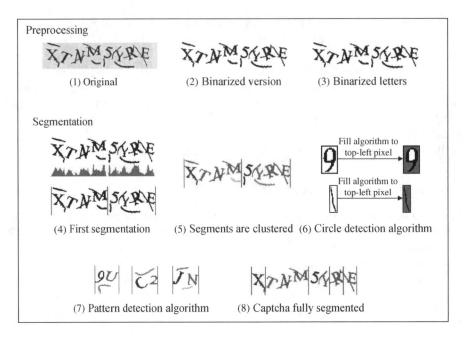

Figure 4.41 Attack steps against the old Microsoft captcha.

4.6.5.2 The Yahoo audio captcha case

We demonstrated another batch of successful automated attacks in 2011 [130] against many audio captchas, including captchas by Microsoft, Recaptcha, and Yahoo. In this section, we will use the Yahoo captcha to illustrate how to attack an audio captcha scheme. The Yahoo audio captchas consist of three beeps followed by seven digits spoken by a child. The captcha is obscured with other children' voices in the background. The waveform presented in Figure 4.43 shows a portion of a captcha containing the digits 1, 7, and 6. The digits are the largest amplitude sections in the waveform. Yahoo captchas' spectrograms have very different patterns than other captchas' spectrograms because of the use of a child's voice. The patterns in children's voices are much clearer than those in adults' voices. This makes digits easier to recognize even though the noise in Yahoo's captchas has more energy than the noise in other captchas. To attack an audio captcha in the preprocessing phase, the audio signal is discretized by applying various audio signal processing techniques,

Figure 4.42 Example of the projection technique applied to an old Microsoft captcha sample. The projection technique is used to improve even further the segmentation accuracy. The histogram in the middle represents the result of the pixel projection to the X-axis. The square represents the pixels that will be removed because they are below the threshold.

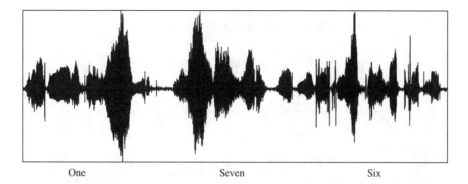

One   Seven   Six

Figure 4.43   The spectrogram (up) and 2D FFT representation of a Yahoo audio captcha. As visible, the signal is very irregular because of the noise.

including at least one discrete Fourier transform [490]. In the Yahoo case, the best audio discretization is the cepstrum representation [489] that helps removing the voice pitch. Once this is done, the segmentation works by finding the energy peaks that represent the voice in the foreground. This segmentation phase can be viewed as a "smart" high-pass filter that isolates the foreground voice from the background voices by only keeping the higher frequencies. The classification part once again relies on a machine learning algorithm to classify the segments. Overall, we were able to solve 45% of Yahoo captchas with a 99% recall on segmentation and 74% precision on digit recognition.

4.6.5.3   The ASIRRA captcha case

As shown in Figure 4.44, the ASIRRA captcha [180] works by asking users to distinguish between dogs and cats. The security of the scheme was based on the idea that it should be hard for a computer to differentiate between two animals. To prevent the attacker from scraping the entire database, Microsoft made a partnership with petfinder.com, which has a very large database of photos of pets that need to be adopted. Note that under each image, a link to adopt the pet was displayed with the hope that the captcha solver would be tempted to adopt the pet he was clicking on. Finding secondary use of a captcha is a trend popularized by recaptcha, which uses text-based captchas to digitalize books [476].

While designing this captcha, the Microsoft research folks went to great lengths and did a lot of testing to ensure that their scheme was resistant to automated attack. Despite their efforts, the "texture" attack (Figure 4.45) invented by Golle in 2008 [217] breaks this scheme. The texture attack works by dividing the images into 5×5 pixel texture tiles, as shown in Figure 4.44, and then analyzing each texture's HSV (hue, saturation, and value) representation. The features used to categorize the images are simply which colors are present in each tile. Surprisingly, the author notes that the presence or absence of a color is a more useful feature than how many pixels have that color. Overall, the texture attack is able to classify the 12 images of an ASIRRA captcha with 12% accuracy.

4.6.6   Crowd-Sourcing: Using Humans to Break Captchas

Because the last few years have been very prolific in terms of new automated attacks against captchas, the barriers to creating automated solvers have been raised considerably. With the increasing resistance of

Figure 4.44 The ASIRRA captcha that tests if you are human by asking you to select either all the cats or all the dogs present in the captchas.

Figure 4.45 Example of texture tiles (5 × 5 pixels) extracted from the ASIRRA images that are used in the attack against it.

text-based captcha schemes to machine learning attacks, many attackers have recently moved to another type of attack: using real humans to solve captchas. This kind of attack, known as crowd-sourcing, comes in three flavors. First, the attacker can hire cheap labor to solve captcha for him via an underground service. Second, he can trick unwilling participants into solving captchas for him, a practice called *captcha farming*. Finally, he can coerce unwilling users to solve captchas via malware installed on their computers. Using cheap labor is currently the attackers' preferred method because it is more reliable and scales better than the other two. Finding defenses against crowd sourcing is a central issue that needs to be addressed to prevent web services from being overwhelmed by bots.

4.6.6.1 Hiring human solvers

As related in Ref. [359], hiring labor to solve captchas *en masse* is becoming easier and cheaper than building an automated solver. In early 2011, the market price was around $1 for 1000 captchas. Overall, workers accuracy are very high: above 80% as reported in Ref. [359]. When these numbers are compared with the price (at least a couple of hundred dollars) and the quick obsolescence of the automated solvers sold on the black market, it is not surprising that most attackers currently prefer to hire real humans to solve their captchas. As illustrated in Figure 4.46, once the attacker gets a captcha, he sends it to human workers through the underground services. Every underground service makes this process easy by providing an API available in many languages (C#, PHP, Java, etc.). As measured in Ref. [359], good underground services will provide the correct answer more than 85% of the time in less than 15. To maintain competitive prices, these underground services have recently moved from eastern Europe to Asia (Bangladesh, China, India, and Vietnam). Because solving captchas is easy by design and does not require specific skills, these underground services have a large pool of workers, which ensure that they can solve a lot of captchas each second at

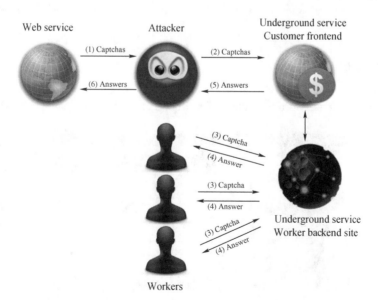

Figure 4.46 Hiring cheap labor via an underground web service to solve captchas.

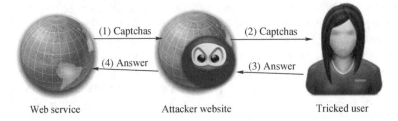

Figure 4.47   Tricking users into solving captchas.

any time of day. Preventing attackers from using these services to reliably solve thousands of captchas per minute is one of the toughest challenges faced by the web security community.

4.6.6.2 Tricking human solvers

A less reliable method to mount a crowd-sourcing attack is to trick users into solving the captchas. This method known as captcha farming is shown in Figure 4.47. First, the attacker creates an "appealing" application/web service to attract users, the usual case being a site that offers adult or illegal content. When the user wants to access or download the content, he is asked to solve a captcha. The trick is that the captcha displayed to the user is in fact a captcha from the site that the attacker wants to attack. The attacker's site acts as a proxy between the attacker's target website and the users. An illustrious example of this kind of attack is the Troj/CAPTCHA-A (Figure 4.48) malicious striptease application that asked users to solve a captcha to continue the striptease. This method is less reliable than paying cheap labor because it depends on traffic to the website. It is also more detectable by the targeted site, because the captchas need to be fetched by the attacker website before being displayed to the user. Sometimes the attackers can get around this issue by exploiting web vulnerabilities (such as CSRF or clickjacking) on the target website, but eventually they will be fixed.

4.6.6.3 Coercing human solvers

Finally, if the attacker has access to a botnet, he can coerce the users into solving captchas for him by locking their computers or threatening to reboot them. The Koobface [99] botnet that specialized in propagating

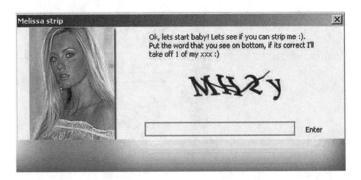

Figure 4.48   Screenshot of the malicious Troj/CAPTCHA-A application.

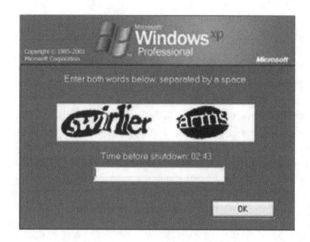

Figure 4.49 The threat displayed by Koobface to coerce the user into solving a captcha.

through social network is famous for using this kind of tactic (Figure 4.49) to allow its bots to send their messages via Facebook despite the captchas Facebook presents for suspicious messages.

Captcha security is a constant arms race between designers and attackers. As the artificial intelligence field progresses, it is becoming increasingly difficult to find novel designs that are both secure and usable. Until now, captcha schemes have been mainly designed around simple ideas, and it is clear that in the near future we will need more complex tests that may increase user friction. Designing this new generation of tests is an open challenge. On the bright side, it is worth noting that having a more complex scheme will offer a lot of room to improve site monetization by tying tests to advertisement. Just as Recaptcha helps to digitalize books, hopefully these new tests will have positive side effects.

4.7 SECURITY QUESTIONS

Ariel Rabkin

Abstract. Security questions (or challenge questions) are commonly used to authenticate users who have lost their passwords. We examined the password retrieval mechanisms for a number of personal banking websites and found that many of them rely in part on security questions with serious usability and security weaknesses. We discuss patterns in the security questions we observed. We argue that today's personal security questions owe their strength to the hardness of an information retrieval problem. However, as personal information becomes ubiquitously available online, the hardness of this problem, and security provided by such questions, will likely diminish over time. We supplement our survey of bank security questions with a small user study that supplies some context for how such questions are used in practice.

4.7.1 Overview

Online financial and email services have deployed increasingly sophisticated authentication mechanisms. Many exhort or require users to pick "strong" passwords, not easily guessed by an attacker. Strong passwords, however, are hard for many users to remember. For usability reasons, these services often couple their password authentication mechanism with some sort of "lost password" mechanism, which users can fall back on if they have forgotten their passwords.

One solution has been to rely on security questions. These come in two varieties. One sort of security questions ask about sensitive information that users generally try to keep secret. This includes Social Security, library card, bank account numbers, and ATM PIN codes. We refer to these as *sensitive* security questions. Another set of security questions, which we term *personal* security questions, ask about personal history and family background, such as one's mother's maiden name. These have also been referred to in the literature as "Personal Verification Questions." Unlike sensitive information, this sort of personal information is routinely and casually shared with others. In theory, the answers to these questions are known only to the rightful user of the account and, therefore, the question serves as an authentication technique. In practice, these answers can sometimes be guessed or discovered by attackers.

> It is a well-known principle that the overall security of a system depends on the strength of its weakest point. Special cases, such as lost password mechanisms, are often less carefully designed than the primary path intended for users and, therefore, they can easily become weak points. The security questions currently in use for password reset are an example of this; too often, they are susceptible to attack, either based on random guessing or on Internet research about the target.

In September 2008, Alaska Governor Sarah Palin became perhaps the most famous victim of the insecurity of security questions. Her experience is worth describing in detail. Palin had a Yahoo! email account, protected by three security questions: asking for her birthday, ZIP code, and "where did you meet your spouse." All of these, it turns out, were inadequate. College student David Kernell was able to discover or guess the answers to all these questions, resulting in Governor Palin's email becoming public. Birthdays of prominent public figures are widely published (e.g., on Wikipedia). Palin's hometown, Wasilla, has only two ZIP codes, allowing the attacker to simply guess. That leaves the spouse question. Here again, the biographies of public officials have enough information, allowing the attacker, after several attempts, to correctly guess "Wasilla high" [505].

This exploit illustrates several important aspects of lost password mechanisms. The strength of a password does not depend on who is using it; the strength of a security question, however, does depend on how much is known about the user. The strength of a security question can change over time, perhaps unpredictably. Before Sarah Palin became a prominent figure, her birthday and marital history would have been less accessible to an attacker. Finally, this example demonstrates that security is a property of whole systems, not just of one component, such as the questions being asked. It took the attacker several attempts to successfully answer Palin's security question. A more cautious email provider might have disabled password reset in response before the attacker succeeded. After Kernell's attack, there were several successive password resets within the space of a few hours by other individuals. These did eventually trigger Yahoo! to disable the password reset mechanism—but too late to maintain the confidentiality of stored email.

4.7.1.1   Threats

> Any security analysis ought to start with an analysis of the relevant threats. Defenses that are useful against one category of attacker may be much less effective against another. Hence, understanding the threat model for a particular context is required to reason about the security of a system.

We can point to two general categories of threats to lost password mechanisms. Some adversaries will try to compromise as many accounts as possible, without caring which particular accounts they succeed on. Other adversaries will be focused on compromising the account of some specific individual. Focused adversaries can be further subdivided into those targeting acquaintances or family and those targeting strangers.

For an adversary interested in compromising as many accounts as possible without being picky about which ones, the best strategy is what is called "bulk guessing"—trying to attack many accounts at the same time, but making only one or two attempts per account. An attacker would start with a list of suspected or confirmed account names and a set of likely guesses for each security question. The attacker would then try a few guesses for each account. By spreading out the guesses over many sites and users, the attacker reduces the chance of a website detecting the attack, given the steady background of legitimate fallback authentication attempts. Several refinements would improve the attacker's odds. Compromised social networking accounts would help generate plausible answers for a given account. Attackers can improve their chances of evading discovery by launching their attack through a botnet. If the malicious login attempts come from thousands of compromised machines, the target website will have a harder time determining whether the client at any particular IP address is behaving suspiciously.

A bulk-guessing attacker might be happy with an attack that succeeds against one account in a thousand, provided that little human time is required to mount the attack and provided that the attacks can be done unobtrusively. Even a low success probability against any particular user could support an economically viable attack if each attempt is nearly free. Suppose, for example, that our attacker is a professional criminal based somewhere in eastern Europe with negligible law enforcement. Suppose attack succeeds one time in a thousand, that the average profit from success is $500, and that the attacker is able to make one attempt per minute. Then the attacker will reap $263,000 per year. The dominant cost will be the attacker's time; compromised machines are available on the black market for pennies a day.

Now turn from our notional criminal to a disaffected employee, estranged family member, or celebrity-obsessed stalker, focused on a particular victim's online presence. Since there is only one target, the attacker will be limited by the lockout mechanism and must make every attempt count. Hence, they are likely willing to commit human time and skill to boost the likelihood of success. The most potent attacker is one who knows the victim well, either by personal acquaintance or because of the fame of the target.

4.7.1.2 An overview of fallback authentication

Any backup authentication system has several parts. The most visible of these is the authentication mechanism itself. This is often based on asking personal knowledge questions. It can also include "sensitive security questions" such as asking users for their bank account number, a government-issued ID number such as a Social Security number, or some other piece of data that users know to keep confidential. Authentication can also include sending email or text messages to a prearranged address or number. It can also include other, more esoteric authentication techniques. (We will give examples of these below.)

Behind the authentication mechanism are other, less visible, parts of the system. There is a lockout mechanism, preventing too many attempts at a particular account. There can be a notification mechanism to tell a user when their account is reset. There can be an anomaly detection mechanism looking at suspicious activity after the password reset. Beyond these, there are other pieces with subtle security consequences. Every system has documentation, explaining to users both how to set up the lost password mechanism and how to use it. There may be a policy restricting the security question answers that users can specify. There may be a way for users to recover a lost user name. (This enhances usability, but can make it easier for a bulk-guessing attacker to find targets.)

These pieces are sometimes mutually reinforcing, but the security of a system is not a straightforward function of the security of the pieces. A lockout policy limiting attempts to reset the password of a particular account helps defeat attacks focused on a particular account, but would do little against a bulk-guessing attacker making just one or two guesses per account. Bad documentation can make systems unusable or result in them being used insecurely.

4.7.2 Vulnerabilities

Sensitive security questions are comparatively easy to reason about. Users generally know who has access to their PIN, library card, or bank account number, and can usually change them if they suspect compromise. The answers are (hopefully) random numbers drawn from a large space, so attackers have only a poor chance of guessing them. This means the attacker must somehow learn the answers to these questions. Sensitive security questions can still have weaknesses. As we will discuss later, Social Security numbers in the United States are comparatively insecure. The key point is that the strength of a sensitive question does not change suddenly and unexpectedly.

In contrast, personal security questions are comparatively difficult to analyze. Their strength can vary widely between users and can change over time. Your birthday might be hard to find today, but might be public in a year if it is present in a public database. Personal questions are far more varied than sensitive security questions, and attackers can learn or guess the answers in a variety of ways. Because such questions are commonly used in practice, they demand careful consideration and analysis. We therefore give a classification of different flaws in personal security questions:

Guessable The answer to a *Guessable* question can be correctly guessed (with significant probability) without knowing anything beyond population-level statistics. For instance, 30% of Americans marry between 25 and 30, and so a random number in that range would be a good guess for the question, "How old were you when you were married?" (All the security questions used as examples in this section were used at one point by email providers or financial institutions.)

Attackable An *attackable* question can be found (with significant probability) by a human adversary with access to the Internet. A great deal of personal information is available online in unstructured or loosely structured documents. Archival copies of old personal webpages, short newspaper profiles, club membership rosters, and the like are all potent sources of personal information to a human attacker and are all growing in volume and coverage. Although reliably answering personal security questions using these sources is beyond the reach of today's commodity information retrieval techniques, human adversaries are able to make use of them . For instance, a victim's resume would reveal the answer to "with which company did you hold your first job?" Employment histories are by no means secret; they are commonly listed on web pages, biographic descriptions, resumes, and the like.

Questions such as "what is your home town" are comparatively easy for humans to answer, if the result is indicated by a document in the first few pages of search engine results. Names of pets or family members are not viewed as private information, and are often made public via personal webpages and the like. Insidiously, users may have little awareness of or control over the information available about themselves online. Genealogical information, for instance, is often published without the subjects being informed; old personal webpages or discussion list emails may be available through archival websites. Hence, users may not have an easy time accurately assessing how secure a particular question would be for them.

Automatically attackable Sometimes, this process of looking up answers to security questions can automated in a straightforward way. We describe a question as *automatically attackable* if the answer would be visible in the structured portion of a user's profile page on Facebook, LinkedIn, or similar social networking sites. Date of birth and ZIP code, which are often mandatory questions, fall into this category. Likewise, "what year did you graduate from college" has an answer that can be automatically mined from Facebook profiles.

There is no simple way to tell how good a question is. The security of a given question can be weakened by seemingly unrelated disclosures and will inevitably deteriorate over time.

Griffith and Jakobsson have demonstrated that mother's maiden names, perhaps the canonical example of a personal security question, can be deduced with significant probability from public records [225]. In most cases, no one public database links individuals to their mother's maiden name. However, combining information from marriage and birth databases enables the attacker to guess mother's maiden names with substantial probability. Note that each of these databases, taken separately, is innocuous: it is the combination that enables the attacker to infer something that otherwise would be hard to guess. The problem extends beyond the single example of "mother's maiden name"; attacks that join information from multiple databases can help attackers guess answers to many security questions. In particular, very similar techniques would likely succeed in answering other security questions that ask about names of family members.

IP addresses are another kind of data, seemingly unrelated to personal security questions, that can weaken the security of a question. If an attacker has compromised one site, they can leverage this information to launch bulk attacks on other sites. Sometimes this is blatant, as in the use of a compromised password databases. In other cases, the attacker's leverage can be more subtle. For example, suppose an attacker has compromised site A. Standard geolocation techniques let the attacker build up a map from IP address to user name for the users of this site. They can then use this mapping to guess the ZIP codes of users at site B, with high probability, even if site A did not ask for ZIP code.

The degree of public information available about the average user is not constant. In the short and medium term, it seems inevitable that it will increase. Digital data do not degrade on its own; if the criminal underworld obtains a database at some point in time, the rest of society must assume that data will remain available to criminals for the indefinite future. And there are many sources of such data. Users sometimes reveal aspects of themselves on Facebook or other social networking sites, only later to decide they have said too much. It sometimes happens that databases with potentially sensitive information are made public, either deliberately or as a result of security breaches. Genealogical data become stale only very slowly; if an attacker learns about the ancestry of a particular user, that information will generally remain relevant for decades.

The salience of these weaknesses will depend on the nature of the attacker. A disaffected spouse or employee mounting a targeted attack might have no ties to organized crime and limited access to stolen databases, but might be willing to invest human time and effort. Conversely, a professional criminal mounting a bulk-guessing attack would avoid security questions that require human effort to compromise. Rather, they would preferentially target guessable or automatically attackable questions, where the work of guessing can be automated.

Some analysts have used the size or entropy of the answer space for a question as a measure of guessability [288]. Both are poor metrics. If 10% of users have the same well-known answer, and all other users have answers chosen uniformly at random from a very large space, the question would have a large answer space and high entropy, but would still be highly vulnerable to guessing. A better metric for security is the fraction of users who give one of the k most common answers, where k is the number of guesses an attacker can make. This captures the intuition that an attacker will try the most likely possibilities, not randomly weighted ones.

4.7.2.1 *Security versus usability*

Even a secure authentication question is no good if legitimate users are unable to consistently give the correct answer. These problems are significant in practice. In a recent study, 57% of the participants were unable to reset their Hotmail passwords because they were unable to remember the answers to the required security questions [416].

Several factors can make questions inappropriate for particular users:

Inapplicability Some security questions rely on circumstances that do not apply to a large fraction of the public,. For instance, "Which high school did your spouse attend?" is inapplicable to unmarried individuals. "In what city is your vacation home?" is another question with limited applicability.

Ambiguity While inapplicable questions sometimes have no truthful answers, ambiguous questions have too many. For most people, "what is the name of a school you attended?" does not have a unique memorable answer. A common source of ambiguity is questions whose answers shift over time. Many security questions ask about preferences, such as favorite restaurants or favorite historical personages. These preferences are not stable over time.

Lack of memorable answers Even if a question has a unique truthful answer, sometimes this answer is just too hard to recall. Users are not able to reliably judge which questions they will remember the answers to. In one study, 22% of users failed to recall the last name of your kindergarten teacher, even after voluntarily choosing the question [416].

Ambiguous questions (and those with easily forgotten answers) exacerbate the tradeoff between security and usability. Because users make mistakes and have fallible memories, they must be allowed to make multiple attempts before being locked out. If a website has ambiguous and hard-to-use the questions, then users will need more attempts in order to authenticate successfully. Maintaining a given success rate for legitimate users will then require a more generous lockout threshold. A generous lockout threshold, in turn, impairs the security of the system. Thus, the presence of hard-to-use questions exacerbates the tension between security and usability of the authentication mechanism.

Inapplicable questions are comparatively benign. A few inapplicable questions in a large bank of options will do little harm. However, if a site offers a limited range of security questions, and some are inapplicable, then users may be forced to choose questions with other more serious defects, such as guessability or lack of memorability.

4.7.2.2 *Estimating vulnerability*

In the previous section, we described some of the potential problems with security questions. Here, we assess how pervasive these problems are in practice at the present time.

Table 4.8   Some examples of weak questions used in practice by banks.

Question	Possible attack	Success rate estimate
In what year did you graduate college?	Guess random years within the last 50	Approximately 2% per guess, assuming users have ages distributed uniformly between 20 and 70
In what year did you graduate college?	Look up victim on Facebook or other social networks.	Depends on quantity of personal information available about target
What college was your college rival?	Manually create table mapping colleges to their rivals. Use Facebook to find where target went to college. Then look up answer in table	Depends on table completeness and available information
What is the name of your first pet?	Guess the most popular pet names in order	Nearly 1% per guess. 1.5% of dogs and cats in New York and San Francisco were named Max. Probabilities fall off from there

In 1991, Haga and Zviran measured the ability of romantic partners to guess security question answers [234]. They succeeded 38% of the time in correctly answering personal security questions about their partners, half as often as those partners themselves. We note, however, that their methodology only allowed one guess, and that subsequent guesses will raise this success rate. Online sources of personal information (not available in 1991) would be helpful even to attackers who are well acquainted with their target.

A 2009 study by Schechter et al. repeated this experiment using web mail security questions [416]. Averaging across the four leading web mail providers, they found that 16% of participants were able to guess the answers to their romantic partners' security questions with five or fewer attempts. There was substantial variance between providers. Google asked about library card numbers, which were impossible to guess. AOL and Yahoo! questions were worse than average, with a 26% success rate for the attacker.

Weak and guessable questions also show up in online banking, perhaps a domain requiring more security than email (Table 4.8). Table 4.9 reports the results of a 2008 examination of security questions from 11 online banking, credit card, and brokerage websites. A large fraction of questions are flawed. Random guessing would succeed (with probability at least 1%) against 39% of questions. Random guessing, supplemented by mining social networking sites, might succeed against 49% of questions. Human attackers would have

Table 4.9   Results of a Study Exploring the Quality of Banking Websites Security Questions

	Ambiguous.	Not memorable	Inapplicable	Guessable	Attackable	Automatically attackable	Automatically accountable or guessable	Secure	Total
Questions	68	29	105	85	144	35	106	75	215
Percentage	31	13	48	39	66	16	49	34	100

Many questions have usability or security flaws. "Attackable" numbers include "automatically attackable" questions.

a nontrivial success chance against two-thirds of questions. See Ref. [394] for details of the methodology and definitions used.

4.7.3   Variants and Possible Defenses

Lost password mechanisms can use other authentication mechanisms to supplement or replace security questions. In particular, email and SMS are commonly used to authenticate users. Unfortunately, these cannot be always used. Some users do not have cell phones. And a web mail provider cannot assume that users have an alternative usable email address. Users change their cell phone numbers and email addresses over time; keeping this information up-to-date is a challenge and an expense. As a result, there is substantial interest in improving security questions, rather than replacing them outright.

4.7.3.1   Alternative forms of questions

Several variants of security questions have been proposed. O'Gorman et al. describe several approaches for using security questions in the context of call centers [379]. They suggest that customers choose a substantial number, perhaps a dozen, multiple choice questions. Each user is supplied with a numbered list of questions to be kept in a safe place. This numbering will vary between users. Rather than asking the question directly, the call center asks, "the answer to question number N." Without the written key with the numbering for a given user, guessing has a low probability of success. If the list is lost or stolen, a new numbered list can be mailed to the customer.

Another variant form of authentication questions is the preference-based technique proposed by Jakobsson et al. and discussed in Section 7.4. In this scheme, users are asked to make a series of preference judgments. If their answers are close enough to the user's previously established preferences, they are authenticated. Users are asked for "like" or "dislike," not asked to volunteer (or identify) favorites. The scheme is motivated by the fact that preferences of the form "do I like cats?" are more durable than memory for facts, and are often harder to guess.

Most security question systems require users to specify the correct answers in advance. A proposed scheme called "Adaptive Challenge Questions" avoids this. Instead, users are asked about their recent browsing history [92]. Unfortunately, this scheme works only in a specific context and against a specific class of adversaries. It requires that the authenticating sites have access to the user's browsing history. It also presumes that adversaries do not have access to the browsing history, either from a centralized site or from observing the network sessions directly.

Several major American credit bureaus authenticate users by asking them multiple choice questions about their past financial activity. This technique exploits the privileged access that credit bureaus have to sensitive information about past financial transactions. A similar technique, sold commercially by RSA Security, asks questions based on public record databases [412]. In both cases, the security of the system depends on the website conducting the authentication knowing much more about users, or being significantly better than the attacker at extracting information from public records. This assumption is hard to validate in practice; the attacker might be able to do the same kind of data mining as RSA did.

4.7.3.2   User-chosen questions

It is tempting to give users themselves the power to write questions. Unhappily, users turn out to be quite bad at writing questions and at remembering answers. Users make all the sorts of mistakes discussed above:

they pick questions whose answers are easily guessed or that can be derived from public sources. In a recent study, a quarter of user-supplied question–answer pairs had answers that were judged vulnerable to guessing [416]. (The threshold for guessability was that the attacker had at least a 4% chance of success on the first guess, without knowing anything about the user beyond general geographical region.) Another quarter of user questions asked about the names and birth locations of family members. A 2009 study by Just and Aspinall found similar results: users pick questions similar to those already used by websites and cannot reliably judge the security of a given question [288].

4.7.3.3 Questions with secret answers

Given the problems with personal security questions, a website might instead ask about something generally considered secret, such as a library card number. While this can be a substantial improvement to security, it is not a perfect defense. For example, the use of Social Security numbers for authentication has surprising weaknesses.

There are two problems with using Social Security numbers to authenticate people. They can be stolen and they can be guessed. Social Security numbers are frequently compromised in institutional data losses and are frequently sold in bulk on the black market [194]. The Social Security Administration has a policy of not assigning individuals a new number unless supplied with proof of fraud [443]. As a result, Social Security numbers cannot be reset to a "secret" value between disclosure and attack. The pool of Social Security numbers available to attackers is therefore likely to grow over time.

An attacker can sometimes guess a user's Social Security number. SSNs are not assigned randomly. They are assigned by blocks to particular regions at particular times. Hence, knowing where and when an individual was born lets an attacker guess the first five digits of their Social Security number with high probability. The current number assignment system came into use in 1989; for individuals born since then, the first five digits of their SSN can be guessed correctly 44% of the time [82]. Allowing the attacker to make multiple guesses improves these odds. As a result, a bulk guessing attacker can partially defeat the use of Social Security numbers for authentication by making more guesses.

While they may be insufficient against a bulk adversary, Social Security numbers can be useful in keeping out targeted attackers. The Social Security numbers of celebrities and politicians are generally not public. Friends will generally not have access to each other's numbers. Unlike a bulk guessing attacker, a focused attacker cannot compensate for a low success probability by making more attempts. The lockout policy will defeat this attack.

4.7.4 Conclusion

Personal security questions, as currently used in fallback authentication in online banking, are surprisingly weak. Optimistically, this suggests that even simple security questions are useful in practice in authenticating users. Less positively, it suggests that even institutions with money on the line have difficulty designing high-quality authentication questions. If current trends continue, questions of the form used today may become dangerously insecure.

There are fundamental problems with conventional personal security questions. Users will seldom share personal information that is truly secret with a website. It is hard to imagine banks posing security questions about a patron's medical or sexual history. Personal security questions must therefore ask about information that is not truly private, but that has not yet been made publicly accessible. This means that the answer must either not have been shared despite being sharable or that finding the answer requires solving a hard information retrieval problem.

One of the hallmarks of the Internet age is that users are willing to share a great deal of personal information online, some of it quite intimate. Another is that data are easy to copy. Once sensitive information is available to attackers, it can be copied by them, and remain available indefinitely. Search technology has been improving rapidly and unpredictably. Hard information retrieval or correlation problems might not remain hard. An answer that was obscure may become easy to find a few years later. As a result, personal security questions cannot reliably keep out motivated adversaries.

They can, however, still be used as part of a larger system. They are able to keep out at least some attackers, while imposing a small burden on legitimate users. In particular, they can be usefully combined with other authentication techniques such as email or SMS to a prearranged address. Security questions can keep out casual attackers who obtain temporary access to a user's cell phone or email. They also make it harder to abuse the lost password system to spam the rightful user with reset emails or SMS. As with so many other security technologies, the context and threat model are all-important.

4.8 FOLK MODELS OF HOME COMPUTER SECURITY

Rick Wash and Emilee Rader

Abstract. Home computer systems are insecure not just because they are administered by untrained users but also because these users make intentional choices that lead to poor security. We describe eight "folk models" of security threats that are used by home computer users to decide what security software to use, and which expert security advice to follow: four conceptualizations of "viruses" and other malware, and four conceptualizations of "hackers" that break into computers. These models are frequently used to justify ignoring expert security advice. One reason why botnets are so difficult to eliminate is that they cleverly take advantage of gaps in these models so that many home computer users do not take steps to protect against them.

4.8.1 The Relationship Between Folk Models and Security

Home computer users are installing paid and free home security software at an increasing rate. These systems include antivirus software, anti-spyware software, personal firewall software, personal intrusion detection/prevention systems, computer login/password /fingerprint systems, and intrusion recovery software. Nonetheless, security intrusions and the costs they impose on other network users are also increasing. Compromised computers often go undetected, and are used as tools in cybercrime enterprises.

One possibility is that home computer users are starting to become well informed about security risks, and that soon enough of them will protect their systems that the problem will resolve itself. However, given the "arms race" history in most other areas of networked security (with intruders becoming increasingly sophisticated and numerous over time), it is likely that the lack of user sophistication and noncompliance with recommended security system usage policies will continue to limit home computer security effectiveness.

To design better security technologies, it helps to understand how users make security decisions, and to characterize the security problems that result from these decisions. To this end, below are identified eight *mental models* [166,285] of attackers and security technologies. Mental models describe how a user thinks about a problem; it is the model in the person's mind of how things work. People use these models to make decisions about the effects of various actions [286].

These mental models are *folk models* for home computer users. Folk models are ideas about how the world works that are not necessarily accurate in the real world, thus leading to erroneous decision making, but are shared among similar members of a culture [166]. It is well known that in technological contexts, users often operate with incorrect folk models [83]. To understand the rationale for home computer users' behavior, it is important to understand what leads them to make the decisions they do. If technology is designed on the assumption that users have correct mental models of security threats and security systems, it will not induce the desired behavior when they are in fact making choices according to a different model.

As an example of folk models, Kempton [297] studied folk models of thermostat technology in an attempt to understand the wasted energy that stems from poor choices in home heating. He found that people possessed one of two different mental models for how a thermostat works. Kempton concluded that "Technical experts will evaluate folk theory from this perspective [correctness]—not by asking whether it fulfills the needs of the folk. But it is the latter criterion [...] on which sound public policy must be based." The same argument holds for technology design: Whether the folk models are correct or not, technology should be designed to work well with the folk models actually employed by users.

Examples from real people   Understanding folk models in the abstract is great. But to really understand how people think, it helps to see it in their own words. Therefore, the discussion below uses numerous quotations from a series of interviews with home computer users to concretely illustrate these mental models [481]. Everyone quoted here has been given a pseudonym (such as Nicole or Irving) for anonymity, but each name corresponds to a real person who is a nonexpert computer user with at least one computer in his or her home.

4.8.1.1 Common elements of all folk models

Folk models of home computer security threats can be divided into two broad categories: (i) models about viruses, spyware, adware, and other forms of malware, which everyone refers to under the umbrella term "virus"; and (ii) models about the attackers, referred to as "hackers," and the threat of "breaking in to" a computer. Everyone seemed to possess at least one model from each of the two categories. For example, the subject we refer to as Nicole believed that viruses were mischievous, and hackers are criminals who target big fish. These models are not necessarily mutually exclusive. For example, a few people talked about different types of hackers and described more than one folk model of hackers.

By listing and describing these folk models, we do not intend to imply that these models are incorrect or bad in any way. They are all certainly incomplete, and do not exactly correspond to the way malicious software or malicious computer users behave. What is important is not how accurate the model is, but how well it serves the needs of the home computer user in making security decisions.

In addition, there is no "correct" model that can serve as a comparison. Even security experts will disagree on the correct way to think about viruses or hackers. To show an extreme example outside the context of security, Medin et al. [348] conducted a study of expert fishermen in the Northwoods of Wisconsin. They looked at the mental models of both Native American fishermen and majority-culture fishermen. Despite both groups being experts, the two groups showed dramatic differences in the way fish were categorized and classified. Majority-culture fishermen grouped fish into standard taxonomic and goal-oriented groupings, while Native American fishermen grouped fish mostly by ecological niche. This illustrates how even experts can have dramatically different mental models of the same phenomenon, and any single expert's model is not necessarily correct. However, experts and novices do tend to have very different models; Asgharpour et al. [93] found strong differences between expert and novice computer users in their mental models of security.

Most people who were interviewed made a distinction between "viruses" and "hackers." These are two separate threats that can both cause problems. Some people believed that viruses are created by hackers, but they still usually saw them as distinct threats. For example, Irving tried to explain the distinction by saying "The hacker is an individual [who is] hacking, while the virus is a program infecting." After some thought, he clarified his idea of the difference a bit: "So it's a difference between something automatic and more personal." This description is characteristic of how many interviewees thought about the difference: Viruses are usually more programmatic and automatic, where hacking is more like manual labor, requiring the hacker to be sitting in front of a computer entering commands.

This distinction between hackers and viruses is not something that most of the respondents had thought about; it existed in their mental model but not at a conscious level. Upon prompting, Dana decided that "I guess if they hack into your system and get a virus on there, itÕs gonna be the same thing." She had never realized that they were distinct in her mind, but it made sense to her that they might be related. She then went on to ask the interviewer, if she got hacked, could she forward it on to other people?

This also illustrates another common feature of mental models. When exposed to new information, most people extrapolate and try to apply that information to slightly different settings. When Dana was prompted to think about the relationship between viruses and hackers, she decided that they were more similar than she had previously realized. Then she began to apply ideas from one model (viruses spreading) to the other model (can hackers also spread?) by extrapolating from her current models. This is a common technique in human learning and sensemaking [413]. Many details of these folk models were probably formed in this way.

4.8.2 Folk Models of Viruses and Other Malware

Almost everyone who was interviewed had heard of computer viruses and possessed some mental model of their effects and transmission. Most focused primarily on the effects of viruses and the possible methods of transmission. The term "virus" was used as a catch-all term for malicious software. Everyone seemed to recognize that viruses are computer programs. Many different types of malicious software were classified under this term: computer viruses, worms, trojans, adware, spyware, and keyloggers were all called "viruses."

Thanks to the term "virus," many people used some sort of medical terminology to describe the actions of malware. Getting malware on your computer means you have "caught" the virus, and your computer is "infected." People who had a Mac believed that Macs are "immune" to virus and hacking problems (but were usually worried anyway).

Overall, we found four distinct folk models of "viruses" through our interviews. These models differed in a number of ways. One of the major differences is how well specified and detailed the model was, and therefore how useful the model was for making security-related decisions. One model was very underspecified, labeling viruses as simply "bad." Interviewees with this model had trouble using it to make any kind of security-related decisions because the model did not contain enough information to provide guidance. Two other models (the *Mischief* and *Crime* models) were fairly well described, including how viruses are created and why, and what are the major effects of viruses. People with these models could use them to extrapolate many different situations and to make many security-related decisions on their computer. Table 4.10 summarizes the major differences between the four models.

Table 4.10 Summary of Interviewee's Folk Models About Viruses, Organized by Model Features

	Folk model			
	Bad Things	Buggy Software	Mischief	Support Crime
Creator	Unspecified	Bad people	Mischievous hackers	Criminals
Purpose of viruses	Unspecified	No purpose	Cause mischief; cause annoying problems	Gather information for identity theft
Effects of infection	General notion of bad things happening	Same effects as buggy software, but more extreme	Annoying problems with computers	No direct harm to computer; stolen information
Method of transmission	"Catch" viruses; miscellaneous methods of catching them	Must be manually downloaded and executed	Passive "catching" by visiting shady websites or opening shady email	Spread automatically, or installed by hackers

4.8.2.1 Virus model 1: viruses are generically "bad"

A few people had an underdeveloped model of viruses. These people knew that viruses cause problems, but could not really describe what problems. They just knew that they were generically "bad" to get and should be avoided.

People with this model knew of a number of different ways that viruses are transmitted. These transmission methods were things that the person had heard about somewhere, but the person did not attempt to understand or organize them into a more coherent model. Zoe believed that viruses can come from strange emails or from "searching random things" on the Internet. She said she had heard that blocking popups helps with viruses too, and seemed to believe that without questioning. Peggy had heard that viruses can come from "blinky ads like you've won a million bucks."

People with this model were uniformly unconcerned with getting viruses: "I guess just my lack of really doing much on the Internet makes me feel like I'm safer." (Zoe) A couple of people with this model used Macintosh computers, which they believed to be "immune" to computer viruses. Since they are immune, it seems that they had not bothered to form a more complete model of viruses.

Because these users were not concerned with viruses, they did not take any precautions against being infected. These users believed that their current behavior does not really make them vulnerable, so they do not need to make any extra effort. These respondents seemed to recognize that antivirus software might help, but were rarely concerned enough to purchase or install it.

4.8.2.2 Virus model 2: viruses are buggy software

One group of people saw computer viruses as an exceptionally bug-ridden form of regular computer software. In many ways, these people believed that viruses behave much like most of the other software that home computer users experience. But to be a virus, it had to be "bad" in some additional way. Primarily, viruses are "bad" in that they are poorly written software. They lead to a multitude of bugs and other errors in the computer. They bring out bugs in other pieces of software. They tend to have more bugs, and worse bugs, than most other pieces of software. But all the effects they cause are the same types of effects you get from buggy software: viruses can cause computers to crash or to "boot me out" (Erica) of applications are running; viruses can accidentally delete or "wipe out" information (Christine and Erica); they can erase important system files. In general, the computer just "does not function properly" (Erica) when it has a virus.

Just like normal software, viruses must be intentionally placed on the computer and executed. Viruses do not just *appear* on a computer. Rather than "catching" a virus, computers are actively infected, though often this infection is accidental. Some viruses come in the form of email attachments. But they are not a threat unless you actually "click" on the attachment to run it. If you are careful about what you click on, then you would not get the virus. Another example is that viruses can be downloaded from websites, much like many other applications. Erica believed that sometimes downloading games can end up causing you to download a virus. But still, intentional downloading and execution are necessary to be infected with a virus, much the same way that intentional downloading and execution are necessary to run programs from the Internet.

Interviewees with this model did not feel that they needed to exert much effort to protect themselves from viruses. Mostly, these users tried not to download and execute programs that they did not trust. Sarah intentionally "limited herself" by not downloading any programs from the Internet, so she did not get a virus. Since viruses must be actively executed, antivirus programs are not important. As long as no one downloads and runs programs from the Internet, no virus can get onto the computer. Therefore, antivirus programs that detect and fix viruses are not needed. However, two respondents with this model ran antivirus software just in case a virus was accidentally put on the computer.

Overall, this is a somewhat underdeveloped folk model of viruses. People who possess this model had never really thought about how viruses are created or why. When asked, they talked about how they had not thought about it, and then made guesses about how "bad people" might be the ones who create them. These interviewees had not put too much thought into their understanding of how viruses work; all the effects they discussed were either effects they had personally seen or more extreme versions of bugs they saw in other software. Christine said, "I guess I would know [if I had a virus], wouldn't I?" presuming that any effects a virus might have would be evident in the behavior of the computer. No connection was made between hackers and viruses; they are distinct and separate entities in the interviewees' minds.

4.8.2.3   Virus model 3: viruses cause mischief

A good number of people believed that viruses are pieces of software that are intentionally annoying. Someone created the virus for the purpose of annoying computer users and causing mischief. Viruses sometimes have effects that are often much like extreme versions of annoying bugs: crashing your computer, deleting important files, your computer would not boot, and so on. Often the effects of viruses are intentionally annoying such as displaying a skull and crossbones upon boot (Bob), displaying advertising popups (Floyd), or downloading lots of pornography (Dana).

While these people believed that viruses are created to be annoying, they rarely had a well-developed idea of who created them. They did not naturally mention a creator of the viruses, just a reason why they are created. When pushed, these interviewees talked about how viruses are probably created by "hackers" who fit the *Graffiti* hacker model below. But the identity of the creator does not play much of a role in making security decisions with this model.

People with this model always believed that viruses can be "caught" by actively clicking on them and executing them. However, most also believed that viruses can be "caught" by simply visiting the wrong webpages. Infection here is very passive and can come from just visiting the webpage. These webpages are often considered to be part of the "bad" part of the Internet. Much like graffiti appears in the "bad" parts of cities, mischievous viruses are most prevalent on the bad parts of the Internet.

Although most believed that care in clicking on attachments or performing downloads is important, these interviewees also tried to be careful about where they go on the Internet. One respondent (Floyd) tried to explain why: Cookies are automatically put on your computer by websites, and therefore, viruses being automatically put on your computer could be related to this.

These "bad" parts of the Internet where you can easily contract viruses are frequently described as morally ambiguous webpages. Pornography is always considered shady, but some people also included entertainment websites where you can play games and the websites that have been on the news like "MySpaceBook" (Gina). Some respondents believed that a "secured" website would not lead to a virus, but Gail acknowledged that at some sites "maybe the protection wasn't working at those sites and they went bad." (Note the passive tense; again, she had not thought about how sites go bad or who causes them to go bad. She was just concerned with the outcome.)

4.8.2.4 *Virus model 4: viruses support crime*

Finally, some people believed that viruses are created to support criminal activities. Almost uniformly, these people believed that identity theft is the end goal of the criminals who create these viruses, and the viruses assist them by stealing personal and financial information from individual computers. For example, people with this model worried that viruses are looking for credit card numbers, bank account information, or other financial information stored on their computer.

Since the main purpose of these viruses is to collect information, interviewees who had this model believed that viruses often remain undetected on computers. These viruses do not explicitly cause harm to the computer, and they do not cause bugs, crashes, or other problems. All they do is send information to criminals. Therefore, it is important to run an antivirus program on a regular basis because it is possible to have a virus on your computer without knowing it. Since viruses do not harm your computer, backups are not necessary.

People with this model believed that there are many different ways for these viruses to spread. Some viruses spread through downloads and attachments. Other viruses can spread "automatically," without requiring any actions by the user of the computer. Also, some people believed that hackers will install this type of virus onto the computer when they break in. Given this wide variety of transmission methods and the serious nature of identity theft, people with this model took many steps to try to stop these viruses. These users would work to keep their antivirus up-to-date, purchasing new versions on a regular basis. Often, they would notice when the antivirus would conduct a scan of their computer and check the results. Valerie even turned her computer off when it was not in use to avoid potential problems with viruses.

4.8.2.5 *Multiple types of viruses*

Some people believed that there are multiple types of viruses on the Internet. These interviewees frequently believed that some viruses are mischievous and cause annoying problems, while other viruses support crime and are difficult to detect. People that talked about more than one type of virus usually included both the previous virus folk models: the mischievous viruses and the criminal viruses. One respondent, Jack, also talked about a third type of virus that was created by antivirus companies, but he apparently felt that this was a conspiracy theory and, consequently, did not take that suggestion very seriously.

When people have multiple mental models, they generally take all the precautions that either model would predict. For example, they would make regular backups in case they caught a mischievous virus that damaged their computer, but they would also regularly run their antivirus program to detect the criminal viruses that do not have noticeable effects. This fact suggests that information sharing between users may be beneficial; when users believe in multiple types of viruses, they take appropriate steps to protect against all types.

4.8.3 Folk Models of Hackers and Break-Ins

The second major category of folk models describe the attackers or the people who cause Internet security problems. These attackers are always given the name "hackers," and everyone seemed to have some concept of who these people are and what they do. The term "hacker" is applied to describe anyone who does bad things on the Internet, no matter who they are or how they work.

People who were interviewed generally described the main threat that hackers pose as "breaking in" to computers. Different people gave different reasons for why a hacker would want to "break in" to a computer, and to which computers they would target for their break-ins, but usually agreed on the terminology for this basic action. "Breaking in to a computer" meant (to most people) that the hacker could then use the computer as if they were sitting in front of it, and could cause a number of different things to happen to the computer. Many people did not understand how this works, but still believed it is possible.

Below are described four distinct folk models of hackers. These models differed mainly in who the interviewees believed these hackers were, what they believed motivated these people, and how they chose which computers to break into. Table 4.11 summarizes the four folk models of hackers.

Table 4.11 Summary of Interviewee's Folk Models About Hackers, Organized by Model Features

	Folk model			
	Graffiti	Burglar	Big fish	Contractor
Identity of hacker(s)	Young technical geek	Some criminal	Professional criminal hackers	Young technical geek
Level of organization	Solo, or to impress friends	Unspecified	Part of a criminal organization	Solo, but a contractor for criminals
Reason for break-ins	Cause mischief	Look for financial and personal information	Look for financial and personal information	Look for financial and personal information
Effects of break-ins	Lots of computer problems; requires reinstall	Possible harm to computer; exposure of personal information	No harm to computer; exposure of personal information	Exposure of personal information
Target(s)	Anyone; does not matter	Opportunistic; could be me	Not me; only looking for rich or important people	Not me; looking for large databases of info
Am I a target?	Possibly	Possibly	No	No

4.8.3.1   Hacker model 1: hackers are digital graffiti artists

Some people believed that "hackers" are technically skilled people who cause a technological version of mischief. Often these hackers were envisioned as "college-age computer types" (Kenneth). They saw hacking computers as sort of digital graffiti; hackers break into computers and intentionally cause problems so that they can show off to their friends. Victim computers are a canvas for their art.

When people with this model talked about hackers, they usually focused on two features: strong technical skills and the lack of proper moral restraint. Strong technical skills provided the motivation; hackers do it "for sheer sport" (Lorna) or to demonstrate technical prowess (Hayley). Some people envisioned a competition between hackers, where more sophisticated viruses or hacks "prove you're a better hacker" (Kenneth); others saw creating viruses and hacking as part of "learning about the Internet" (Jack). Lack of moral restraint is what makes them different from others with technical skills; hackers were sometimes described as maladjusted individuals who "want to hurt others for no reason" (Dana). These hackers were often described as "miserable" people. Interviewees felt that hackers do what they do for no good reason, or at least for no reason they can understand. Hackers were believed to be lone individuals; although they may have hacker friends, they are not part of any organization.

People with this model often focused on the identity of the hacker. This identity—a young computer geek with poor morals—was much more developed in their mind than the resulting behavior of the hacker. As such, people with this model usually gave clear examples of who hackers are, but seemed less confident in information about the resulting break-ins that happen.

These hackers like to break stuff on the computer to create havoc. They intentionally upload viruses to computers to cause mayhem. Many interviewees believed that hackers intentionally cause computers harm; for example, Dana believed that hackers will "fry your hard drive." Hackers might install software to let them control your computer; Jack talked about how a hacker would use his instant messenger to send strange messages to his friends.

These mischievous hackers were seen as not targeting specific individuals, but rather choosing random strangers to target. This is much like graffiti; the hackers need a canvas and choose whatever computer they happen to come upon. Because of this, the respondents felt like they might become a victim of this type of hacking at any time.

Often, victims like this felt there was not much they could to do protect themselves from this type of hacking. This was because they did not understand how hackers were able to break into computers, so they did not know what could be done to stop it. This would lead to a feeling of futility; "if they are going to get in, they're going to get in" (Hayley).

4.8.3.2   Hacker model 2: hackers are opportunistic burglars

Another set of people believed that hackers are criminals that happen to use computers to commit their crimes. Other than the use of the computer, they share a lot in common with other professional criminals: they are motivated by financial gain, and they can do what they do because they lack common morals. They "break into" computers to look for information much like a burglar will break into houses to look for valuables. The most salient part of this folk model is the behavior of the hacker; interviewees talked in detail about what the hackers were looking for, but spoke very little about the identity of the hacker.

Almost exclusively, the criminal activity they described was some form of identity theft. For example, some interviewees believed that if a hacker obtained their credit card number, then that hacker can make fraudulent charges with it. But others were not always sure what kind of information the hacker was specifically looking for; they just described it as information the hacker could use to make money. Ivan talked about how hackers would look around the computer much like a thief might rummage around in an attic, looking for something useful. Erica used a different metaphor, saying that hackers would "take a digital photo of everything on my computer" and look in it for useful identity information. Usually, people envisioned the hacker himself using this financial information (as opposed to selling the information to others).

Since hackers target information, people with this folk model believed that computers are not harmed by the break-ins. Hackers look for information, but do not harm the computer. They simply rummage around, "take a digital photo" (Erica), possibly install monitoring software, and leave. The computer continues to work as it did before. The main concern of interviewees was how the hacker might use the information that they steal.

These hackers were believed to choose victims opportunistically; much like a mugger chooses his victims, these hackers will break into any computers they run across to look for valuable information. Or, more accurately, people who believed this folk model do not have a good model of how hackers choose, and believed that there is a decent chance that they will be a victim someday. Gail talked about how hackers are opportunistic, saying "next time I go to their site they'll nab me." Hayley believed that they just choose computers to attack without knowing much about who owns them.

Respondents with this belief were willing to take steps to protect themselves from hackers to avoid becoming a victim. Gail tried to avoid going to websites she was not familiar with to prevent hackers from discovering her. Jack was careful to always sign out accounts and websites when he was finished. Hayley shut off her computer when she was not using it so that hackers cannot break into it.

4.8.3.3   Hacker model 3: hackers are criminals who target big fish

Another group of interviewees had a conceptually similar model. This group also believed that hackers are Internet criminals who are looking for information to conduct identity theft. However, this group thought more about how these hackers can best accomplish this goal, and have come to some different conclusions. These respondents believed in "massive hacker groups" (Hayley) and other forms of organization and coordination among criminal hackers.

Most tellingly, this group believed that hackers only target the "big fish." Hackers primarily break into computers of important and rich people in order to maximize their gains. Almost every person who held this model believed that he or she is not likely to be a victim because he or she is not a big enough fish. They believe that hackers are unlikely to ever target them, and therefore they were safe from hacking. Irving believed that "I'm small potatoes and no one is going to bother me." Interviewees with this model often talked about how other people are more likely targets: "Maybe if I had a lot of money" (Floyd) or "if I were a bank executive" (Erica).

For these people, protecting against hackers was not a high priority. Mostly they found reasons to trust existing security precautions rather than taking extra steps to protect themselves. For example, Irving talked about how he trusts his preinstalled firewall program to protect him. Both Irving and Floyd trusted their passwords to protect them. Their actions indicated that they believed in the speed bump theory: by making it slightly hard for hackers using standard security technologies, hackers will decide it is not worthwhile to target them.

4.8.3.4   Hacker model 4: hackers are contractors who support criminals

Finally, there is a sort of hybrid model of hackers. In this view, hackers are very similar to the mischievous graffiti hackers from above: They are college-age, technically skilled individuals. However, their motivations are more intentional and criminal. These hackers are out to steal personal and financial information from people.

Interviewees with this model showed evidence of more effort in thinking through their mental model and integrating the various sources of information they had. This model can be seen as a hybrid of the mischievous graffiti hacker model and the criminal hacker model, integrated into a coherent form by combining the most salient part of the mischievous model (the identity of the hacker) and the most salient part of the criminal model (the criminal activities). Also, everyone who had this model expressed a concern about how hacking works. Kenneth stated that he does not understand how someone can break into a computer without sitting in front of it. Lorna wondered how you can start a program running; she believed you have to be in front of the computer to do that. This indicates that these people are actively trying to integrate the information they have about hackers into a coherent model of hacker behavior.

Since these hackers are first and foremost young technical people, interviewees with this folk model believed that these hackers are not likely to be identity thieves. They believed that the hackers are more likely to sell this identity information for others to use. Since the hackers just want to sell information, the reasoning goes: they are more likely to target large databases of identity information such as banks or retailers like Amazon.com.

People with this model believed that hackers were not really their problem. Since these hackers tended to target larger institutions like banks or e-commerce websites, people's own personal computers are not in danger. Therefore, no effort is needed to secure their personal computers.

However, all respondents with this model expressed a strong concern for who they do business with online. These people only make purchases or provide personal information to institutions they trusted to get the security right and figure out how to be protected against hackers. These users are highly sensitive to third parties possessing their data.

4.8.3.5 *Multiple types of hackers*

Some interviewees understood that there are multiple types of hackers. Most of the time, these people believed that some hackers are the mischievous graffiti hackers and that other hackers are criminal hackers (using either the burglar or big fish model, but not both). People with this belief then tried to make the effort to protect themselves from both types of hacker threats as necessary.

Some amount of cognitive dissonance occurred when interviewees had heard about both mischievous hackers and criminal hackers. There are two ways that respondents resolved this: The simplest way was to believe that some hackers are mischievous and other hackers are criminals and, consequently, keep the models separate. A more complicated way was to try to integrate the two models into one coherent belief about hackers. The "contractor" model of hackers is the result of this integration of the two types of hackers.

4.8.4 Following Security Advice

Computer security experts have devoted much time and effort to simplifying security advice so that home computer users can easily understand and follow it. There are many websites and other online resources available to nonspecialist users, including support forums where home computer users can ask security-related questions. However, many home computer users still do not follow available advice.

There is a disagreement among security experts as to why computer security advice directed at "regular" users is not followed. Some experts believe that home computer users do not understand the security advice, and therefore more education is needed. Others believe that these users are simply incapable of consistently making good security decisions [162,450].

However, none of these explanations account for the fact that certain types of security advice tend to be followed by home computer users, while other advice is not. The folk models described above begin to provide an explanation of what expert advice users choose to follow, and what advice is ignored. By better understanding why people choose to ignore certain pieces of advice, we can better craft advice and technologies to have greater security.

Table 4.12 lists 12 common pieces of security advice for home computer users. This advice was collected from the Microsoft Security at Home website,[5], the CERT Home Computer Security website,[6] and the US-CERT Cyber-Security Tips website,[7] and much of this advice is duplicated across websites. The content of the table represents the distilled wisdom of many computer security experts. It then summarizes, for each folk model, whether that advice is "important to follow," "helpful but not essential," or "not necessary to follow." The table illustrates how home computer users apply their folk models to determine for themselves whether to follow a given piece of advice.

The most notable rows in the table are labeled "xx," indicating when users believe that a piece of security advice is not necessary to follow. In addition, rows labeled "??" denote instances where users having a given folk model believe that advice will help with security, but do not see the advice as so important that it must always be followed. Often, users will decide that following advice labeled with "??" is too costly in terms of effort or money, and ignore it. Finally, advice labeled "!!" is extremely important, and users feel that it should never be ignored, even if following it is inconvenient, costly, or difficult.

4.8.4.1 Antivirus use

Security advice for home computer users often includes the recommendation to run antivirus software and make sure it is updated regularly (rows 1–3 in Table 4.12). People mostly use their folk models of viruses to make decisions about antivirus use, for obvious reasons. A belief that viruses are just buggy software is likely to lead to the idea that it is possible to keep viruses off a home computer by tightly controlling what software is installed on it. This tight control combined with the belief that viruses need to be executed manually to infect a computer (and if a virus is never executed, a computer cannot be infected) means antivirus is unnecessary.

Users with the underdeveloped folk model of viruses, who refer to viruses as generically "bad," also do not use antivirus software. These people understand that viruses are harmful and that antivirus software can stop them. However, they have never really thought about specific harms a virus might cause to them. Lacking an understanding of the threats and potential harm, they generally find it unnecessary to make an effort to follow the best practices around antivirus software.

> In contrast to people with other models, the burglar folk model leads to a belief that antivirus software can help detect and stop hackers. Users with the burglar model of hackers believe that regular antivirus scans can be important because these burglar hackers will sometimes install viruses to collect personal information.

---

[5]http://www.microsoft.com/protect/default.mspx., retrieved July 5, 2009

[6]http://www.cert.org/homeusers/HomeComputerSecurity/ retrieved July 5, 2009.

[7]http://www.us-cert.gov/cas/tips/, retrieved July 5, 2009.

Table 4.12 Summary of Expert Security Advice

	Virus models					Hacker models		
	Viruses are bad	Buggy software	Mischief	Support crime	Graffiti	Burglar	Big fish	Contractor
1. Use antivirus software	??	xx	??	!!		!!	xx	xx
2. Keep antivirus updated	xx	xx	??	!!				xx
3. Regularly scan computer with antivirus	xx	xx	??	!!				xx
4. Use security software (firewall, etc.)	xx	??	??		??	??	??	xx
5. Do not click on attachments	!!	!!	!!	!!	!!	!!		
6. Be careful downloading from websites	??	!!	??	!!	??	??	xx	xx
7. Be careful which websites you visit		xx	!!	??	!!	!!	??	!!
8. Disable scripting in web and email								xx
9. Use good passwords					??		??	xx
10. Make regular backups		??	!!	xx	!!	xx	xx	xx
11. Keep patches up-to-date		??	xx	!!	!!	!!	xx	xx
12. Turn off computer when not in use	xx	xx	xx	!!	??	!!	xx	xx

Rows contain common security advice. Each column represents a different folk model. Each folk model responds to this advice differently:

!!	Important	It is very important to follow this advice
??	Maybe	Following this advice might help, but it is not all that important to do
xx	Not necessary	It is not necessary to follow this advice
	Not applicable	This model does not have anything to say about this advice, or there are insufficient data from the interviews to determine an opinion

4.8.4.2   Other security software

There are other types of security software in addition to antivirus, and home computer users are commonly advised to do things like run a firewall or other more comprehensive Internet security software suites (row 4 in Table 4.12). Most folk models incorporate an unsophisticated concept of what security software other than antivirus does: it provides general "security." Because the purpose of software such as firewalls is vague and unspecified by these models, people do not treat security software as an important part of protecting their computers. People who hold the graffiti hacker or burglar hacker models believe that this software must help with hackers somehow, even though they do not know how, and would suggest installing it. But since they do not understand how it works, they do not consider it of vital importance.

Another interesting belief about this software comes from the big fish model of hackers. People with this model believe that hackers only go after big fish, and that security software can serve as a speed bump that discourages hackers from casually breaking into their computer, making them a more unattractive target. In this way, it is not necessary for the model to be correct or for people to understand how security software protects, for value to be placed upon using it.

4.8.4.3   Email security

Nearly all folk models incorporate the idea that bad things can happen if you open email attachments from people you do not recognize (row 5 in Table 4.12). All the virus models support the belief that viruses can be transmitted through email attachments, and therefore not clicking on unknown attachments can help prevent viruses. People with the big fish and contractor folk models do not believe that they would be targeted, and therefore are not worried about receiving bad email from hackers.

4.8.4.4   Web browsing

Browsing the web involves the potential for encountering many security risks, and much advice is provided to home computer users about how to avoid situations where one's computer might be compromised (rows 6–9 in Table 4.12). Overall, most folk models are consistent with this expert advice; however, the models also do not incorporate a clear cause-and-effect relationship between the advice and better security. In particular, the idea of a "web script" is not explicitly part of any folk model, and therefore is largely ignored because it is not understood.

Because downloads are strongly associated with viruses in most of the virus-related folk models, it naturally follows that the advice about careful downloading would make sense in the context of these models. However, only users with well-developed models of viruses (the *Mischief* and *Support Crime* models) believe that viruses can be "caught" simply by browsing webpages. People who believe that viruses are buggy software do not see browsing as dangerous because they are not actively clicking on anything to run it.

In addition, all the folk models are consistent with the idea that passwords are important, but like the advice about browsing the web, the association between passwords and better security is only vaguely defined in several of the models. For example, people with the *graffiti* hacker model sometimes put extra effort into their passwords so that mischievous hackers cannot mess up their accounts. And people who believe that hackers only target big fish think that passwords could be an effective speed bump to prevent hackers from casually targeting them. But most folk models do not support a belief that it is important to make good, strong passwords.

Finally, the contractor folk model, in which hackers are believed to work for criminals, supports the idea that people who are not logically the target for criminals are therefore safe from hackers. Web browsing is relevant to security in this view of the world in that one's choices about websites to do business with might make one more or less of a target. For example, a belief that hackers target web businesses with lots of personal or financial information is consistent with advice to be careful about which websites you visit, because it is important to only do business with websites that are trusted to be secure.

4.8.4.5 Computer maintenance

Finally, security experts often give advice to home computer users concerning computer maintenance (rows 10–12 in Table 4.12). Different folk models vary dramatically in terms of how consistent they are with this type of computer security advice. For example, mischievous viruses and graffiti hackers can cause data loss, so users with these models feel that backups are very important. But, users who believe in more criminal viruses and hackers do not feel that backups are necessary; hackers and viruses steal information but do not delete it.

Keeping patches up-to-date is a very important behavior for maintaining a secure computer; however, most of these folk models are not directly consistent with this advice. Most people experience patches only through the automatic updates feature in their operating system or applications, and therefore cannot form an idea of what these patches are for. The hacker folk models are more consistent with the advice about patching: If a person feels that he or she would be a target of hackers, then he or she also feels that patching was an import tool to stop hackers. Also, people who believe that viruses are buggy software folk model associate viruses with the appearance of more bugs in other software on the computer; therefore, patching the other software makes it more difficult for viruses to cause problems.

4.8.5 Lessons Learned

Across all the models, everyone worries about how hackers and viruses would affect them. People primarily see the danger to themselves, and do not really consider how malicious people can use them to attack third parties. This self-focus leads people to take precautions only when they feel they are directly at risk. Clever attackers have exploited this feature to form large-scale botnets, and as long as people continue to focus solely on personal risk, botnets will continue to be a problem.

These folk models also illustrate one major problem with many security education efforts: They do not adequately explain the threats that home computer users face; rather, they focus on practical, actionable advice. But without an *understanding of threats*, home computer users intentionally choose to ignore advice that they do not believe will help them. Security education efforts should focus not only on recommending what actions to take but also on why these actions are necessary.

Finally, following the advice of Kempton [297], security experts should not evaluate these folk models on the basis of correctness, but rather on how well they meet the needs of the folk that possess them. Likewise, when designing new security technologies, we should not attempt to force users into a more correct mental model; rather, we should design technologies that encourage users with limited folk models to be more secure. Effective security technologies not only need to protect the user from attacks but also expose potential threats to the user in a way the user understands, so that he or she is motivated to use the technology appropriately.

4.9 DETECTING AND DEFEATING INTERCEPTION ATTACKS AGAINST SSL

Christopher Soghoian and Sid Stamm

Abstract. The notion of *compelled certificate creation attack*, in which government agencies may compel a certificate authority to issue false SSL certificates, can be used by intelligence agencies to covertly intercept and hijack individuals' secure web-based communications. Although there is not direct documented occurrences of this type of active surveillance taking place in the wild, there are products already on the market that are geared and marketed toward this kind of use—suggesting such attacks may eventually occur, if they are not already occurring. To help mitigate against these attacks, a lightweight browser add-on called CertLock can be used to detect and thwart such attacks.

4.9.1 Introduction

Cryptography is typically bypassed, not penetrated.

—Adi Shamir [434]

Just because encryption is involved, that doesn't give you a talisman against a prosecutor. They can compel a service provider to cooperate.

—Phil Zimmerman [438]

Consider a hypothetical situation where an American executive is in France for a series of trade negotiations. After a day of meetings, she logs in to her corporate web mail account using her company-provided laptop and the hotel wireless network. Relying on the training she received from her company's IT department, she ensures to look for the SSL encryption lock icon in her web browser, and only after determining that the connection is secure does she enter her login credentials and then begin to upload materials to be shared with her colleagues. However, unknown to the executive, the French government has engaged in a sophisticated man-in-the-middle attack, and is able to covertly intercept the executive's SSL encrypted connections. Agents from the state security apparatus leak details of her communications to the French company with whom she is negotiating, who use the information to gain an upper hand in the negotiations. Although this scenario is fictitious, the vulnerability is not.

The security and confidentiality of millions of Internet transactions per day depend upon the SSL/TLS protocol. At the core of this system are a number of *Certificate Authorities* (CAs), each of which is responsible for verifying the identity of the entities to whom they grant SSL certificates. It is because of the confidentiality and authenticity provided by the CA-based *public key infrastructure* (PKI) that users around the world can bank online, engage in electronic commerce, and communicate with their friends and loved ones about the most sensitive of subjects without having to worry about malicious third parties intercepting and deciphering their communications.

Although not completely obvious, the CAs are all trusted equally in the SSL public key infrastructure, a problem amplified by the fact that the major web browsers trust hundreds of different firms to issue certificates for any site. Each of these firms can be compelled by their national government to issue a certificate for any particular website that all web browsers will trust without warning. Thus, users around the world are put in a position where their browser entrusts their private data, indirectly, to a large number of governments (both foreign and domestic) whom these individuals may not ordinarily trust.

The *compelled certificate creation attack* enables government agencies to compel (via a court order or some other legal process) a CA to issue false certificates that are then used by law enforcement and intelligence agencies to covertly intercept and hijack individuals' secure communications. The interception can be performed in many ways, including network-controlled man-in-the-middle attacks or by deploying malware onto target computers or network devices.

In 2010, there were already surveillance products advertised in a way that suggests that this attack is more than a theoretical concern, but is likely in active use; at least one private company is supplying government customers with specialized covert network appliances specifically designed to intercept SSL communications using deceptively created certificates.

In order to protect users from these powerful government adversaries, we introduce a lightweight defensive browser add-on that detects and thwarts such attacks. Finally, reductive analysis of governments' legal capabilities is used to perform an adversarial threat model analysis of the attack and the proposed defensive technology.

In Section 4.9.2, a brief introduction to CAs, web browsers, and the man-in-the-middle attacks against them is provided. In Section 4.9.3, the presence of government-controlled CAs in the browsers is discussed. In Section 4.9.4, the compelled certificate creation attack is introduced, and in Section 4.9.5, evidence is presented that suggests it is being used. In Section 4.9.6, a browser-based add-on to mitigate this attack is described, and in Section 4.9.7, its effectiveness is analyzed via a threat model-based analysis. Finally, related work is discussed in Section 4.9.8 and the whole lot is summarized at the end.

4.9.2 Certificate Authorities and the Browser Vendors

This section provides a brief overview of the roles played by the Certificate Authorities in the public key infrastructure, the browser vendors in picking the certificate authorities that they include in the browsers, and existing man-in-the-middle-attack techniques that circumvent SSL-based security.

4.9.2.1 Certificate Authorities

[Browser vendors] and users must be careful when deciding which certificates and certificate authorities are acceptable; a dishonest certificate authority can do tremendous damage.

—RFC 2246, The TLS Protocol 1.0 [171]

CAs play a vital role in the SSL *public key infrastructure*. Each CA's main responsibility is to verify the identity of the entity to which it issues a certificate. The level of verification performed by the CA depends upon the type of certificate purchased. A domain registration certificate can be obtained for less than $15, and will typically only require that the requester be able to reply to an email sent to the administrative address listed in the WHOIS database. Extended Validation (EV) certificates require a greater degree of verification. When a user visits https://www.bankofamerica.com, her browser will inform her that the bank's certificate is valid, was issued by VeriSign, and that the website is run by Bank of America. It is because of the authenticity and confidentiality guaranteed by SSL that the user can continue with her transaction without having to worry that she is being phished by cyber criminals (Figure 4.50).

Figure 4.50   Various browsers' SSL UI when visiting an EV HTTPS site (Bank of America) and a site with a standard HTTPS certificate (Chase). Country information (US—shown in the EV UI) presented by the browsers refers to the owner of the certificate, not the location of the Certificate Authority.

CAs generally fall into one of three categories: Those trusted by the browsers ("root CAs"), those trusted by one of the root CAs ("intermediate CAs" or "subordinate CAs"), and those neither trusted by the browsers nor any intermediate CA ("untrusted CAs"). Furthermore, intermediate CAs do not necessarily have to be directly verified by a root CA—but can be verified by another intermediate CA, as long as the *chain of trust* eventually ends with a root CA.

From the end users' perspective, root CAs and intermediate CAs are functionally equivalent. A website that presents a certificate signed by either form of CA will cause the users' browser to display a lock icon and to change the color of the location bar. Although certificates verified by an untrusted CA and those self-signed by the website owner will result in the display of a security warning, which for many nontechnical users can be scary [373], confusing, and difficult to bypass in order to continue navigating the site [460].

As the CA system was originally designed and is currently implemented, all root CAs are equally trusted by the browsers. That is, each of the 264 root CAs trusted by Microsoft, the 166 root CAs trusted by Apple, and the 144 root CAs trusted by Firefox is capable of issuing certificates for any website, in any country or top-level domain [186]. For example, even though Bank of America obtained its current SSL certificate from VeriSign, there is no technical reason why another CA cannot issue another certificate for the same site to someone else. Should a malicious third party somehow obtain a certificate for Bank of America's site and then trick a user into visiting their fake web server (e.g., by using DNS or ARP spoofing), there is no practical, easy way for the user to determine that something bad has happened, as the browser interface will signal that a valid SSL session has been established. Even if the user examines the more complex security information listed in the browser's SSL interface, she will still lack the information necessary to make an informed trust decision. Since other CAs are equally valid certificate authorities and probably issue many other valid certificates, there is no way for the user to determine that any one particular certificate was improperly issued to a malicious third party.

Of course, a second CA is extremely unlikely to knowingly provide such an illegitimately issued certificate to a malicious third party. Doing so would almost certainly lead to significant damage to its reputation, a number of lawsuits, as well as (in theory) the ultimate threat of having its trusted status revoked by the major web browsers. Therefore, it is in each CAs' self-interest to ensure that malicious parties are not able to obtain a certificate for a site not under their own control.

It is important to note that there are no technical restrictions in place that prohibit a CA from issuing a certificate to a malicious third party. Thus, both the integrity of the CA-based public key infrastructure and the security users' communications depend upon hundreds of CAs around the world choosing to do the right thing. Unfortunately, as will soon be clear, any one of these CAs can become the weakest link in the chain.

4.9.2.2 Man-in-the-middle

Any website secured using TLS can be impersonated using a rogue certificate issued by a rogue CA. This is irrespective of which CA issued the website's true certificate and of any property of that certificate.

—Marc Stevens et al. [454].

Although an exhaustive explanation of man-in-the-middle attacks against SSL is beyond the scope of this text, it is important to at least provide a brief introduction to the subject. Over the past few years, the SSL protocol has been subject to a series of successful attacks by security researchers, some exploiting flaws in deployed systems, while others making use of social engineering and other forms of deception [290,338,401,419,447].

It is because SSL protected web connections flow over a number of other insecure protocols that it is possible for attackers to intercept and hijack a connection to a SSL protected server (these are known as *man-in-the-middle-attacks*). It is only once the browser has received and verified a site's SSL certificate that the user can be sure that her connection is safe.

However, this step alone is often not enough to protect users. Sites that supply self-signed certificates or that exploit unpatched vulnerabilities in the certificate handling code in the browsers can still trigger the display of the SSL lock icon, yet without providing the user with the associated security protections that they would normally expect.

Security researcher Moxie Marlinspike has repeatedly attacked the SSL-based chain of trust, revealing exploits that leverage both browser design flaws and social engineering attacks against end users. His *sslsniff* [339] and *sslstrip* [340] tools automate the task of performing a man-in-the-middle attacks, and when supplied with a valid SSL certificate (obtained, for example, via a rogue CA), can be used to intercept users' communications without triggering any browser warnings.

4.9.3   Big Brother in the Browser

Microsoft, Apple, and Mozilla all include a number of national government CA certificates in their respective CA databases [53]. These government CAs, like all other root CAs included by the browsers, must satisfy the requirements detailed in each browser vendor's CA policies, and are included for legitimate reasons: Many governments embed cryptographic public keys in their national ID cards, or do not wish to outsource their own internal certificate issuing responsibilities to private companies.

Although it may be quite useful for Estonian users of Internet Explorer to trust their government's CA by default (thus enabling them to easily engage in secure online tasks that leverage their own national ID card), the average resident of Lebanon or Peru has far less to gain by trusting the Estonian government with the blanket power to issue SSL certificates for any website. Thus, users around the world are put in a position where their browser entrusts their private data, indirectly, to a number of foreign governments whom these individuals may not ordinarily trust.

As an illustrative and *hypothetical* example of what is currently possible, consider the Korean Information Security Agency who is able to create a valid SSL certificate for the Industrial and Commercial Bank of China. However, the legitimate certificate whose actual certificate is issued by VeriSign, United States), that can hypothetically be used to perform an effective man-in-the-middle attack against users of Internet Explorer.

While this might at first seem like an extremely powerful attack, there are several reasons why governments are unlikely to use their own CAs to perform man-in-the-middle attacks.

First, while *some* governments have successfully petitioned the browser vendors to include their CA certificates, not all governments have done so. Thus, for example, the governments of Singapore, the United Kingdom, and Israel (among many others) do not have state-run CAs that are included by any of the major browsers. These governments are therefore unable to create their own fake certificates for use in intelligence and other law enforcement investigations where snooping on a SSL session might be useful.

Second, due to the fact that the SSL chain of trust is *nonrepudiable*, any government using its own CA to issue fake certificates in order to try and spy on someone else's communications will leave behind absolute proof of its involvement. That is, if the Spanish government opts to issue a fake certificate for Google Mail, and the surveillance is somehow discovered, anyone with a copy of the fake certificate and a web browser can independently trace the operation back to the Spanish government.

4.9.4   Compelled Assistance

Many governments routinely compel companies to assist them with surveillance. Telecommunications carriers and Internet service providers are frequently required to violate their customers' privacy—providing the government with email communications, telephone calls, search engine records, financial transactions, and geolocation information.

In the United States, the legal statutes defining the range of entities that can be compelled to assist in electronic surveillance by law enforcement and foreign intelligence investigators are remarkably broad [444]. Examples of compelled assistance using these statutes include a secure email provider that was required to place a covert back door in its product in order to steal users' encryption keys [438] and a consumer electronics company that was forced to remotely enable the microphones in a suspect's auto-mobile dashboard GPS navigation unit in order to covertly record their conversations [345].

Outside the United States, and other democratic countries, specific statutory authority may be even less important. The Chinese government, for example, has repeatedly compelled the assistance of telecommunications and technology companies in assisting it with its surveillance efforts [265,337].

Just as phone companies and email providers can be forced to assist governments in their surveillance efforts, so too can SSL certificate authorities. The *compelled certificate creation attack* is thus one in which a government agency requires a domestic certificate authority to provide it with false SSL certificates for use in surveillance.

The technical details of this attack are simple, and do not require extensive explanation. Each CA already has an infrastructure in place with which it is able to issue SSL certificates. In this compelled assistance scenario, the CA is merely required to skip the identity verification step in its own SSL certificate issuance process.

For the purposes of this analysis, assume that a CA cannot refuse to comply with a lawful court order. However, it may be possible, via a *warrant canary* or a similar technique, for a CA to communicate the existence of a secret court order to the Internet community. For example, a representative from one CA has informed us that his organization's disaster contingency plans include court orders and that his technical infrastructure includes a "kill switch" that enables him to move to a new physical location and nullify data at the data center [372]. The effectiveness of such measures is not evaluated here.

When compelling the assistance of a CA, the government agency can either require the CA to issue it a specific certificate for each website to be spoofed, or, more likely, the CA can be forced to issue a intermediate CA certificate that can then be reused an infinite number of times by that government agency, without the knowledge or further assistance of the CA.

In one hypothetical example of this attack, the U.S. National Security Agency (NSA) can compel VeriSign to produce a valid certificate for the Commercial Bank of Dubai (whose actual certificate is issued by Etisalat, UAE), that can be used to perform an effective man-in-the-middle attack against users of all modern browsers.

4.9.5 Surveillance Appliances

In October 2009, at an invitation-only conference for the surveillance and lawful interception industry in Washington, DC, Packet Forensics staffed a booth advertising the products and services from their Arizona-based company that sells extremely small, covert surveillance devices for networks.

The marketing materials for the company's 5-series device reveal that it is a 4 sq. in. "turnkey intercept solution," designed for "defense and (counter) intelligence applications," capable of "packet modification, injection and replay capabilities" at Gb/s throughput levels. The company proudly boasts that the surveillance device is perfect for the "Internet cafe problem." Most alarming is the device's ability to engage in active man-in-the-middle attacks:

> Packet Forensics' devices are designed to be inserted-into and removed-from busy networks without causing any noticeable interruption [. . .] This allows you to conditionally intercept web, email, VoIP and other traffic at-will, even while it remains protected inside an encrypted tunnel on the wire. Using 'man-in-the-middle' to intercept TLS or SSL is essentially an attack against the underlying Diffie-Hellman cryptographic key agreement protocol [. . .] To use our product in this scenario, [government] users have the ability to *import a copy of any legitimate key they obtain (potentially by court order)* or they can generate 'look-alike' keys designed to give the subject a false sense of confidence in its authenticity. [383]

The company has essentially packaged software equivalent to *sslstrip* into a 4 sq. in. appliance, ready for government customers to drop onto networks, at a price that is "so cost effective, they're disposable." When contacted by a journalist from *Wired News* in March 2010, Packet Forensics spokesman Ray Saulino initially denied the product performed as advertised in its sales materials, or that anyone used it. But in a follow-up call the next day, Saulino changed his stance, telling the journalist that

> The technology we are using in our products has been generally discussed in Internet forums and there is nothing special or unique about it [. . .] Our target community is the law enforcement community [439].

Furthermore, while Packet Forensics has not disclosed a list of its customers, the firm's website reveals that the 5-series device was authorized for export to foreign firms and governments by the US Bureau of Industry and Security on July 7, 2009 [382].

4.9.6 Protecting Users

The major web browsers are currently vulnerable to the compelled certificate creation attack, and it does not appear that any of the existing privacy-enhancing browser add-ons sufficiently protect users without significantly impacting browser usability.

In an effort to significantly reduce the impact of this attack upon end-users, *CertLock* has been created as a lightweight add-on for the Firefox browser. This solution employs a Trust-On-First-Use (TOFU) policy (this is also known as "leap-of-faith" authentication) [91,451], reinforced with a policy that the country of origin for certificate issuing does not change in the future. Specifically, this solution relies upon caching CA information, which is then used to empower users to leverage country-level information in order to make common sense trust evaluations.

In this section, the motivations that impacted the design of CertLock are discussed as is the assertion that users can make wise country-level trust decisions; to understand fully, the technical implementation details of the prototype add-on are briefly summarized.

4.9.6.1 Design motivations

The compelled certificate creation attack is a classical example of a low probability, high-impact event [133]. A vast majority of users are extremely unlikely to experience it, but for those who do, very bad things are afoot. As such, it is vital that any defensive technique have an extremely low false positive rate, yet be able to get the attention of users when an attempted SSL session hijacking is detected.

Most users are unlikely to know that this threat even exists, and so it is important that any protective system not require configuration, and maintenance, nor introduce any noticeable latency to users' connections. Given the low likelihood of falling victim to this attack, most rational users will avoid any protective technology that requires configuration or slows down their web browsing [242].

Furthermore, to achieve widespread adoption (even more so if the browser vendors are to add similar functionality to their own products), any protective technology must not sacrifice user privacy for security. Information regarding users' web browsing habits should not be leaked to any third party, even if that party is "trusted" or if it is done so anonymously. The solution must therefore be self-contained, and capable of protecting the user without contacting any remote servers.

The research suggests most consumers are unaware of how SSL functions, what a CA is, the role it performs, and how many companies are trusted by their browser to issue certificates. Expecting consumers to learn about this process or to spend their time evaluating the business practices and trustworthiness of these hundreds of firms is unreasonable. Nevertheless, the security of the current system requires each user to make trust decisions that that they are ill-equipped (nor willing) to perform.

It is reasonable to believe that consumers do not directly trust CAs. Aside from the biggest CAs such as VeriSign and large telecommunications companies local to their country, it is unlikely that consumers have ever heard of the vast majority of the hundreds of companies entrusted by their web browser to issue certificates. Thus, it is just as unreasonable to expect an American consumer to make a trust decision regarding a certificate issued by Polish technology firm Unizeto Technologies as it is to expect a Japanese consumer to evaluate a certificate issued by Bermuda-based QuoVadis. However, both of these CAs are trusted by the major browsers, by default.

Consumers are simply told to look for the lock icon. What happens in the browser to produce that lock icon is assumed by users to be reliable. It is the responsibility of security technologists to ensure that what happens behind the scenes does in fact protect the average users' privacy and security.

This is not to say that most users are clueless—merely that browsers currently provide them with little to no useful contextual information without which such complex decisions are extremely difficult.

4.9.6.2 Country-based trust

Many believe consumers are quite capable of making basic trust decisions based on country-level information. Since March 2010, Google has been providing country-level warnings to users of its Google Mail service when it detects that their account has been accessed from a potentially suspect IP address in a different country [173].

Thus, a consumer whose banking sessions are normally encrypted by a server presenting a certificate signed by a US-based CA might become suspicious if told that her US-based bank is now using a certificate signed by a Tunisian, Latvian, or Serbian CA.

To make this trust evaluation, she does not have to study the detailed business policies of the foreign CA, she can instead rely on common sense, and ask herself why her Iowa-based bank is suddenly doing business in eastern Europe. In order to empower users to make such country-level evaluations of trust, CertLock leverages the wealth of historical browsing data kept by the browser.

Individuals living in countries with laws that protect their privacy from unreasonable invasion have good reason to avoid trusting foreign governments (or foreign companies) to protect their private data. This is because individuals often receive the greatest legal protection from their own governments, and little to none from other countries. For example, the US law strictly regulates the ability of the US government to collect information on the US persons. However, the government can freely spy on foreigners around the world, as long as the surveillance is performed outside the United States. Thus, Canadians, Swedes, and Russians located outside the United States have absolutely no reason to trust the US government to protect their privacy.

Likewise, individuals located in countries with oppressive governments may wish to know if their communications with servers located in foreign democracies are suddenly being facilitated by a domestic (or state-controlled) CA.

4.9.6.3 Only blocking bad certificates

A simplistic defensive add-on aimed at protecting users from compelled certificate creation attacks could simply cache all certificates encountered during browsing sessions, and then warn the user any time they encounter a certificate that has changed. In fact, such an add-on, Certificate Patrol, already exists [39].

The problem with such an approach is that it is likely to suffer from an extremely high false positive rate. Each time a website intentionally changes its certificate, the browser displays a warning that will needlessly scare and soon desensitize users. There are many legitimate scenarios where certificates change. For example, old certificates expire; certificates are abandoned and or revoked after a data breach that exposed the server private key; and many large enterprises that have multiple SSL accelerator appliances serving content for the same domain use a different certificate for each device [289].

By adopting a Trust-On-First-Use policy, CertLock assumes that if a website starts using a different certificate issued by the same CA that issued its previous certificate, there is no reason to warn the user. This approach enables us to significantly reduce the false positive rate, while having little impact on our ability to protect users from a variety of threats.

Because of the way sites operate their businesses, there is little reason to warn users if a website switches CAs within the same country. As the threat model is focused on a government adversary with the power to compel any domestic CA into issuing certificates at will, it is appropriate to consider CAs within a country to be equals. That is, a government agency able to compel a new CA into issuing a certificate could just as easily compel the original CA into issuing a new certificate for the same site. Since CertLock does not warn users in that scenario (described above), there is no need to warn users in the event of a same-country CA change.

By limiting the trigger of the warnings to country-level changes, this implementation has struck a balance that will work in most situations.

4.9.6.4   *Implementation details*

The CertLock solution is currently implemented as an add-on to the Firefox browser. Because the Firefox browser already retains history data for all visited websites, the add-on has simply modified the browser to cause it to retain slightly more information. Thus, for each new SSL-protected website that the user visits, a CertLock- enabled browser also caches the following additional certificate information: (a) a hash of the certificate, (b) the country of the issuing CA, (c) the name of the CA, (d) the country of the website, (e) the name of the website, and (f) the entire chain of trust up to the root CA.

When a user revisits a SSL-protected website, CertLock first calculates the hash of the site's certificate and compares it with the stored hash from previous visits. If it has not changed, the page is loaded without warning. If the certificate has changed, the CAs that issued the old and new certificates are compared. If the CAs are the same or are from the same country, the page is loaded without any warning. On the other hand, if the CAs' countries differ, then the user will see a warning.

At a high level, this algorithm is quite simple. However, there are a few subtle areas where some complexity is required.

Because governments can compel CAs to create both regular site certificates and intermediate CA certificates, any evaluation of a changed site certificate must consider the type of CA that issued it.

Although the web browser vendors do not vouch for the trustworthiness of any of the root CAs that they include, it is reasonable to assume that the browser vendors do at least verify the country information listed in each of their root CAs. Therefore, users are able to trust this information as the add-on evaluates changed certificates.

When CertLock detects a changed certificate, it must also determine the type of CA that issued the new certificate. If the new certificate was issued by a root CA, then CertLock can easily compare the country of the old certificate's CA with the country of the new root CA. However, if the new certificate was issued by an intermediate CA, then the add-on has no way of verifying that the issuing CA's country information is accurate.

As an illustrative and hypothetical example of what is currently possible, the Spanish government could compel a Spanish CA to issue an intermediate CA certificate that falsely listed the country of the intermediate CA as the United States. This rogue intermediate CA would then be used to issue site certificates for subsequent surveillance activities. In this hypothetical scenario, let us imagine that the rogue CA issued a certificate for Bank of America, whose actual certificate was issued by VeriSign in the United States. Were CertLock to simply evaluate the issuing CA's country of the previously seen Bank of America certificate and compare it with the issuing country of the rogue intermediate CA (falsely listed as the United States), CertLock would not detect the hijacking attempt. In order to detect such rogue intermediate CAs, a more thorough comparison must be conducted.

Thus, in the event that a new certificate has been issued by an intermediate CA, CertLock follows the chain of trust up to the root CA, noting the country of every CA along the path. If any one of these intermediate

Table 4.13 A trust matrix evaluating CertLock. In short, the tool only protects users from compelled certificate creation attacks when the spying government and the country of the actual CA are not the same.

Spying Government	Country of Actual CA	CertLock Protects?
country1	country1	No
country1	country2	Yes

CAs (or the root CA itself) has a different country than the CA that issued the original certificate, then the user is warned.

4.9.7 Threat Model Analysis

In this section, several *hypothetical* scenarios are presented wherein a man-in-the-middle attack may be desired. In each example scenario, the government's available surveillance options are examined, the suitability of the compelled certificate creation attack is considered, and the ability of CertLock to detect and thwart the attack is evaluated. A condensed summary of the threats that CertLock defends against is also presented in Table 4.13.

Scenario A

Actual CA	VeriSign (United States)
Compelled CA	VeriSign (United States)
Website	Citibank (United States)
Location of suspect	United States
Spying government	United States

In this scenario, the United States government compels VeriSign to issue a certificate for use by a law enforcement agency wishing to spy on communications between a suspect located in the United States and Citibank, her US-based bank.

This attack is impossible for CertLock to detect, because the CA issuing the fake certificate is also the same that issued the legitimate certificate. However, it appears this scenario is extremely unlikely to occur in the investigations of end users. This is because if a government adversary is able to obtain a court order compelling VeriSign's cooperation, it can just as easily obtain a court order compelling Citibank to disclose the suspect's account information.

While there are perhaps a few volunteer-run Internet providers that will do anything possible to avoid delivering user data to government agents, it is likely that the vast majority of corporations will eventually comply. Outright refusal could potentially result in seizure of corporate assets, and the jailing of executives—consequences that profit focused shareholders would likely wish to avoid. As a related example, in 2006, Google very publicly fought a subpoena from the US Department of Justice requesting aggregate search request records. However, once a court ruled on the matter, the company complied and provided the government with 50,000 URLs from the Google search index [495]. As such, the threat model specifically excludes the rare category of ISPs willing to say no to government requests at all costs, and instead focuses on typical, law-abiding corporations that provide services to most users.

Scenario B

Actual CA	VeriSign (United States)
Compelled CA	GoDaddy (United States)
Website	Citibank (United States)
Location of suspect	United States
Spying government	United States

In this scenario, the US government compels GoDaddy, a CA located in the United States to issue a certificate for an intelligence agency wishing to spy on communications between a suspect located in the United States and a bank also located in the United States (CitiBank), which obtained its legitimate SSL certificate from VeriSign.

Just as with Scenario A, this attack is extremely unlikely to occur. This is because any government agency able to compel GoDaddy is also capable of obtaining a court order to compel VeriSign or Bank of America. By simple reduction, any attacker capable of Scenario B is also capable of Scenario A. CertLock does not detect attacks of this type.

Scenario C

Actual CA	VeriSign (United States)
Compelled CA	VeriSign (United States)
Website	*Poker.com* (United States)
Location of Suspect	United States
Spying Government	United States

In this scenario, the US law enforcement agents are investigating a US-based online gambling website and the US-based users of the service. The agents wish to first obtain evidence that illegal activity is occurring, by monitoring the bets as they are placed via SSL-encrypted sessions, before they later raid the offices of the company and seize their servers. In order to survey the communications between users and the gambling website, law enforcement officials compel VeriSign to issue an additional certificate for the site, which is then used to intercept all communications to and from the website.

In this scenario, where both ends of the SSL connection are under investigation by the government, the compelled certificate attack is a highly effective method for covertly gathering evidence. However, because the issuing CA does not change, CertLock is unable to detect this attack and warn users.

In general, attack scenarios in which both the end user and the website are under surveillance are beyond the scope of the threat model.

Scenario D

Actual CA	VeriSign (United States)
Compelled CA	TeliaSonera (Finland)
Website	Aktia Bank (Finland)
Location of suspect	Finland
Spying government	Finland

In this scenario, a resident of Finland is accessing her Aktia Savings Bank online account, which obtained its legitimate SSL certificate from VeriSign, a US firm. The Finnish intelligence services are interested in getting access to the suspect's online transaction data, and thus seek to compel TeliaSonera, a domestic CA to issue a certificate for the surveillance operation.

This scenario is not identical to scenario A, however it is quite similar. Again, if the Finnish government is able to compel a domestic CA into assisting it, it is safe to assume that it could just as easily compel the Finnish bank into providing the suspect's account details. While this attack scenario is unlikely, should it occur, CertLock will detect it.

Scenario E

Actual CA	VeriSign (United States)
Compelled CA	TeliaSonera (Finland)
Website	Google Mail (USA)
Location of suspect	Finland
Spying government	Finland

In this scenario, a US executive is traveling in Finland for business and is attempting to access her secure, US-based web mail account using the Internet connection in her hotel room. Finnish authorities wish to intercept her communications, but due to Google's use of SSL by default for all web mail communications [421], the government must employ a man-in-the-middle attack. This scenario is thus an ideal candidate for a compelled certificate creation attack, since the Finnish authorities have no leverage to compel the assistance of Google or VeriSign. This scenario is also one that is easily detected by CertLock.

Scenario F

Actual CA	VeriSign (United States)
Compelled CA	VeriSign (United States)
Website	CCB (China)
Location of suspect	United States
Surveilling government	United States

In this scenario, a Chinese executive is traveling in the United States for business and is attempting to access her China Construction Bank account using the Internet connection in her hotel room. The US government authorities wish to get access to her financial records, but are unwilling to let the Chinese government know that one of their citizens is under investigation, and so have not requested her records via official law enforcement channels.

This scenario is almost identical to scenario E, however, there is one key difference: The legitimate certificate used by the Chinese bank was issued by a CA located in the United States and the US government has turned to the same US-based CA to supply it with a false certificate. Thus, while this scenario is an ideal candidate for a compelled certificate creation attack, it is not one that can easily be detected by looking for country-level CA changes. As such, CertLock is not able to detect attacks of this type.

4.9.7.1   Why sites should consider the country of the CA they use

Building on the information presented thus far, the following conclusions emerge:

- Users are currently vulnerable to compelled certificate creation attacks initiated by the government of any country in which there is at least one certificate authority that is trusted (directly or indirectly) by the browser vendors.

- When users provide their private data to a company, the government of the country in which their data are located may be able to compel the provider to disclose their private data.

- When users provide their private data to a company that holds the data in country1, but uses a SSL certificate provided by a CA in country2, users are vulnerable to both the compelled disclosure of their data by the government of country1 and interception of their private data through a compelled certificate creation attack by country2.

- Thus, when a company that uses a certificate authority located in a country different than the one in which it holds user data, it needlessly exposes users' data to the compelled disclosure by an additional government.

Based on this, it follows that websites best serve their users when they rely on a SSL certificate from a CA located in the same country in which their private data are stored. (e.g., all the Hungarian banks surveyed by the authors use certificates provided by NetLock Ltd., a Hungarian CA.) Unfortunately, this is not a widespread practice in the industry; instead, American CAs totally dominate the certificate market and are used by many foreign organizations.

As just one example—a number of big banks in Pakistan, Lebanon, and Saudi Arabia (countries in which the United States has a strong intelligence interest) all use certificates obtained from the US-based CAs to secure their online banking sites.

It is because of the dominance of US CAs that CertLock is not able to equally protect users from different countries. CertLock can effectively protect users of US-based services from compelled certificate disclosure attacks performed by non-US governments. Thus, it is useful for Americans traveling out of the country who may be subject to surveillance by the national government of the country in which they are traveling and for non-US persons who use US-based services and who do not wish for their own governments to get access to their data.

However, as long as companies around the world continue to rely on SSL certificates issued by American CAs, the US government will maintain the ability to perform man-in-the-middle attacks that are practically impossible to detect with CertLock or any other country-based detection mechanism.

4.9.8   Related Work

Over the past decade, many people in the security community have commented on the state of the SSL public key infrastructure and the significant trust placed in the CAs [100,211,213].

In 1998, James Hayes of the US National Security Agency published a paper that focused specifically on the threat of rogue insiders within a Certificate Authority [240]. Although the technical details of the threat outlined by Hayes are largely the same as the scenario on which this work focused (albeit with vast different legal and policy consequences), Hayes did not address the threat of government compelled certificate creation. It is unclear if he was simply unaware of this scenario, or if the topic was too sensitive for him to discuss, given his employer. In his paper, Hayes proposed a technical solution to address the insider threat, which relied on users configuring various per-site attributes within their browser that would be used to evaluate each new site's certificate.

Crispo and Lomas also proposed a certification scheme designed to detect rogue CAs [164], while the Monkeysphere project has created a system that replaces the CA architecture with the OpenPGP web of trust [47].

Ian Grigg has repeatedly sought to draw attention to both the potential conflict of interest that some CAs have due to their involvement in other forms of surveillance and the power of a court order to further compel these entities to assist government investigations [226–228]. In particular, in 2005, Grigg and Shostack filed a formal complaint with ICANN over the proposal to award VeriSign control of .net domain name registration, arguing that the firm's surveillance products created a conflict of interest [229].

In recent years, several browser-based tools have been created to help protect users against SSL-related attacks. Kai Engert created Conspiracy, a Firefox add-on that provides country-level CA information to end users in order to protect them from compelled certificate creation attacks. The Conspiracy tool displays the flag of the country of each CA in the chain of trust in the browser's status bar [182]. Thus, users must themselves remember the country of the CAs that issue each certificate, and detect when the countries have changed. Herley [242] claims that this is an unreasonable burden to place upon end users, considering how rarely the compelled certificate creation attack is likely to occur.

Wendlandt et al. created Perspectives, a Firefox add-on that improves the Trust-On-First-Use model used for websites that supply self-signed SSL certificates [486]. In their system, the user's browser securely contacts one of several notary servers, who in turn independently contact the web server and obtain its certificate. In the event that an attacker is attempting to perform a man-in-the-middle attack upon the user, the fact that the attacker-supplied SSL certificate and those supplied by the Perspectives notary servers differ will be a strong indicator that something bad has happened.

Unfortunately, the Perspectives system requires that users provide the Perspectives notaries with a real-time list of the secure sites they visit. Modern browsers already leak information about the secure websites that users visit, as they automatically contact CAs in order to verify that the certificates have not been revoked (using the OCSP protocol). While this is currently unavoidable, it is best to avoid providing private user web browsing data to any additional parties. Although the Perspectives project's designers state that "all servers adhere to a strict policy of never recording client IP addresses, period," it is unwise to provide users' private web browsing data to a third party, merely based on the fact that they promise not to log it.

Alicherry and Keromytis have improved upon the Perspectives design with their DoubleCheck system [87], substituting Tor exit nodes for special notary servers. Because the Tor network anonymizes the individual user's IP address, there is no way for the Tor exit nodes to know who is requesting the certificate for a particular SSL website. While the authors solved the major privacy issues that plague the Perspectives scheme, their choice of Tor carries its own cost: latency. Their system adds an additional second of latency to every new SSL connection, and up to 15 s for visits to new self-signed servers. This additional latency is too much to ask most users to bear, particularly if the chance of them encountering a rogue CA is so low.

Herzberg and Jbara created TrustBar, a Firefox add-on designed to help users detect spoofed websites. The browser tool works by prominently displaying the name of the CA that provided the site's certificate, as well as allowing the user to assign a per-site name or logo, to be displayed when they revisit to each site [244].

Tyler Close created Petname Tool, a Firefox add-on that caches SSL certificates, and allows users to assign a per-site phrase that is displayed each time they revisit the site in the future. In the event that a user visits a spoofed website or a site with the same URL that presents a certificate from a different CA, the user's specified phrase will not be displayed [156].

In May 2008, a security researcher discovered that the OpenSSL library used by several popular Linux distributions was generating weak cryptographic keys. While the 2-year-old flaw was soon fixed, SSL certificates created on computers running the flawed code were themselves open to attack [86,501]. Responding to this flaw, German technology magazine Heise released the Heise SSL Guardian for the Windows operating system, which warns users of Internet Explorer and Chrome when they encounter a weak SSL certificate [461].

In December 2008, Stevens et al. demonstrated that flaws in the MD5 algorithm could be used to create rogue SSL certificates (without the knowledge or assistance of the CA). In response, CAs soon accelerated their planned transition to certificates using the SHA family of hash functions [454]. As an additional protective measure, Márton Anka developed an add-on for the Firefox browser to detect and warn users about certificate chains that use the MD5 algorithm for RSA signatures [90].

Jackson and Barth devised the ForceHTTPS system to protect users who visit HTTPS-protected websites, but who are vulnerable to man-in-the- middle attacks due to the fact that they do not type in the https:// component of the URL [264]. This system has since been formalized into the HTTP Strict Transport Security (HSTS) standard proposal [247], to which multiple browsers are in the process of adding support. While this system is designed to enable a website to hint to the browser that future visits should always occur via a HTTPS connection, this mechanism could be extended to enable a website to lock a website to a particular CA or CAs of a specific country.

4.9.9 Conclusion

Compelled certificate creation attack is shown to be a way for governments and other authorities to subvert the CA-based public key infrastructure based on a variety of evidentiary data points. In an effort to protect users from these powerful adversaries, CertLock was created as a lightweight defensive browser-based add-on that detects and thwarts such attacks. The reductive analysis of governments' legal capabilities to perform an adversarial threat model analysis of the attack and the proposed defensive technology shows how technology like CertLock can be used to help reduce the threat of eavesdropping through compelled certificate creation.

Ultimately, the threats posed by the compelled certificate creation attack cannot be completely eliminated via the simple CertLock add-on. The CA system is fundamentally broken, and must be overhauled. DNSSEC may play a significant role in solving this problem or at least reducing the number of entities who can be compelled to violate users' trust. No matter what system eventually replaces the current one, the security community must consider compelled government assistance as a realistic threat and ensure that any solution be resistant to such attacks.

ACKNOWLEDGMENTS

Thanks to Kevin Bankston, Matt Blaze, Kelly Caine, Jon Callas, Allan Friedman, Jennifer Granick, Markus Jakobsson, Dan Kaminsky, Moxie Marlinspike, Eddy Nigg, Eli O, and Adam Shostack for their useful feedback.

Chapter 5

The Mobile Problem

Until recently, if you asked consumers whether smartphones are computers, they would immediately respond that they are not; they are phones. At the same time, if you asked typical computer scientists the same question, they would respond that they *are*—nothing but small computers that people use to make phone calls. Both of these views are a bit unfortunate.

Smartphones are computers, and they suffer all the drawbacks of computers. They can be targeted by malware. They can be used in botnets. And of course, users of smartphones can be targeted by phishing attacks. So smartphones are not just phones. But at the same time, they are not just small computers that are used to make calls. They have limited battery resources, which makes some software (and security software in particular) potentially unsuitable. Their limited and different user interfaces open us up to new risks. And they are used in a different way than computers are. Phones are used in a much more social context, which actually affects bottom-line security. And they are used so much more often, which means that users will have a much greater exposure to evil if we do not dramatically improve our takedown speeds.

To give a flavor of the differences, we begin by describing mobile phishing (Section 5.1) and how it is different from traditional phishing. We then describe why the mobile problem is severe (Section 5.2), but why it has not yet (as this is written) been commonly recognized as such. In Section 5.3, we describe the problem of tapjacking, and how it has the potential of becoming a much greater threat on mobile platforms than what clickjacking is on traditional platforms. Later on, in Chapter 7 of the book, we present some solutions to existing and evolving security problems, many of which are also very relevant in the mobile context.

5.1 PHISHING ON MOBILE DEVICES

Adrienne Porter Felt and David Wagner

Abstract. Mobile operating systems and browsers lack secure application identity indicators that are present in traditional operating systems and browsers. Consequently, a user cannot always identify whether a link on a mobile device has taken her to the expected application. This makes users vulnerable to phishing attacks when they enter payment information or passwords after following links on mobile devices. To evaluate this risk, we study 85 websites and 100 mobile applications and discover that websites and applications regularly ask users to type their passwords into contexts that are vulnerable to spoofing. Our implementation

The Death of the Internet, First Edition. Edited by Markus Jakobsson.
© 2012 John Wiley & Sons, Inc. Published 2012 by John Wiley & Sons, Inc.

of sample phishing attacks on the Android and iOS platforms demonstrates that attackers can spoof legitimate applications with high accuracy, suggesting that the risk of phishing attacks on mobile platforms is greater than has previously been appreciated.

5.1.1   The Mobile Phishing Threat

User interfaces for mobile devices are constrained by the devices' small screens. In particular, mobile operating systems and browsers lack secure application identity indicators. A user cannot definitively tell what mobile application or website she is interacting with, yet 40% of smartphone users enter passwords into their phones at least once a day [280]. This exposes users to the risk of mistaking a malicious application for a trusted one.

Mobile applications and websites often link to each other to share data or refer the user to a related service. For example, a music-themed website might link the user to the iTunes application to buy a song. In a normal interapplication link, the *sender* application links to a second *target* application. After following the link, the user might provide the target application with authentication credentials or payment information.

We discuss phishing attacks that imitate normal interapplication links between mobile applications and websites. In this type of phishing attack, the user clicks on a link and is delivered to a spoofed version of the expected target. The lack of secure identity indicators on a mobile device means that the user would be unable to tell that she had been sent to the wrong target. The unaware user might then provide authentication credentials or payment information to the phishing page. In a *direct* phishing attack, the sender is a malicious application that links the user to its own spoof screen instead of the real target application. In a *man-in-the-middle* attack, the sender is benign, but another party intercepts the link and loads a spoofed target application in place of the intended target application. Figure 5.1 illustrates the direct and man-in-the-middle attack models. (For more background of the general phishing problem, please see Section 3.3.)

Users become accustomed to entering their passwords or payment information in familiar, repeated settings [294]. Successful phishing attacks mimic these familiar settings. We can evaluate the risk of phishing attacks by examining (1) whether users frequently encounter legitimate links whose targets prompt them for private data and (2) whether attackers can build convincing replicas of these legitimate transactions. We study 50 Android applications, 50 iOS applications, and 85 websites to evaluate how often they link users to password-protected or payment-related applications. We find that websites and mobile applications commonly link the user to password-protected social network and payment applications, thus conditioning users to reflexively enter their credentials after following links. Based on this analysis of common behavior, we identify new phishing attacks against mobile platforms. We demonstrate that it is possible to build phishing attacks for Android and iOS that convincingly mimic the types of interapplication links that our study found to be common.

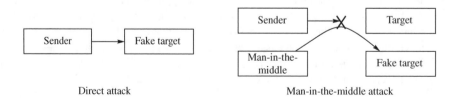

Direct attack   Man-in-the-middle attack

Figure 5.1   Phishing attacks can be launched directly by the sender, or by a man-in-the-middle.

5.1.1.1 User interfaces on mobile devices

Smartphone operating systems and browsers have minimalist user interfaces to accommodate the small size of mobile devices. In particular, their user interfaces lack application identity indicators that are available in desktop operating systems and browsers.

Only one mobile application can control the screen at a time, even in platforms that support multitasking. The *foreground application* fills the screen and receives all user input, with the exceptions of input-method applications (e.g., alternate keyboards) and the Apple App Store (which uses popup dialogs for in-application purchases). No major smartphone operating system displays the identity of the foreground application. Users can find a list of running processes, but no part of the screen identifies the current foreground application.

Mobile browsers display only one browser window at a time. The Android and iOS browsers display the URL of the current window at the top of the screen, similar to desktop browsers. However, websites can hide the URL bar once the page has loaded; this commonly used feature allows the website to fill the available screen. (For example, Figure 5.4 shows `weather.com` in mobile Safari without the URL bar.) If a user wants to see the URL bar, she can tap the top of the screen.

5.1.1.2 Mobile security measures

Mobile applications are less trusted than their desktop counterparts. In Android and iOS, applications are isolated from each other by default; for example, applications cannot read each other's databases or network traffic. Additionally, Google and Apple attempt to prevent users from installing malware by controlling how users install applications.

Android applications are restricted with an application permission system. Permissions control access to privacy- and security-relevant parts of the system API, such as the ability to read a user's contacts or send a text message. When a user installs an application, the application's desired permissions are displayed to the user. The user can then decide whether to grant all of the permissions and continue with the installation. This informs users of the risks of installing an application. Users of iOS devices can only install applications from the App Store. In order to be listed in the App Store, applications must undergo a formal review process. Although specific details of the App Store review process are secret, the process likely includes a security review.

Websites in mobile browsers are also treated as potentially untrustworthy. They must obey the standard Same Origin Policy [504], meaning that websites on different domains are isolated from each other. Neither Android nor Apple review or restrict access to mobile websites.

5.1.1.3 Application control transfers

A *control transfer* occurs when a user clicks on a link and the foreground application or website changes. As a result of a control transfer, the user stops interacting with one application and begins interacting with another. Although mobile applications and websites are isolated, interapplication communication via explicit channels can lead to control transfers. Control transfers can happen in four ways, classified according to whether the sender and target are mobile applications or websites:

Mobile Sender ⇒ Mobile Target Android and iOS applications can optionally choose to accept communication from other applications by registering a receiver with the operating system. In response to a message, the OS transfers control to the target application.

Mobile Sender ⇒ **Web Target**   A mobile application can send the user to a website by invoking the phone's native browser with the target URL. The browser will come to the foreground with the target website.

Alternately, a mobile application can *embed* web content. As a result, the web content is rendered as part of the mobile application's screen. For example, Figure 5.3 shows Groupon embedding a Twitter login page. Embedding can be done by communicating directly with a website's data API or by asking the OS to load a website in a WebView. A *WebView* is similar to an iframe: the embedding application can control the size and placement of it within the screen, and browser chrome is not displayed (including the address bar). Mobile applications can additionally insert arbitrary JavaScript into a WebView. The two types of embedded web content are difficult to visually differentiate. For both, the mobile application retains control of user input and the screen while the user interacts with the embedded web content.

Web Sender ⇒ **Mobile Target**   A website can send the user to a mobile application if the mobile application registers a data scheme with the OS. A *data scheme* is a nonstandard URL protocol. For example, the mobile Skype application registers the skype scheme. Thereafter, clicking on a skype:// link in any website will send the user into the Skype application if it is installed. While this example involves explicit user action, user involvement is not necessary for such a transfer; a website can automatically launch an application by embedding an iframe with the appropriate scheme. (The target application will take full control of the UI, despite the use of an iframe.)

Applications can also register for HTTP(S) domains. For example, the mobile Google Maps application registers maps.google.com. When a website links to an application-registered domain in Android, the user is asked to choose between the browser and the alternate application. After choosing the first time for a domain, the user can set a default application. In iOS, only a small number of Apple-approved applications (like the App Store and YouTube) can register themselves for HTTP(S) domains, and the registered applications always override the browser and receive control.

Web Sender ⇒ **Web Target**   Web-to-web control transfers are standard links. As on the desktop, websites can link to each other, automatically redirect, and embed each other in iframes. The primary difference in a mobile setting is that either the target or sender can hide the URL bar.

A developer may not be responsible for a link, for example, a link in an email. However, we focus on control transfers that developers have intentionally inserted into their applications.

5.1.2   Common Control Transfers

As users interact with legitimate applications, they become conditioned to enter their passwords and payment information in certain types of settings [294]. Phishing attacks prey on user expectations by mimicking and then subverting legitimate application behavior. We study popular Android, iOS, and web applications to identify how often and when control transfers lead to password or payment entry. Asking a user to enter a password after a control transfer raises phishing concerns because the user may not know the correct identity of the post-transfer application.

To understand links that originate in mobile applications, we studied the control transfer patterns of the 50 most popular free Android 2.2[1] and iOS 4.3[2] applications. We manually exercised each application and

---

[1] The Android applications were collected in October 2010.

[2] The iOS applications were collected in March 2011. We tested iPhone/iPod Touch applications.

Figure 5.2   A screenshot of Pandora in iOS. Pandora's song description screen includes a menu with two interapplication links: one opens iTunes to the song, and the other opens the Mail application with a precomposed email. If the user decides to purchase the song, she will be asked for her iTunes password.

recorded whether it links the user to other mobile applications, opens websites in the browser, or embeds web content. Manual testing provides a lower bound on the number of control transfers. We found that 89 of the 100 mobile applications contain links that send the user to another application or website.

To understand links that originate in websites, we studied 85 of the 100 most popular Alexa-ranked domains[3] to evaluate website link behavior. For each domain, we collected the links on the home page and one representative page of content, linked from the home page. We used iPhone and Nexus One browser user-agent strings to receive the appropriate mobile versions of the websites. We built a Firefox extension to crawl each loaded page and find link target values. Some websites use JavaScript to create links in a nonstandard way; as a heuristic for finding these cases, the extension also collected onclick values for div, span, and img elements. We then reviewed the onclick JavaScript to find links, but we did not follow method calls referenced in the onclick event handler. We may have missed complex onclick links or links that are dynamically generated after load.

For both mobile and web links, we observed whether each control transfer involves the entry of information pertaining to the following:

- **Passwords**   Is the target application's content only visible to logged-in users? (For example, a user must log in to Facebook to post to her Facebook "wall".) If so, this indicates that the user will not be surprised if the target application requests a password.

- **Payment**   Does the sender link to the target for the explicit purpose of payment? (For example, Amazon sells books and music.) If so, the user is prepared to enter payment information into the target application.

We present the findings of our study next.

5.1.2.1   *Mobile Sender* ⇒ *Mobile Target*

A majority of the studied mobile applications contain functionality that will send the user to other mobile applications. In Figure 5.2, Pandora provides an example of a mobile-to-mobile control transfer. Table 5.1

---

[3]We omitted adult and advertising websites from the list of 100. Advertising home pages do not reflect the content that users typically see from that domain.

Table 5.1 The Rate at Which 50 Android and 50 iOS Applications Link the User to Another Mobile Application

	Mobile Sender–Mobile Target	
Mobile target	Android	iOS
Another mobile application	56%	72%
A password-protected application	36%	60%
An application for payment	10%	34%

Targets may be both password protected and payment related. We do not include the browser as a target mobile application; the browser is considered separately in Table 5.2.

summarizes the results of our mobile-to-mobile study. We observed four common types of control transfers that involve passwords or payment: social sharing and the purchase of upgrades, music, and credits.

Sharing Some applications encourage users to share content (e.g., high scores) with their Facebook, Twitter, or email contacts. This involves transferring the user to a Facebook, Twitter, or email application. These target applications are password protected.

Upgrades Developers sometimes publish two versions of an application: a free version with limited functionality or banner advertisements, and a paid version with full functionality or no advertisements. The free versions of these applications link to the Android Market or Apple App Store to "Upgrade" or "Remove ads." In order to complete the upgrade, the user may need to enter password or payment information into the store. The Android Market asks the user for payment information for paid upgrades, and the Apple App Store prompts the user for a password for both free and paid downloads. The Apple App Store also frequently asks the user to verify stored payment information. Consequently, users will likely be accustomed to entering their password after control transfers to an application store. All of the applications in our sample set were free at the time of download; users of paid applications will see fewer payment links than our results suggest. However, the most popular free applications are downloaded orders of magnitude more often than the most popular paid applications.

Music Music-centric applications typically contain links to purchase songs. In iOS, these links point to the Apple iTunes Store. For Android, some devices come with a preinstalled Amazon MP3 application for this purpose. Both target applications may require passwords or payment.

Credits Our sample of popular iOS applications includes 34 games, many of which sell game credits through the Apple Game Center or App Store. Game credits are required to progress through the games. The Game Center and App Store both immediately request a password to complete the sale. Periodically, they will also ask the user to verify her payment information. We did not observe the sale of game credits in our sample of Android applications. However, our sample includes only one game, so our analysis may undercount the rate at which game applications can transfer control to a payment application.

Our study demonstrates that users of mobile applications are accustomed to seeing links to other mobile applications for social sharing, upgrades, music, and credits. Links to email, Facebook, Twitter, and the platform stores are particularly prevalent. Users are conditioned to enter their passwords for these operations.

Table 5.2   The Rates at which 50 Android and 50 iOS Applications Embed Websites or Open Websites in the Browser

Mobile Sender–Web Target		
Embedded web target	Android (%)	iOS
Another company's website	16%	46%
A password-protected website	8%	38%
A website for payment	2%	0%
Web browser target	Android	iOS
A website	30%	18%
A password-protected website	3%	4%
A website for payment	2%	0%

Targets may be both password protected and payment related. We suspect that Android web payment rates are low because of biases introduced by sampling only the most popular applications.

Phishing attacks could therefore mimic these control transfers and prompt for a password without deviating from user expectations.

Mobile applications (with the exception of financial applications) commonly store their users' passwords so that users won't need to re-enter them. However, users must enter their passwords into the web versions of these applications, either in the browser or as embedded web content. Thus, users are still conditioned to enter passwords when they see an appropriate login screen for a mobile target.

5.1.2.2 Mobile Sender ⇒ Web Target

Mobile applications can display web content by sending the user to the browser or embedding the content. Table 5.2 summarizes how often the sampled applications use either approach, and Figure 5.3 displays an

Figure 5.3   A screenshot of Groupon in iOS. Groupon invites users to share daily deals with friends. The Twitter button takes the user to this screen, which is still part of Groupon. Groupon created the top "Twitter Connect" bar, and the Twitter login is embedded below.

example from our sample set. For embedded web content, we only report the inclusion of web content from other companies; many mobile applications seamlessly embed their own web content, but that practice is not relevant to phishing.

Passwords Social sharing accounts for nearly all of the links from mobile applications to password-protected websites. For iOS applications, social sharing is primarily implemented with embedded web content. Within our Android sample set, applications do not commonly link to password-protected websites. Instead, they prefer to implement social sharing with links to mobile applications. This is because many Android devices come with preinstalled Facebook and Twitter mobile application clients.

Payment Within our sample set, websites are not commonly used for payment. The iOS applications rely on Apple-provided applications (e.g., iTunes and the App Store) to handle financial transactions; this obviates the need for web-based payments. Two Android applications refer users to websites for purchases, but most of the Android applications that we studied either process their own payments within the application or rely on the Android Market. We suspect that this is an artifact of popularity; many of the very most popular Android applications are developed by large companies with their own payment processing services. We have independently observed other, less popular Android applications using PayPal for donations and non-Market upgrades. For example, PayPal's website showcases several PayPal-enabled applications with a few hundred to a few hundred thousand users [386]. If our sample had included less popular applications, we expect we would have observed a higher rate of web payments among Android applications.

Our analysis indicates that users who participate in social sharing are at a high risk for falling for a phishing attack. Thirty-eight percent of the sample iOS applications embed password-protected web content, and all of them do so for social sharing. Furthermore, a user must log in to a website every time she encounters it in a new application because there is no cross-application cookie store for embedded web content. This means that social users may enter their social networking site passwords into more than a third of the applications they install, thereby acclimating them to this workflow. On the other hand, we find that popular mobile applications do not commonly link users to websites for payment. This reduces the likelihood that people are conditioned to enter their passwords or payment information into a phishing application that subverts the web-to-mobile scenario.

5.1.2.3 *Web Sender ⇒ Mobile Target*

We studied the rate at which websites link to the schemes associated with applications (Figure 5.4). We separate these links into two categories. First, some applications are guaranteed to be present on every phone. iOS and Android phones have common applications like Google Maps, YouTube, and an email client. Each operating system also has its own applications (e.g., iOS includes the iTunes store) that are guaranteed to be present on every phone of that platform type. We refer to these applications as *core* applications. Links to core applications are guaranteed to succeed. Second, we also consider links to noncore applications; these links may fail if the user does not have the target application installed on the phone. Table 5.3 presents the rates for both types of links. The Android and iOS rates differ partly because of differences in their sets of core applications.

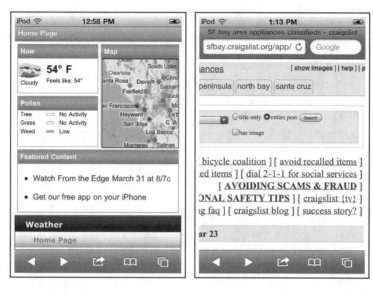

Figure 5.4 Websites with links to mobile applications, in iOS. The Weather Channel links to the Apple App Store, and Craigslist links to YouTube for Craigslist TV.

Passwords Websites link to mobile applications for the same reasons as mobile applications link to other mobile applications. Many websites contain mailto or twitter.com links to share content with friends; mailto links open the mobile email client (a core application), and the twitter.com domain is registered by a popular and often preinstalled Android application. mailto links are also sometimes used to contact the website staff.

Table 5.3 The Rates at which 85 Websites Include Links to Mobile Applications

Web Sender–Mobile Target		
Core application target	Android	iOS
A core mobile application	38%	47%
A password-protected application	22%	41%
An application for payment	6%	25%
Total application target	Android	iOS
A mobile application	49%	48%
A password-protected application	38%	42%
An application for payment	6%	25%

The top counts only links to core applications (which are present on every phone). The bottom counts all links to any application, core or not. Targets may be categorized as both password protected and payment related.

Payment Some websites link to the Apple App Store or Android Market to let the user download their application or buy related items. (In fact, some websites such as Hulu are not fully functional on mobile browsers, so the user must install the application to use the service.) The user may need to enter his or her account password or verify payment information to install the given application.

Our web analysis shows that websites commonly link to mobile email and Twitter applications. Twitter, in particular, is an attractive phishing target. We also found that websites often link users to the Apple App Store or Android Market to install the company's mobile application, which indicates that the web-to-mobile installation process could become a target for phishing attacks.

5.1.2.4 Web Sender ⇒ Web Target

Web-to-web links are a standard, familiar part of the Internet. All but one of the websites we crawled contain multiple links to external domains. Although we did not measure their use in our dataset, external payment services like PayPal and Google Checkout are widely incorporated into websites.

5.1.3 Phishing Attacks

We discuss how phishing attacks can be mounted against each of the four control transfer scenarios enumerated in Section 5.1.1.3. For each scenario, we present two types of attacks: direct attacks and man-in-the-middle attacks. In a *direct* attack, the sender application is malicious and loads a fraudulent target application. In a *man-in-the-middle* attack, the sender and target applications are both benign, but a malicious party intercepts the control transfer and responds in place of the legitimate target.

The goal of our attacker is to mimic the legitimate application behavior that we identified in the application survey (Section 5.1.2). An accurate attack should not deviate from the user's expected workflow, and the fake user interface should be indistinguishable from the target user interface. The user should have few or no opportunities to differentiate the phishing attack from legitimate behavior. We evaluate how well each attack meets these accuracy goals.

5.1.3.1 Mobile Sender ⇒ Mobile Target

In this scenario, the user believes that one mobile application links to another, trusted application. In addition to mimicking a normal workflow and user interface, malicious mobile applications must face the Android permission model and Apple review process.

Direct attack As presented in Section 5.1.2.1, mobile applications commonly include social sharing and payment buttons. A malicious application could similarly include "Share on Facebook" or "Upgrade this application" buttons. Clicking on one of the buttons would send the user to a screen that spoofs the target application. The phishing screen could request the user's password or payment credentials, enabling the malicious application to steal the data. The phishing application would then load the real application. If the user does not have an existing session with the real application, then the real application will ask the user to enter her password. This resembles normal application behavior after a failed login attempt, so the user might naturally assume that she had mistyped her password.

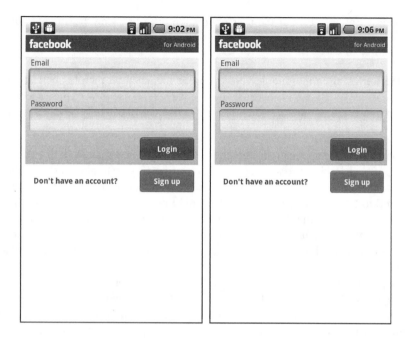

Figure 5.5   The Facebook login screen for Android (left), accompanied by our phishing version of the same screen (right). In our attack, the user's credentials are captured before invoking the real Facebook application. The other buttons (e.g., "Sign up") lead directly to Facebook's corresponding page.

Mobile login screens are often very simple, which makes them easy to copy. Figure 5.5 shows a fake Facebook login screen, which we constructed in several hours using images and layout values copied from a disassembled version of the legitimate Android Facebook application. It is highly unlikely that any user could differentiate between the real Facebook login screen and our fake Facebook login screen.

Android's permission system would do little to warn users of this attack; the attack requires no permissions, which might give users a false sense of security. At most, the malicious application might request the INTERNET permission to send the stolen data to the attacker. The permission request would not be anomalous: 87% of free applications request Internet access [185]. However, the INTERNET permission is not required because the Android API provides several ways to submit web requests and exfiltrate captured data without the INTERNET permission. For example, a MediaPlayer object can be created to load an arbitrary HTTP URL [89].

The Apple application review process might prevent this attack from appearing in the App Store if reviewers detect the fraudulent screen. However, the review process is not perfect [424] and there is no guarantee that reviewers would detect such an attack. More dangerously, the attacker could use web content to evade detection during review. The fraudulent screen would be constructed with an embedded website that is the full size of the screen, served by the attacker. (Recall that embedded websites do not have browser chrome.) During the application review, the website could immediately redirect the user to the legitimate application with no signs of any malice. Once the application has been added to the store, or at any subsequent date of the attacker's choice, the attacker could change the website to a fraudulent copy of the target. Web content can be styled to mimic the look and feel of an application. Alternately, the attacker could try to evade detection by targeting only a subset of the user population or not serving the attack to users in a certain geographic region (e.g., Apple's headquarters in Cupertino).

Man-in-the-middle   Man-in-the-middle attacks can be launched on mobile applications in two ways. The first attack, scheme squatting, is weak because it changes the user's workflow and cannot be hidden from application reviewers. Task interception is a strong attack, but it can only be implemented on Android.

> **Scheme squatting**   Some applications register to handle URI schemes. A links to a URI scheme will open the registered application. If the real application for a scheme is not installed, a malicious application could register for the scheme instead. Messages intended for the target would instead be delivered to the attacker, and the attacker could present the user with a phishing screen upon launching. Scheme squatting is a form of an attack named "Activity hijacking" [148].
>
> One strength of this attack is that it does not require any Android permissions. However, it suffers from three weaknesses. First, to evade detection, the application would need to emulate the intended target after the login screen completes. Otherwise, the user's expected operation would abruptly halt, raising suspicion. Emulation may be implausible, and this problem is intrinsic to the attack. Second, the real application might be installed. If so, iOS and Android would give the user a choice between the real application or the phishing application. Consequently, the phishing application would need to convince the user to prefer it to the real application, which would likely fail. Third, it would not be possible to hide this behavior from reviewers because applications must declare their schemes upfront in a file that is bundled with the application.

> **Task interception**   If an OS lets applications view the list of running processes, then a malicious application could poll the task list and wait for a target application to become active. The attacker could then launch itself and display a phishing screen when it is brought to the foreground. When the user enters credentials into the phishing screen, the fraudulent application can exit, leaving the original target application visible. We implemented this attack for Android and found that the application needs to poll the running task list every 5 ms to prevent the transition to the phishing screen from being visible to the naked eye.
>
> Task interception is a very effective attack for Android. The attack requires two permissions: one to start the application in the background after the phone has booted, and another to request the task list. However, both permissions are considered nondangerous, and neither is displayed to the user during installation. We are not aware of a way to launch this attack on iOS because applications are not allowed to view the task list.

5.1.3.2   *Mobile Sender ⇒ Web Target*

In this scenario, the user believes that a mobile application is displaying or linking to a trusted website, and the target website solicits private information.

Direct attack   A malicious application could present the user with buttons to share content or purchase an item. The attacker can then eavesdrop on the user's interaction with an embedded website or present the user with a site in a fake browser.

Embedded web content Many iOS applications embed pages from password-protected sites, such as Facebook and Twitter, into their screens. This trains users to type their password wherever they see a password prompt, despite the lack of security indicators. The risk is obvious: a malicious application can embed a website and then eavesdrop on any exchanged credentials. Both Android and iOS allow applications to insert JavaScript into embedded WebViews, and there is no mechanism for websites to prevent this.

This attack is close to indistinguishable from legitimate behavior. The inserted JavaScript could be obfuscated to thwart application analysis. The Android version of this attack would require the INTERNET permission to load the target, but so would the legitimate version.

Web browser If the target website hides its URL bar, then the mobile application could load a phishing website in the browser. The phishing website would then hide the URL bar. Many password-protected websites (such as Bank of America, Amazon, and Facebook) hide their URL bars [376].

If the target website does not hide its URL bar, then the attacker can spoof the trusted browser chrome. There are two ways to do this. First, the attacker could launch the browser, hide the URL bar, and then present a fake URL bar. We discuss how to build fake URL bars in Section 5.1.5. Alternately, the attacker could display a fake browser that looks identical to the real browser, except it lies about the current URL. Unlike their desktop counterparts, mobile browser interfaces are not customizable; this makes them easier to falsify. The fake browser could load the real website in a WebView and listen to the user's keystrokes. If the user were to try to use features of the browser that the fake browser can't implement (e.g., history), then the attacker needs to end the attack and launch the real browser. We implemented this for Android (see Figure 5.6).

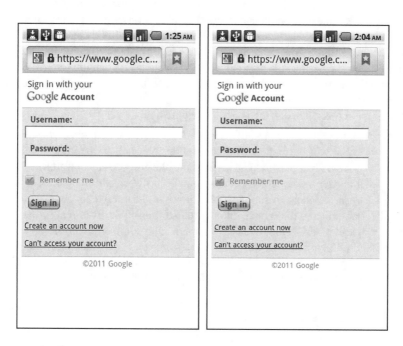

Figure 5.6 The real Android browser (left), alongside our fake Android browser for a Nexus One phone (right). It displays the legitimate Gmail website.

The first attack is extremely simple and could be effective with users who do not check browser chrome for security indicators. It does not require any notable Android permissions, and the target website could be benign until after Apple's review process. A security-conscious user could detect the ongoing attack by deciding to check the URL bar, although a user study shows that users do not do this in practice [376]. The second attack is more complete, although the user might notice that the bookmarks button next to the URL bar is not functional. Niu et al. previously demonstrated that spoofed URL bars can be convincing enough to trick security experts [376]. The third attack would likely fool users despite some shortcomings. Real browsers have data and functionality that a fake browser cannot replicate (e.g., history). For example, the Nexus One browser has 14 menu items, 3 of which our fake browser cannot handle smoothly. However, it is unlikely that a user would press these buttons before entering her password.

Man-in-the-middle   When users of mobile devices connect to the Internet over insecure WiFi hotspots, they are at risk of man-in-the-middle attacks. For instance, in one well-known active attack [388], if a user navigates to an HTTP website with an HTTPS login form, then the network attacker can change the HTTP web content so that the login form submits the password to the attacker's server. Security-conscious websites defend against this attack by not including login forms in HTTP pages. Instead, the user must click on a link to go to a separate, all-HTTPS login page. If the attacker redirects the user to a login page on a different domain, the user has the opportunity to notice that the login page in the URL bar is from the wrong domain. This defense against network attacks relies on the presence of a trusted URL bar, which may not be present on a phone.

Embedded web content   Consider a legitimate mobile application that embeds a webpage served over HTTP. A network attacker could change the "login" button on this page so that it links to a page owned by the attacker. When the user clicks this button, she will be taken to a phishing page within the embedded web frame. Since there is no URL bar for embedded content, there is no way for the user to detect that she has left the original website. The attacker can thus steal the user's credentials. To better mimic the user's expected workflow, the attacker could then relay the credentials to the valid website and sign the user in. Of our 100 sampled applications, 4 applications embed HTTP content with login links. This attack is not detectable by the user.

Web browser   A similar attack is possible when a legitimate mobile application links the user to an HTTP webpage that will be rendered in the browser. Normally, when not under attack, a browser would display a URL bar that indicates what site the user is currently browsing. However, this does not pose a barrier to the attack because mobile browser chrome can be hidden and spoofed. (Section 5.1.5 describes how to spoof mobile browser chrome.) This attack tricks the user with a spoofed URL bar, which can be made almost indistinguishable from real browser chrome. Of our 100 sampled applications, 7 link to HTTP content with login links in the browser. For example, the popular Android application Shazam links to songs on http://www.amazon.com for the user to purchase them. Applications can prevent these attacks by only sending users to HTTPS webpages, and never to a HTTP webpage. The site must support HTTPS for all of its pages.

5.1.4   Web Sender ⇒ Mobile Target

In this scenario, the user interacts with a website in the browser. The website links to a trusted mobile application.

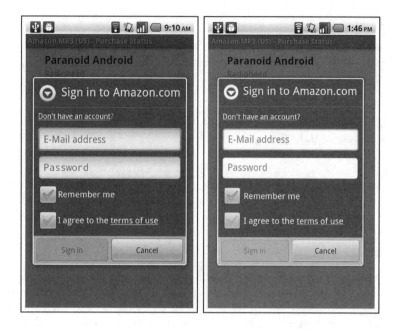

Figure 5.7 The real Amazon MP3 Store Android application (left), alongside our spoof website in the default Nexus One browser (right).

5.1.4.1 *Direct attack*

Websites often link the user to mobile applications, as discussed in Section 5.1.2.3. Malicious websites could mimic this behavior without appearing suspicious. For example, a phishing site might provide a link to buy a song from the iTunes Store. When the user clicks on the button, the website can pretend to transfer the user to the target application, but actually display a fake version of the target application. The malicious website must hide the URL bar and style the website to respond to user touch in the same way as the mobile application. For example, in Android, form fields should have rounded edges and turn orange when selected. Title text and dialog boxes need subtle drop shadows, and the browser's zoom feature should be disabled unless the application also supports zooming.

As we demonstrate in Figure 5.7, it is possible to build a website that looks very similar to a mobile application. However, the degree to which a website can emulate an application differs by platform. In iOS, the mobile Safari browser places a navigation bar on the bottom of the screen. This makes it impossible for a normal website to occupy the entire screen. However, users can "install" websites to their home page (i.e., add an icon that launches the browser to that page). Installed websites can remove the navigation button to mount an attack that would be close to undetectable. However, it may not be feasible for an attacker to convince a user to install a website.

In Android, one unavoidable difference is how the spoofed web application responds to the physical Menu button on the phone. A website cannot change the options that the browser presents, and the browser will have different Menu options than the target application. However, few users will try to use the Menu when presented with a login screen that does not allow any other actions. The user will likely be focused on the task of logging in.

5.1.4.2 Man-in-the-middle

Web-to-mobile links are vulnerable to the same man-in-the-middle attacks as mobile-to-mobile links (Section 5.1.3.1), with the same strengths and weaknesses. A malicious mobile application can scheme squat or watch the task list for the start of a target application.

5.1.5 Web Sender ⇒ Web Target

In this scenario, the user interacts with a website in the browser. The website links the user to another website in the browser, and the user expects to trust the target website.

5.1.5.1 Direct attack

Niu et al. present detailed web-to-web phishing attacks on mobile devices [376]. They discuss how phishing attacks can be built by hiding the browser URL bar or spoofing the URL bar. URL bar spoofing has three steps: (1) the attacker hides the legitimate URL bar, (2) the attacker adds a spoofed URL bar to the visible top of the page, and (3) the attacker catches any attempts to scroll to the real top of the page and instead jumps to the fake URL bar [376,415].

Niu et al. describe several differences between the behavior of their spoofed URL bar and the real browser user interface. We find that we can reduce the obviousness of two of these glitches. First, they always send the user to the fake top of the page whenever the user attempts to scroll in any direction. The users in their user study find this annoying. We ease the intrusiveness of our scrolling control by always scrolling a fixed amount away from the current location in the document, but not to a specific location. The scroll event therefore might scroll slightly more or less than the user intended, but the screen will never unexpectedly shift a large amount. Second, they observe that the URL bar is visible while the page loads and renders, giving the user the opportunity to see the real URL. We reduce the URL loading and rendering time by delivering a phishing page that is empty except for a script. The page load will complete very quickly, so the user cannot read the real URL bar. After the page load event completes, the script dynamically adds all of the visible elements to the phishing website.

An observant user could unmask the URL bar hiding attack by scrolling up to view the URL. There are also two weaknesses in the spoofing attack. First, the bookmarks button is placed next to the URL bar. In iOS, the bookmarks cannot be faked, and the user might notice a nonfunctional bookmarks button. (In Android, an application with the appropriate bookmark permissions can access the browser's bookmark storage.) Second, both browsers have a window selection feature that lets the user view the URLs of the open windows.

Despite these shortcomings, Niu et al. found that the URL bar hiding and spoofing attacks were very successful on a set of 37 users that included security experts. None of the users identified the phishing attacks when the URL bar was hidden, and only one noticed the fake URL bar. The user who noticed the fake URL bar did so because of a small implementation error in their emulation of the browser chrome. The near-perfect success rate of their phishing attacks on primed, expert users indicates that these techniques have the potential to enable highly successful phishing attacks. Their user study found that small glitches were attributed to browser or website bugs and did not raise suspicion.

5.1.5.2   *Man-in-the-middle*

In Section 5.1.3.2, we describe an active attacker that subverts HTTPS form submission after a mobile application has linked the user to an HTTP site. An even more powerful network attack is possible in the web-to-web setting. If the user ever visits any HTTP page in the browser while there is an active attacker tampering with the network connection, then all subsequent browsing can be compromised. A network attacker could subvert all HTTP webpages so that all links to HTTPS pages point to an attacker-controlled server. In a desktop browser, the user would have an opportunity to detect the attack by looking at the URL bar. However, in a mobile browser, the attacker can suppress visual indicators of the attack with a fake URL bar. This attack could be automated by a tool like Ettercap [4].

This attack is unobtrusive and would likely go undetected by users. It relies on the mobile browser URL hiding and spoofing techniques, which are demonstrably effective at tricking users. The only way for the user to avoid the attack is to manually enter HTTPS URLs directly into the browser URL bar (or with a saved bookmark).

5.1.6   Attack Prevention

The phishing attacks in this paper all exploit the mobile platform's pervasive lack of application identity indicators. A user cannot reliably tell what application is currently running or what website is currently loaded in the browser. In the absence of identity indicators, applications and websites can mimic each other with a high degree of accuracy.

One solution is to permanently dedicate some small portion of the screen to application identity. The operating system could provide an always-present identity bar that displays the name of the current foreground application, and the browser could similarly provide a minimalist, always-present address bar that simply displays the domain in a small font. However, there are three significant problems with this solution: mobile screen space is limited, users ignore security indicators [170], and users will still be conditioned to fall for embedded phishing attacks as long as legitimate applications continue to embed login forms.

An alternate solution is for the operating system to support a trusted password entry mechanism. SpoofKiller is a proposal for such a trusted login mechanism [274]; also see Chapter 7.6. When using SpoofKiller, a user presses the "Home" button when she wants to log in to a website or application. The operating system then presents the user with a standardized login screen that displays security information and any other relevant security indicators (e.g., SSL status). The primary challenges for this approach are usability and adoption; users must be convinced to always press the button before supplying a password, and applications and websites must support this form of password entry.

In general, phishing is an open problem, and the constraints of mobile devices make it more difficult. As an immediate measure, we recommend that companies stop using embedded login forms. Companies like Facebook and Twitter should encourage developers to implement social sharing using their mobile applications instead of embedded logins. Embedded logins exacerbate the problem of training users to ignore security indicators.

5.2   WHY MOBILE MALWARE WILL EXPLODE

Markus Jakobsson and Mark Grandcolas

Abstract. We describe why mobile malware is not a big threat—yet—and why we believe it will be.

5.2.1   Nineteen Eighty-Six: When it all Started

Once upon a time, malware authors wrote code to infect thousands of machines for entertainment and intellectual stimulation. Today, it's all about the money, and the greatest threat may lie in the silence, making a far more dangerous landscape.

Let's look back at the brief history of malware. It is 1986, and the first computer virus has just been released. The "brain virus"—a benevolent-acting boot sector virus that immediately declares its presence on an infected machine. Ten years later, Adam Young and Moti Yung predicted that crypto-enabled ransomware may strike—and later, the Archiveus Trojan fulfilled the prophecy. It encrypts files on infected machines and offers the decryption key for sale. Yet a few years later, keyloggers become part of the everyday threat on the Internet. What changed? Malware stopped announcing its presence. It hides. It spies. This is an important change in functionality, in particular when we talk about security attitudes of typical Internet users. To many, if the malware does not announce its presence, it simply is not there.

5.2.2   A Glimpse of Users

With practically no worries, people will install "fun applications"—games, screensavers, and other cute things that will put their machines in harm's way. Many people do not realize that a game may moonlight as capturing and recording user keystrokes. People will click "yes" if they are asked to install something time after time after time, and the question just won't go away as long as they click "no." If people are offered convenience or security—then security will lose. The average Internet user is more lazy than security aware.

Average Internet users will play full-screen movies sent by friends, even if it means running self-signed executables. They will buy and install pirated software, which of course can have been gently augmented to include malware. Ironically, a large portion of pirated antivirus software may not help the user too much. And of course, it does not matter whether the original version was made by a respectable antivirus vendor or not. And people will put up their own websites, but not quite know how to manage their security. Many of these sites (unwittingly to their owners) become hosts for malware.

People do not know that their machines have been infected nowadays because it is not in the best interests of the malware authors that they do. The silence is deadly. And because money is the main motivator, the game is different now than in 1986.

5.2.3   Why Market Size Matters

As this is written, mobile malware is still in its infancy—but is starting to receive media attention. Why is it not here, and why do we think it will soon change?

It is helpful to look at what has happened to traditional computing platforms to predict what may happen to handsets. It is commonly known that the Windows platform is the most attacked by malware. While malware existed before the Internet, the development of the Internet has fueled malware tremendously. Windows was the biggest platform when the Internet was developed. Windows was also the biggest platform when e-commerce saw the light of day; e-commerce permits a *monetization* of infection. It is commonly believed that this has greatly contributed to the shift in malware generation from a largely innocent hobby to a tool of organized crime. Currently, malware authors often rely on an existing code base. This makes them remain attached to Windows.

So let's go back in time and look at the development of malware for traditional platforms, to understand why things happen as they do.

> In 1998, around the time that malware took a serious hold of the Internet, the market share of desktop personal computer operating systems in the United States during the year was as follows: Windows 95: 57.4%; Windows 98: 17.2%; Windows NT: 11%; Mac OS: 5%; DOS: 3.8%; Linux: 2.1%; Windows 3.11: 1.1%; Unix: 0.8%; OS/2: 0.5%; others: 1%. No wonder malware authors turned to Windows!

There *is* malware for Macs—although two orders of magnitude less than for Windows. Some argue that this is not due to a higher security of these machines. For example, in hacking competitions in recent years, teams attacking Macs have been approximately as victorious as teams attacking Windows machines.

The fact that Macs are not inherently better than Windows is also supported by the fact that Trojans are more common on Windows than on Macs. A Trojan does not depend on a machine vulnerability to install itself, but on user misjudgment, and therefore does not relate to code vulnerability (i.e., detailed knowledge of code), but only to code development (requiring less detailed knowledge). This supports the argument that malware is written for common platforms. That also explains the relative absence of mobile malware to date: traditional cell phones are inherently less vulnerable, and smartphones are still relatively uncommon.

Malware authors are writing malware for the dominant platforms in order to maximize the number of machines they target, and to reuse their code base and domain-specific knowledge. Once smartphones become common platforms to access the Internet, they will be targeted at a large scale.

5.2.4 Financial Trends

By the end of 2012, estimates suggest that the global population will hover around 7 billions, with the world's mobile subscriber base will approaching 4.8 billion.

The widespread adoption of ubiquitous mobile devices and their capacity to act as a general purpose computing platform make them ideal candidates for mobile commerce (m-commerce)—particularly mobile money transfer services (e.g., mobile banking, mobile payments, and mobile remittance). For example, in India with a mobile device subscription rate of 261 million by March 2008 and with an estimated growth of about 8 million per month, banks have been exploring the feasibility of using mobile phones as an alternative channel of delivery of banking services. A few banks have started offering information-based services like balance enquiry, stop payment instruction of checks, record of last five transactions, location of nearest ATM or branch. The increasingly popularity of m-commerce is now demonstrable.

5.2.5 Mobile Malware Outlook

As this is being written, the threat of mobile malware is marginal, and there is no meaningful market for products to address the threat. However, there will soon be more smartphones than PCs—if not already. This will cause a change of what platforms are targeted by malware authors, particularly if a small number of mobile operating systems come to dominate the market.

Once the smartphone market is big enough to attract the attention of malware authors, they will enter in earnest. At first, most exploits will hit slightly more vulnerable devices and more common types of operating systems. There will also be cross-platform malware, which may use and exploit vulnerabilities in Java 2 Micro Edition, or other code that exists on multiple operating systems.

A handset is a much more desirable target to malware authors than a laptop or desktop. It is always connected—being a phone. It is a payment platform—also, due to being a phone, but also due to the likely use for many as a mobile wallet. It can be used to physically move infection being mobile. It also has much more personal data, and is used in a much more social manner (and therefore, with less security.) And at least at the time of writing it has weaker protection. Finally, it has intrinsic limitations on computation due to power limitations that affects the type of security software it can run.

There are several "tectonic shifts" occurring in the mobile industry landscape that, taken together, are likely to cause a perfect storm of malware development; at least as far as there is a dearth of protection during the period the new trends take hold and become mainstream. Let us describe some of these trends:

- **Trend #1 Mobile payments**   It has long been known that malware creators covet two primary targets above all others; access to credit cards (and the associated PINs), debit cards, and bank accounts. Thus, banking and retail sectors have suffered disproportionately from online fraud. But until now, mobile credit and debit payments have only been offered (and used) in a very limited capacity, and while that is expected to change dramatically in the next few years, it also ushers in one of the most attractive incentives for malware creators to go mobile. Up until now, there have been many reasons why mobile payments have not taken off; not the least of which has been the credit card industry moving slowly in adopting and implementing mobile standards and solutions. But with the past issues around NFC having been mostly nontechnical, and finally settled, the expectation is that retailers will be rolling out NFC enabled terminals for mobile transactions in earnest. Not to be outdone, almost coincident with the credit card industrys public and united rally around NFC, Google has announced a mobile wallet initiative. While the biggest players have now placed their bets in mobile payments, it remains to be seen how the winners and losers will shake out. As is so often the case, the opportunity the larger players have created by putting the mobile market in play, has also given rise to several new startups (with alternative approaches) funded by the venture community. Thus regardless of who wins, the malware producers will win as well, unless there are proven effective counter measures that emerge along with the mobile payment solutions.

- **Trend #2 Personalization via mobile context**   The mobile revolution has also given rise to a valuable new commodity that did not exist in the PC world; it is what I like to refer to as the mobile context. When you turn on your phone, your carrier knows who you are, where you are, who your friends and relatives are, and many other highly personal aspects about you. In some sense, they can know more about you than anyone you are closest to. All of this exists as digital data either on the handset or stored in the cloud, and all of it is highly attractive to the malware creators, and fraudsters skilled in the art of spear phishing. While the mobile context offers advertisers the ability to become much more targeted with their promotions and messages, it also presents an attractive opportunity to malware creators one that can be leveraged to much greater effectiveness by the bad guys.

- **Trend #3 Moving content to the edge of the network**   At the time of writing, managed service providers are locked in the early stages of an ongoing battle with OTT (Over The Top) broadcasters of popular content. While the managed service providers are currently able to leverage their subscriber base and secure premium content deals funded by their business model of monthly subscription and advertising, they are at a significant cost disadvantage to the OTT players. As the use of video explodes, the big service providers know that they must reduce the capacity costs of their networks and one of the best ways to do that is to cache popular content out at the edges close to where it is requested. Many schemes (both at the application level and at the underlying communication protocol layer) are being tested, all with this goal in mind. The new security challenge this will create then, is that any security measures based on traffic analysis will have to adapt to this new architecture, as the centralized command and control structure is going to evolve to content stored at the edge, and backbone filters are circumvented. As many of these managed networks will have cellular communication reaching the client, and these mobile networks move to 4G LTE and IP at the edge, the traditional purveyors of worms will have a familiar architecture to work with.

It is almost a given that any new and large technology trends will give rise to a whole new set of winners and losers including fraudsters, of course. Mobile computing will not be an exception.

5.3 TAPJACKING: STEALING CLICKS ON MOBILE DEVICES

Gustav Rydstedt, Baptiste Gourdin, Elie Bursztein, and Dan Boneh

Abstract. HTML lets one webpage load another page as a subframe called an iframe. An ad, for example, can be loaded as an iframe inside a larger page. A broad category of attacks, called *framing attacks*, exploit the framing capabilities of HTML to harm users. A standard defense, called *frame busting*, is deployed on several popular websites, but often only on the nonmobile version of the site, leaving mobile users vulnerable to framing. In this section, we survey a number of framing attacks against mobile web browsers. We show that the limited screen space of a mobile browser greatly helps the attacker in mounting framing attacks. We hope these examples will encourage more sites to deploy framing protection for both mobile and nonmobile sites.

5.3.1 Framing Attacks

Framing attacks take place in the browser and begin with a malicious page loading a victim page in an iframe. Once the victim page is iframed, the framing page can mount a variety of attacks. The most common example is clickjacking [238] where the victim page is loaded as a transparent iframe over a benign-looking page that tempts the user to click on the screen. For example, the attacking page can implement a game that encourages the user to click on various parts of the screen. The victim page is loaded as a *transparent* iframe that is positioned on top of the game so that all user clicks are sent to the victim page. Since the victim's iframe is transparent, the user only sees the game and has no idea that an iframe is overlayed on top of the game. Now, if the framed page is an e-commerce or social website then the user may think she is playing a game, but in reality she is clicking on the framed page and potentially initiating actions such as purchasing an item or sending a tweet.

Real-world exploits using clickjacking include social networking worms such as Tweetbomb [330] and Likejacking [491]. Tweetbomb fools anyone visiting a malicious page into tweeting the URL of that malicious page, thereby enticing other twitter users to visit and retweet the malicious URL. Similarly, Likejacking tricks users into clicking on the Facebook like button hosted on a malicious page thereby "liking" the malicious page and exposing their friends to it. These clickjacking URLs quickly propagate through the social graph. As another demonstration of clickjacking, Huang and Jackson [253] show that a website can identify visitors to the site by clickjacking the Facebook like button hosted at the site.

Another framing attack called UI redressing [214] proceeds with the attacker opening the victim webpage in a subframe and positioning frames on top of the victim page so that the appearance of the victim page is changed. For example, the attacker can hide a transaction confirmation message on the framed page by placing a benign question over it. The user is then fooled into authorizing a potentially harmful action at the victim site.

Other attacks include drag-and-drop attacks [457] and scrolling attacks [457]. We discuss these attacks later on in the chapter.

5.3.1.1 Defenses

The standard defense against framing attacks, called *frame busting*, refers to code or annotation in a webpage intended to prevent the webpage from being loaded in a subframe [414]. One approach to frame busting uses the following simple JavaScript code:

```
if (top.location != location)
    top.location = self.location;
```

The code checks if the page is opened in a subframe and if so makes the browser load the page as a top-level frame. A 2010 survey of clickjacking defenses [414] found that only 14% of the Alexa Top-500 sites implement some form of frame busting. More disturbing, the survey shows that current JavaScript-based methods, including the code above, can be easily defeated. That is, webpages can be framed despite using frame busting JavaScript as above. The paper [414] proposes more robust frame busting methods.

Another approach to performing frame busting is to use the HTTP header called X-Frame-Options [319]. This header tells the browser that the served page should not be opened in a subframe. Best practice suggests that web developers use both JavaScript code and the X-Frame-Options header to prevent framing.

These defenses are not always adequate. Web tools, such as the Facebook like button, are intended to be framed on other sites. Consequently, frame busting is not an option for protecting these tools from clickjacking.

5.3.1.2 Framing attacks on mobile websites

In this section, we describe framing attacks on mobile sites and show that smartphones are highly vulnerable, much more so than desktop browsers and public websites. Despite these vulnerabilities, at the time of this writing few mobile sites defend against framing. In Ref. [415], it is shown that mobile sites are prevalent: 53% of Alexa-Top 500 sites have mobile alternatives to their primary site designed to render better on a phone. These are most often served in the .mobi domain, or in m.*, mobile.*, wap.* subdomains. A majority deliver a significant subset of their functionality to their mobile sites.

While 14% of the top 500 sites do some form of frame busting on their main site, virtually none use frame busting on their mobile sites ([415] only reports two sites that frame bust their main and mobile site). As a result almost all mobile sites are vulnerable to framing attacks on the phone.

In the next section we present *tapjacking*, a framing attack on mobile websites that is far more effective than its clickjacking cousin on desktops. These attacks on the iOS and Android phones show that without frame busting, mobile sites can be easily compromised. Surprisingly, the Opera mini browser seems immune to tapjacking, despite its full support for JavaScript and frames. We discuss this in more detail in Section 5.3.2.2.

5.3.1.3 Lessons

Why do sites frame bust on their main but not on the their mobile equivalents? There are two predominate arguments:

1. "Older mobile browsers do not support the JavaScript needed for frame busting." The concern is that frame busting code will cause the mobile site to render incorrectly on older phones. However, this concern is easily addressed by selectively rendering based on user-agent. That is, inject frame busting code when the user agent is an iPhone or Android and do not inject it if the browser is an older phone.

2. "Clickjacking is not an issue on cell phones." We hope this section demonstrates that this assumption is simply not true. In fact, we show that quite the opposite holds: framing attacks are more effective on smartphones than on desktops.

As an aside we note that many mobile sites do not check that the user agent is a mobile phone and happily render the mobile site in a desktop browser. Moreover, many sites do not differentiate sessions between the main site and the mobile site. That is, a user logged in at the main site is also logged in at the mobile site and vice versa. As a result, if a site frame busts on the main site but not on the mobile site, an attacker can frame the mobile site on a desktop browser and mount a framing attack of its choice on the site. For example, if a user is logged into a web mail site on the desktop, an attacker on the desktop browser can frame the mobile version of the web mail site and use the user's credential from the main site to send mail on behalf of the user.

Clearly mobile sites should frame bust if the user agent indicates a phone that supports frame busting. If this is not possible for some reason then at the very least we recommend that sites not share sessions between the main site and the mobile site.

5.3.2 Phone Tapjacking

In this section, we present Tapjacking—a clickjacking attack that leverages the accessibility features implemented in mobile browsers. Tapjacking illustrates the importance of frame busting on mobile sites. We hope this section will convince more sites to do so.

5.3.2.1 Tapjacking the iPhone web browser

The iPhone Safari browser supports all the basic functionality to pull off a classic clickjacking attack: transparency and iframes. Transparency is supported through the CSS opacity attribute in Safari Mobile. We now show that extra features of the iPhone make the attack far more dangerous.

Zooming On desktop browsers an attacker must ensure that the user clicks at the right place in the victim iframe (e.g., on the submit button on the victim page). One approach is to move the victim iframe into place after every MouseMove event is detected so that the mouse always points to the button that the attacker wants clicked on the victim page. Since this method is more difficult to pull off on the iPhone we instead demonstrate a different approach: the iPhone's zooming functionality.

Figure 5.8 Tapjacking Twitter with a zoomed button. The Twitter publishing button has been enlarged in a transparent iframe so that clicking anywhere on the screen publishes a tweet.

Recall that scaling on smartphones is often done via the viewport meta tag:

```
<meta name = "viewport"
  content = "width = 320,
             initial-scale = 10,
             user-scalable = no">
```

In this example, the initial scaling of the entire viewport is set to 10 (maximum). At this level of zoom, any regular button will cover the entire width of the screen. By putting this enlarged button in an iframe, the clickjacking attack becomes much more efficient since the "tappable" area is very large. Interestingly, scaling properties of the top frame takes precedence over those of framed sites. Hence, after opening the victim site in an iframe, the attacker can scale his own top frame, thus also scaling the victim site.

Figure 5.8 shows an example where the Twitter publishing button has been enlarged in a transparent iframe. To further ensure the user is constrained to click the targeted area, we can disable any further scaling by setting the user-scalable attribute to 0.

Hiding or faking the URL bar When mounting a clickjacking attack in a desktop browser the address bar points to the attacker's page. Therefore, the attacker needs to somehow host his page on a legitimate-looking URL. The attacker's life is much easier on the phone: he can easily cause the address bar to disappear. Even better, from the attacker's point of view, he can spoof the address bar and make it appear to contain whatever URL he wants.

The following code hides the URL bar as soon as the site is loaded by scrolling the URL navigation bar out of the visible window:

```
<body onload="setTimeout(function()
   { window.scrollTo(0, 1) }, 100);">
</body>
```

Figure 5.9   Faking the URL bar. The left figure shows the fake address bar under the real one. Note that the page is served from badguy.com. The middle figure shows what happens when the attacker scrolls the page so that the fake URL bar replaces the real one: Although the page is served from badguy.com the address bar now shows google.com. The right figure shows that by further scrolling, the URL bar can vanish completely.

Once the real address bar is off the visible window, the attacker can embed a picture of a fake URL address bar in the framing page, thereby making the page appear to come from a legitimate site. Figure 5.9 gives an example. Niu et al. [376] also used this feature of the iPhone browser to study phishing attacks on the iPhone.

Abusing normal phone behavior   An attacker can abuse normal phone behavior to fool the user into clicking on the screen. For example, Figure 5.8 shows a webpage that presents the exact same dialog that comes up when an SMS text message is received. Phone users are trained to click "Close" or "Reply" upon seeing this dialog. In Figure 5.8, the user is interacting with the web browser, not the messaging application. Clicking will not acknowledge the text message, but instead publish a tweet. If the user clicked "Close" then the dialog closes as expected and the user cannot tell that something out of the ordinary took place.

Strengthening tapjacking by turning off gestures   The attacker can disable any touch gesture, such as scrolling or zooming, by telling the browser to ignore touch gestures. This is done by calling the function preventDefault as shown in the code below:

```
function touchMove(event) {
    event.preventDefault();
}
```

As a result, the user cannot undo the dynamic scrolling and zooming set by the attacker.

Session handling   Without a session to hijack clickjacking attacks are of no value to the attacker. On desktop browsers sessions often expire when the user closes the browser. This is not the case on the iPhone where sessions persist after Safari Mobile is closed. This helps the attacker since sessions lay dormant for potential tapjacking attacks. Whenever the user visits a malicious page, a tapjacking attack can take place on any live session in the browser.

While analyzing the Alexa Top 100 top sites, we noted that some "mobile cookies" expire further in the future than their desktop counterparts. Presumably this is designed to minimize the number of times that the user needs to log in on a cell phone. These longer lived sessions help the attacker.

To conclude our tapjacking discussion of the iPhone we note that the attacks presented here use main stream features of the browser that are unlikely to change much over time. Resig [406] describes an iPhone clickjacking attack that exploits a specific bug in an old version of the iPhone browser (iPhone OS 2.2) that was fixed shortly thereafter.

Defenses: the X-Frame-Options HTTP header   This header instructs modern versions of all main browsers not to render the page in a subframe. Both the iPhone 3.0's Safari Mobile and the Android 2.1 browser support this header. When appropriate, the header should be added whenever the user agent is one of these browsers to prevent tapjacking on active sessions.

5.3.2.2   Other mobile browsers

The Android browser   All the tapjacking techniques we outlined for the iPhone are applicable to the Android browser. Support for iframes, opacity changes, scaling, viewport meta tags, makes the Android browser a prime target for tapjacking.

Opera Mini   Opera Mini uses a proxy-rendering system to display webpages faster. Although Opera Mini has growing JavaScript and CSS support we conclude that a traditional clickjacking attack is not possible on the Opera Mini (we tested on version 5.0.5 on the iPhone). Although iframes are supported, reliably changing their opacity and size is not. This makes the classic approach to clickjacking difficult since the attacker cannot effectively redress clickable UI of the target page.

5.3.3   Framing Facebook

Figure 5.10 shows Facebook's clever clickjacking defense that places a semitransparent div overlay on top of the page. Users can see their session content but not interact with it. When the div is clicked, Facebook attempts to frame bust using standard techniques. While this defense works reasonably well against standard clickjacking attacks, an attacker can exploit it to leak private user information using a scrolling attack due to Stone [457].

Stone presented a technique for defeating the same origin policy on pages that do not frame bust. Roughly speaking, the idea is that the attacking page loads the victim page victim.com in a small iframe. The attacking page then navigates the victim frame to victim.com#test. If the hashtag 'test' exists on victim.com then the browser will scroll the victim frame to the position of that hashtag. If the hashtag does not exist, the victim frame is unchanged. By reading the frame's scroll position, the attacking page can learn if the hashtag 'test' exists on the victim page. This violates the DOM same origin policy.

Here we briefly explain how an attacker can use Stone's frame leak attack (FLA) to exploit overlay-based frame busting. We use Facebook as an example.

Figure 5.10   Facebook's translucent div defense. When framing a Facebook page, Facebook inserts a translucent div that overlays the entire page. The user can read the text underneath the div, but clicking anywhere activates frame busting code that makes Facebook the top frame.

Let's now take a look at how the attack works. When the user—whom we will call Alice—visits the attacker's page, an invisible double iframe with a small width and height is displayed. The inner iframe is redirected to Facebook with a specified hashtag: #pagelet_intentional_stream. If Alice is logged-in the scrollbar of the inner iframe will move. This movement can be dynamically detected by the attacker's outer frame letting the attacker learn if Alice is currently logged in. Next, the attacker can test if Alice is the one currently visiting his page. To do so, the attacker navigates the Facebook iframe to an arbitrary Facebook page and tests if the hashtag #box_app_2305272732 is present on the page, where 2305272732 is Alice's Facebook ID. If so, then the attacker leans that Alice (user 2305272732) is currently visiting. Even more, the attacker can test if another Facebook user, say Bob, is a friend of Alice by navigating the Facebook iframe to a hashtag corresponding to Bob's Facebook ID. If the scrollbar of the inner iframe moves then indeed Bob is one of Alice's friends. Many features of Alice's profile can be extracted this way.

This issue was fixed by Facebook by adding randomness to their hashtags so that the attacker cannot predict what hashtags to test. Nevertheless, this privacy leak serves as a good illustration of the difficulty in verifying the security of novel framing defenses.

5.3.4   Summary and Recommendations

This section discusses a vulnerability in mobile websites that is easily corrected by introducing frame busting on mobile sites. Mobile websites that do not use frame busting are vulnerable to tapjacking and expose their users to unnecessary risk. We hope that our brief survey of tapjacking will encourage more sites to embed frame busting in their pages.

Beyond mobile sites, we examined the effectiveness of overlay-based frame busting as used by Facebook. While this defense may prevent traditional clickjacking, it can result in exposure of private user information. When possible, it is much safer to use traditional frame busting, as discussed in Ref. [414], to prevent user content from rendering in a subframe of an unknown domain.

ACKNOWLEDGMENT

This work was supported by NSF.

Chapter **6**

The Internet and the Physical World

This chapter describes how Internet problems have the potential of "reaching out" into the physical world.

We start (Section 6.1) by describing how a person's location privacy can be affected by corrupted mobile devices. Here, it is important to recognize the impact of location. If you can see my address book, you can conclude a bit about who I am. If you can see what numbers I am calling, how often, and for how long, then you may be able to build a better understanding of me. But if you know where I am, at what times, and *with whom*, then you know much more. The second thing to recognize is that a person's location privacy would not only be affected by that person's poor "security hygiene"—but by that of other people as well. In other words, if other people's mobile devices get infected by malware, or their owners agree against better knowledge to install abusive applications—then *your* privacy may suffer.

We turn (Section 6.2) to looking at how social networks are abused by Internet fraudsters, and how an attacker can build a profile about a victim—simply by befriending the victim. This is surprisingly simple to do—nobody wants the embarrassment of turning down a friend request from somebody whose name was just forgotten, and everybody wants to be popular and have friends. Few people recognize the impact spurious friendships may have on their privacy, and security, too.

We then turn to politics, and how it can be manipulated on the Internet (Section 6.3). This is a terrifying prospect, if we think of fraudsters as politically motivated activists, terrorist organizations, and foreign governments—all of which have good reasons to affect political developments. However, internal manipulation of the political process and propagation of lies—which has already been witnessed—is not that much more desirable for a society that wishes to rely on the opinions of informed citizens.

Clearly, we cannot think of the Internet as "a technology playground" for those who like gadgets. Whether we want it or not, most of us rely on the Internet for our daily lives, as does society in general!

6.1 MALWARE-ENABLED WIRELESS TRACKING NETWORKS

Nathaniel Husted and Steven Myers

Abstract. Modern smartphones provide computing power and sensor capabilities that were unheard of in previous mobile devices. The new power and sensor capabilities provide the potential for many useful applications, but also many new attacks. These new forms of attacks can leave the traditional computational or virtual realm, where previous computer security attacks have existed, and begin to interact with us in the physical world. The result is that computer security problems will now result in not only attacks on our finances and data, but can extend out to affect our privacy and physical security. In this section, we consider the ability of software to track users' physical movements through a city, not due to any security flaws on their own device, but potentially due to the flaws in the devices of *others*. We do this by introducing the notion of a tracking network, and then show simulation results based on human validated data, which shows that there is some potential for such networks to exist in the future.

6.1.1   Introduction

Modern smartphones barely resemble their precursors, traditional cell phones. Some of the evolution from cell phone to smartphone is visible. For example, the relative size of a modern phone versus one form the 1980s and the inclusion of large displays. Changes in the computational power, data storage capability, network connectivity, and the default inclusion of a myriad of sensors are less evident from physical inspection. The increase in features have made smartphones more computers with sensors that happen to have a phone functionality, rather than traditional phones with some computing functionality. These changes have significant potential when put into the context of security and privacy: (i) the ability of malicious code to attack the phones increases with their computational power and complexity and (ii) the value in attacking the phones increase as they acquire more valuable data such as through their sensors and user interaction.

While traditional cell phones dominated the marketplace in the early 2000s, smartphones (e.g., Research in Motion's Blackberry) were a niche market catering primarily to business people and the IT crowd. This changed dramatically in 2007. This is when Apple released the iPhone, a phone inspired by Apple's iPod. It provided a number of very useful computational abilities along with an intuitive user-interface, and Apple's famous marketing. (For more discussion on the general value of User-Interfaces, see Section 8.1.) The result was that smartphones were pushed into the larger consumer market. Other companies soon aimed to compete in this growing market. For example, Google produced its Android operating system to power families of new consumer-friendly smartphones.

Smartphone and mobile phone usage have increased greatly over the last decade. Approximately 68% of the world's population have a cell phone subscription in 2011. The figure was only 12% in 2000 [46].

In 2012, more Americans will have smartphones than traditional cell phones [390]. Further, from the perspective of a computational platform, this new smartphone market is very homogenous: Android, Apple, and Research in Motion (RIM) accounted for roughly 91% of the smartphone market share in early 2010 [296]. This has serious consequences, as homogeneity of the platform suggests an attack on one device is likely to work on the population at large, leading to epidemic attacks. The information that is either stored on or accessible by a smartphone is of high value, thus making smartphones more likely targets of malicious attacks than traditional cell phones.

Smartphones are becoming the primary tool for communication and personal data storage for many individuals. People use them to place and receive calls, manage their email and social networking, finances, and medical and organizational data. Additionally, smartphones play important parts in peoples entertainment. They contain music, videos, games, and supporting general Internet surfing. Further, they enhance or help monitor many of physical activities, be it for sport or physical fitness. Finally, we use them to capture photos and videos of important moments in our lives. The centrality of smartphones to our interpersonal communication and our lifestyles means that they generally contain huge amounts of personal and confidential data, and are potentially—if not likely—central points of failure for personal and confidential information to be leaked. For example, the loss of a modern smartphone to an adversary can communicate communication habits, future and past appointments, contacts, access to social networks, financial transactions, and access to private networks through stored passwords. The aggregation of a user's personal information and information on members of their social network in a central point on the smartphone creates a high-value target for malicious individuals wanting this information. The information is valuable for attacks such as identity theft and other forms fraud.

The value of data on smartphones, and the homogeneity of the phones' operating systems suggest that phones will quickly become targets of traditional malware. However, traditional malware (see Section 3.4) is not the only way that such phones can leak private information about their users. The smartphone's connectivity to the Internet via WiFi and the cellular network, in conjunction with cloud-computing, is another weakness. Due to this connectivity, a malicious individual does not even need physical access to the smartphone; they must only be able to create a digital connection! Many smartphone providers use this digital connection to maintain a central repository or backup "in the cloud" for their users' data. These repositories are also subject to attack, and the security of such repositories is beyond users' control. One highly publicized example of smartphone information leakage is when data from the socialite Paris Hilton's smartphone was stolen. The attackers stole contact information and private pictures originally stored on the phone that were then published on the Internet. The phone itself was never attacked, but rather its cloud backup was targeted by taking advantage of a flaw in the T-Mobile webpages to reset a users passwords. (Details on password reset attacks are in Section 4.7.) Yet, this is still a rather traditional attack taking advantage of the phone's programming to backup its data to an external source. The ubiquity of computing power and sensors leads to new types of attacks, just as distributed denial of service attacks could only appear once a significant fraction of the population had connections to the Internet.

This section focuses on one such potential attack. We describe an attack that uses the location finding capabilities of the smartphone as a sensor platform, which are then used to violate the privacy of phone users who are in close physical proximity. In particular, we show how a large number of individuals can coordinate their behavior to track the physical location of someone in a metropolitan area. This is done by having each coordinating smartphone look for unique identifiers transmitted by other smartphones, and reporting their observations along with current locations and time to a central system. This central system can then interpolate the relative positions of individuals. Such abilities might be of use to a number of organizations including paramilitary groups, botnet operators, advertisers, and aid agencies. We will give specific examples shortly. In the remainder of this section we describe the capabilities of a modern smartphone and the information they can collect (or leak). Next, the tracking capabilities of a smartphone will be enumerated as well as scenarios where such networks might be used. A specific example will be given in regards to a WiFi-based tracking unit, and their properties will be investigated.

We should mention that while we motivate our discussion in this section with smartphones, any devices with similar mobility, connectivity, sensing, and computational powers can be thought of as synonymous with smartphones. Thus, the recent explosion of tablet computers, such as Apple's iPads and iPod touches, Android-based tablets and RIM's Playbook, can all be considered as smartphones for the purposes of the discussion in this section.

6.1.2 The Anatomy of a Modern Smartphone

The modern generation of smartphones should be considered computers that happen to have a phone functionality incorporated into them. Those currently on the market have processing power that could rival desktop PCs from several years earlier. Soon smartphones will ship with multicore processors, further increasing their peak computational abilities, while allowing for aggressive and adaptive power management.

Most smartphones are able to take full advantage of the high-speed always-on data connections that are inherent in most modern cellular networks. In the United States 3G (including LTE) and 4G networks are the standard for cellular wireless connectivity. These standards provide transfer capabilities rivaling many low-end home broadband connections. High-speed 3G and 4G cellular connections allow users to stream high definition multi-media and perform large data downloads on their mobile phones, capabilities that were not previously possible.

In addition to data networks provided over the cellular radio, smartphones almost universally come with both some form of WiFi (802.11b/g/n) and Bluetooth capability. The WiFi capability permits phones to connect to the Internet through wireless access points (WAP) just like any other laptop or tablet PC. A user can arrive at a coffee shop, connect to the free WiFi, check their email, and perform the plethora of other activities that high-speed Internet access allows. The range of WiFi is significantly smaller than that of the cellular network, and the battery usage is significantly higher. The bandwidth of WiFi connections is significantly higher than 3G connections, and the latency is less than that of 4G connections. Further, there is no usage charge for WiFi by cellular providers, therefore we can expect their presence on phones to continue, especially as unlimited data plans become a relic of cell phone history. Bluetooth provides no direct competition as Bluetooth has been relegated to personal networks of small devices such as hands free headsets or in-car audio.

Smartphones commonly provide a number of multimedia and sensor devices that laptops and many other mobile computing devices do not include. Examples include at least one camera that can be used both for high definition (720p) video and high-quality digital camera pictures (5 megapixels), temperature and light sensors, accelerometers, compasses , global positioning systems, and microphones. Additionally, the wireless radios used for WiFi and Bluetooth are forms of sensors when receiving data. The collection of all these capabilities create a powerful sensor platform on any smartphone that can collect an immense amount of personal data. The personal data is not necessarily stored safely and is at least retained on the local device, if not also by a cloud provider.

Some smartphones also support Near Field Communications (NFC). NFC can be used for local communications, but can also be used to power traditional RFID devices, and their anticipated use is in wireless payment systems that are incorporated into smartphones. However, NFC can also be used to receive signals. Therefore, once incorporated NFC communications will provides both new transmission, and sensing capabilities to phones.

In addition to their physical anatomy, a word on the software on smartphones is order. This is especially true due to its implications for the security of these devices. In order to provide a robust environment for all the new physical and software (i.e., application) functionality provide by modern smartphone, their operating systems are extremely complex. Google's Android operating system has over 12 million lines of code (no official counts were found for Apple's iOS and Windows Phone 7) [43]. For a comparison, the Linux kernel, the brain of the Linux operating system, has nearly 14 million lines of code [45]. The size and complexity of the code means that there are certainly security vulnerabilities in the systems (for more detail see Gary McGraw's writings in Ref. [278]). This, combined with the previously mentioned homogeneity of the market suggests that there will be a number of attacks that emerge that target large segments of users phones, and which can spread in an epidemic fashion.

6.1.3   Mobile Tracking Networks: A Threat to Smartphones

We focus on one particular example of how a large number of smartphones in a given vicinity can be used to track the location of others. We call such a grouping of smartphones that is working in concert to track the movements of others a *tracking network*. Such networks pose potential physical security and/or privacy threats.

Global tracking networks are able to geolocate others as follows. The individuals in the tracking network know their geographical positions through the use of their own positioning systems. These systems may use GPS systems, or they may be based on other technology such as cellular or WiFi positioning systems. To position others that are *not* in the tracking network, the tracking network uses the existence of short-range radio broadcasters on the tracked individuals. The communications standards for most of these short-range radios embed unique identifiers into most, if not all, communications. When a member of a tracking network observes radio transmissions, it reports all the identifiers to a centralized system, along with its current location. A centralized collector of the data can then triangulate positions of individuals as they are observed. We go into more detail on how this is done in Section 6.1.3.3.

We consider a tracking network that tracks individuals that are broadcasting through the 802.11b/g/n WiFi networking standards to locate nearby individuals that are not part of the tracking network. We consider WiFi for several reasons: (i) it is ubiquitously deployed in smartphones, (ii) the radio transmits a broadcast identifier to find open access points (APs), and (iii) the phones have the ability to receive communications not directly targeted at them. These three factors combine to make 802.11 a perfect communications standard with which to attempt to track people. The scenario we consider is a wide-scale, potentially malware formed, WiFi-based tracking network in a dense metropolitan area. We consider dense metropolitan areas because they are the scenarios where such a network is most likely to be effective: it is exactly a user's proximity to many other people that allows her short-range radio broadcasts to be picked up.

Roadmap A brief overview of this section follows. In Section 6.1.3.1, we provide a sample of scenarios where tracking networks could be used. In Section 6.1.3.2, we provide an overview of the 802.11 wireless standard, so those who are unfamiliar with it can gain a better understanding of how a WiFi-based tracking network can detect individuals. Section 6.1.3.3 explains what a WiFi-based network might look like and a high-level description of its operations. Section 6.1.3.4 explains the methodology we used to study the performance of a WiFi-based tracking network. The results of our performance tested tracking network can be found in Section 6.1.3.5. The current defenses to WiFi-based tracking networks and their drawbacks can be found in Section 6.1.3.7.

6.1.3.1 *Tracking network scenarios*

We briefly consider some of the motivations for tracking networks, by people using them to attack others in various means.

Insurgent army In many cases a military will be operating in an urban environment in which there is a large insurgent population. In modern armies, many soldiers will travel with cellular phones, laptops, and other modern electronic paraphernalia. The insurgents can then deploy a tracking network to track the positions of some solders in the occupying force. The threat of an insurgent created tracking network will become greater as more battles are fought in urban areas.

Botnet operators In modern cybercrime, information about individuals has value. It increases the ability of attackers to perform successful identity theft attacks, and other forms of fraud, by being able to provide accurate information about individuals, such as their place of residence. A botnet operator whose controlling a tracking network could track the locations of potential fraud victims.

Advertisers Modern online advertising is all about customizing delivery of adds to those who are likely to make use of them. Advertisers are acutely aware of the potential power of using geolocation to target adds and incentives. Many users are willing to indiscriminately provide their geographic location, but some users with a legitimate concern of privacy are unwilling to provide such data to advertisers, say through a smartphone app. However, if a number of an advertiser's clients are willing to deploy such an app, they more form a tracking network. The network could be formed explicitly by asking the users if they are willing to report the positions of others, or implicitly without the users explicit willingness to do so. The resulting tracking network can be used to track those that are not willing to share their position with the advertiser.

However, we would like to point out that there are potentially legitimate uses for a WiFi-based tracking network. Below we consider some such scenarios.

Amber alert networks Amber alert networks are networks that are used to find children that have gone missing. Many of today's children's toys contain WiFi transmitters as part of their function (e.g., personal gaming devices). A large portion of the public might be encouraged to join a tracking network that can be used to scan for devices connected to lost children.

Theft recovery network Many high-cost digital electronic devices now incorporate WiFi. Many of these devices are mobile in nature, and prone to theft. Examples include laptops, tablets computers, cars, and others. Many of these devices do not necessarily include GPS systems, and we may wish to position them in the case of theft. A tracking network could be used to find such stolen goods.

Note that how a tracking network is formed is completely dependent on the scenario of usage. An insurgent army or advertiser might simply have supporters install the software or attempt to hide the functionality in a popular piece of software targeted at their opponents. An advertiser might pay users to install the software or provide some incentives to use the software, such as providing some beneficial service at a discounted cost. A botnet operator would take advantage of security flaws, or social engineering to have tracking software installed on users phones.

A word of caution We would like to note that while all of the above scenarios seem like potential uses of tracking networks, the authors are unaware of an actual deployment of a tracking network. *However,* there are currently a large number of smartphone apps that make use of a smartphone's geolocation capabilities and record the user's location. It is unknown what they do with this data, nor what future trends in the usage of such data will be. For example, the Pandora personal radio station application on smartphones came under fire due to the location information and other personal information of its clients that it transmitted to advertisers.

6.1.3.2 *An overview of the 802.11 wireless standard*

The fact that 802.11 devices can listen to signals from other devices is a key requirement for the proposed wireless tracking. Each 802.11 device has a unique identifier called its basic service set identifier (BSSID), which allows for the appropriate routing of wireless communications to appropriate wireless devices.

In layman's terms, each phone that supports WiFi has a unique identifier called a BSSID. All communications sent by an 802.11 device contain this BSSID. An attacker can use that BBSID to determine when that *specific device* has been seen within the range of their wireless receiver. This can be used to track and uniquely identify an individual carrying a smartphone with WiFi enabled.

There is a limited physical range within which an 802.11 radio can broadcast communications before the signal degrades. While this range is dependent on a host of factors (e.g., geography, landmarks, and interference), it is limited to a radius of about 100 m under optimal conditions, and about half that in a metropolitan urban setting. Therefore, detecting an 802.11 communication with a given BSSID tells us that the device is within close proximity (i.e., within the 802.11 standard's broadcasting range). Note that while the quality of a normal 802.11 connection decreases with distance, the detecting device need only detect a frame with the specified BSSID, and not actually form a paired connection with the device. The range at which the phone can be detected is slightly higher than the range at which a connection can be established. One can be at a range where enough communications can be detected to observe a BSSID, but not enough communications are transmitted in an *uncorrupted* fashion to actually permit a handshake between devices, allowing for normal two-way communication.

The actual broadcast range is dependent on the specific value of X in the 802.11X standard considered. For most of the discussion herein we are discussing 802.11g, the most commonly deployed standard for smartphones, and home and office routers in 2011. The range will increase as the standards change. For example, the 802.11n standard greatly expands the broadcast radius, and is available on some smartphones and many home and office routers.

In order to use the ability to detect communications from a phone with a given BSSID, we obviously require both the tracked phone to *broadcast* communications, so the phone can be detected, and the tracking phones to be able to *detect* such communications. We note that if a tracked phone is actively using its WiFi connection then it is sending out a continuous series of data, management and control communications, each of which contains the phone's specified BSSID. However, in the case that the phone is not actually communicating over its WiFi connection it can still be actively sending out communications with its associated BSSID contained within: When a wireless device is turned on and operational, it will send out *probe requests*. The purpose of these requests is to find wireless access points that the phone may be interested in connecting to. For example, when one wishes their phone or laptop to connect to a wireless access point, the user is generally presented by the operating system with a list of nearby access points that are available for connection. This list is the result of these access points responding to a probe request. Specifically, the 802.11 standard permits 802.11 APs to reply to such probe requests to make their presence known and inform on the standards they support. Probe Requests can ask to receive a *probe response* from a specific AP by sending a probe request with that BSSID listed as a target. Otherwise, a phone can send a probe request to a broadcast BSSID asking for probe responses from all routers in the area. This is referred to as *active scanning*. We note that many smartphones perform active scanning when they are not currently connected to an AP, in order to allow users to promptly connect to such APs. Thus, smartphones are frequently broadcasting their BSSIDs even when they do not have an active communications session with an AP or other 802.11 device. There is also a form of *passive scanning* where a phone waits on each wireless channel to hear a *beacon frame* from an access point, which regularly transmits beacons. If smartphones used passive scanning, this would mean that phones are not broadcasting their BSSIDs when they look for APs, which would lower the time in which a phone could be detected by a tracking network. It also means less accurate lists of nearby APs are presented to the user. We will discuss this more when detailing countermeasures for tracking networks.

For those readers interested in a more comprehensive overview of 802.11, one can be found in standard books such as [206].

6.1.3.3 *The design and implementation of a WiFi-based tracking network*

We consider a simple scenario with two individuals, Alice and Eve, to provide a convenient way to illustrate the workings of a WiFi-based tracking network. Assume Alice is a resident who lives and works in downtown Chicago. Alice walk to work in the morning and walks home in the evening. She will walk to lunch a few times a week or the corner grocer. Sometimes she will work or relax at a local coffee shop. Alice owns a smartphone and keeps her wireless radio on as her office has WiFi capabilities and she chooses to make use of open WiFi networks.

Eve controls a tracking network of smartphones and chooses to target Alice. Eve has previously obtained the BSSID identifier of the WiFi device in Alice's smartphone. There are many ways in which such a BSSID might be learned, we will speculate on a few shortly. Eve sends a request to all the bots in her botnet ordering them to report back the time and their current location whenever they spot signals sent from Alice's smartphone. Eve, over a given period of time, is able to conglomerate the information. Using triangulation, she can track Alice's position over time.

Eve's ability to track Alice increases depending upon three different properties of the botnet: (i) the coverage of the malnet over Alice's general pattern of human mobility; (ii) the broadcast range of Alice's WiFi device; and (iii) the frequency (over time) at which Alice's smartphone broadcasts any communications.

The performance of a wireless tracking network such as Eve's is simplified both because of the common behaviors of smartphone users and the WiFi protocol itself. In particular, to find Alice, Eve needs for Alice's WiFi radio to be broadcasting. Alice's WiFi is enabled and broadcasting whenever its WiFi radio is actively being used. The radio is used when the user is checking their email, browsing the web, downloading data files, or scanning for access points. For most smartphones, anytime the phone's screen is on and WiFi has not been totally disengaged the phone will actively scan for wireless access points. Thus for a significant fraction of time, a user's phone is actively transmitting. We speculate that the amount of time in which phones are actively broadcasting will only increase. For example, applications now exist for the Apple iPhone that will keep the phone from disabling the wireless (phones attempt to deactivate wireless in order to conserve battery power). Many casual users do not bother to turn off WiFi during day-to-day use, especially if they are heavy WiFi users, unless battery life is an issue. Companies that produce phones are actively working on increasing the duration phones can be used with WiFi active. Therefore, the number of users who deactivate WiFi to reduce battery usage will likely decrease in the near future. If this trend continues, then on the majority of users phones WiFi will only be disabled if a user consciously disables it.

In order to track Alice while she is broadcasting her BSSID, every device in Eve's botnet works as a sensor to enable triangulation. The smartphones in the botnet can use either internal GPS units or an external locating service to position themselves (e.g., the locating service Skyhook [22] that positions WiFi devices using WiFi signals and an Internet connection). When a bot sees a transmission of Alice's BSSID, it can then report its current position to Eve. After Eve receives the position, very simple trilateration algorithms can be use to find Alice's position with a certain level of accuracy. If Eve is able to measure the signal strength of each of those detections, she can further improve the accuracy of the tracking network [95,96].

How Eve builds a tracking network   The above suggests that Eve already has a tracking network, and one might question if Eve can even *build* such a network to begin with. Many of the issues that Eve faces are the same as those of traditional botnet operators.

For Eve to build such a tracking network there are three main requirements. First, Eve must find a way of installing tracking software on a large number of smartphones in a given region. This could be done by creating an application that has its malicious function hidden by legitimate behavior, or by releasing malicious software that spreads over a wireless vector, making it likely that infections occur within a small geographic region. Second, Eve must have a control mechanism to issue commands to the smartphones in her tracking network. For example, she needs to be able to communicate the BSSID addresses of the phones that should be tracked, or geographic regions of interest to listen for BSSIDs in. Third, Eve must provide a central data repository that the smartphones send their data to so that Eve can perform the required tracking trilateration analysis, and any other inference she might wish to perform. We note that the only requirement that is different than a typical botnet is that the infections should be localized in a given geographic region, and that the bots are now mobile smartphones.

Botnets that satisfy the above properties have already been studied in the research community under the name of *Malnets* (mobile botnet) [467]. A malnet consists of a number of smartphones interconnected through a central command and control server or potentially communicating between each other via Bluetooth or other wireless radios [440]. Eve would set every smartphone in the malnet into *monitor mode*, a mode that allows the smartphone WiFi device to see all WiFi traffic within range. Monitor mode is very similar to how a radio works in that you can tune to a specific frequency and hear anything being broadcast on that frequency. While most phones do not have the ability at this time, smartphone enthusiasts are attempting to create software for smartphones that allows them to operate in monitor mode. One such example is the monitor mode patch for the Nokia N900 [44]. Another option is to take advantage of a modern smartphone's ability to act as a WiFi access point. Part of the 802.11 WiFi standard states that access points must respond to probe requests with probe responses as discussed in Section 6.1.3.2. If a malnet operator can take advantage of this standard and record information from the probe requests that are received by phones in the tracking network that can act as APs, and in these cases she does not require these phones to be in monitor mode.

Eve only requires one pieces of information from the WiFi frames she collects: the BSSID contained in the frame. Another piece of information that can be of value to a tracking network operator, such as Eve, is the received signal strength indication (RSSI) value. The RSSI values gives her a very rough estimate of the quality/strength of the signal received by the phones in her tracking network. This can potentially be used to infer the distance of the tracking smartphone from the target smartphone, ad result in more precise triangulation of positions.

There have been works that suggest that the SMS network and Bluetooth are insufficient for operating as a botnet control network for cellular phones and thus smartphones [440,468], and thus the reader may wonder if controlling a botnet of smartphones is feasible. We note that this is not a concern for tracking networks. The assumption is that the phone will be working on a 3G or 4G network, with significant bandwidth, and constant network connectivity. Further, the smartphones in the network, by definition, will have WiFi capability. Finally, the actual bandwidth that would be required for the transfer of tracking information is very small, meaning that if a botnet did transfer data over the cellular network, and did not have an unlimited data plan, they would likely not notice the extra traffic. The only information required to be transferred would be a time stamp, the RSSI value, the GPS coordinates of the phone in the tracking network, and the BSSID address of the target smartphone. For a mass surveillance of all nearby devices, the data could be packaged and sent in batch form when the smartphone accesses a WiFi network or at the end of the day when the phone is not being used (e.g., when it detects it has been plugged in to recharge).

Determining a target's BSSID   Earlier it was assumed Eve had access to Alice's unique identifier, her phone's BSSID. A tracking network operator could get this BSSID in a number of ways. To point out the simplicity of getting the data, we suggest several methods for different scenarios. Advertisers might buy the BSSIDs from public hotspot providers who can gain the information by pairing BSSIDs used to communicate with one of their access points and the credentials used to pay for hotspot service. In an alternate scenario of botnet operators, if a malicious botnet operator knew the location of their target(s) during some part of the day, the operator can use the tracking network to report all BSSIDs in the given area, at the appropriate time. Collecting this data multiple times, and using standard data-mining technology, can allow a tracking network operator to determine an individual's BSSID easily. An insurgent army, might just want to know the location of all BSSIDs that are not known to be "friendly," by belonging to one of the insurgents.

6.1.3.4 *Methodology for Evaluating Effectiveness of Tracking Networks*

In the remainder of this section, we show experimental evidence that shows that tracking networks are feasible in certain circumstances, and under differing technology scenarios. We have used the following high-level methodology in order to study the performance of a WiFi-based tracking network:

1. We simulate a number of human location traces, T. These location traces represent the position, both indoor and outdoor, of each individual in a dense metropolitan area over a given period of time with a granularity of 1 s. That is, every individual in the simulation has their position recorded every second.

2. In order to define the individuals in the tracking network we do the following: we uniformly at random take a subset of a given fraction of the population of individuals from T and put them in a set of individuals called N. The set N will represent those individuals who have tracking software installed on their smartphone, and thus are members of the tracking network.

3. For each second in the simulation, we determine the set of users in T that can be detected by those in the tracking network N, given the specified range for WiFi communications.

4. For each user in T that is detected, we determine how accurately they can be positioned due to multiple observations by the tracking network.

Step 1 is done in three dimensions using the UDelModels mobility simulator. This is a high-fidelity mobility simulator that provides stochastic simulations of peoples' movements over time, and validated to human movement statistics in a number of fields. The simulator uses a geographical and industrial map of the area to be simulated. The simulator is discussed later in Section 6.1.3.6 in more detail.

Step 3 determines who can be tracked by the tracking network. The wireless transmission radius is chosen to be a fixed distance representing the capabilities of 802.11-based WiFi. In our simulations, we considers radii between 15 and 45 m as they are conservative representatives of the 802.11g/n standards. One note, is that we perform detection volumes using bounding cubes as opposed to spheres. Using a sphere would already be a gross approximation, as real radio transmissions due to not broadcast uniformly in all directions due to interference and structures. Using an inner and outer bounding cube corresponding to a sphere of a specific diameter provides a very small decrease in accuracy, but provides an immense speedup in determining proximity. See Figure 6.1 for a 2D visualization of this process.

Step 4 narrows down the area in which a detected individual can be in by using trilateration when multiple devices in the tracking network detect the same individual .

Two cities: Chicago and Dallas   We performed simulations of two different cities: Chicago and Dallas. This was to determine if building distribution, geography, and relative density of population in the cities has a noticeable affect on the efficacy of the tracking networks. The two cities are in some sense at opposite

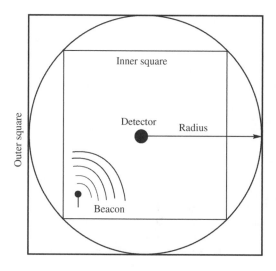

Figure 6.1 Depicted is a smartphone, and a bounding circle representing the area in which a smartphone could be detected assuming broadcasts traveled a fixed distance in all directions. It is computationally more expensive to detect if an individual is a circle than a square. Therefore, we instead determine if an individual is in the smallest square that bounds the circle. In the simulation, we uses corresponding spheres and cubes, due to the 3D nature of the simulation.

ends of the axis in terms of density, and results for both cities give us an indication of the range of efficacy tracking networks might provide in dense urban centers. We provide no guidance on their efficacy in suburban environments. Our tools do not adequately model these populations, and there is good reason to believe that the densities of suburban environments would be insufficient to support tracking networks.

In Figures 6.3 and 6.5, we see the area modeled in Chicago. In Figures 6.2 and 6.4, we see the area modeled in Dallas. In Figures 6.2 and 6.3, we see aerial photography of the regions, whereas in Figures 6.4 and 6.5 we see the simulators representation of the areas. With the latter two figures, we can see inscribed on the buildings some of the UDelModels simulator's parameters. Specifically, the numbers indicate the number of floors of the building in question. Further, its designation as an office (OF), residence (RE), or service building (SR) is also indicated. Some buildings have multiple designations, as services are provided on ground and lower levels, and other uses for higher levels. The UDel simulator makes use of this information in its path and destination planning during simulations.

Figure 6.2 The simulated area in the 16 block area of Dallas. The area is bound on the north by Pacific Ave., the south by Jackson St., the west by N Field St., and the east by North St. Paul St. (Photo from USGS Urban Area Ortho.)

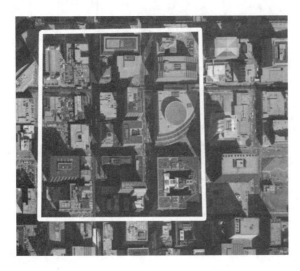

Figure 6.3 The simulated area in the 9 block area of Chicago. The area is bound on the north by W. Wacker Dr., the south by W. Washington St., the east by N. Clark St., and the west by N. Franklin St. (Photo USGS Urban Area Ortho.)

Population density   In order to simulate tracking networks in a dense city, we must have some idea of the realistic population density for the area being simulated to feed into our simulator. In our studies we simulated subsections of two large metropolises downtown cores: Dallas and Chicago. Specifically, the simulation areas used were a 16 block region of Dallas (population 2988) and a 9 block region of Chicago (population 9056). To determine population densities for these areas we got data from the LandScan project that gives the number of individuals who *live* in the area.

LandScan's population estimates are likely conservative, as they average an area's population during a 24 h period. Many metropolitan areas have significantly higher day-time populations than evening populations, due to the influx of workers during the day, and drain of workers to the suburbs in the evening. Strengthening the assumption that the population estimates are conservative is the fact that the chosen areas in Dallas and Chicago are both primarily business districts that don't have much housing.

Three dimensions versus two dimensions   One method one might consider to simplify the experiments is to consider only a 2D simulation, ignoring the vertical dimension, and projecting all individuals on

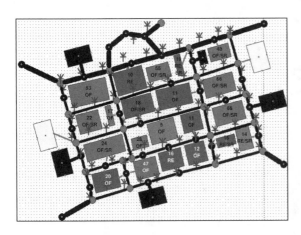

Figure 6.4 Map of the Dallas area created by the UDel Models group [51]. This map shows the placement of buildings and their functionality so that it is representative of the actual Dallas area. Compare the similarity of the simulated buildings to the actual corresponding buildings in the white rectangle in Figure 6.2.

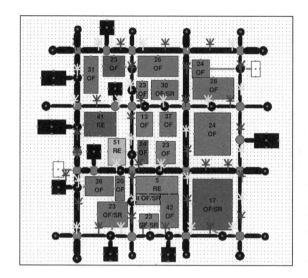

Figure 6.5 Map of the Chicago area created by the UDel Models group [51]. This map shows the placement of buildings and their functionality so that it is representative of the actual Chicago area. Compare the similarity of the simulated buildings to the actual corresponding buildings in the white rectangle in Figure 6.3.

to the floor. We performed early experiments in two dimensions by flattening the every simulated individual on to a plane, and compared the results to 3D results. These results showed that while this strategy may be reasonable in a suburban context or a context with a small range of z-values, it created an unrealistically high level of detections in the metropolitan simulation areas we considering.

All experiments we mention were done in three dimensions to take into account the varying number of floors in the Dallas and Chicago buildings. These three-dimensional simulations showed a distinct drop in detections and thus more conservative estimates of detection.

Assumptions on phone usage The modeling in this section is dependent upon a liberal assumption on smartphone usage: a smartphone's WiFi is constantly on and transmitting various information. This is a strong assumption as if phones are not transmitting, they cannot be detected. The assumption raises natural questions on how actively individuals use their phones, and when are their WiFi radios active? There has been some research done on phone usage, although there remain a large number of open questions. We briefly overview the known material. Uninterested readers can safely skip this section.

Karlson et al. [295] have studied smartphone habits of business professionals. Their results confirm that most businesses users use their smartphones to remain connected to their office via email and other applications. The amount of use varied greatly between individuals. Some used their phones constantly, others intermittently, but nearly all users used their phones over large parts of the day. This study was done with early model Windows smartphones. These phones provide limited user functionality compared with today's phones. We believe it very likely that current usage is much more intensive. In regards to specific WiFi usage specifically, ABI Research showed that 74% of smartphone users used their phone's WiFi [449].

These disparate pieces of research suggest that smartphone users frequently use their devices to connect through the Internet to Internet sources. A large majority of these users will use WiFi to do this assuming there are available access points. When the WiFi capabilities of the phone are used, the smartphone user opens themselves up to monitoring via the tracking network.

We believe it is reasonable to conjecture that peoples' movement patterns and geographic positions will be discernible to a tracking network, based on current general WiFi usage patterns.

6.1.3.5 Performance results

Simulations were performed representing a number of different scenarios as follows. Simulations were structured to look at varying levels of tracking network size as a percentage of the full population (1%, 5%, 10%, 25%, 50%, 75%, and 100%), so we can determine the fractions of the population that are necessary to achieve fairly comprehensive tracking networks. We considered modifications in broadcast diameter of the mobile devices (15, 30, and 45 m), to determine the effects newer technologies with larger broadcasting radii might have on the effectiveness of the tracking networks. Simulations were performed for 30 min intervals throughout the day to show the effects of human circadian activity. We used 30 min intervals due to the intense computational requirements of performing one continual 24 h simulation.

Figures 6.6 and 6.7 show the respective detection percentages for a tracking network in both Chicago and Dallas over the course of a day. The network is comprised of 10% of the available population with a broadcast radius of 15 m using the outer bounding box mentioned in Section 6.1.3.4. This is a conservative estimate of broadcast range that fits well with an urban setting due to the many physical boundaries to transmission often encountered, such as concrete buildings. While a network comprised of 10% of the population may seem particularly high, it is not wholly unreasonable for many of the scenarios we've proposed.

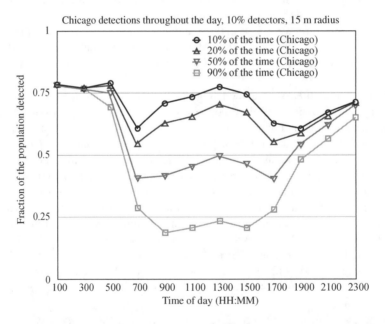

Figure 6.6 Results of a day of simulation of a tracking network in Chicago that comprises 10% of the population. The tracking network is more effective than Dallas, especially when only low frequencies of detection are required. The increase in effectiveness is caused by the increased population density in the Chicago area. The tracking network's effectiveness is tied to circadian rhythms of peoples movement patterns.

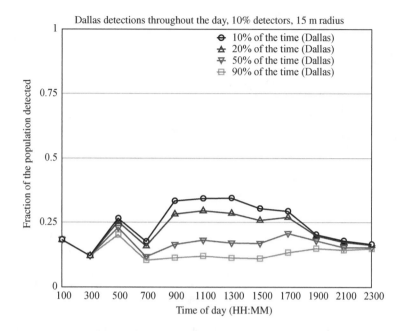

Figure 6.7   Results of a day of simulation of a tracking network in Dallas that comprises 10% of the population. The tracking network is less effective than Chicago due to the sparse population given the larger geographic area. The tracking network's effectiveness is still tied to circadian rhythms in movement patterns.

The performance of the tracking network depends significantly on the time of day and the performance is the lowest when the population is the most mobile. These mobile periods correlate to rush-hour and are when the population is the most spread out throughout the simulation area. Note that since 10% of the population is in the tracking network, the minimum percentage detected is 10%.

Detection frequency   One, potentially worrisome, aspect about WiFi tracking networks is that they do not need to detect any of their targets 100% of the time. Instead, they can track a target only a portion of the time and infer their positions in between detections. The inference of a target's position works because the mean distance they travel between detections is small. In Figure 6.8 we show the mean distance a user goes undetected by the tracking network in Chicago between 7:00 and 7:30 a.m. Broadcast radii of 15 and 45 m are shown for a bounding comparison. While the standard deviations are not shown for clarity, they are at worst 3.2 s for a 15 m radius and as little as 2.9 s for 45 m.

At least 95% of the time a user will never go undetected for more then 18 s when 10% of the population are in the tracking network. As the tracking network's relative size increases (as a percentage of the population), the mean time between detections, and its associated standard deviation will decrease.

Dallas versus Chicago   As previously presented, simulations were done focusing on both Dallas and Chicago. Again, these cities were chosen for their differing properties, representing in some sense different

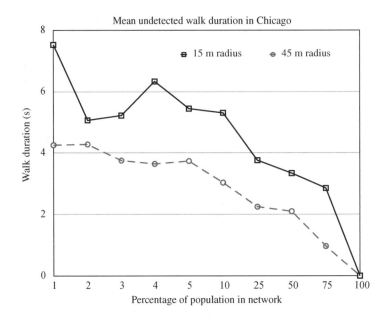

Figure 6.8   Low detection rates are sufficient to accurately place most individuals, for even with detection rates as low as 10% of the time, the average gap between observations is less that 8 s, even when considering very small broadcast radii on the smartphones, and low rates of participation in the tracking network. Formally, a depiction of the average length of time for an undetected walk in Chicago from 7:00 to 7:30 a.m. when tracked individuals detection rates are at least 10% of the time. The percentage of the population in the tracking network is varied.

ends of a density spectrum for large metropolises. Both cities have differing densities and different building usages (split between residencies, stores, and offices). Dallas has on average a higher number of floors in its building than Chicago. Dallas and Chicago also have different topographies. For example, Dallas has a number of very tall buildings surrounded by a number of shorter buildings, but Chicago contains a number buildings of roughly the same height. These differences between cities create considerable differences in the effectiveness of tracking networks. While the ambient population of Dallas is roughly one third that of Chicago, and Dallas's simulation area is greater, the rate of detection in Dallas is only about half that of Chicago. Full results are shown in Figures 6.6 and 6.7, respectively.

The different detection rates between cities shows that the privacy intrusions caused by WiFi tracking networks are largely dependent upon intrinsic in the metropolitan area relating to geography, and building use. The worst privacy intrusions will occur in larger denser cities like Chicago, New York, Boston, and San Francisco.

Large cities that are less dense will, obviously, have a lower level of privacy intrusion. However, in all cases tracking networks will be able to position individuals a fraction of the time that is perhaps distressingly high, with a high degree of accuracy.

Effects of population density   Figure 6.9 shows the effects on tracking when the number of individuals in the simulation area increases while the percentage of individuals in the tracking network remains constant.

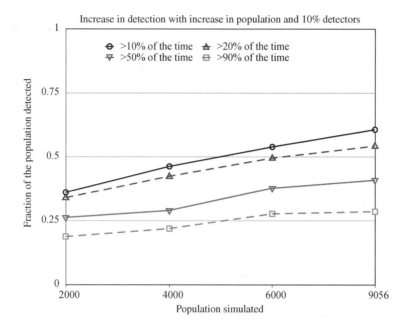

Figure 6.9 A plot showing the effect of modifying the population density in a simulation. Increases in population density lead directly to higher tracking rates. Note that even relatively low densities of individuals can still have somewhat effective tracking rates. The simulations graphed are of Chicago from 7:00 to 7:30 a.m. for 15 and 30 m broadcast radii. The tracking network comprises 10% of the population.

As expected, as the density increases the fraction of the population detected increases – independent of the percentage-of-time detected rate. The increase in detection rates makes sense, as the amount of volume covered in the simulation volume increases with the number of individuals. However, perhaps surprisingly, we see even relatively low densities of individuals in the Chicago area can have somewhat high tracking rates if the tracking network is willing to have lower percentage-of-time detected rates.

Thus, density is a key factor that affects the efficacy of the tracking network, and within a given location higher density definitely leads to higher tracking rates. In fact, we see that as the density levels in Chicago approach those that are represented in Dallas in Figure 6.7, that detection rates become fairly comparable. It suggests that the efficacy of tracking networks may be able to be estimated by a general value of the density of the population of a given area, with only minor effects of topography and geology.

That high tracking rates can be achieved even with very low densities may seem counterintuitive, but can be explained by the clustering behavioral patterns of people. When individuals cluster, the entire cluster can be observed by a single member of the tracking network that is close by. Further, the larger the cluster, the more likely there is a tracking network sensor in the cluster.

Effects of tracking network size on detections It is expected that, everything else being equal, as the tracking network size increases, so will the percentage of the population that the network detects.

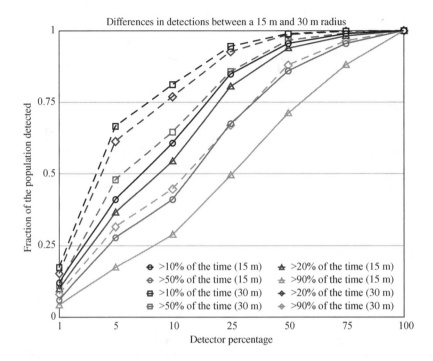

Figure 6.10   The biggest payoff in detection rates for tracking networks comes when their relative size is increases from ≈1% to ≈10%. Thus, tracking network operators do not need huge penetration rates in order to be successful. The graph represents simulations of 9056 people in Chicago from 7:00 to 7:30 a.m. with a 15 m broadcast radius on WiFi radios.

Figure 6.10 shows a simulated period between 7:00 and 7:30 a.m. in Chicago with a wireless broadcast radius of 15 and 30 m. As expected it shows an increase in tracking network performance as the population in the tracking network increases (and the population in the area as a whole remains constant). If the tracking network is comprised of at least 10% of the population, then the network is able to track a significant fraction of the population a significant fraction of the time. With a 15 m broadcast radius, 41% or of the population can be positioned to within 30 m^2 at least 90% of the time. If we require less persistent positioning, 65% of the population can be positioned to 30 m^2 at least 50% of the time. These percentage of the time individuals are observed is independent of any interpolation on position that a tracker might perform.

The effect of broadcast range   Broadcast range should have a significant effect on the performance of a tracking network. As mobile devices increase their WiFi ranges, they should be able to detect more mobile devices. The increased range creates an increased level of coverage. The increase is effectively linear. Figure 6.11 shows a simulation at 7:00 – 7:30 a.m. in Chicago with a tracking network comprised of 1% of the population. The broadcast radius of the WiFi devices is either 15, 30, or 45 m. The radii 15 and 30 m signify conservative estimates for the minimum and maximum range of the 802.11g standard, and 45 m is a conservative minimum range for the 802.11n standard.

This linear increase in detection rates has significant affects when consider tracking networks. For example, if we reconsider the day-long simulations of tracking networks in Chicago and Dallas that were

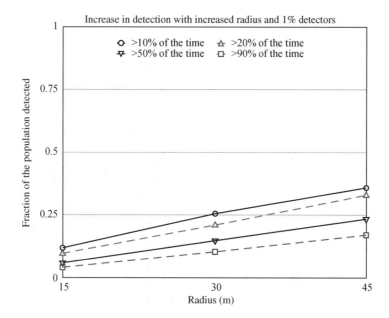

Figure 6.11 There is linear growth in detection rates as a function of increased range in broadcast radius of the WiFi standard. The graph depicts simulations of 9056 people in Chicago from 7:00 to 7:30 a.m. The tracking network is comprises only 1% of the population.

reported in Figures 6.6 and 6.7, but reduce the tracking network population to only 1% of the entire population, we get the results shown in Figures 6.12 and 6.13.

It is conceivable that an attacker could infect 1% of the population with an advertising network on malnet, and in these scenarios, when the 802.11n standard becomes dominant, tracking networks could be quite effective. Therefore, the adoption of 802.11n creates the real possibility of a widespread rise of tracking networks. This could especially be true in countries outside the United States where cell phone use is more prevalent and cities are far denser. For example in Hong Kong or Tokyo.

Triangulation performance The increased performance of the tracking networks achieved by increases in WiFi range has a negative side effect: it decreases the average area in which a person is triangulated. For example, if a 15 m broadcast radius triangulates a position to approximately $(30m)^2 = 900m^2$ then a detection with a 45 m broadcast radius triangulates a position to approximately $(90m)^2 = 8100m^2$. Some loss of accuracy is mitigated by an increase in multiple detections of the same individual caused by the increase in range.

While detection for tracking occurs in three dimensions, triangulation was done in only two dimensions. The z-coordinate (i.e., altitude) was dropped as, in most cases, it is far more interesting to know what building an individual is in and not necessarily the range of floors they are potentially on. Table 6.1 shows the average triangulation performance for a tracking network with 10% of the population as detectors in Chicago at 7:00–7:30 a.m. with a population of 9056 individuals. It displays the tradeoff between increased coverage from

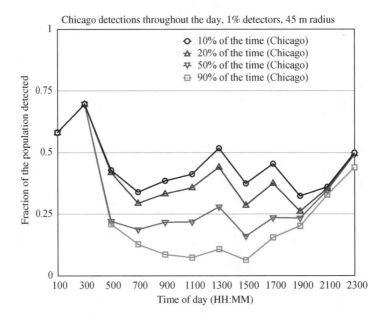

Figure 6.12 Results of a day of simulation of a tracking network in Chicago that now comprises 1% of the population, but WiFi has a broadcast radius of 45 m. We see that effective tracking networks are possible with botnet levels of penetration in Chicago when the 802.11n standard becomes dominant. The improvement over Dallas is due to Chicago's increased population density.

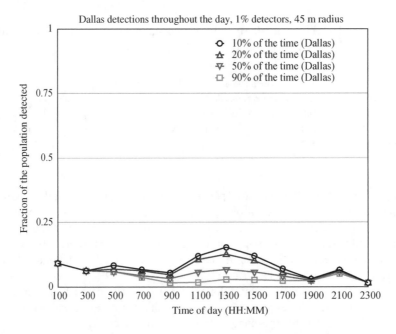

Figure 6.13 Results of a day of simulation of a tracking network in Dallas that now comprises 1% of the population, but WiFi has a broadcast radius of 45 m. Less dense cities, such as Dallas, are not as susceptible to botnet tracking, even though the WiFi range is increased. The decrease in performance compared to Chicago is due to the much lower population density in Dallas.

Table 6.1 The Number of m^2 a User can be Triangulated to Given the Number of Concurrent Sightings in the *Con. Obs.* Column

Device	Average Detection Area in Square Meters for 10% Detectors and 9056 Pop., 7 a.m.								
	15 m radius			30 m radius			45 m radius		
Con. Obs.	μ	σ	%	μ	σ	%	μ	σ	%
≥ 1	734	239	73	2323	1107	84	4655	2377	88
≥ 2	559	219	18	1709	849	41	3815	1864	61
≥ 3	498	172	7	1437	742	24	3509	1736	44
≥ 4	481	184	3	1335	706	14	3097	1619	28

Columns labeled μ is mean, σ is std. dev., and % indicates the percentage of observations with the appropriate radius and minimal number of observations.

larger radii and decreased triangulation areas in m^2. The table shows that while the triangulation accuracy decreases with increased radii it does not do so to the extent that the naive calculations above show: larger detection radii, correspond to more frequent cases of multiple observation, which through triangulation reduce the area of possible locations of the individual being tracked. There is a similar percentage of observations for two detectors in the 15 m radius case and four detectors in the 30 m radius case, and the difference in triangulation area is slightly less then double ($559.39m^2$ vs. $1335.73m^2$).

6.1.3.6 *The UDelModels simulator*

The UDelModels simulator is part of the UDel Models project from the University of Delaware [51]. The mobility simulator simulates realistic human mobility patterns for a metropolitan area at both a micro and macro level. An example of micromobility is the behavior that occurs when an individual walks up fast behind a large group of pedestrians and must slow down until they can pass. The same example is useful to discuss cars where a fast car must slow down and wait to pass a slower moving car. The mobility traces created are based on a number of different data sources using stochastic processes. A full description of UDel Models including the probabilistic models used and their validations to observed behavior, as well as details on the simulator's implementation can be found in Kim et al. [298,299].

A high-level overview of the data that the models are developed to correspond to are now explained. The UDel Mobility simulator simulates pedestrian movement. The simulator uses accurate Geographic Information System (GIS)-based maps of the metropolitan areas. Each building of the map is assigned its own building material, function, and number of floors. The pedestrian mobility is recreated based on data sources from the fields of urban planning and meeting analysis. Data models are also created from statistics in the 2003 Bureau of Labor Statistics (BLS) Use of Time study. Urban planning research informs on pedestrian movements between buildings. Worker meeting analysis data informs on how workers move inside and between floors in their offices. The BLS study provides information on when workers arrive at work, go to lunch, and leave work, as well as what they do during their breaks and how long those breaks are. To give some evidence of the fidelity of the data produced by the simulator we give a comparison between a Brownian motion walk and a UDel Models walk in Figure 6.14.

6.1.3.7 *Defending against mobile location tracking networks*

There are several defenses that can be implemented to protect users from illicit tracking networks that have been investigated in the research community. We note that these defenses were investigated solely

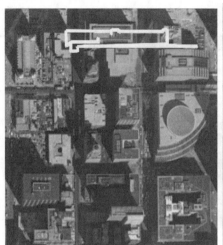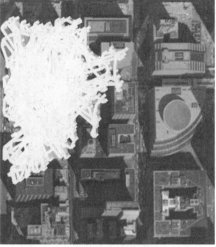

Figure 6.14   A visualization of the distinction between a sample UDEL Walk and Brownian motion. Both represent approximately 1000 steps.

with respect to concern about the privacy loss of broadcasting unique identifiers, and did not consider the possibilities of tracking networks. Nonetheless, the defenses should be considered.

One of the simplest solutions, but not necessarily the most usable, is for Alice to keep her wireless radio turned off when she is not actively using her wireless connection. This minimizes the amount of time that Alice is tracked, but does not eliminate it. The downsides to this solution is that automatically connecting to access points when in range is not a possibility due to the fact that the wireless radio would need to be initiated, and a beacon sent out enquiring about close access points. This will make access point switching more complicated.

There are a number of more in-depth solutions. Jiang et al. [283] propose three specific defenses. First, pseudonyms should be created for WiFi devices whenever they connect to a WiFi access point. That is, instead of using fixed unique identifiers, a randomly chosen identifier would be used instead. The pseudonyms would need to be randomly chosen, and from a domain large enough to ensure collisions did not occur between different users attempting to access the same access point (for traffic routing purposes, each device connected to an access point needs a unique identifier). However, this would require changing the 802.11 wireless standard, and deployed hardware is beyond this protection. A second defense they propose to work in conjunction pseudonyms is the concept of an *opportunistic silent period*: when a specific period of time elapses (the silent period) where the WiFi device has had no activity, the WiFi device takes the advantage of this to negotiate a new pseudonym. The perceived advantage of this scheme, over pure pseudonyms is that there is a more frequent rotation of pseudonyms for a given individual. This makes it harder for an attacker to attempt to derive the sequence of pseudonyms a given user has used, thereby negating the privacy they are suppose to provide. The third proposed defense is a limitation of transmission range for the WiFi device, so that it only transmits to the nearest access point thereby preventing unneeded broadcast of the pseudonym.

Opportunistic silent periods and pseudonyms would provide some protection against the tracking network described in Section 6.1.3.3. The defenses do not, however, provide any consideration for users under constant surveillance in which their identity can be learned from an aggregation and analysis of surveillance records. If a user travels between two known end points their pseudonym can be followed from each end point and the user will lose any benefit the pseudonym provides. The third part of Jiang et al.'s defenses, modifying transmit power, also provides some, but incomplete protection. While providing some strong protection against trilateration via access point, it does not provide any against mobile devices. The problem is that there are frequently times when there are members of the tracking network closer than a nearest access point. Additionally, it is not clear how a decrease in power might affect errors in transmission, and thus effective bandwidth of end users.

6.1.4   Conclusion

In this section, we've demonstrated that there are potentially new forms of threats to privacy, and thus physical security, that can result from unintended uses of ubiquitous computing infrastructure. We have focused on tracking networks, showing their potential to locate individuals in metropolitan areas a large degree of the time, to a high degree of accuracy. While we are unaware of any tracking network actually having been deployed, there have numerous cases of different phone applications harvesting location and network information, and we would not find it unlikely to see such networks pop into existence in the next few years, if countermeasures are not implemented to prevent such attacks.

> While there has been some limited investigations into countermeasures, we believe that more work in this directions needs to be done. We note that coming technological evolution, such as the inclusion of 802.11n into phone standards, and fast communication of phones via 4G networks, is likely to make the threat more severe in the short term.

While the focus of this section has been on tracking networks, we believe that the larger conclusion one must draw is that there is a great potential for completely novel forms of attacks on individuals as the computing infrastructure becomes ubiquitous. We believe that tracking networks are just one possible instantiation of such new attacks, and that the security community and society as a whole need to consider the many possible unintended ways that the new ubiquitous computing infrastructure can be put to use for unintended consequences, and develop strategies to handle attacks that result from emergent unwanted properties and/or behaviors. Most importantly, it is important to consider attacks *before* they happen, consider the likelihood that the attacks will materialize, and proactively develop countermeasures. Failing to develop countermeasures for attacks because they have yet to materialize is a way to guarantee, by definition, that our systems continue to be successfully attacked, and is a failed security strategy.

Finally, we note that because the ubiquitous computing infrastructure is now controlling and interacting with so much of our physical world, future attacks on computer infrastructure are going to have security and privacy consequences in the physical world. That is, the consequences will no longer be constrained to the virtual world. This is a truly concerning thought, given the track-record of individuals, companies, corporations, organizations, and governments to keep the cyber-infrastructure secure.

6.2   SOCIAL NETWORKING LEAKS

Mayank Dhiman and Markus Jakobsson

Abstract. Social networking sites have changed the way people interact and communicate, and have become part of daily life. They are already giving competition to search engine giants like Google in terms of popularity and are changing the way people perceive and use the Internet. However, due to their sudden burst in popularity, security and privacy may have taken a back seat. Scammers see social networking sites as a huge database of personally identifiable information. They see it as a vehicle to collect information about their potential victims as well as to carry out various attacks in an automated and distributed manner.

In this section, we are going to discuss various security and privacy related issues associated with the usage of social networking sites. We describe various motivations of attackers to turn to social networking sites to carry out attacks like spamming, spreading malware, sending phishing messages, crawling personal information, and stalking and bullying. We also present a case study of how personal information leaked from social networking sites can provide an insight into the physical world as well as sociopsychological behavior of users. We do this by studying the timings and online/offline behavior of people on social networking sites.

6.2.1   Introduction

Social networking sites try to digitize real-world connections by creating virtual representations of social networks where people can interact, build new or maintain existing relationships, exchange information, and find like-minded people. The three main concepts related to the success of online social networks are as follows:

1. Ability to share information
2. Ability to build new and maintain existing relationships
3. Ability to search for people

The basic idea that unifies these three concepts is the *profile*. The profile is a representation of a user's identity. While registering, users are asked basic questions like name, age, sex, location, profile picture, and interests, which become part of their profiles. Profiles act as gateways for interactions, as they can be used to identify, to search and to introduce people. Most people think that their information is private and undervalue the extent to which their information is exposed. As such, social networking sites pose a threat to users' privacy.

Social networking sites have developed a bad reputation for protection of users' privacy due to continued news of privacy issues. Popular media stories usually involve disclosure of embarrassing personal information to employers and universities, blackmailing using photos found online, and social scams. Other stories involve divorces, suicides, the spreading of false rumors, and a user backlash against newly introduced features or automatic changes in privacy settings. Such incidents and their frequency of occurrence underline the sensitive nature of information that users are exposing on their profiles.

6.2.2   Motivations for Using Social Networking Sites

There have been various attempts to identify motivations of people to share personal information on their profiles. The two main reasons are as follows:

1. The profiles are part of the digital identity of the person. People consciously or subconsciously tend to use it to enhance their self-worth by reminding themselves of important aspects of their lives; like identity, past achievements, friendships, and group memberships [465].

2. People are more likely to be connected with those who include verifiable identity cues in their profiles [174]. Thus, the more elements are included, the more successful one is in making new connections.

However, networks of people on social networking sites are less tight than the networks in the physical world. Hence, there can be a lot of weak ties [174]. Usually, people are willing to accept more people as friends on social networking sites than in the physical world, and the strength of these relationships can be varying. Thus, it can lead to various privacy issues. Social networking sites have also attracted the attention of attackers. The various motivations of attackers to use social networking sites are as follows:

1. The popularity of social networking sites.

2. The vast amount of personal information shared by users using their profiles and postings.

3. The ability to befriend potential victims.

4. The ability to query social networking sites to find more users.

5. The ease to identify social circles.

6. The inherited trust associated with the information and links shared among friends in these social circles.

7. The highly connected nature of social networking sites, which can be used to automate attacks.

Typically, attackers try to exploit the inherited trust associated a person within the victim's social circle—rather than from a complete stranger, as is done in traditional online social engineering.

6.2.3 Trust and Privacy

Trust and privacy go hand in hand.

> **Trust** is defined as the willingness of a party to be vulnerable to the actions of another party based on the expectation that the other will perform a particular action important to the trustor, irrespective of the ability to monitor or control that other party [341].

Trust is the central concept in social exchange theory [408] that presents a cost-benefit analysis with respect to social interactions. If the exchange is perceived to be beneficial, then the individual is likely to enter into an exchange relationship. However, on social networking sites, users postpersonal information on their profiles and inadvertently share their information with lots of entities, without going through the trust-building and information exchange cycles. Hence, social networking sites are very lucrative for attackers as they don't have to go through those cycles and can remain completely anonymous to their potential victims.

Some relationships on the social networking sites are stronger and more active than others. Even though a user may be friends with a large number of people, she might not trust sharing her information with all of them. However, social networking sites aren't well designed to reflect this, and as a result, broadcast activity to all friends by default. This may lead to privacy issues. To the extent that the sites have categories of contacts—as Google+ does, for example—everybody within the same category of connections has the same access rights. While the notion of categories is a step forward, it remains to be seen to what extent it can curb abuse.

Privacy is defined as the ability to be free from observation by others. It usually involves the ability to control the type and amount of personal information shared and who may access the information and hence, expose themselves selectively [230].

Privacy is a topic constantly linked with social networking sites. Social networking sites are known to store every piece of information shared by a user, including text, photos, videos, and IP address. They are known to share parts of personal information with third party marketing companies [472]. These companies use such information to display targeted advertisements. This has come under constant criticism as social networking sites usually do not reveal the nature and extent to which personal information of their users is shared.

Privacy is a concept often misunderstood by typical users. Even though most users state that they are concerned about their privacy, it has been shown that they act in a contradictory manner [190]. Several studies have revealed that users are unaware about the potential risks associated with sharing information about themselves [81,309]. This indicates that users have difficulties in estimating short-term and long-term risks regarding the disclosure of private information as well as lack of awareness regarding privacy issues.

Social networking sites provide default privacy settings, but users usually have the freedom to *change* their privacy settings. It has been found that a high percentage of users never do, for example, 79% users on MySpace [287]. Reasons for maintaining default privacy settings may be poor interface design, peer pressure, and inherited trust from offline communities. The constant changes in features of social networking sites further complicates the matter. While some users have modified their privacy settings, there is still a significant portion of users who have not and who therefore allow unknown users to view private bits of information.

6.2.4 Known Issues

Social networking sites have been riddled with security-related issues. Most of these are related to information disclosure. Here we discuss a few of them:

1. **Spam** The spreading of unsolicited messages through a medium like social networking sites, email, or instant messaging. Spam is very useful for marketing purposes as it is very cheap to send. A list of email addresses is collected usually from a malware or bought from the underground market. According to a study, about 90% of the email traffic is spam [36].

Spammers try to build attractive fake profiles and send out vast number of friend requests to lots of people. After they have a sufficient number of friends, spammers start posting links and comments to external websites. This may be a simple marketing strategy, or it may be a way to propagate malware. Since social networking sites contain a plethora of personal information, spammers use this information to create more original and trustworthy-looking spam messages, called *context-aware spam*.

In the traditional method of spreading spam via emails, spammers were restricted to email addresses in their database, which is not the case for social networking sites. Also, unlike email spam filters, no highly developed strategies are being implemented by social networking sites to combat spam. Spam messages usually come from friends within their social circles and hence, more trust is associated with them in comparison to spam from unknown email addresses.

URL shortening services have played a big role in spam campaigns as they make it increasingly difficult for normal users to differentiate between a good URL and a malicious one. This makes it easy for attackers to mask malicious URLs. Since users can't by default preview the actual page beforehand, they can be directed by a shortened URL to a malicious website.

In fact, it is being said that social networking spam that is context aware is already the most commonly used method by spammers, as opposed to simple bulk email spam [68].

2. Phishing is a way of attempting to acquire sensitive information such as user names, passwords, and credit card details by posing as a trustworthy entity [276]. Phishing is typically carried out by email or instant messaging and often directs users to enter details at a fake website whose look and feel is almost identical to the legitimate one. Therefore, phishing is an example of social engineering that is used to fool users to give up personal information.

The success of phishing attacks depends on establishing trust with potential victims and trying to avoid any suspicion. In common phishing attacks, a general message is sent to a potential victim to request personal information, for example, to activate an account, change password, and so on. These messages trick many users to divulge personal information. However, to improve the success rates of these attacks, phishers have started crafting more personalized messages.

Spear phishing is a targeted version of phishing [268]. Instead of giving general information to the potential victim to obtain trust, an attacker first tries to collect background information about the potential victim, either manually or automatically. She then constructs messages that use this information. Since the messages are highly targeted and based on a potential victim's personal information or known behavior, they have much higher success rates.

Spear phishing can be automated using bots. These bots may collect information from user profiles and then send them highly targeted phishing messages. One entity—the "friend"—may collect the information, while another—the "service provider"—may use it. The goal of the attack may be to steal a user's password for his or her email account. The attacker may then automatically scan old messages and identify memberships, affiliations, and other relevant pieces of information. This may allow him or her to target the user in a second round of attack, for example, with an email appearing to come from the user's financial institution, and containing the same information as these emails typically do. Experiments conducted at Indiana University showed that by using data available on social networking sites, email phishing attacks can achieve a success rate of up to 72%, or more than 10 times than that of regular phishing attacks [267].

3. Malware is a piece of malicious code written to gain unauthorized access to system resources, to gather information and to abuse privacy. A typical piece of malware may report web surfing habits, personal behavior, and financial information such as credit card numbers [278]. Machines infected by malware can also be used to carry out other attacks like spamming, phishing, and identity theft.

Social networking sites have become a rich ground for malware to spread. This is because of the nature of communication and the ease of broadcasting information. Malware is known to spread by exploiting various vulnerabilities in social networking sites. One example vulnerability is XSS—

see Sections 4.2 and 4.3 for more details on XSS attacks. One of the best examples is the SAMY worm [313], which spread by exploiting an XSS vulnerability in MySpace. It infected more than 1 million profiles within 20 h, making it one of the fastest spreading instances of malware of all time. It ultimately forced MySpace to temporarily shutdown.

Instead of depending on various vulnerabilities in social networking sites, various malware has been designed to use social engineering 6.2.4 and spam to spread. A good example is KoobFace [98], which spreads over Facebook, Twitter, MySpace, Bebo, and Friendster. It usually begins with an interesting message or a post from a friend, containing a link to an external website (which is hosting the malware.) On visiting the website, the user is tricked to download a seemingly benign program. As soon as the user downloads the program, her machine gets infected. The malware then uses this infected machine to launch new attacks, to propagate itself and to steal the personal information stored on the victim's computer. Malware can be part of a botnet and can be controlled by an attacker through a command and control (C&C) server. Then it can be used as a zombie computer for spreading spam and for mounting DDoS (Distributed Denial of Service) attacks.

4. **Information crawling** involves using a bot to crawl profiles of users, either through friend lists or by directly querying the social networking site. In the process, a huge database can be built, containing personal information that may include profile picture, name, location, friend list, and more.

Social networking sites provide methods to search users. Information like name and profile picture cannot be hidden and thus, certain parts of the information is not under the direct control of the user. Even if a user deletes the information posted on her profile or changes her privacy settings, there is still a possibility that the information was already crawled and stored. Information crawling can lead to various other attacks like identity theft and spamming. People have lost employment opportunities [42] and there have been various reports of blackmailing [387] as a potential result of these types of access.

5. **Cyber stalking** is the use of social networking sites, instant messaging or email to stalk or harass an individual, a group of individuals, or an organization. It may include false accusations, monitoring, making threats, identity theft, damage to data or equipment, or gathering information to perform any of these abusive actions [28].

The same phenomenon in the age group of children is called *cyber bullying*. Cyber bullies may disclose victims' personal data (e.g., real name, address, or workplace/school). They may obtain the password of the victim and then pose as the victim to publish material in the victim's name, directly defaming or ridiculing the victim. Some cyber bullies may send threatening and harassing emails and instant messages to the victims, while others postrumors or gossips, and instigate others to dislike and gang up on the target. Research has shown that cyber bullying due to social networking is on the rise [246]. Cyber bullying has even lead to suicides [24] and is a growing concern among parents when their children use social networking sites [17].

6. **Social engineering** is the act of manipulating people into performing actions or divulging confidential information, rather than by breaking in or using technical techniques [276]. It exploits people and their trust. This typically is the weakest link of security. Social engineering is often combined with mining of personal data.

Attackers can use social networking sites to gather initial background information of their targets. Social networking sites serve as communication platforms by offering services such as private messaging and chat. These services can be used by automated social engineering bots. Social engineering attacks in the physical world are very expensive to carry out and are often very time consuming as they may involve building trust and relations with potential victims. Social engineering bots quicken this process.

Social engineering can be very dangerous for corporations. Professional social networking sites like LinkedIn can provide a whole directory of employees of a corporation. This information can be used by attackers to study the internal structure of a corporation, relationships among employees or even to find former employees who can potentially leak information. With the advances in face recognition algorithms, photos of employees can be downloaded from professional social networking sites like LinkedIn and then, their profiles on other social networking sites can be automatically identified. Information gained from their personal profiles maybe used to blackmail or gather internal details of the corporation.

6.2.5   Case Study: Social Networking Leaks in the Physical World

We will now present a case study of how information leaked from social networking sites can expose information about sleeping patterns, diurnal rhythms, daily routines, physical location, and the professional life of a user. In our case study, we only consider social networking sites that have a built-in IM chat applications, such as Facebook, MySpace, and Orkut/Gmail. We focus on analyzing states and timings of users on social networking sites by monitoring their activities on associated chat applications.

Chat activity is different from other pieces of information like wall posts, images and videos as it is not explicitly shared/posted by the user. However, if an attacker can befriend a user on a social networking site, then she can log this information and use it to further build a profile of the potential victim. After accepting the friend request of an attacker, the user becomes vulnerable by just logging in and following her daily usage pattern.

The information gathered from our experiments was only used to show vulnerabilities and wasn't used to carry out any kind of malicious activity. We never used the information. An attacker, of course, would.

6.2.5.1   Experiment

For our experiment, we chose Facebook due to its vast popularity and built-in chat application. We began by creating a fake profile. We did not send out friend requests, though. Manually crawling and sending friend requests is a slow process and requires breaking the CAPTCHA. Also, Facebook is often alerted when an account sends a large number of friend requests, especially if a reasonably large portion is turned down. Such accounts are usually suspended for a certain period and all pending friend requests are canceled. *However*, Facebook places no restrictions on *accepting* large number of friend requests.

Facebook identifies bad accounts by detecting large number of friend requests within a short period of time, possibly combined with an unusually low acceptance rate of these. To avoid detection, an attacker can instead make it known that he/she is willing to accept friend requests, and wait for gullible users to send *him* friend invitations. Why would they, you may ask? Simply because in some games, it is an advantage to have large number of connections. That is what we did in our experiment.

Our fake profile posted requests to add her as a friend on various communities/pages of popular games – Farmville and Mafia Wars. In these games, the profile of a user on social networking site acts as her avatar. Thus, she can play these games with others in her friend list. The more friends she has in the game, the more she is able to proceed. Thus, in order to advance to higher levels, people often tend to add more friends to their profiles. This can be taken advantage of, as we demonstrated.

For the benefit of one more friend in the game, people started sending friend requests to our fake profile. Within one week, our fake profile had around 725 friends—without sending *any* friend requests. Another advantage of this method over crawling and sending friend requests, at least in the context of our experiment, is that the test subjects are reasonably random. Also, they may already be vulnerable to various attacks, as they sent a friend request to a complete stranger.

This technique to get friends again underlines the well-known fact that no matter how secure algorithms are, humans still remain the weakest link of the chain. Instead of only focusing on developing stronger security algorithms, we should keep human aspects of security in mind. It also underlines how much users undervalue their personal information and privacy. Finally, it shows how unintended incentives (making progress in a game) undermines security.

After 1 week of accepting friend requests, we crawled the profiles of our new-won friends. Being friends, we were able to access most of the information on the profiles of these users. We did not do that, but simply logged all the changes in their states and associated activities on the chat service of Facebook.

6.2.5.2   *Technical details*

Here we describe the technical details of our attack. When a user has a profile on Facebook she can be in either of these three states: available, idle, or offline. Facebook has a built-in chat application that users can use from within their profiles. Thus, their state information can be viewed from their activity on the chat application. Usually, IM applications show popups as notifications whenever a user in the friend list changes state. These notifications can be logged. However, the built-in chat application does not support notifications. Hence, it is difficult to extract activity information using the built-in Facebook chat application.

However, Facebook chat also supports XMPP, which is an open-standard chat protocol based upon XML. Since, XMPP is open standard, any chat client that supports XMPP can be used as a substitute to the built-in Facebook chat application. For gathering activities of victims, we chose the open-source chat application Pidgin, which supports XMPP. There is an open-source plugin called Guification for Pidgin, which shows various notifications. We modified the plugin to log all the notifications along with their associated timestamps.

The notifications from friends of our fake profile were logged for one week. Using these logs, we plot two graphs for each user. In one graph, all the activity of the user for the 7 days is superimposed, for example, see Figure 6.15.

In such scatter plots, various clusters emerge—both in terms of activity and inactivity. Namely, we can clearly identify the gaps in activities. Thus, from these clusters and gaps, we can identify times when there are high and low probabilities of changes in state. We can predict to a certain extent that at a given time during a day, the user will be in a particular state. For example, in Figure 6.15, the user in never active between 6:00 and 12:00. This kind of data can be extremely helpful to study the sleeping patterns and diurnal rhythms of a user, as discussed in the next section.

In the other graph, activities for various days are clearly visible so that we can analyze the behavior for each day, see for example, Figure 6.16. Since we can see the various activities for each day, we can understand how the pattern changes within the week. Longitudinal information collection could also attempt to identify

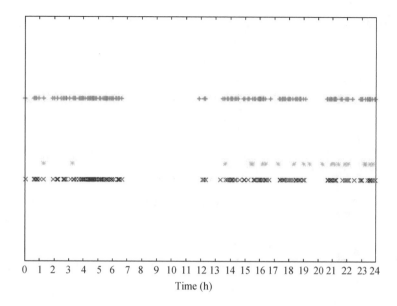

Figure 6.15   A scatter plot representing the various changes in activities of a user over a period of 1 week. The top strip represents activities of switching to online state, the middle strip represents activities of switching to idle and the bottom strip represents activities of going offline. Clearly, this particular user sleeps between 7:00 and 12:00 in her time zone, and has regular breaks around 17:00 and 20:00. She is distracted at work and quite addicted to Facebook.

changes in such patterns, which may be indicative of change in employment, vacation, and so on. It can also be used to study the physical location, professional and private life of the user, as discussed next.

By combining the analysis from both types of graphs for a user we can identify the daily routines and exceptions to these routines for specific days, for example, usage on weekdays versus weekends.

6.2.5.3 *Analysis and potential misuse*

We are able to identify various pieces of information about the users, which are not necessarily shared directly by the users on their profiles:

1. **Sleeping patterns**   Many users are logged into their Facebook accounts for most of the time, as a means to stay connected. It is easy to track down and identify sleep timings and sleeping patterns of such people. The sleeping hours can be identified as the longest stretch when the person is idle/offline, coupled with the location of the user. (Their location gives us the offset from the observed time—our time—and their time zone.) For example, see Figure 6.15: The person associated with this scatter plot usually sleeps between 7:00 and 14:00, that is, for 7 h. Users whose computer is logged in all the time will show this interval as idle. Those who don't prefer to be logged in all the time will be shown as being offline. Breaks in activity can expose information such as if the person is an early riser or late riser, if the person is getting enough sleep or not. Research has already been done to link sleeping patterns with health, social life and efficiency at work [108].

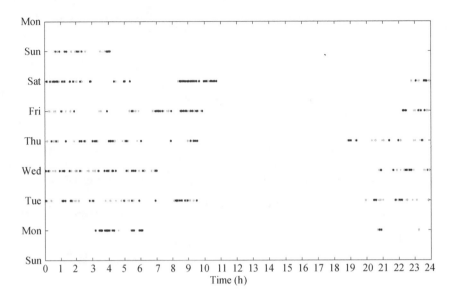

Figure 6.16 A scatter plot describing the activity of a user, displaying activity for each day of 1 week. Each point marks a change of state of the user at a given time of a given day. Lighter dots mark when a user switches to available or idle state, darker dots mark the time when user is offline. From this we can understand that this user's sleeping pattern is not fixed, and as the week progresses she sleeps in. The activity on Thursday gives an indication that she sleeps for around 8 h. She is a heavy user, except on Sunday and Monday. Her usage on Friday and Saturday doesn't change much, suggesting she doesn't go out. The information on her profile supports this, stating that she is a housewife.

2. **Diurnal rhythms and daily routines** Scatter plots can be used to predict daily routines of people. A common observation after analyzing scatter plots is that people have a high probability of activities around time boundaries, that is, at xx:00 or xx:30. For example, see Figure 6.15, where the user takes a break around 17:00, 21:00, 23:00, 00:30, and 1:30 in her time zone. These breaks can be seen as gaps in her scatter plot. These gaps can be interesting as they may specify work/break hours and daily routine. Another interesting observation is the activity of users on weekends. It may specify weather a person goes out on weekends or prefers to stay at home. Diurnal activity can be used to find when a person is at work, at home or sleeping, and when she usually goes out. This information can be important for stalkers and robbers, and to fraudsters wishing to carry out "love scams." These are attacks in which synthetic relationships are produced, with the goal of eventually asking the victim for money— for example, for an airline ticket to come and visit. These attacks are surprisingly common—and emotionally devastating to victims

3. **Professional life** An interesting observation is the number of times a user switches states between available and idle. If the frequency is too large then it could mean that the person is distracted or not enjoying work, as in Figure 6.16. The scatter plot of a user's access behavior can be used to identify her normal working hours, that is, how many hours she spends in office. The time required to travel from home to office may also be extracted, and hence, a rough estimate of distance between them can be calculated.

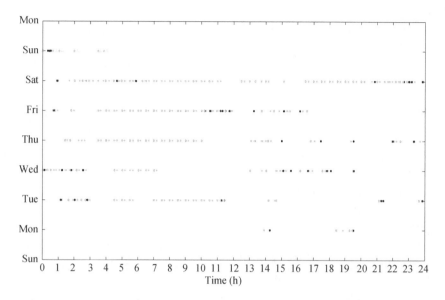

Figure 6.17   A scatter plot showing the daily usage by a highly addicted user for 1 week. Each point marks a change of state of the user at a given instance of time on a given day. Lighter dots mark when a user switches to available or idle state, darker dots mark the time when user is offline. From this we can clearly identify that this user is addicted to Facebook. She is not getting enough sleep and the patterns are quite inconsistent. She is very active on most days however, not on Sunday and Monday.

4. **Physical location**   Various location-based social networking sites like Foursquare have been launched. These websites are mostly used by people with GPS enabled smartphones. Users can use these social networking sites to "check in" at various places they visit. In February 2010, a website called Please Rob Me [20] launched. It scraped real-time tweets from Twitter, originated from Foursquare and other location-based social networking sites. It pointed out the vulnerability that whenever a user checks in at a place other than home, there is a potential risk of robbery. Thus, by giving out their exact locations, users may invite robbers to their home. Scatter plots can be used to identify when a person is likely to be on vacation, as there may be shifts in the scatter plots due to a potential change in timezone and different daily routines.

5. **Socio-psychological behavior**   Scatter plots can also be used to identify addictive behavior of a person, for example, see Figure 6.17. The number of periods and the length of periods of activity, along with frequency of changes in activity and inactivity may be used to identify users addicted to social networking sites. However, if such behavior only lasts for short periods of time (say a few days), it may suggest changes in behavior or environment.

6. **Private life**   Activities on social networking sites may give an insight into private lives. The activity of a user on weekends can be a pointer to her success in finding new or maintaining existing relationships. If a user is online more or less all the time—except when obviously sleeping—then it may imply a current inability to make/maintain relationships; or weak friendship ties in the physical world; or an introvert nature of the person. For example, many friends of our fake profile preferred to play games on Facebook on weekends to going out. Figure 6.18 represents a user who is mostly active on weekends.

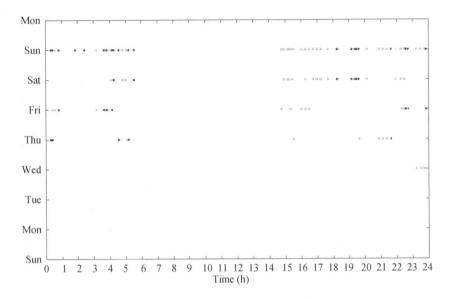

Figure 6.18 A scatter plot showing a person who is more active on weekends than on weekdays. Each point marks a change in state of the user at a given instance of time on a given day. Lighter dots mark when a user switches to available or idle state, darker dots mark the time when user is offline. We can clearly see that this user is only active on weekends. She is employed as a manager (information from her Facebook profile), and rarely uses Facebook during weekdays. She sleeps between 6:00 and 14:00 and doesn't go out much on weekends. It is fair to assume that she is single.

Ex-girlfriends and ex-boyfriends may use this kind of information for stalking. A report suggests that the information leaked on Facebook leads to 20% of all divorces in United States [204], pointing to the sensitive nature of information shared by many users.

6.2.5.4 Potential uses

Apart from malicious uses, our method can be used to design experiments in the fields of security, sociology, cyber-psychology and human-computer interaction. It may be useful for advertising companies and social networking sites to display advertisements depending upon the current mood (working or relaxing) of a person. Also, our method has potential security benefits. During our analysis we were able to locate fake profiles and bots, with one such example shown in Figure 6.19. The states of certain users changed at exact times—every day! Such precision, of course, is humanly impossible.

Spying can be used for protection purposes. Parents can spy on their children to check if they are using smartphones while driving or accessing social networking sites when they should be studying. Users can use their own graphs to check if their computer is being used when they are not around, or their accounts are being accessed by anyone else. Psychologists and doctors can keep an eye on their patients. In the United States, there are already laws that allow government officials to befriend suspects on social networking sites in order to gather evidence [49]. Information posted on social networking sites is already being used in many trials in the United States [41].

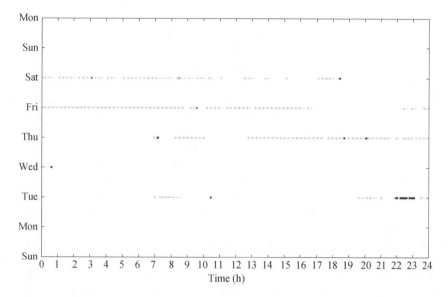

Figure 6.19   A scatter plot for 1 week of a potential bot. The state changes of this user were extremely precise—beyond what a human can achieve. Information posted in this profile like, wall posts and pictures, also point to the conclusion that it is a fake profile. Any click from this account must be considered invalid for purposes of billing, and the IP address of such an account should be blacklisted or at least be put on bot and spiders lists.

6.3   ABUSE OF SOCIAL MEDIA AND POLITICAL MANIPULATION

Bruno Gonçalves, Michael Conover, and Filippo Menczer

Abstract. With the exploding popularity of online social networks and microblogging platforms, social media have become the turf on which battles of opinion are fought. This section discusses a particularly insidious type of abuse of social media, aimed at manipulation of political discourse online. Grassroots campaigns can be simulated using techniques of what has come to be known as astroturf with the goal of promoting a certain view or candidate, slandering an opponent, or simply inciting or suppressing the vote. Such deception threatens the democratic process. We describe various attacks of this kind and a system designed to detect them.

6.3.1   The Rise of Online Grassroots Political Movements

The 2008 presidential election will go down in history as the first to be dominated by grassroots movements organized and coordinated online. The ultimate success of Senator Obama's campaign was due in no small part to its pioneering use of social media. An approach of direct dialog with his grassroots supporters captivated and connected with untapped layers of society and initiated a new era of political participation in American politics. On the other side of the aisle, the aftermath of the election brought about a reaction culminating in the Tea Party movement [397]. In both cases, it was clear that citizens would no longer be content as passive targets of political messages. They demanded an increased role in defining political discourse.

As individuals gradually turn to the Internet in search of political and economic information, they naturally use existing social networks and platforms to discuss their views and ideals with their peers. Microblogging tools such as Twitter play an important role in this movement by allowing individuals to act as media aggregators and curators who are able to influence their followers and who are, in turn, influenced by the people that they elect to follow. Over time, trust develops between followers and followees making the latter more likely to accept content and information provided by the former.

Perhaps the most striking demonstration of the relevance of this type of discourse, and of how aligned it is with public opinion at large, can be found in a 2010 paper by Tumasjan et al. [470]. By analyzing over $100,000$ tweets containing direct political references to parties or politicians in the ramp-up to the German Federal Election in 2009, they found that the fraction of activity within Twitter corresponding to each party closely matched the vote shares in the final election results. If this result could be generalized, this would imply that Twitter can be used as a real-time public sentiment monitoring tool. Based on this finding, Tumasjan et al. proposed that Twitter be used as a distributed real-time campaign monitoring tool.

If it is true that Twitter truly mirrors public perception, then perhaps it is also true that by manipulating perception within Twitter one is also able to manipulate it in the real world. This inference has not escaped the attention of institutions and groups interested in promoting specific topics or actions. Mustafaraj and Metaxas [364] studied in detail one such case that occurred during the 2010 special Massachusetts senate election. They observed how a network of fake, computer controlled, accounts produced almost 1000 tweets in just over 2 h, containing a specific URL smearing one of the candidates. The goal of the perpetrators was to generate as much traffic as possible to reach a wide audience and thus influence the outcome of the election. To achieve this goal, specific users perceived as influential were they targeted in hopes that they would retweet the URL, thus bestowing upon it an added layer of credibility. Blunt as it was, this attempt was extremely successful, generating such a large number of retweets to briefly place the URL in the first page of Google results for the query *Martha Coakley*—the name of the smeared candidate. Coordinated deception of this sort, where a single agent forges the appearance of widespread support for an idea or position, is known as *astroturfing*, a name that stems from the parallel between fake grassroots movement and the common type of artificial grass used in sports stadiums.

In this section, we look in detail at several tactics being used to promote misinformation in a covert way and a system that aims to automatically detect and track such attempts.

6.3.2 Spam and Astroturfing

As anyone with an email inbox is well aware, spammers have decades of experience in reaching huge audiences. Their techniques range from simple mass email campaigns to sophisticated techniques that automatically customize each message to avoid detection by automated countermeasures. As with other communication media in the past, spammers have descended upon Twitter and adapted their toolbox to this new medium. Many of these techniques and potential countermeasures have been analyzed in detail [113,223,479,499].

Although there seems to be limited amounts of collusion between spammer accounts [223] in the form of spam campaigns designed to make users click a specific URL, there are specific characteristics that can identify spammer accounts. Defining features include the frequency of tweets, the age of the accounts, and their periphery in the social graph [499]. The combination of content and user behavior attributes makes it possible to train machine learning algorithms to automatically detect spam accounts with a large accuracy [113]. This is likely due to the fact that spam relies on large numbers of accounts controlled by a small number of spammers.

At first glance the goals of spammers and astroturfers might seem similar. They both want to communicate a message to a large audience of users, and both want to effect action (clicks, votes, changes of opinion) in the targeted users. However, there are several fundamental differences between the two types of attacks. Astroturfers, to create the illusion of widespread autonomous support, must retain some degree of credibility and appear independent with respect to commercial or political interests. Likewise, while spammers can use a single account to target many users, astroturfers rely on the fact that users are more receptive to messages they perceive as coming from multiple independent sources. These different techniques necessitate distinct approaches to the detection problem. Spam detection systems often focus on the content of messages—for instance, determining whether the message contains a certain link or set of tags. In detecting astroturf, the focus must be on how the message is delivered rather than its content. The fact that the message is delivered in the guise of legitimate online chatter instead of an organized campaign is more relevant than its veracity. Content may be a legitimate opinion or information resource; the fraud is not a product of the content but rather the distribution mechanism. Further, many of the users involved in propagating a successful astroturf message may in fact be legitimate users who are unwittingly complicit in the deception, having been deceived themselves. Thus, methods for detecting spam that focus on properties of user accounts, such as the number of URLs in tweets originating from an account or the interval between successive tweets, are likely to be unsuccessful in the detection of astroturf. A normal user may come to believe and disseminate a piece of information that had its origins on a campaign of this type. As more and more normal users join the dissemination of this message, any information that could potentially be extracted from analyzing the properties of the accounts spreading it will become increasingly muddled.

6.3.3 Deceptive Tactics

Anyone trying to increase their visibility on Twitter has an obvious strategy: create an account, start tweeting and gradually accumulate followers. However, the egalitarian nature of the platform means that they are just one voice in a crowd of millions. When the goal is to have your voice heard no matter what the cost, several deceptive tactics can be used to quickly gain a large number of followers and obtain an aura of influence or importance within the community [141].

6.3.3.1 *Centrally and computer controlled accounts*

The old tenet, "nothing attracts a crowd like a crowd" holds true online. Astroturfers take advantage of this fact to catalyze faux grassroots activity by creating the illusion that a large number of people are behind a message or movement. The simplest way to achieve this effect is the creation of multiple centrally controlled accounts, known as *sockpuppets*, which are used to simulate several independent actors promoting a coherent message. These accounts can then be used to broadcast a message seemingly independent of one another, or be manipulated to appear as though they are engaged socially with one another. One advantage of the first approach is that it creates the appearance of independent actors responding to an exogenous influence at the expense of the credibility that comes with a rich social circle. The second approach relies on social expectations to create the appearance of authenticity at the expense of appearing independent. Common to both of these approaches is a reliance on a large number of centrally coordinated accounts.

To effectively astroturf at scale requires automation, and Chu et al. [153] studied the behavioral differences between real users and *bots* on Twitter. They distinguish between two types of bots: "benign" bots, which often self-identify as automated processes and simply relay information from RSS feeds or other automated sources; and "malicious" bots, which spread spam or malicious content while acting as real users. One of the key distinguishing features between humans and bots is that bots tend to generate a large number of tweets over the course of a short period of time and then hibernate for extended periods, presumably to avoid detection. Humans, on the other hand, tend to follow more regular patterns of online activity [218,219]. While bots can gradually improve their behavior to more closely mimic that of a human, it is not clear if they will ever be able to be completely successful in this task. At the same time, our understanding of human behavior also undergoes a process of continuous refining that further complicates the task of any bot creator.

A large number of emails from HBGary Federal, a security consulting firm, were leaked in early 2011 by a loosely organized group of Internet activists, known as *Anonymous*. Included in these emails are accounts of the development of commercial software to manage large numbers of online personas [459]. The software would keep track of every account associated with each persona as well as its main characteristics. The user of a persona could then rely on a dashboard of personal information necessary to allow him or her to adopt each persona on various social media and easily switch among them. The software package was marketed to companies looking to deceptively manage their online identities as well as government agencies trying to covertly monitor or help shape public opinion [187].

In a related scheme, organizations may recruit volunteers and ask them to donate access to their social media accounts. In doing so, volunteers allow the organization to post on their behalf, making detection much harder while amplifying the potential reach of the message. As these accounts are often unrelated to one another, it's possible to reach separate regions of the social network and potentially expose large portions of the population to a single unified message. Recently this tactic has been employed by groups such as the Christian Coalition of America (CCA) and the Human Rights Campaign (HRC) [251,378]. CCA claims that their "Educate Voters" campaign leading up to the 2008 presidential election involved 1111 Facebook users and 147 Twitter users resulting in 4339 posts and 458 tweets, respectively. HRC's "National Coming Out Day" Facebook campaign involved more than 125, 000 people and generated over 16.3 million posts on National Coming Out Day.

6.3.3.2 *Content injection*

Twitter is famous for limiting messages to 140 characters, and the need for users to compress messages has led the community to create ways of squeezing as much information in as little space as possible. As a result, users created "hashtag" annotations, terms prefixed by a # (hash) sign, that serve to identify a stream of information associated with a topic or intended audience, such as #dadt for "Don't Ask Don't Tell" or #gop for "Grand Old Party." Their quick adoption by the Twitter community eventually forced Twitter to officially support them and as a result, tweets associated with a given hashtag can be accessed by clicking on the hyperlink embedded in any tweet annotated with the tag or through the official Twitter search tool. For example, clicking on the #gop hashtag in the Twitter website will take the users to https://twitter.com/#!/search?q=%23gop, a constantly updating page containing all recent tweets marked with this hashtag.

Since hashtag streams are not centrally controlled there is nothing stopping any individual user from contributing to a content stream by including the corresponding hashtag in his or her tweets. The potential for abuse is clear: if I'm a political activist trying to reach a large audience of users interested in the Republican party, appending the #gop hashtag to my tweets is a straightforward way to accomplish this. Using multiple centrally controlled sockpuppet accounts in this way amplifies the effect.

As for hashtags, the use of URL shortening services became widespread in response to the space constraints of a communication medium originally designed to be accessed via SMS. Services such as bit.ly and Twitter's t.co provide URLs containing unique hashes that redirect to the original target. For example, www.example.com would be represented by http://bit.ly/3hDSUb making it difficult to rapidly inspect tweets for suspicious domains for both end users and filtering tools alike.

Twitter has developed spam detection mechanisms that will prevent a single user from simply reposting the same URL over and over again. A simple countermeasure is to slightly modify the URL that is posted by adding meaningless query-string parameters to a shortened URL. Any query parameters in the original URL are already contained within the shortened URL. Extra query parameters are ignored by the shortening service, while providing a simple way of averting detection by Twitter. The predominance of this tactic is demonstrated in Kandylas and Dasdan [292]. They studied the quality of tweeted URLs and found that they are bimodally distributed between high-quality URLs and spam. This highlights the volume of spam that flows through Twitter daily.

The combination of URL obfuscation and content injection makes it possible for spammers and astroturfers alike to target well-defined populations with content that may be, at first glance, difficult to distinguish as being fraudulent.

6.3.3.3 *Followback groups*

Classic sociological theory holds that public opinion and perception is shaped by leaders that are able to influence a large fraction of the remaining population (see [407] for an in depth description). In social media in general and on Twitter in particular, having a large number of followers is often associated with reputability or importance. Although the applicability of this idea in modern social networks has recently been questioned [141,482], there is still a widespread belief that popular people are necessarily more influential or reliable than others. This perception, fuelled by the fact that well known or influential individuals such as Barack Obama or Oprah Winfrey have several million followers, has led to the development of numerous strategies to increase the numbers of followers.

One of the better known techniques to increase the number of followers is identified by the #FollowFriday hastag. Micah Baldwin in credited with having created this trend in 2009 when he suggested to his followers that they should follow two other users. The idea of promoting other users quickly caught on and led Mykl Roventine to coin the hashtag #FollowFriday. It, and its variation #FF, have endured as a regular trend ever since [97]. This was only one of the first among several hashtags that have been created for this same end.

Another notorious example is that of #TeamFollowBack, a hashtag meant to identify anyone who will reciprocally follow any new follower. Users will add #teamfollowback to a tweet or their profile information as a way of requesting new followers and demonstrating that they will return the favor (follow back). In this way, Bob upon seeing a #teamfollowback tweet by Alice is assured that he will also receive a follow link and have his own number of followers increased if he chooses to follow Alice. Several derivative tags, such as #FollowMe and #InstantFollow, have also been created failed to achieve the same levels of popularity. This trend is the Twitter equivalent of link exchange programs that were developed to influence the PageRank algorithm [241]. PageRank relies on the number of links that a page receives to evaluate its quality, under the assumption that the more pages link to it, the higher its quality is. As a result, webmasters started to exchange links among themselves as a way of boosting their PageRank score.

These mechanisms for developing a large though perhaps fake social circle have clear appeal for spammers and astroturfers. A spammer can draw attention to a particular website by following a large numbers of users and placing a short message along with a URL in the biographical information section of their profile. By default, Twitter notifies users by email whenever they acquire a new follower, and these messages not only include the biographical details of the user but also easily get through automatic spam detection filters as coming from a trusted source. This task is usually carried out by bots, which will stop following the target person after a certain amount of time if the person does not follow them back. This is to avoid having too high a follower to followee ratio, a feature that has been used to detect this type of spam attack in the past [153]. These idiosyncrasies of typical spam bots result in measurable network differences between spammers and nonspammers [499].

6.3.4   The Truthy System for Astroturf Detection

In the previous section, we illustrated some of the tools and techniques commonly employed by malicious users to acquire an aura of respectability and to inject spam and astroturf in online discussions. In this section we describe a system designed to track the spread of political information on Twitter, with the intent of detecting organized astroturf attempts (Figure 6.20). The system is called Truthy, a nod to a term coined

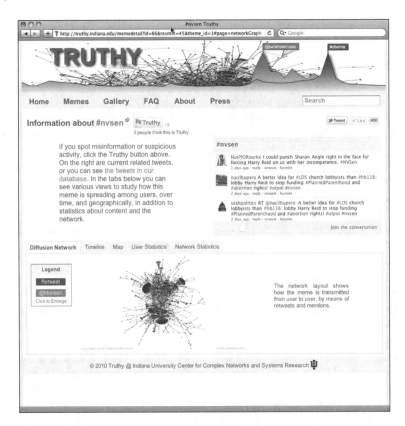

Figure 6.20   Screenshot of a meme detail page on the Truthy website.

by comedian Stephen Colbert to describe something that a person claims to know based on emotion rather than evidence or facts.

Snippets of information that are passed from person to person by word of mouth or common usage are dubbed *memes*, a term originally introduced by Richard Dawkins as the cultural transmission analogous of the gene [169]. In the context of the Internet, a meme is usually meant to refer to a small element of information that has become popular, such as a specific video that has gone viral or a sound byte that has became prominent in online forums.

In light of the characteristics of astroturf discussed above, we need a definition that allows us to discriminate falsely propagated information from organically propagated information originating at the real grassroots. We then define our task as the detection of truthy memes in the Twitter stream. Not every truthy meme will result in a viral information cascade like the one documented above [364], but we wish to test the hypothesis that the initial stages exhibit common signatures that can help us identify this behavior. Of particular interest to this end is the identification of differences in the diffusion patterns of organic and injected memes. For example, a comedians sound byte might become popular and be used by various sources, thus starting many independent cascades. On the other hand, two accounts can try to initiate a cascade by producing many identical tweets in hopes of starting a trend with varying degrees of success. These two examples illustrate some of the obvious differences that we might look for.

Such fingerprints are also likely to concern the way in which Twitter is used as a conversational medium [120,249], but emphasis must be given to the way these conversations lead to the diffusion of information. While usually referred to as "viral" [94,102,138,183,323,324,396], the way in which information or rumors diffuse in a network has important differences with respect to infections diseases. Rumors gradually acquire more credibility and appeal as more and more network neighbors acquire them. After some time, a threshold is crossed and the rumor becomes so widespread that it is considered as "common-knowledge" within a given community and hence, true [199].

We should note that, unlike other systems [139], Truthy does not attempt to make any claims with respect to the factuality of the content in the memes that it tracks. Our goal is simply to be able to distinguish between naturally occurring and injected memes regardless of the validity of the information they might contain. For example, if the sentence "The moon is made of cheese" were to become a meme, it could be considered to be "Truthy" based solely on whether such a surge of popularity was orchestrated by a third party.

Truthy was originally deployed in the run up to the 2010 US midterm elections with the explicit purpose of detecting and tracking political astroturfing attempts in real time. However, the system is general in scope and can easily track multiple themes. An in-depth description of the system and of several analyses performed on the data it generated are available elsewhere [158,399,400]. In the remainder of this section we focus on an overview of the system and some of the main results obtained.

6.3.4.1 *Data collection*

When a user visits the Truthy website[1], he finds both a list of all the memes detected for each theme, and in-depth information on each meme (Figure 6.20). This presentation allows users to use statistical and visual information to make judgments about the provenance of each meme. The number of nodes and the thickness of edges connecting them in the representation of the diffusion network give a quick indication of how many users are involved and how much traffic each of them is generating. The streaming box of tweets containing that meme that is displayed on the right hand side of the page illustrates the latest contributions and help to

---

[1] http://truthy.indiana.edu.

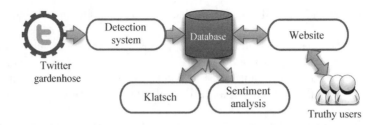

Figure 6.21   Architecture of the Truthy data collection and analysis system.

convey a better understanding of what the meme is about. A more in-depth exploration can also be made by analyzing the information contained in the other tabs, such as the geographical location of users contributing to this meme, statistics on the structure of the network and of more significant users and on how the traffic has changed over time. The website also provides a "Truthy" button that allows any visitor to mark a meme as being truthy, in hopes that these crowdsourced annotations may provide a useful feature in the automatic classification of truthy memes.

The Truthy systems relies on Twitter's streaming API to collect relevant tweets. The overall architecture of the system is illustrated in Figure 6.21. As tweets arrive through the stream, they are processed by a filtering system that looks for political keywords such as the names of all candidates running for US federal office, as well as any common variations of their names and known Twitter account usernames. We also include the top 100 hashtags that co-occurred with the tags #tcot (Top Conservatives On Twitter) and #p2 (Progressives 2.0), the top conservative and liberal tags, respectively, during the last 10 days of August 2010. Any tweet that matches one of more of these keywords it is added to the database [400].

We also consider as a meme any hashtag, URL, username, or phrase that co-occurs with any of our keywords at least one time. These memes are further filtered to extract only those tweets that pertain to memes of significant general interest. To this end, we extract all memes from each incoming tweet, and track activity over the past hour. If any meme exceeds a threshold of traffic in a given hour it is considered "active" and any tweets containing that meme are then stored in the database, until the meme becomes inactive. Note that a tweet can contain more than one meme, and thus the activation of multiple memes can be triggered by the arrival of a single tweet.

Properties of the diffusion network are computed by a system referred to as "Klatsch," the German term for gossip (Figure 6.21), while the sentiment analysis is performed using the GPOMS systems [118]. The end result of these analyses is further added to the database that is also used by the web frontend to produce the page presented to visitors.

The streams provided our system with up to 8 million tweets per day during the course of the study. These were scanned in real time by our system. In total, our analysis considered over 305 million tweets collected from September 14 until October 27, 2010. Of these, 1.2 million contained one or more of our political keywords; detection of interesting memes further reduced this set to 600, 000 tweets actually entered in our database for analysis.

6.3.4.2   Detection of astroturf

We focused on the analysis of three sets of features in our effort to detect truthy memes. The first set of features originates from the network properties of each meme, computed by Klatsch. Considering the nodes corresponding to users, we can observe how a particular meme spreads among users by way of retweets and

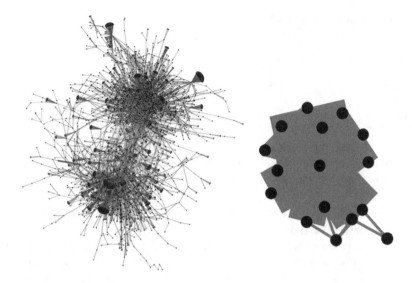

Figure 6.22 Diffusion networks of sample memes from our dataset. Edges represent propagation of memes by way of retweets as well as mentions. Each edge has a weight (width) determined by the number of tweets related to a meme exchanged between two users. Left: a legitimate meme corresponding to a popular, grassroots tag (#gop). We can observe two clusters representing the conservative and liberal communities. Right: a truthy meme boosted by accounts that collude by retweeting each other to promote a particular website. Different tweets include links to different pages from the promoted site, as well as popular but irrelevant hashtags in an effort to catch public attention.

mentions, that is, actions by which a meme can be transmitted from a user to another. For example, when a user Bob retweets a post from Alice containing the meme Charlie, we can see that Charlie has propagated from Alice to Bob. We extract a number of features from the topology of the largest connected component of each meme's diffusion graph. These include the number of nodes and edges in the graph, the mean degree and strength of nodes in the graph, mean edge weight, mean clustering coefficient, and the standard deviation and skew of each network's in-degree, out-degree, and strength distributions. Additionally, we track the out-degree and out-strength of the most prolific broadcaster, the in-degree and in-strength of the most focused-upon user, and the number of unique injection points of the meme. Figure 6.22 illustrates the differences between the diffusion networks of a legitimate and a truthy meme.

A second set of meme features comes from a sentiment analysis system (Figure 6.21) that extracts a six-dimensional vector of mood attributes from the content of the tweets corresponding to a meme [118]. The crowdsourced truthy annotations provide a final feature.

A binary classifier was trained to automatically label legitimate and truthy memes, based on a training set of hand-labeled memes [399]. We used semisupervised learning (bootstrapping) and resampling to deal with class imbalance between truthy and legitimate memes in the labeled examples. AdaBoost, an ensemble classifier as implemented by Hall et al. [235], yielded excellent results as shown in Table 6.2. Our system identified several truthy memes, resulting in many of the accounts involved being suspended by Twitter. Below we elaborate on a few representative examples of particular relevance.

Example 1: #ampat This hashtag, meaning "American Patriots" is widely used by conservatives on Twitter, however we observed bursts of activity driven by just two accounts (@CSteven and

Table 6.2 Average Performance of the AdaBoost Classifier in the Detection of Truthy Memes, Based on 10-fold Cross-Validation

Accuracy	96.4%
Area under ROC curve	0.99
False negative rate	1%
False positive rate	2%

@CStevenTucker) that belong to the same person. This activity generated traffic around this hashtag and gave the impression that more people were tweeting about it. These two accounts had generated a total of over 41,000 tweets.

Example 2: @PeaceKaren_25 This account generated over 10,000 tweets in just 4 months in support of several Republican candidates, boosting for example the popularity of the site gopleader.gov. A separate colluding account @HopeMarie_25 retweeted all the tweets generated by @PeaceKaren_25 supporting the same candidates and boosting the same websites. This is an example of a successful Twitter bomb similar to the one observed by Mustafaraj and Metaxas [364]. For a short period, Google searches for "gopleader" returned these tweets in the first page of results. Both accounts were subsequently suspended by Twitter.

Example 3: How Chris Coons budget works From an analysis of the injection points of this meme we uncovered a network of about 10 bot accounts that injected thousands of tweets with links to posts from the freedomist.com website. These accounts also used several of the tactics described above, such as adding different hashtags to tap into different content streams and appending junk query parameters to the URLs to avoid automatic detection by Twitter. This particular meme was part of a campaign smearing a Democratic candidate for US Senate from Delaware. After the scheme was uncovered by our system, the website administrator admitted to the astroturf behavior in response to a reporter [212].

These are just a few instructive examples of characteristically truthy memes our system was able to identify. Two other networks of bots were shut down by Twitter after being detected by Truthy. In one case we observed the automated accounts using text segments drawn from newswire services to produce multiple legitimate-looking tweets in between the injection of URLs. These instances highlight several of the more general properties of truthy memes detected by our system. A gallery with detailed explanations about various truthy and legitimate memes can be found on the Truthy website.

6.3.5 Discussion

Our social nature makes us vulnerable to attacks that target deep-seated expectations about group consensus and perceptions about source objectivity. In this section, we have explored a variety of techniques malicious attackers can employ to prey on these vulnerabilities, and highlighted several characteristics that make these attacks particularly difficult to defend against.

The ease with which dummy accounts can be created across different social media platforms and the existence of low-cost mechanisms for quickly developing an aura of credibility all but ensure that the scope of this problem is not likely to decrease in coming years. Likewise, as more users turn to social media for information about products, politics, and public opinion, the potential impact of such deceptive attacks may continue to increase.

Short of the undesirable outcome of unique identifiers for digital content creators, the challenge going forward will be the development of new techniques for the real-time identification of coordinated deception as discussed here. While no one solution can be expected to address these attacks entirely, improved reputation systems, crowdsourced detection mechanisms, and traditional machine learning approaches will all likely play a role in reducing the negative impact of astroturf attacks on the digital ecosystem.

ACKNOWLEDGMENTS

Jacob Ratkiewicz, Mark Meiss, and Snehal Patil have contributed to the development of the Truthy system. We are also grateful to Alessandro Flammini, Johan Bollen, Alessandro Vespignani, Takis Metaxas, Eni Mustafaraj, Ciro Cattuto, Jos Ramasco, and Matt Francisco for critical discussions of the material presented here. We acknowledge support from the Lilly Foundation (Data to Insight Center Research Grant) and the Center for Complex Networks and Systems Research at the IUB School of Informatics and Computing.

Part II

Thinking About Solutions

Until quite recently, many organizations would respond to security-related questions with the answer that "we have no problems because we encrypt all data using such-and-such long keys." This is, of course, a very naive answer. Security is not a matter of encryption alone, and even less so purely a matter of key length. For example, encrypted data need to be decrypted at some point. Where is the key stored? Who has access to it? Can they be coerced to give it out? Can they be tricked? Can a program they have installed steal the key and access the data? But even if there *were* good answers to these follow-up questions, relying on encryption would still be unsatisfactory in most situations. Security is complex.

> If we think that the answer is "encryption," then we probably have not understood the question, or we have not yet appreciated the complexity of the threat.

Part 1 of the book described what the problems are—or some of them, at least—and how we can identify and anticipate them. Understanding the problem allows us to pose the right questions. Part II of the book, which you are embarking on now, is about attempting to *answer* the questions we pose ourselves.

Please do not read this second part and think that the proposed solutions are the answers to your questions. They *may* be, but then again, they may *not*.

What is covered in this part are some unconventional solutions and some less well-known approaches. In other words, things you may not know about. The real goal of this part is to inspire you to go beyond the basics. To deal with an increasingly complex situation (as online security represents), I think we have to get used to venturing into that territory more often.

The Death of the Internet, First Edition. Edited by Markus Jakobsson.
© 2012 John Wiley & Sons, Inc. Published 2012 by John Wiley & Sons, Inc.

Chapter 7

Solutions to the Problem

This chapter begins with a focus on authentication. First of all, we look at how a person's actions and whereabouts can be used to *implicitly* authenticate him or her (Section 7.1). To some extent, this may do away with the need for user authentication—and to some extent, it may simply be used as a second factor.

We then consider the problem of user authentication from another angle. Sometimes, clearly, users have to enter credentials—but passwords are frustrating, especially on handsets. In Section 7.2, we describe an alternative to passwords: The solution, so-called *fastwords*, offers an alternative to passwords that is more secure, faster to enter, and has higher recall rates.

Another alternative to passwords are PINs—but organizations that rely on passwords already may find it difficult to make users register PINs, too. In Section 7.3, we describe how one can derive PINs from passwords (or other credentials, for that matter) in order to reduce the amount of friction.

We then tackle another angle of the authentication problem: *backup authentication*, also commonly referred to as password reset. In Section 7.4, we describe a backup authentication scheme that improves on traditional security questions (see Section 4.7 for an analysis of these.)

After having described these various angles of authentication, we take a step back and consider the question of how to design security protocols with the users in mind (Section 7.5). This is a central concept in Section 7.6, where we describe how to mitigate web spoofing and app spoofing—and thereby address the phishing problem. (The importance of the user experience is also a focus of Section 8.1, although in a more general sense.)

We then shift gears and look at another aspect of authentication—of devices. Section 7.7 describes how this works, and what it can be used for.

We end the chapter (Section 7.8) by looking at how to determine that a machine is not infected—with a focus on mobile devices. Think of these three parts: Authentication of a user; authentication of a device; and validation of the execution environment. These are all crucial for many security tasks.

7.1 WHEN AND HOW TO AUTHENTICATE

Richard Chow, Elaine Shi, Markus Jakobsson, Philippe Golle, Ryusuke Masuoka, Jesus Molina, Yuan Niu, and Jeff Song

The Death of the Internet, First Edition. Edited by Markus Jakobsson.
© 2012 John Wiley & Sons, Inc. Published 2012 by John Wiley & Sons, Inc.

Abstract. Usable authentication on mobile devices faces different challenges compared to traditional computers. For example, due to the constrained user interface, traditional passwords are awkward at best (see Section 7.2). Auxiliary hardware is generally cumbersome, but even more so for users on the go. We believe in the need for a new approach to authenticating users. Extending the traditional authentication paradigm beyond "what you have—what you know—what you are," we propose that "what you do" is a practical way to control access. We refer to this as *implicit authentication*, which identifies users by their *habits*, as opposed to their belongings, memorized data, and biometrics.

7.1.1   Problem Description

As online access to services becomes ubiquitous and the cloud access model gains momentum, authentication is increasingly becoming a focal point for security professionals. With bank accounts, health records, corporate intellectual property and politically sensitive information being just a few clicks away—no matter where in the world you are—it is natural to worry about the identity of those wishing to gain access. At the same time, as penetration rates of cell phones approach (and oftentimes surpass) 100% in industrialized nations [13], more and more of these accesses are made from handsets. This introduces security vulnerabilities and complicates matters, given that handsets abide by entirely different usability, computational, and power limitations than traditional computers.

Besides computational power and battery consumption, there are other important differences between the traditional computing framework and its mobile counterpart that affect bottom-line security. In particular, mobile devices are constrained in terms of text input and are more prone to theft than traditional computers. The input constraints make it difficult for users to input complex passwords, often leading to the use of password managers, short passwords, and simple PINs. Approximately 20% of users use a birthday as a PIN, a number with only 366 possibilities (however, see Section 7.3 for more on deriving stronger PINs). The higher risk for theft, in turn, makes these practices increasingly dangerous, as they threaten to put "open" devices in the hands of criminals.

We argue the need for a new approach to authentication of users. Extending the traditional authentication paradigm beyond *"what you have—what you know—what you are,"* we suggest that *"what you do"* is a practical way to control access. We refer to this as *implicit authentication* [222,280]. Implicit authentication allows us to identify users by their *habits*, as opposed to their belongings, memorized data, and biometrics. User habits can be encapsulated by behavioral models, learned through contextual data on the phone such as location, phone logs, and website visits.

Contextual data can also originate from sources other than the phone, such as laptops/desktops, automobiles, or smart devices in the home. The greater the variety and quantity of contextual data available, the more accurate the implicit authentication. In the logical extreme, if every action of the user is tracked, authentication becomes nearly trivial. In practice, an implicit authentication system must balance error rates and incomplete data (due in no small part to a respect of user privacy).

This statistical nature of the authentication must be accounted for. The effortless nature of implicit authentication makes it very usable, but error rates need to be acceptable, and users must not be frustrated by the occasional error. We believe user frustration over remaining errors can be reduced through appropriate policies, in particular, explicit backup authentication methods in the case of an implicit authentication error.

7.1.2 Use Cases

We present here a sampling of the use of implicit authentication technology.

7.1.2.1 Lost/stolen device

Consider the problem of losing possession of one's device. For instance, strangers may steal the legitimate user's device or find it in a public place. Friends or coworkers may happen to get hold of the legitimate user's device. The paradigm of authentication based on implicitly observed behavior offers protection against unwanted access from stolen handsets.

The traditional remedy for a lost or stolen device is a "device unlock" password, where a device requires a password after a period of inactivity. However, standard passwords on mobile devices are sufficiently annoying that most users don't use them [8]. Using implicit authentication, a mobile phone in a safe location, for instance, might be used without first requiring an unlock password.

7.1.2.2 Primary factor authentication

A handheld medical device can be protected by observing its use in the context of location, schedules, and more. This allows automated authentication of medical staff, protecting access to privacy-sensitive medical data (see, e.g., information in HIPAA [25]) in a context where stressful working conditions would otherwise make account sharing tempting.

7.1.2.3 Secondary factor authentication

Consider a bank customer using his phone to check his bank account, with his regular password. If the recent history of the device is inconsistent with the user's habits, then implicit authentication flags the login as a potentially high-risk event. The bank can use the implicit authentication score in its authentication policy to determine how to process the request, potentially involving a customer service call or another form of authentication. Thus, implicit authentication is not used as a replacement of regular authentication in this setting, but rather, as a *second factor*.

Implicit authentication may also be used in conjunction with "what you have." For instance, implicit authentication could enhance security of mobile payments or paying subway fares with your phone, which are usually secured through simple possession of the device.

Auxiliary hardware tokens such as the SecurID one-time password have been commonly used as a second-factor, especially in corporate environments. The main drawback is the usability. There are software versions of one-time passwords, but then the risk of a lost/stolen device increases. Certificate-based authentication has the same risk profile.

Another related approach is known as device fingerprinting [19], as detailed in Section 7.7. A device fingerprint might include the browser type ("user-agent" string), clock settings, fonts, installed software, screen sizes, and so on. Companies building device fingerprinting technologies include BlueCava [2] and 41st Parameter [1]. BlueCava claims to have assembled unique signatures for over 10 billion devices. These efforts are consistent with implicit authentication, which one can view as incorporating all available contextual information, user behavioral signals as well as static device signals such as fingerprint data.

7.1.2.4 *Collective authentication*

Implicit authentication can also make use of collective contextual data for a user. For instance, suppose a consumer performs a credit card transaction at a point-of-sale (PoS). The authorization request is redirected to the credit card clearing organization that inquires about the recent behavior of the consumer. If the user's phone appears to be in use (i.e., the accelerometer sensor is activated), and its recent location traces are inconsistent with the PoS location, then the transaction may be rejected or require further corroboration, depending on policy. Or, the transaction may also be rejected if the user is visiting websites on his desktop at work. On the other hand, if everything is consistent with the legitimate user making the purchase, the clearing house may signal to the PoS that no signature is needed—resulting in a fast-track checkout.

7.1.3   System Architecture

We propose a cloud-based implicit authentication service, that is, a service that collects user behavioral data (suitably anonymized), builds machine-learned individual behavioral models, and evaluates the likelihood of recent data based on these models by producing a "score" for a particular event of interest. For example, a score may be produced that indicates the probability that a phone's user is the legitimate user. A score may also be produced indicating the probability that a particular user is at a given geographic location. The service is naturally cloud-based because of the need to collect and consolidate data from multiple devices.

   In deployment, we envision these implicit authentication scores to be often considered together with other authentication credentials. For instance, a service provider may consider a sufficient authentication measure a valid short numeric password and good implicit authentication score. In particular, we see the ability to match a password that is relatively weak (but easy to type on a mobile device) with an effortless second factor as an attractive option. Also, implicit authentication is a statistical test whose output is not binary, and the thresholds and amount of uncertainty allowed depend on the particular application. Also, because false positives cannot be eliminated, implicit authentication works best with a well-defined fallback authentication technique. Thus, the use of implicit authentication implies a policy-based authentication framework that can integrate multiple kinds of authentication data, such as TrustCube [446].

   Our proposed architecture is shown in Figure 7.1. Phones (and other devices) periodically upload contextual data to an implicit authentication server. In some deployments, this type of data would already be collected, say by a cellular carrier, allowing us to avoid explicitly exporting it from client devices. The implicit authentication server exposes two web service interfaces: *report* and *query*. The report interface allows client side agents to report context and activity information routinely; the query interface allows other entities (e.g., the authentication service) to get a score for a device that indicates, for example, how normal the behavior of the device is at the moment. The score depends on current data and a machine-learned model of past behavior, based on a sliding window of data collected in the past.

   The authentication service exposes two interfaces: a web-based user interface for authentication consumers to define and maintain policies and a web service interface to authenticate client devices. The Authentication Service scales effortlessly because it itself is a cloud service. Policies should be easily uploaded, modified, and monitored using the authentication service's user interface. Policies can also be based on the platform, enabling mobile and desktop clients to share the same authentication engine with different policies.

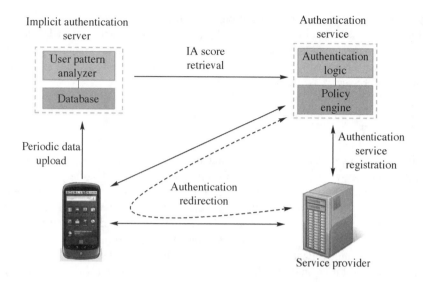

Figure 7.1   System architecture. Devices periodically upload contextual data to an implicit authentication server in the cloud. Authentication requests are redirected to a policy-based authentication service. An IA score is one input into the authentication service; other inputs may be passwords or device posture.

We suggest a federated identity protocol such as OpenID to redirect an access request between a service provider and the authentication service is OpenID. We observe that OpenID includes methods for a service provider and an authentication service to exchange a secret before authentication using the Diffie–Hellman key exchange method. Later, the service provider can use the shared secret to verify authentication results. For more details on our proposed architecture, see Ref. [150].

7.1.3.1 Data types

Modern mobile phones are rich sources of data. As a result, we can leverage a variety of data types to model a user's behavioral patterns. Examples are listed in Table 7.1.

More broadly, implicit authentication can make use of a virtually unlimited variety of data. For instance, all user devices produce data that help in building behavioral patterns; these are not just laptops and desktops,

Table 7.1   Sample Mobile Phone Data

Location, for example, GPS, cell tower ID, WiFi SSIDs
Phone calls and SMSs
Application usage, for example, browsing patterns, software installations, and email
Accelerometer measurements
Bluetooth/USB connections and battery charging activities
Biometric-style measurements, for example, typing patterns and voice data
Contextual data, for example, calendar entries, held on the phone or in the cloud
Colocation, for example, distance to other users or devices

but also home entertainment devices, car navigation and entertainment systems, and even public kiosks. The advent of the smart home and smart meters implies the availability of data that gives detailed insight into the daily routines of inhabitants, including sleep habits of inhabitants and the use of individual appliances [393]. Of course, accessing and aggregating this data across devices and systems faces multiple challenges, not the least of which is user privacy.

7.1.4   User Privacy

The elephant in the room in any discussion of implicit authentication is user privacy. Even if authentication becomes effortless, privacy risks may make the concept unacceptable to the end user. Naturally, the most identifying data is the most sensitive. Location traces are a well-known example of behavioral data that can have drastic privacy impact. In the architecture proposed in Figure 7.1, behavioral data becomes available and potentially at risk in the cloud. One can modify the architecture to hold data on the device and compute implicit authentication scores locally. One drawback is the inability to combine data from multiple sources. We propose instead to use anonymization or obfuscation measures on the data before upload. These measures would protect the privacy of users and yet still retain utility for our algorithms. For example, some measures might be

- removing identifying information (such as names or phone numbers) from the data being reported;
- pseudonyms, for example, "phone number A, location B, area code D";
- coarse-grained or aggregate data, for example, reporting a rough geographic location rather than precise coordinates, and reporting aggregate statistics rather than full traces.

Concretely, one approach we have employed is to hash data with a random key at the time of collection. This key is device-specific, generated and stored on the device, and never exported. The system cannot infer the actual data from the hashed data, nor can it test a piece of data to see if it agrees with the original data. In this way, the system balances security and privacy: unusual patterns can still be detected while the user keeps private the phone numbers called and the websites visited. We will see later that one can adopt measures like these and yet still retain utility for implicit authentication purposes.

7.1.5   Machine Learning/Algorithms

The task of machine learning is to use past behavior to train a *user model* that characterizes an individual's behavioral patterns. Given a user model and some recently observed behavior, we can compute the probability that the device is in the hands of the legitimate user, or the probability that a user performs a certain action at a certain point of time. We refer to this probability as an *authentication score*. The score is used to make an authentication decision: for example, when implicit authentication is used as a primary means of authentication, we can use a threshold to decide whether to accept or reject the user, and the threshold can vary for different applications. The score may also be used as a second-factor indicator to augment traditional password-based authentication.

In the remainder of this section, we describe some concepts and suggestions on the design of the machine learning algorithms. We note that there exists a large body of literature on relevant machine learning and behavioral modeling algorithms. The ideas and approach described below are merely what worked well for us in our preliminary user studies; there are numerous other approaches that could be equally or even more effective.

7.1.5.1 *Feature selection*

Our machine learning algorithms greatly benefit from the selection of a set of good features. Potential features include but are certainly not limited to the following:

Example Features Characterizing Good Events

G_{phone} := *number of phone calls to familiar numbers within the past hour*

G_{sms} := *time elapsed since last SMS sent to a familiar number*

$G_{browser}$:= *time elapsed since last visit to a familiar website*

Example Features Characterizing Bad Events

B_{phone} := *time elapsed since last phone call to an unfamiliar number*

B_{sms} := *number of SMS messages sent to unfamiliar numbers in the past k hours*

$B_{browser}$:= *number of unfamiliar websites visited in the past k hours*

Examples of Other Features

Location as (*latitude, longitude, time*) tuples,

Biometrics,

. . . . . .

For many features, one can take into consideration the *time-of-the-day* and the *day-of-the-week* effect. For example, a user may place and receive phone calls frequently in the afternoon, but she may not have much phone activity at night. For a user like this, typically the authentication score should decay faster in the afternoon during periods of silence; but should decay very slowly at night, if there is no activity. In other words, this user's authentication score should be punished more if we observe no phone calls to familiar numbers in the afternoon than the same condition at night. Another typical example for the day-of-the-week effect is the following. Many people are usually in the same work location on weekdays, but their location can vary on weekends, for example, in shopping malls, at the movie theater, or in a museum. To incorporate the time-of-the-day and the day-of-the-week into our behavioral models, one simple method might be to divide the time into different epochs depending on the time-of-the-day and the-day-of-the-week. For example, we can divide each day into several epochs, including morning, afternoon, and evening, and train a different model for each time epoch. One challenge is that different users have different daily or weekly schedules. For example, user A may sleep from midnight to 8 a.m., and work from 9 a.m. to 5 p.m.; while user B may sleep from 2 a.m. to 10 a.m., and work from noon to 8 p.m. Therefore, the granularity and boundaries of the most appropriate time epochs are user dependent, should ideally also be learned from each individual's past behavior.

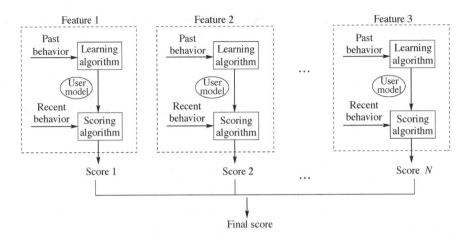

Figure 7.2 A machine learning model for incorporating multiple independent features. Although different features may exhibit dependencies in reality, the independence assumption proves to be effective in our experiments. The simplicity of the independence assumption allows for fast training and learning algorithms, and avoids overfitting.

7.1.5.2 Integration of multiple features

The existence of multiple features and their interdependent nature can complicate the task of user behavior modeling. In reality, multiple features may have intricate dependencies. Consider a user who typically browses her email while waiting for a train at around 5 p.m. every day. This example demonstrates the dependence of the user's email activities and her location. While there exist machine learning models and tools (e.g., Bayesian networks, Markov random fields) for modeling dependence between variables, we opted for a simpler and yet effective approach, that is, disregarding the dependence between features, and simply assuming that each feature is independent. The advantage of the independence assumption is that it creates compact models, allows for fast training and scoring algorithms, and avoids overfitting.

Figure 7.2 depicts an algorithmic framework where we train a separate user behavioral model for each individual feature. In the scoring phase, we also compute a separate score for each of the N features, and then combine all N scores into a final score. In particular, if each separate score represents the probability of seeing certain recent behavior corresponding to an individual feature, then the final score would be the product of all N probabilities, under the independence assumption.

7.1.6   User Study

To study the feasibility of this approach, we developed a data collection application which we posted in the Android Marketplace [377]. We recorded the following types of activities from each user: (1) phone calls; (2) SMS activity; (3) website browsing activity; and (4) location. To protect users's privacy, we took measures to obfuscate the data collected, and to allow users to opt out of data collection for certain periods of time or for certain data types.

Among the 276 users who downloaded our data collection program, we filtered out those who did not contribute enough data, for examples, users who immediately uninstalled our application. We selected roughly 50 users to model as legitimate users, and about 70 to model as adversaries.

7.1.6.1 Modeling adversarial behavior

We studied the accuracy of implicit authentication under two different adversarial models: an *uninformed adversary* who is unaware of the existence of implicit authentication; and an *informed adversary* who is aware of implicit authentication, and tries to game the system by imitating the behavior of the legitimate user.

As the data collected contains no adversarial behavior, one challenge was how to model an adversary's behavior in our analysis. To model an uninformed adversary, we adopted a splicing approach—we chose a user to be the legitimate user, and another user to model as the adversary. We spliced a segment of the legitimate user's trace with a segment of the adversary's trace. The splicing moment, that is, the point at which the two traces are concatenated, can be regarded as the time of device capture.

Note that our data obfuscation algorithm described earlier introduces some intricacy in the splicing operation. Specifically, the data collector computed a keyed hash of phone numbers and URLs where the key differs and remains secret on each device. As a result, we were not able to detect when two users called or SMSed the same phone number, or visited the same website. While it may be safe to assume that each user calls or texts a disjoint set of phone numbers, we cannot assume the same for the browser history, since there is a set of common websites that many people visit (e.g., major search engines and social networks). To address this issue, we take a lower and upper-bound approach (Figure 7.5). We first assume that all websites visited by the adversary are disjoint from the legitimate users' websites, thus obtaining a lower bound on the adversary's advantage. Then, we assume that all websites visited by the adversary are familiar websites, thereby obtaining an upper bound on the adversary's advantage.

Another difficulty arises when splicing location, as the selected legitimate user and the adversary are typically located in different cities. Therefore, when splicing location, we add an offset to the adversary's locations after the splicing moment, such that the adversary would be colocated with the legitimate user at the splicing moment. While this approach may yield locations that are semantically impossible (e.g., driving in the middle of the ocean), it is fine in our analysis, as our implicit authentication algorithms did not make use of any semantic information associated with location.

We were also interested in the robustness of implicit authentication against an informed adversary. Obviously, if the informed adversary can perfectly imitate the legitimate user's behavior over all features, it is theoretically impossible to detect the adversary through behavioral analysis. However, in practice, some features can be difficult to imitate, such as location. Moreover, the adversary also does not gain much utility if it merely imitates the legitimate user's behavior without doing anything else with the captured device. Therefore, our analysis focused on the advantage of an informed adversary who is able to pollute a small number of features.

7.1.6.2 Results

Figure 7.3 shows the effectiveness of implicit authentication in detecting an adversary who captures a legitimate user's device. In particular, Figure 7.3 clearly demonstrates the power of fusing multiple features. The five different curves represent using each feature alone and combining all features. The *x*-axis represents the number of times the legitimate user used the device before a failed authentication, and the *y*-axis represents the number of times the adversary used the device before being detected.

Figure 7.4 shows that an informed adversary gains only a small advantage by actively injecting good browsing events to keep its browsing score at a maximum. Recall that our prototype utilized only four

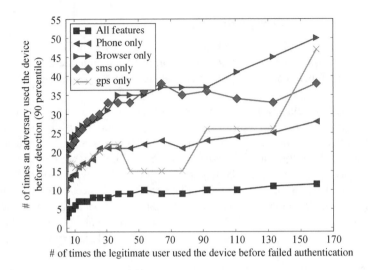

Figure 7.3 Power of fusing multiple features. The five curves represent using each feature alone, and combining all features. A point (x, y) on the curve means that if we set the threshold such that a legitimate user will fail implicit authentication 1 out of x times, then the adversary will be detected with 90% probability after y times of usage.

categories of data. When we incorporate more features into the model, we expect that implicit authentication will become even more robust to the pollution of a small fraction of features.

Figure 7.5 corrects for the bias introduced due to the obfuscation of the browser activities. Specifically, we plot an upper bound of the adversary's advantage assuming that the adversary always visits familiar

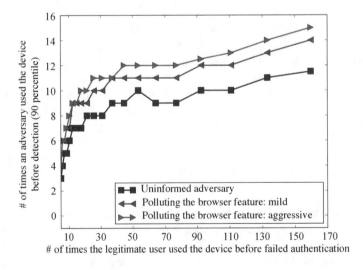

Figure 7.4 Robustness to feature pollution. An adversary who can pollute the browser features by imitating the legitimate user's behavior does not gain a significant advantage. This suggests that implicit authentication is robust to the pollution of a small fraction of the features.

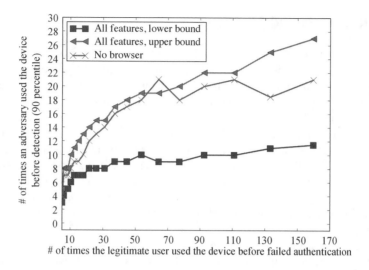

Figure 7.5   Correction of bias for the browser features. Due to data obfuscation, our collected data cannot detect when two users visit the same website. To correct for such bias, we plot an upper bound and a lower bound for the adversary's advantage. The upper bound is obtained assuming that the adversary always visits a familiar website, while the lower bound is obtained assuming that the adversary always visits an unfamiliar website. In reality, the adversary's advantage is somewhere in between the upper and lower bounds. Not surprisingly, the upper bound curve is also comparable to the "no browser" curve in which we simply discard the browser features.

websites; and we plot a lower bound of the adversary's advantage assuming that the adversary always visits unfamiliar websites.

7.2 FASTWORDS: ADAPTING PASSWORDS TO CONSTRAINED KEYBOARDS

Markus Jakobsson and Ruj Akavipat

Abstract. In this section, we describe and analyze an alternative to the traditional password scheme . The new approach takes advantage of standard error-correcting methods of the types used to facilitate text entry on handsets. We call the new approach *fastwords* to emphasize their primary feature compared to regular passwords. Compared with passwords of the same length, fastwords are approximately twice as fast to enter on mobile keyboards, and approximately three times as fast on full-size keyboards. Furthermore, fastwords also have considerably greater entropy than passwords, and their recall rates are dramatically higher than that of passwords and PINs. The new structure permits a memory jogging technique in which a portion of the fastword is revealed to a user who has forgotten it. We show that this results in boosted recall rates, while maintaining a security above that of traditional passwords. We also describe the notion of equivalence classes—whether based on semantics or pronunciation—and describe uses, including voice-based authentication. The new technology does not need any client-side modification.

7.2.1 The Principles Behind Fastwords

Security protocols have developed at a pace largely matching the development of online threats, but passwords remain the same—in spite of increasing pressure on authentication mechanisms [243]. Mobile authentication, in particular, poses new problems due to the limitations of handset keyboards.

Text entry on handsets is time consuming and error prone. A study [329] estimates that the mean entry rate is typically in the range of 15–30 words per minute, which is much slower comparing to an average of 33 words per minute on a regular keyboard [293]. The handset market is also increasingly moving toward soft buttons, as opposed to hardware keyboards as is standard for traditional computers. This leads to a higher rate of errors. Lee and Zhai [322] report that when data is entered using fingers (as opposed to a stylus), then the error rate is 8% higher for soft buttons than for hard buttons. (This result is for a situation without tactile or audio feedback, and where the sizes of the soft and hard buttons were approximately the same.) As a result, autocorrection and autocompletion methods are ubiquitous. With them, users can reach an average of 45 words per minute on on-screen keyboards [310] .

However, autocorrection and autocompletion only work for *text*—not for password entry. This is due to the fact that good passwords are much like poorly spelled words, and that error-correction techniques help *remove* poor spelling. While the dictionaries used by error-correction techniques can be augmented with words they should recognize, it is naturally not a good idea to augment them with passwords—even though it *would* help entering these. Therefore, better error correction techniques help maintain usability of text entry as we move toward smaller, feedback-free on-screen keyboards; they do *not* help us enter traditional passwords, which therefore are becoming *harder* to input. This is likely to give rise to increased reliance on password managers and short passwords—neither of which bode well for bottom-line user security.

A recent study by Jakobsson et al. [280] reports that consumers are only *slightly* less frustrated by entry of text and passwords on handsets than they are of slow web connections on such devices, and much more annoyed with all of these than lack of coverage and poor voice quality. In a survey we performed, two of five users expressed annoyance with entering passwords on handsets, and one of five stated that they avoid situations that require them to enter passwords on handsets.

Therefore it is important to address the question of how to facilitate human-machine authentication on input-constrained devices. To benefit from error correction techniques, we need to permit dictionary words.

At the heart of our solution is the insight that dictionary words are easy to enter if error-correction is enabled—and that a *sequence* of dictionary words becomes a secure credential. We refer to this as a *fastword*.

To make our proposal concrete, let's consider an example. As a user sets up an account or changes access credentials, he is offered the possibility of selecting a "mobile friendly" credential. A particular user who opts to do this may choose the fastword "frog work flat," which might correspond to a mnemonic of "I ran over a frog on my way to work, and now I have a flat frog under the tire." Research into human memory suggests that colorful phrases are easier to recall than more mundane ones, but this is orthogonal to the work described herein.

In order to analyze the strength of fastwords, we use the Microsoft N-Gram Service [480] to assess word frequencies; alternative services may result in slightly different estimates. From frequency analysis, our example system would accept the fastword "frog word flat" as a strong credential, given that the frequencies of the three words in English language are $2^{-17.0}$, $2^{-10.6}$, and $2^{-14.5}$ (resulting in a *product* of frequencies of $2^{-42.3}$); and that the 3-gram frequency is $2^{-49.5}$. The latter is the frequency in English language of the three words *together*. In contrast, the four-word fastword "I love you honey" might be rejected in spite of the fact that the product of word frequencies ($2^{-7.8}$, $2^{-11.8}$, $2^{-7.8}$, and $2^{-16.3}$) is $2^{-43.7}$, since the frequency of the 4-gram is only $2^{-25.8}$.

The frequency measures described above do not reflect how secure a credential is against an adversary who tries the k most common credentials, but how secure it is *on average*. However, by using a database of frequencies of keywords in previously registered fastwords—and not only considering their frequencies in English language—the system can turn down fastwords that are starting to become too common, thereby avoiding the "most popular credential" attack. This is analogous to the work by Schechter et al. [418] in the context of traditional passwords.

We do not permit keywords to be selected as names, or many users may be tempted to select names of friends and family members—which are often possible to gather from social networks. We can enforce this by allowing only words from dictionaries to be entered. As many names are not found in dictionaries; those who are can easily be excluded in an automated manner, given the labeling of words in common dictionaries. In Webster, for example, all names are labeled *biographical name*.

It is possible to implement any such policies by simple changes on the backend; it is also much easier to enunciate the policies in the context of our proposed solution than it is for traditional passwords since we can easily parse fastwords on a component level. Any fastword that is considered insufficiently strong will be refused; the user can either simply be told to enter a new one, or be told of the rule that caused the fastword to be rejected.

It should be stressed that in the fastwords scheme, credentials are not assigned to users. The user is advised to selects his or her own credential using words from their own memorable story. In this way, a fastword is easier to remember than a technique that assigns a collection of words to a user [101] because the more concrete and meaningful information is, the easier it is to remember [177].

The proposed solution has three main benefits:

1. The *increased speed and convenience* it provides—measured in terms of the time it takes to enter a credential.

2. The *improved security*—both in terms of the average and minimum security.

3. Substantially *higher recall rates* than passwords and PINs.

These rates are further boosted by the use of hints given to a user who has forgotten his or her fastword—for the fastword "frog work flat," the hint might be the word "frog." This maintains sufficient security as long as the frequency measures of the *remaining* words are sufficiently low. For a particular fastword, one and the same word would always be the hint. This could be the first word or the least common word, for example.

Our new structure allows for a class of new features that are not supported by the traditional password paradigm—such as voice-based entry and the use of equivalence classes. Equivalence classes—such as normalizing different tenses of verbs—permits the adaptation of the authentication mechanism to how people remember and enter credentials. This includes order invariance—"flat frog work" is considered equivalent to "frog work flat." It also includes synonyms (making "fat cat bite" equivalent to "chumpy kitty bite") and homophones and their approximations (making "red flower fly" equivalent to "read flour fry"). The latter helps with voice entry of credentials.

There is a trivial way to improve traditional password security without having to write one line of code. If users are encouraged to choose their regular password as three words—representing a story of significance to them—then the security of the resulting credential will increase, and the credential become easier to remember. Of course, many of the other benefits of fastwords require that the backend is modified—not much, but still.

Yet another benefit of our proposed technique is that it allows for a crude determination (on the backend) of the *degree* of correctness of a given login attempt, in contrast to what can be done in traditional password systems. While this type of data should never be fed back to the user (or it can be used as an oracle to attack the system), it can aid in the collection on analytics on the backend. The fuzziness is achieved at the cost of a slight expansion of the records used to store salted and hashed credentials, but without any associated reduction of security.

Outline We detail the basic structure of our proposal in Section 7.3.3—both from the point of view of the user experience and in terms of the backend solution. We then describe how to achieve an extended feature set in Section 7.2.3. As examples of such extended features are voice entry of fastwords and hints given to users who fail to log in. We describe our adversarial model and provide security analysis of our proposal in Section 7.2.6. In Sections 7.2.6–7.2.8, we report on usability experiments that let us establish security, recall rates and speed of entry.

7.2.2 Basic Feature Set

7.2.2.1 *User experience*

The user experience of entering fastwords will be very similar to that of entering passwords—except with the added benefits endowed by error-correction and autocompletion features. Instead of entering a password, the user would simply enter a sequence of words, separated by spaces. As a user completes a word, the word can be shown for an instance before each letter of the word is replaced by a star. Like for traditional passwords, the user would press enter at the end of the sequence. This user experience is the same when fastwords are *registered* (enrollment) and when they are *used* (authentication.) A credential strength meter can be used to indicate the quality of what has been entered during enrollment. A sample user interface is shown in Figure 7.6.

7.2.2.2 *Client-side process*

In contrast to text entry, traditional password entry does not rely on error-correction techniques. The incorrect password submission simply triggers the event that asks the user to try again. Fastword entry is instead implemented like regular text entry, which means that autocorrection and autocompletion are not *disabled*, and are therefore *automatically* performed in the selected language.

Figure 7.6 What the user may see when entering a fastword. The first word has been replaced by black dots, and the second word is shown with an autocorrect suggestion. The use of autocorrect and autocomplete allows users to type faster and with less precision. To accept a suggestion, the user simply presses space and continues writing the next word—or presses enter or submit to conclude. To turn down a suggestion—which should typically not happen in the context of fastword entry—the user taps the X next to the suggestion.

Analogous to how characters are often replaced by stars or other characters during password entry (whether immediately or as the next character is entered), completed words can be replaced by stars during fastword entry. This can be achieved using Javascript or an embedded program such as Flash or Java applet.

The credential is transmitted over an encrypted channel to a backend server in charge of enrollment or authentication; this can be done in installments (e.g., after each keyword) or after the entire fastword has been entered. The backend server then signals back whether the credential is accepted or not. For enrollment, this corresponds to communicating the result of a credential strength check (described below). For authentication it is simply a matter of signaling success or failure.

7.2.2.3 Backend process

Credential strength checker As a new credential is submitted, whether as an account is set up or to replace another credential, the credential strength checker is used to verify that the credential is sufficiently strong.

The credential strength checker determines the product of single-word frequencies of the words in a credential, and uses that as one strength estimate. The strength checker also determines the N-gram frequency of the sequence, and uses that as a second estimate. These two security assessments are performed relative to frequencies in English language (e.g., using the Microsoft Web N-Gram Service [480]) and relative to already registered fastwords. If any of these measures indicates that the new credential is more likely than a system security threshold (such as 2^{-30}) then the credential is rejected.

The output of the credential strength checker is the inverse of the maximum of the result of the different checks, which is the estimated probability with which the adversary is expected to be able to guess the credential. Alternatively, it can be represented as the minimum of the bits of security of the two tests, that is, the negative second logarithm of the associated frequency.

Dictionary words In contrast to typical passwords, it is not desirable for the user to include non-dictionary words in a fastword. This is because the autocompletion feature on the client device would *learn* these new terms eventually—which inevitably means to *store* them. This is undesirable from a security stance. To avoid this, the server-side will verify that all words are dictionary words when the user registers a fastword. (It would either have to ask the user what language is used, or infer it from the words used.)

Enrollment After a credential has been determined to be strong, it is accepted—and then stored on the backend. Just as passwords are salted and hashed to reduce the risk of internal exposure, so are fastwords. More specifically, if the credential is a k-tuple of words, $W = (w_1, w_2, \ldots, w_k)$, then $hash(W, salt)$ is stored, along with the unique value *salt*.

Normalization of credentials We assume the use of some amount of normalization, whether for robustness or to add system features. An example of the former type of normalization is for all credentials to be converted to lower case representations before they are salted and hashed. As an example of a feature-extending type of normalization, one may sort the words of the fastwords in order to obtain order invariance.

Conventional authentication The server looks up the appropriate user record (given the user name or other identifier), and salts and hashes the normalized credential to be verified, comparing the result with the stored result. More specifically, the value *salt* is extracted from the database, $hash(W, salt)$

is computed, where W is the normalized credential to be verified. If the result of the hash matches the stored result, the authentication is said to succeed.

Application The technique we describe can be used both to authenticate from handsets to remote sites, and to the handsets themselves. In the latter case, an external service could to be involved during the fastword registration phase in order to verify the strength of the credential—it is not practically feasible to house this database on the handset. If no strength check is needed, this outsourcing is also not required.

We report on relative recall rates for different types of credentials in Section 7.2.5; analyze the security of our construction in Section 7.2.6; and the speed on credential entry in Section 7.2.8. In the next section, we describe an extended feature set based on the techniques we have just described.

7.2.3   Extended Feature Set

There is an array of new features that are made possible by the new structure we use—and, in particular, by the decomposability of the credential. We will now describe some of these features.

Use of conceptual equivalence classes One can use conceptual equivalence classes to allow for *variants* of a word to be accepted, which aims as establishing the intent of the user when she enters a credential. The use of conceptual equivalence classes addresses a situation in which some words are largely interchangeable to users, a situation that could otherwise potentially create difficulties if a user has to remember the exact word she used. As a simple example, an equivalence class may contain different tenses of a given verb—in order, for example, to avoid a distinction to be made between the word "run" and the word "running." Equivalence classes may also be used to allow substitution of words of similar meaning. For example, a user entering a fastword (mother, stroke, wedding) during enrollment may later attempt to authenticate using the sequence (mom, stroke, wedding) or (mother, rub, wedding)—depending on whether the person uses multiple terms to refer to his/her mother, and based on the intended meaning of "stroke." (There is no attempt to infer the meaning of a word on the backend in the current proof-of-concept implementation.)

Given a credential $W = (w_1, w_2, \ldots, w_k)$, the backend computes the equivalence class $E(W) = E(w_1), E(w_2), \ldots, E(w_k)$, where E is the function that maps a word to its equivalence class. Instead of computing $hash(W, salt)$ for a given value $salt$, the backend would compute $hash(E(W), salt)$—whether for the purposes of enrollment or authentication.

Use of homophonic equivalence classes One can use a normalization corresponding to homophonic equivalence classes to simplify voice-based entry of credentials. We assume the use of standard dictation tools to create a mapping from the audio sample to a homophonic equivalence class; this corresponds to the error-correction processing of text inputs. To avoid having to train the tool on individual speakers (as dictation tools need), we will combine this with wide equivalence classes. This will map a large number of words to the same equivalence class, which will result in the same selection of equivalence class for different pronunciations and accents. One might argue that it is enough that the sequence sounds *the same* during registration and authentication; however, the use of wide equivalence classes permits text-based registration followed by voice-based authentication. The resulting equivalence classes are phonetic representations of the words of the fastword. To process the credential, the backend would salt and hash the sequence of phonetic representations to create the credential record. However, the issue of eavesdropping is an orthogonal problem to the management of audio authentication, and is not addressed in this work.

The creation of homophonic equivalence classes, and the associated credential records could be done *in addition* to the other credential records created and maintained on the backend. During voice-based authentication, the candidate credential would be verified by being represented by its phonetic description, salted, hashed, and compared to the stored record.

Implementing fuzzy authentication Instead of storing a salted hash of the *full* credential W during the enrollment process, the backend server stores salted hashes of all acceptable variants, using the same salt for each such variant. This is done in a manner that does not reveal the number of words k of the credential, where $k \leq k_{max}$. If we set $k_{max} = 4$ words, then there are no more than four subsets of the credential in which one word has been omitted—and one verbatim credential. If a credential has fewer than k_{max} words, then the remaining slots in the record would store random strings of the correct format. This way, one cannot infer the value k from a user record on the backend.

To perform *fuzzy* verification of a submitted credential during an attempted login, it is checked against each of the stored credentials by salting and hashing it, comparing the result to the stored values. One can also verify that it has no more than k_{max} words, and test all subsets of size $k_{max} - 1$ to see if either matches the stored values.

If the submitted credential, after being salted and hashed, matches the stored full credentials then the login attempt is successful. If either of the comparisons with the subset-credentials results in equality, then the submitted credential is known to be *almost* correct. It is a matter of policy how to react to *almost* correct credentials: The backend server may consider it a successful login attempt; may permit limited access; or other system actions may be taken. Users are not given any feedback describing the degree to which their credential was correct, or this could be used as a password breaking oracle.

Implementing hints If a user forgets her fastword, she can be given a hint, which is one of the words in her fastword. It would always be the same word for a particular user and fastword; it could be either the first word or the word with the lowest frequency—this is fairly likely to provide the most help to the user. The hint is also selected so that the frequency measures of the *remaining* words in the fastword correspond to a sufficiently secure credential. If a hint has *ever* been given for a given fastword, without a successful authentication following in the same session, then the word that corresponds to the hint should be considered public. This must be considered in the context of fuzzy verification. In Section 7.2.5, we report on the extent to which hints help users recall a credential, based on a user study we performed.

Implementing fuzzy blacklists If a given user's credentials are believed or known to have been compromised (e.g., by a phisher or malware), then the exposed credential can be placed on a user-specific blacklist. This would block the user from using this credential—or one with a large overlap—later on. This is to address the problem that users have "credential classes" and there is a large degree of reuse—even after a credential has been corrupted!

7.2.4 Sample Stories and Frequencies

We are interested in understanding how people choose fastwords. In a separate experiment not related to experiments reported later in this section, we asked subjects to write down a memorable story and then, from this, select three words that would constitute their credential. We did this to understand how well people can extract the important words from their memorable stories. We give an example of the stories here. In the story, we underline the three keywords (provided by the user) that make up the fastword for that story and provide the associated single-word frequencies in parenthesis. The story starts with a label that is the biggest of the 3-gram frequency of the word sequence, and the product of its single-word frequencies, the latter which is listed after each word.

(Frequency $2^{-43.2}$) "My mother (frequency $2^{-13.8}$) had a stroke (frequency $2^{-15.7}$) 1 week before my wedding (frequency $2^{-13.7}$)."

(Frequency $2^{-53.4}$) "Up until recently, I always thought penguins (frequency $2^{-17.5}$) were the size of humans (frequency $2^{-15.9}$). I'm in my twenties (frequency $2^{-20.1}$)."

(Frequency $2^{-50.4}$) "One day I was driving on the freeway in a major city. I was driving an older model car that only had a lap belt for a seat belt. As I was driving along, a highway patrol pulled up in the lane next to me, pointed at me, and then indicated his shoulder strap. He was motioning me to put on my seat belt. I tried to motion back to him that I was wearing a seat belt by pointing down at my lap. The cop immediately put on his lights and made me pull over. When he came up to my car window, I was puzzled by why I was pulled over. He said in an angry voice, 'You think you're pretty funny?' I then realized: When I had pointed down at my lap, he thought I was making an obscene gesture! He thought I was pointing down at my private parts and was making a crude suggestion. When he realized I was only trying to explain I was wearing a lap safety belt, he burst out laughing and so did I. 'Okay,' he said. 'Get the hell out of here'."—*This subject provided the keywords "cops, driving, goofy." While these keywords are actually not part of the expanded story, that is not a problem—the real system would not ask for the long story, but only for the keywords. The frequencies of the three keywords are* ($2^{-17.2}, 2^{-14.1}, and\ 2^{-19.2}$).

We note that a user would never have to write down an entire story when creating a fastword; the above examples illustrate how people select words from stories they know, and what the associated security levels are. In a real application, the user would simply enter the three words that make up his or her fastword.

7.2.5 Recall Rates

We performed an experiment in which we recruited users to set up a collection of different credentials, and to attempt to authenticate between 2 and 3 weeks later. (On average, the authentication took place 20 days after the setup.) A total of 147 subjects enrolled in the study; 105 completed it.

The aim of the study was to determine what types of credentials are easiest to recall, relative to each other. For this reason, we asked subjects not to reuse credentials from elsewhere, as this would bias their ability to recall these (and provide the authors with valid real-life credentials for these subjects, which we did not want to obtain.) Furthermore, we asked the subjects to promise that they would not write down any credentials.

We asked subjects to create five types of credentials: a "simple password" (such as what they might use for a social networking service); a "strong password" (such as what they may use for financial transactions); a 4-digit PIN; a 6-digit PIN; and a three-word fastword. We also asked them to remember a "super-strong password"—a complex password we assigned to them. For each credential, we asked them to assess how likely they would be to remember it after 2–3 weeks. In the second phase of the experiment, we asked them to recall the credentials and state whether they believe they managed to do so.

Table 7.2 Recall Rates for Various Types of Credentials

Credential	Recall rates	
	User estimate	Measured
Simple passwords	24%	14%
Strong passwords	22%	6%
Total after a hint		0%
Super-strong passwords	5%	2%
4-digit PIN	47%	26%
6-digit PIN	28%	29%
3-word fastword	25%	36%
Total after a hint		48%

User estimates are derived from users answering I think I did, very likely and certain in a questionnaire. The results show that fastword is easier to recall than other types of credentials. The amount of fastword recall also increases further to 48% after a hint.

Subjects were considered to have succeeded with an authentication if they managed to enter the credential verbatim during the authentication stage, except for the fastwords, where capitalization, tense, and order were not considered, and where subjects who entered at least two of the three words of the fastword were passed. This matches the way real authentication would be performed. Subjects who failed the fastword authentication were given a hint—the first word of their fastword—and asked to try again. Subjects who failed the strong password authentication were given a second chance, too, but no hint. This, to matches the way real authentication would be performed.

The recall rates of the various credentials are shown in Table 7.2. The subjects's guess whether they correctly recalled a credential was done on a 5-point Likert scale, where we count the responses "I think I did," "very likely," and "certain" as a vote of confidence, while "maybe" and "I did not" were counted as a lack of confidence. We see that people remember passwords to a lesser extent than they expect, and fastwords to a greater extent.

While this does not show how well people would recall any of these credentials in a real-life scenario, it shows how well they remember them relative to each other, in a setting where they are not strongly incentivized to do well. The experiment shows that users are able to recall fastwords to a much greater extent than passwords, and that close to half of those who forget their fastword are helped by the hint they are given.

As part of the study, we collected some demographic information. Among other things, we asked subjects to indicate their profession. We could not identify any relation between profession and performance, and in particular, did not see different recall rates among technical people, who were overrepresented in the study in relation to their relative number in society.

As the experiment shows that a recall rate of fastwords is better than that of passwords, more than half of the users still could not remember their fastword. Therefore, it is an interesting problem of how to automatically assess—*at the time of enrollment*—the likelihood that a user will be able to recall a given credential. For example, considering a user who thinks of using a rocket to fly out into space and plant a flag on the moon. He could either enter a credential "fly space flag" or "rocket moon flag". The latter credential is arguably better from the perspective of recall, given a user who requests a hint. "Fly" could refer to an insect or what a bird does, and "space" could refer to a key on a keyboard or a distance between teeth. However, "rocket" and "moon" are less ambiguous, which makes them better memory joggers. This example suggests that one may be able to build *credential recall estimators* and ask users with credentials that do not seem likely to be remembered to provide another credential. Like many of the features described in this paper, such a feature is made possible by the fact that credentials can be broken down into components that can be processed.

7.2.6 Security Analysis

We want to compare the strength of the fastword with that of traditional passwords. We will begin by reviewing the approximate security of passwords (Section 7.2.7), followed by an adversarial model for our context (Section 7.2.7.1), and an analysis of the security of fastwords (Section 7.3.5).

7.2.7 The Security of Passwords

NIST [128] estimates that the distribution of passwords corresponds to an entropy of 4 bits for the first character, 2 bits for the next 7 characters, and 1.5 bits per character for the 9th to the 20th character, and 1 bit per character for the remainder of the password. Six bits of entropy is added when the user is forced to use both upper case and nonalphabetic characters. This is for traditional passwords—mobile passwords are likely to have lower entropy due to the complications of entering them—at least in contexts where the user is aware of later having to enter the password on a mobile platform when first selecting it. It is also an average: There are indications that users select passwords of different strength on different types of sites. Analysis [275] of passwords from raided dropboxes (files used by fraudsters to store stolen credentials) suggests that the average password length was 7.9 characters, which corresponds to an entropy of approximately 18 bits. While this indicates that the *average* probability of guessing a password is 2^{-18}, an attacker can gain access to a fairly large portion of accounts simply by trying the most common credentials—this probability is on the order of 0.22%–0.9% [262,422]. (While we do not have any evidence to support it, there are plenty of indications that passwords used on handsets are weaker than traditional passwords.)

7.2.7.1 Understanding the adversary

We consider a remote adversary attempting to gain illegitimate access to an account. We assume that the adversary knows the rules used to approve and reject fastwords as they are first established, and that he knows system-wide weights and parameters. We also assume that he knows the frequencies of individual words and N-grams. We make the pessimistic assumption that the system does *not* know the true frequencies, but that it mis-estimates the true frequencies by up to a factor c.

The adversary wishes to guess the fastword of a given user. Since we may assume that an adversary will behave rationally, we know that he will try the most likely candidate fastwords (that would be accepted by the system) in order of decreasing likelihood, and that he will try as many as he is allowed before the account gets locked down.

The adversary will request to get the hint for the fastword (claiming to be the user to be targeted and claiming to have forgotten the fastword.) Let's say that the hint is displayed to the adversary—as opposed to being sent to an email address associated with the account. The adversary then attempts to guess the two missing words in a manner that maximizes his probability of success. We say that the adversary *wins* if he manages to get access to the targeted account.

Note that we neither focus on security against shoulder surfing or eavesdropping, nor attacks in which the adversary knows his victim. It is also worth noting that most systems are rather vulnerable against adversaries who know the victim, due to the poor security of many password reset schemes [416]. These are interesting attacks to consider, but are not the primary threats in most systems.

7.2.7.2 The security of fastwords

We have assumed an adversary who knows the true frequencies and distributions of words and fastwords, obtains the hint for a given fastword, and who then attempts to guess the remaining two words. Let us also assume that a person will be given n chances to log in to an account from an unknown IP address.

We will let $\hat{f}$ denote an upper bound of the actual frequencies of the n most likely fastwords, conditional on the hint. This corresponds to a probability of success for the adversary of no more than $p = 1 - (1 - \hat{f})^n$. This is the same as stating that $\hat{f} = 1 - (1 - p)^{1/n}$. Since we have assumed that the system's understanding of frequencies would be off by a factor c, this corresponds to requiring that the system's belief of the conditional frequency of a fastword, given the hint, is $f \le (1 - (1 - p)^{1/n})/c$.

For concreteness, we may set the maximum probability of success for the attacker to $p = 2^{-20}$. Recalling the analysis in Section 7.2.7, this corresponds to a *minimum* security of the solution exceeding the *average* security of typical passwords by two bits. We further assume $n = 5$ and $c = 2$. These parameter choices corresponds to a conditional frequency of the fastword—given the hint—of at most $2^{-23.3}$.

In Figure 7.7, we show the cumulative distribution of fastwords in our study, where hints are *not* given or where these are sent to the account owner in a way that can be established not to be possible to intercept by a typical attacker. All of these measures use the minimum-security estimate after both the N-gram frequency and the product of frequencies are computed.

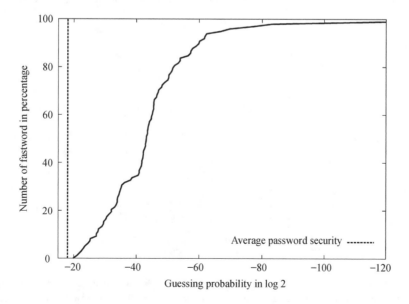

Figure 7.7 The figure shows a cumulative distribution of probabilities of the fastwords in our user study. The average security of passwords (2^{-18}) is shown as a reference point.

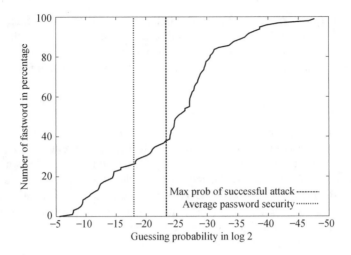

Figure 7.8 The figure shows a cumulative distribution of the conditional probabilities of the fastwords in our user study, after the word with the *lowest frequency* has been given as a hint. Sixty-one percent of the fastwords have a security—after the hint is given—that exceeds the maximum probability of success for the attacker ($2^{-23.3}$). The average security of passwords (2^{-18}) is shown as a reference point.

In Figure 7.8, we show the conditional probabilities of fastwords used by subjects in our study, given the word with the lowest frequency as a hint. In Figure 7.9, we instead plot the conditional probability based on using the *first* keyword in the fastword as a hint. In both graphs, we draw a line at the probability of $2^{-23.3}$, as described above. The reduced guessing probabilities shown in both graphs represent the situation

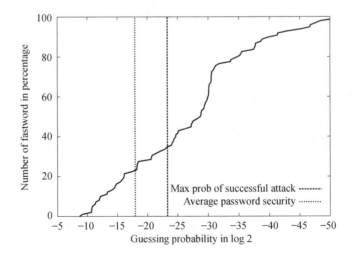

Figure 7.9 The figure shows a cumulative distribution of the conditional probabilities of the fastwords in our user study, after the *first* keyword of the fastword has been given as a hint. Sixty-four percent of the fastwords have a security—after the hint is given—exceeds the maximum probability of success for the attacker ($2^{-23.3}$). The average security of passwords (2^{-18}) is shown as a reference point.

when an adversary knows the hints that is possible through a weak hinting system such as those that show the hint right away after a user indicates that he/she forgets the password.

We see that 61% versus 64% of the fastwords have conditional probabilities (for the adversary to succeed) that correspond to a fastword security that is better than the *average* password security—and *much* better than the *lowest* password security. If this is the minimum acceptable security, then fastwords that do not comply can either be rejected during the enrollment phase, or the system may refuse to disclose hints for these values.

We have not discussed the security against an adversary who gains access to the salted and hashed fastwords. However, this can easily be seen to correspond to the security shown in Figures 7.8 and 7.9. We note that if the system policy is to never give out a hint if the resulting security would fall below a system threshold, however, then these hints do not need to be stored.

Turning now to the security of the extended feature set, we observe that this depends on the number and sizes of the equivalence classes. For simplicity, we assume that *all* words belong to equivalence classes, and that each such class contains exactly s elements. The probability of being able to guess the sequence will be increased by a factor of s^n where n is a number of words in a sequence. For $n = 3$ words in a fastword, as we have used, and for equivalence classes of size $s = 8$ words, this means a reduction of security by a factor 2^9 for the entire fastword, and 2^6 for the fastword given a hint.

In other words, a fastword whose probability of being guessed is 2^{-42} would be guessable with a probability of 2^{-33} if equivalence classes are used, and these each have the maximum size of $s = 8$. Similarly, if the probability of success for an adversary would be 2^{-27} after seeing the hint, then the use of equivalence classes of size $s = 8$ would increase this to a probability of success of 2^{-21}.

In Figure 7.10, we show the effects on security of using such equivalence classes. The graph describes the conditional fastword probabilities, given the first keyword as a hint. We note that a realistic implementation

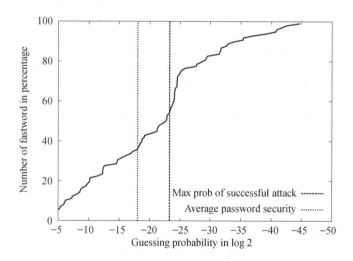

Figure 7.10   What happens when we introduce equivalence classes and the adversary has obtained the *first* keyword of the fastword from a password hint. The figure shows a cumulative distribution of the conditional probabilities of the fastwords in our user study, with equivalence classes of size $s = 8$ added. Forty-five percent of the fastwords have a security that exceeds the maximum probability of a successful attack ($2^{-23.3}$) and the average password security (2^{-18}). We note that fastwords with lower security can be rejected at enrollment. Alternatively, hints can be disabled for these credentials, or smaller sets of equivalence classes be used.

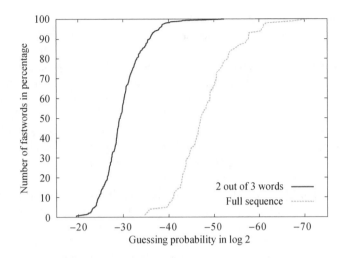

Figure 7.11   The figure shows the cumulative distribution of the strengths of partial fastwords of 100 subjects where two out of the three keywords are entered and the third is left out. We show all combinations; thus, the above corresponds to the average security. For comparison, we also show the strengths of the complete fastwords for the same set of subjects. Recall that typical passwords are believed to have 18 bits [128] of security.

will have differing sizes of equivalence classes. While we use a somewhat simplified analysis by assuming that all equivalence classes are of the same size, this does not affect the underlying principles. Moreover, we note that the sizes of equivalence classes can be set to balance usability needs and security expectations.

Similarly, if the system accepts a login attempt with only a partial match to the registered fastword, this affects security. It is possible to set a threshold for the minimum security required. For example, if *one* subset of keywords correspond to a sufficiently low frequency measure, while *another* does not, then the first would be accepted but the second would not. (At least not without any additional support for the login attempt.) It is also possible that an authentication above one level gives access to certain resources, whereas an authentication above another level gives access to others. To illustrate the effect of partial matches on security, we plot the security resulting from inputting only two out of the three keywords for the fastwords of our 100 subjects. In Figure 7.11, we show all combinations of keyword selections herein—in other words, a total of 300 partial matches for our 100 subjects.

7.2.8   Entry Speed

In addition to being able to assess the security and recall rates of fastwords relative to traditional passwords, we *also* wish to estimate how long it takes to enter these types of credentials on a typical handset.

This was done in a second user study. We recruited participants to enter three fastwords and three passwords on a device, where the credentials used were drawn at random from the credentials obtained from the study described in Section 7.2.5. Half of the passwords were what we refer to as "simple" passwords, and the other half were "strong" passwords. This corresponds to passwords the participants in the first study gave as example passwords for social networking sites and for financial sites. Subjects were told to enter the credentials as fast as they could, and were shown the times taken to enter these.

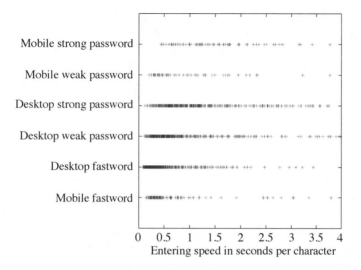

Figure 7.12   The figure shows a scatter plot of how long participants in the study took to enter passwords and fastwords on handsets and traditional keyboards. All times in seconds. Note that we did not implement error correction for the desktop fastwords in this study; this could easily be done in a real-world application, using a scripting language.

We recruited total 234 PC users and 45 mobile users from Amazon Mechanical Turk, friends and family, and by tweets. The browser agent was read to determine what type of device each subject used. The resulting timings are shown in Figures 7.12 and 7.13. The timings clearly shows that entering fastword on a desktop is about twice faster than on a mobile device. The difference in speed can be greater if error-correction is

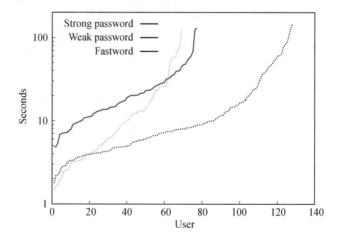

Figure 7.13   This plot shows the time taken to enter each type of credential (strong password, weak password, and fastword) by different users. The plot is sorted in ascending order. It should be noted that points with the same "User" number do not come from the same user. Also, please note the logarithmic y-axis. Fastwords are quicker to enter for most users; however, could be slower for users who do not use their phone to type; these users "peck out" any credential, and the entry time depends to a large extent on the length of the credential.

added to desktop text entry using plugins or backend correction, this was not done herein, and therefore, the timings for fastwords on desktops are upper estimates.

We note that the subjects entered unknown credentials—therefore, there is no speedup due to the "motoric memory" of having entered the same string time after time. That effect has to be determined through follow-up studies. However, we note that it is reasonable to expect that motoric memory will affect both fastwords and passwords—the extent to which it will reduce the entry times is likely to depend largely on the length of the credential.

7.2.9   Implementation of Fastword Entry

There are two principal approaches one can take when implementing fastword entry: (1) using client-side browser scripting (JavaScript or VBscript) and (2) using plugins (Java applet, Flash, ActiveX, etc.). This section describes how to implement fastword entry using JavaScript to control an HTML form. JavaScript approach is preferable over others because it is supported by all modern browsers available on mobile devices. (iPhones, iPods, and iPads cannot execute any plugins or VBscript at the time of writing.)

As shown in Figure 7.14, a fastword entry requires two HTML form components: a *text area* and a *hidden field*. A hidden field is for storing fastword content, and a text area, such as a *textarea* tag or an *input* tag, is for displaying a masked fastword and accepting input from the user. A textarea tag is better than an input tag in supporting a long fastword. The reason is that some web browser implementations, input tags have a limited size, which will prevent a user from entering a long fastword.

A fastword entry requires JavaScript to help mask the portion of a fastword that is already completed. To do that, the event handler *onkeyup* has to be attached to the text area. As shown in the flowchart in Figure 7.15, when a user types, the handler checks the changes in the text area. If it is a deletion, then the handler updates the fastword in the hidden field accordingly. If it is an addition, then the handler checks whether the user has completed a word. For simplicity, we decide that a word is completed and should be masked by "*"s when the user types a white space. There are two reasons why we wait until the user completes a word before masking: First, we want to allow the autocorrect/autofill feature of the mobile device to assist the user. Second, it is more likely for a user to make a mistake if we mask the character immediately.

We note that the autocorrection and autocompletion can be done by the device itself, or it can be done on the server side. The latter has benefits for devices (such as Android devices) where the autocompletion/autofill functionality depends on past behavior. This is not beneficial for security reasons, and so, one can disable that functionality by implementing the features on the backend.

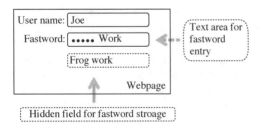

Figure 7.14   Implementing fastword entry on a webpage using an HTML form. A text area (textarea or input tag) is used for fastword entry. A hidden field (not visible to the user) is used for storing the content of a fastword because a text area and a password field cannot leave one the last word unmasked as shown in the figure.

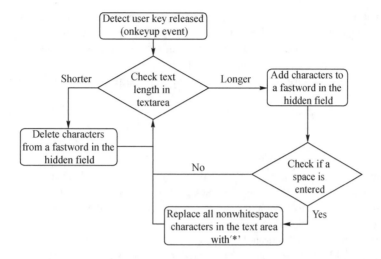

Figure 7.15   Flowchart describing how to use JavaScript to process fastword entry in the context of an HTML form.

7.2.10   Conclusion

We have described a new authentication scheme and argued that it offers benefits over traditional passwords in terms of speed of entry; security; and recall. It also enables features not currently available for passwords, such as voice entry, credential strength checking, and robustness against mistakes.

It is also of interest to consider additional features. For example, if a user faces a camera and *mouths* his fastword (i.e., speaks it with no sound), can the device infer the credential from his lip movements with sufficient precision? If that were possible, it would provide us with an elegant way of avoiding attacks based on eavesdropping and shoulder surfing, given that the average person is not very good at lip reading.

We believe the novel structure we have proposed has the potential of offering many new helpful features; we have described some, but believe that there are many more possibilities to be unearthed, given the possibilities offered by being able to identify and process conceptual components of the credential.

ACKNOWLEDGMENTS

Many thanks to Richard Chow, Lucky Green, Bill Leddy, Debin Liu, Alon Nir, and Liu Yang for helpful feedback on previous versions of the manuscript, and to Hampus Jakobsson for helping to recruit subjects.

7.3   DERIVING PINs FROM PASSWORDS

Markus Jakobsson and Debin Liu

Abstract. In this section, we describe a method of deriving PINs from passwords. We assume that the user already has a password. The method is useful to obtain friction-free user onboarding to mobile platforms. It has significant business benefits to organizations that wish to introduce mobile apps to existing users—but which are reluctant to make the users authenticate with passwords. From the user's perspective, a PIN is easier to enter than a password, and a *derived* PIN does not need to be remembered. Even though the PINs are derived from passwords, they do not contain sufficient information to make the passwords easy to infer from compromised PINs. We quantify exactly how much information about the passwords and the derived PINs contain, and how much information is *lost*—based on real-life password distributions. We also show that our proposed method is easy to use.

7.3.1   Introduction

Consumers do not like passwords, especially if they have to be entered on a handset [280]: users find password entry on handsets more annoying than lack of coverage, small screen size, and poor voice quality. It has been shown that the time to enter a typical strong password is on the order of two to three times longer on a handset than a regular keyboard (see Section 7.2).

Financial service providers *also* do not like passwords for handsets, but for a different reason: handsets are believed to be more likely to be targeted by fraudsters than PCs are—at least in the near future. This is based on a shift from phishing to malware [103,210], an explosive growth of the mobile market [239], and structural vulnerabilities in the current malware defense paradigm [271] for battery-constrained devices. It has been shown that trusted computing [488] may help address the problem. Handsets are also vulnerable to threats that PC are not exposed to—such as malware propagation over Bluetooth [137]. Although the threat is nascent, it has started to get attention [236].

Having *both* passwords and PINs allows for a tiered authentication approach where certain types (and sizes) of transactions can be performed on mobile devices, and rely on PINs for authentication—while more secure devices and authentication could be required for other transactions. In a way, PINs therefore *improve* security relative to only using passwords: they can be used in contexts where passwords should not be exposed, and such PIN-authenticated transactions could be treated differently by the backend risk model than password-authenticated transactions would. This is contrary to the traditional wisdom that PINs, being shorter than passwords, are simply less secure.

As a result of user preferences and provider concerns, there is an industry trend toward using PINs instead of passwords on handsets, gaming consoles, store checkouts, and other appliances with similar constraints and security profiles. Many phone apps ask for a PIN instead of a password.

While PINs offer improved convenience to users and has security benefits in comparison to passwords, using PINs instead of passwords come with a multitude of drawbacks. From a business point of view, *any* increase of the end user friction is worrisome. Having to force millions of existing users to create PINs is not desirable at all. Moreover, PINs are not as easy to remember as passwords, unless the number represents something to the user. As a result, approximately one user in five selects a birthday as her PIN [115]. This not only means that database-scraping attackers have an edge, but also leads to a restricted distribution of PINs: There are only 365 days in a year. It is also well understood that people commonly reuse PINs, just as they reuse passwords. This means that if one PIN is compromised, then that may put others at risk as well. For those who do not use any of these tricks to remember PINs, it is relatively common to *forget* them: Roughly 1 in 10 report having forgotten their PINs [115]. Forrester research [165] estimates the average costs of help-desk assisted reset at $70 per reset, making forgotten credentials a commercially very expensive security problem.

We describe a method that *bootstraps* the generation of PINs to create an automated onboarding of an overwhelming majority of users. We achieve this by deriving the PINs from already established passwords—

Figure 7.16   The figure shows the user interface. To the left is an image of what the user might see when arriving at the authentication stage; in some contexts, the user name may be autofilled or obtained from a drop-down menu. The image to the right shows what she would see after tapping on the PIN window. To log in, the consumer would simply enter the first four characters of her password, using the numeric keypad. If a password character is "2", "A", "a", "B", "b", "C", or "c", then the user presses the 2-button—we are not case sensitive. A password starting with "Blu2" would correspond to the PIN 2852.

without explicit user involvement. The user would, in fact, not even be aware of the PIN creation until she is told that she *has* a PIN, and should use it to log in. The PIN is set as the first four characters of the password, mapped to a numeric keypad. A screenshot of a possible user interface is shown in Figure 7.16.

> The mapping from passwords to PINs is analogous to how alphanumeric phone numbers are mapped to a 10-button keypad—like 1 – 800 CALL ATT *becomes* 1 – 800 225 5288. Similarly, the password "Blu2thrules" becomes the PIN "2582".

We show that the method is easy to use. We also analyze how much information a derived PIN reveals about the underlying password. This is relevant to consider in order to understand the consequences of a PIN being compromised. The analysis is based on tens of thousands of actual passwords, and their associated derived PINs. In addition, we give a first-order estimate that derived PINs have approximately the same entropy as traditional PINs do. Therefore, derived PINs do not reduce the security of traditional PINs.

7.3.2   A Brief Discussion of Passwords

Before we start explaining in detail the method of derived PINs, you probably have some questions about passwords and PINs you use everyday: How good is my password? How do people measure it? Let's have a brief discussion of passwords!

How do people measure the strength of passwords?   People usually use *entropy* as a measure of password strength. The entropy of a password in bits is the binary logarithm of the number of guesses needed to find the password with certainty. For example, a password with 42 bits of strength would require 2^{42} attempts to exhaust all possibilities. Thus, adding one bit of entropy to a password doubles the number of guesses required, which makes an attacker's task twice as difficult if he uses brute force.

Today, many websites require the users to avoid simple passwords. This is enforced by their password rules. A typical password rule, for example, requires a minimum password length of eight characters. Other rules require users to include upper case letters, special letters, or numerical characters.

7.3.3   How to Derive PINs from Passwords

In this section, we describe how to derive PINs from passwords.

7.3.3.1   Derivation approach

The derived PINs are set as the first four characters of the passwords, mapped to a numeric keypad. As the users authenticate to the system using their passwords, their PINs are derived from their passwords without their knowledge. When a user for whom a PIN has been derived arrives to the mobile authentication interface (or another PIN authentication interface), she would be told that she has a PIN—and how to determine it from her password. As a result, users do not have to remember the PIN—it is enough to remember the password.

7.3.3.2   Managing special cases

There are several rare cases that the method cannot be applied directly. For example, you might wonder how we deal with special characters, or what if people change their passwords. We list these special cases below, along with some suggested approaches for dealing with them.

1. **How do we deal with unmappable characters?**   An unmappable character is a character that is not on a typical numeric keypad. The frequency of passwords containing unmappable characters is marginal—less than 1.4% according to our study. This special case can be addressed in at least two ways: (a) one can map all special characters to one digit (e.g., to "0") or (b) one can simply "disqualify" passwords containing unmappable characters among the first four characters. The latter would force the owners of such passwords to create a PIN manually—in the old-fashioned way—or to update his/her password. One approach to increase automatic enrollment is to augment password strength checkers to reject unmappable characters in the first four positions of passwords that are created. Given the very low rates of unmappable characters in the first four positions, this has no practical impact on the security of the derived PINs.

2. **What if a strong password becomes a weak PIN?**   A password is considered *strong* if it is sufficiently uncommon—otherwise *weak*. Similarly, some PINs are so commonly used that they are considered weak. For example, "1234" is one such PIN. There is a case that strong passwords result in weak PINs. For example, both passwords "1234GreyFrieS#" and "1Beg2Cry" make the derived PIN "1234".

To avoid weak derived PINs, we could reject the associated password (as is commonly the policy); accept the password but not derive a PIN; or derive a PIN but demand that it is updated on its first use. The approach taken is a matter of security policy.

> Many password strength checkers will reject passwords with "weak" sequences—independently of the strength of the remainder. For example, many password strength checkers will already reject the above example password. This is because it contains the sequence "1234", which is considered an *indicator* of a weak password—whether the password is actually weak or not. Similarly, many password strength checkers reject passwords that contain the name of the registered user, his or her zip code, and similar elements.

3. **What if users change their passwords?** If a PIN is derived from a password, and then used for some time and the user may either think of the PIN in terms of the password it is derived from or she may learn the PIN. In the latter case, the PIN would become independent of the password in the mind of the user. The backend cannot know whether this has happened or not. Therefore, if the user were to change her password, the backend could create two "parallel universes"—with the *old* derived PIN and the *new* derived PIN. Both are valid until one of them is used, at which point the other one is erased.

4. **How do we derive PINs for hardware keyboards?** Some handsets, like Blackberries, have hardware keyboards. When the user is asked to enter her password, the hardware keyboard would be momentarily turned off, and the PIN entry would be done using the touch-screen keyboard.

> Old Blackberries do not have touch screens. Since apps are platform aware (if not platform specific), apps on noncompliant platforms would simply not offer users to log in using a derived PIN, but would require them to create a PIN out of band (OOB)—as is currently required for *all* users.
>
> Other handsets, such as the typical 4–5 year old phone, have hardware keyboards with the proper mapping; however, people are used to pressing each button one or more times in a row to advance to the right character. This can be detected and compensated for on the backend, or the user can be instructed to only press each button once for each character.

7.3.4   Analysis of Passwords and Derived PINs

Now you have learnt how one can derive PINs from passwords. In this section, let's derive some PINs from a large number of real passwords obtained from raided dropboxes, and then have a closer look at these passwords and the derived PINs.

> A *dropbox* is a file created and used by hackers to temporarily store stolen credentials. Many financial organizations and security vendors attempt to raid dropboxes, that is, locate them and copy their contents. This is done to restrict access to compromised accounts.

Let's look at the contents of three dropboxes, corresponding to a large financial service provider (denoted as FSP with 8359 credentials); a large Social Networking Provider (denoted as SNP with 2873 credentials); mixed credentials (denoted as malware with 16192 credentials). The contents of the groups are not combined since the distribution of each class is different. The difference in distribution may be attributed to different rules of what a good password is on the various domains, and to differing user security mentalities for the three different types of domains.

7.3.4.1 How do we compute password entropy?

We want estimate the entropy of passwords of each group, corresponding to the three groups described above. For all the credentials in the dropboxes, we truncate them to the four first characters, resulting in what we refer to as *pwd*4. We then count—within each group of passwords—the relative frequencies of each value *pwd*4. For example, the password "Blu2thrules" would be truncated to become *pwd*4 ="Blu2," and a counter for this very string would be increased. After that, given the relative frequencies, we would estimate the entropies for the different groups.

We then perform what we refer to as the *phone pad mapping* for all the truncated passwords *pwd*4. For example, this would map the *pwd*4 string "Blu2" to "2582", using the mapping resulting from the common interface shown in Figure 7.16. As a result, there are exactly 10,000 possible mapped strings. For each of these, we determine the relative frequency, given the mapped and truncated passwords of the three groups. Like the entropy assessments from the unmapped passwords, the entropy assessments of the mapped passwords will be slight under-estimates (but closer to the truth given that the mapping increased the density.)

7.3.4.2 What have we learnt from our computations?

Figure 7.17 shows the entropies of the first four characters of *unmapped* passwords and the derived PINs, that is, the *mapped* and truncated passwords. It also shows the information loss during the mapping process.

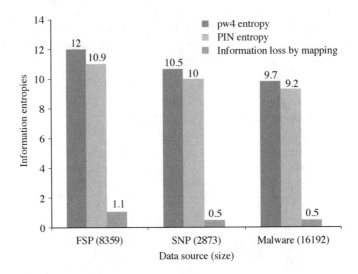

Figure 7.17 The figure shows the entropies of the first four digits of the studied passwords; the entropies of the corresponding PINs; and the information loss during the mapping process from passwords to PINs. The numbers are different for our three sources of passwords; most probably due to differing rules governing what passwords are accepted, and different security mentalities among end users. The first two groups correspond to phishing dropboxes for FSP and SNP, while the third group corresponds to a malware dropbox containing credentials to any domain that was accessed from the infected machines.

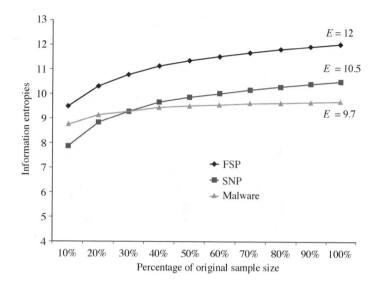

Figure 7.18   The figure shows a strong sample size dependency of entropy estimation for all three data sources. We know that the true entropies of the three sources are *at least* as big as the estimates for the 100% sample measurements, but extrapolation of these curves tell us that still bigger sample sizes would most likely have shown yet higher source entropies. It is an interesting open problem how to extrapolate estimates of this kind to assess the true entropy, given only samples of rather small sizes.

These entropy estimates are 12, 10.5, and 9.7 for the three groups of *pwd*4 from the three dropboxes, and for the derived PINs, they are 10.9, 10, and 9.2. This means that the *differences* between the entropies of the unmapped and mapped password collections correspond to the amount of information that is removed by the phone pad mappings. These are 1.1, 0.5, and 0.5 for the three groups. (The reason they are not the same are due to different sample sizes, different requirements on passwords, and potentially, due to different efforts among the users to select good passwords for the associated domains.)

A note for those who want to replicate this The sample sizes play a substantial role when producing entropy estimates—especially for the unmapped samples, where the density is sparser than for the mapped samples. To determine the effects of this, we sampled down the first group (8359 samples) to the size of the second group (2873 samples). We do this 10 times for different randomized samples and averaged the associated entropy measures. The result is 10.9 for the down-sampled group of financial service provider, to be compared to the 10.5 of the group of Social Networking Provider, and 12 for the full financial service provider.

In addition, the three data sources are sampled from 10% to 100% of their original size. Figure 7.18 shows a strong dependency on the sample size when estimating the entropy. This is due to the fact that low densities of samples create an artificially low estimate of the entropy, given how entropies are estimated.

We know that even larger sample sizes are likely to further increase the estimates of entropy. Therefore, the estimates are very likely *lower* estimates.

7.3.4.3 How commonly are people using special characters?

Since special characters make it impossible to derive PINs, you must want to know how common they are. It turns out among the passwords reviewed, on average approximately 32% had both upper and lower case among the first four characters; only 3.2% had at least one nonalphanumeric character.

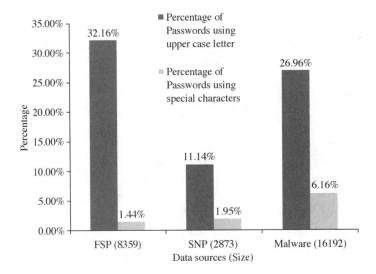

Figure 7.19 The figure shows the percentages of the passwords that contain upper case and special characters at any of the first four positions. Passwords with special characters in the first four positions can either have such symbols mapped to 0 or 1, or these passwords could be excluded from the PIN derivation process.

The method that we have described only considers the mapping of alphanumerical strings, and does not account for special characters (such as "@", "$", "+") among the characters to be mapped to generate the derived PIN. However, we find that the frequency with which one or more of the first four characters is "unmappable" is rather marginal: It is between 1.4% and 1.9% for all three sources. Figure 7.19 shows the percentages of passwords using upper case and special characters.

7.3.4.4 What type of characters do people usually use?

Microsoft researchers Florêncio and Herley [192] found that typical users hardly use upper case and special characters. All three sources exhibit similar character type distributions: lower case characters dominate among all positions; numerical characters are consistent around 10%; upper case characters are used more often as the first digit around 7%, then reduced to 2–3% at other positions. Figure 7.20 shows the character type distribution in the first four positions of financial service provider passwords.

7.3.5 Security Analysis

You might still wonder why our method can generate more secure PINs. In this section, we will take a look at the security of the derived PINs!

7.3.5.1 Security impact of compromise

We know that an adversary gains on average 10 bits of information about a password if he compromises the corresponding PIN. The exact amount of information lost by the truncation depends on the length of the

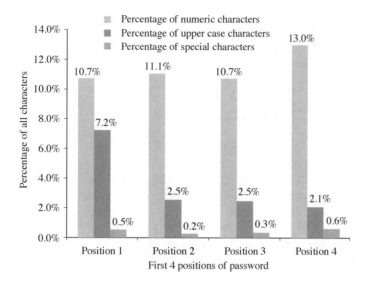

Figure 7.20   The figure shows the character type distribution at first four positions of financial service provider passwords. It is interesting to note that upper case is much more common in the first position than elsewhere. The percentage of numeric characters is fairly even for the different positions.

password. The average password length we analyzed was roughly 8 characters, which according to NISTs entropy estimates [375] corresponds to an entropy of 18 bits.

Our findings suggest that the actual entropy is a bit higher than what was estimated by NIST. Our estimate of the entropy of the entire password is 19.3 bits instead of 18 bits.

The attacker learns on average 10 bits out of the on average 19.3 bits of information, resulting in a *conditional entropy* of between $18 - 10 = 8$ bits (using NIST's estimate) and $19.3 - 10 = 9.3$ bits (using our estimate). This means that there are at least $2^8 = 256$ possibilities left to the attacker who does not know which one to guess. This is the security of a password for which the derived PIN has been compromised. While this is not terrific, it ought to be compared to the much starker situation in which the entire password is compromised, should passwords be used on insecure devices instead of derived PINs.

7.3.5.2 *How people choose PINs?*

Before we compare the security between derived PINs and regular PINs, it would be interesting to see how people choose their PINs. To find out, we built another survey asking 100 subjects to answer one simple question: "How do you choose PINs to make them easy to remember?"

The responses we got can be categorized into four groups: PINs generated using years, PINs generated using dates, PINs generated by keypad mapping, and PINs generated by other methods.

To estimate a first-order approximation of the entropy of a 4-digit PIN number, let's assume people can randomly choose a year between 1900 and 2010 as their PINs. This would give us an entropy value of $E_1 = \log_2(110) = 6.6$ for any PIN chosen as a year. We also assume there are 365 days a year. People can randomly choose a month and a date to create a 4-digit PIN whose entropy value would be $E_2 = \log_2(12 \times 30) = 8.5$. According to the previous section, a 4-digit PIN mapped from a password has an entropy value of $E_3 = 10$.

Table 7.3 How to choose PINs?

Method	Percentage	Entropy
Using years	21%	6.6
Using dates	27.4%	8.5
Keypad mapping	12.9%	10
Others	38.7%	13.3

We use this value for any PIN created by keypad mapping. This is based on the approximation that the mnemonics that are mapped will have a similar distribution as passwords. We treat all the other PINs that are not generated by years, dates, or keypad mapping as *uniformly random* PINs, which again, of course gives us an upper bound on the entropy. Those PINs have an entropy value of $E_4 = 4 \times \log_2(10) = 13.3$.

The percentages and entropy estimates are presented in Table 7.3.

Therefore, a not-very-precise estimate of the upper bound of the average entropy for a 4-digit traditional PIN is 10.15.

7.3.5.3   *Comparing derived PINs and traditional PINs*

Now we know that traditional PINs that are *not* derived from passwords have an entropy of no more than approximately 10.2 bits. From previous sections, we also know the entropies of derived PINs were 10.9, 10, and 9.2 for the FSP, SNP, and mixed domains. Therefore, our derived PINs do not reduce security, but have approximately the same average security as traditional PINs. (There is anecdotal evidence suggesting that the lower quartile of derived PINs is notably more secure than the lower quartile of traditional PINs, though. This is due to the lack of very common combinations for derived PINs, and the relatively common use of years and dates as traditional PINs.)

Moreover, if the (beginning of the) password is not reused, then the derived PIN is independent of other PINs created from other related passwords.

An iPhone app developer, Daniel Amitay, analyzed the PINs used in his app. In his blog of "Most Common iPhone Passcodes" [88], he presented the top 10 PINs he found, out of 204, 508 recorded PINs: 1234, 0000, 2580, 1111, 5555, 5683, 0852, 2222, 1212, and 1998. Most of them follow typical formulas, such as four identical digits, moving in a line up/down the pad, or repetition. These 10 PINs represent 15% of all PINs in use. Their frequencies are shown in Figure 7.21.

In his blog, Amitay observed that a thief could safely try 10 different PINs on an iPhone without initiating the data wipe. With a 15% success rate, about 1 in 7 iPhones would easily be unlocked.

7.3.6   Usability Experiments

It's important to know how users would understand the derived PINs method. In this section, we will look at the two human subject studies. The subjects were asked by the question shown in Figure 7.22.

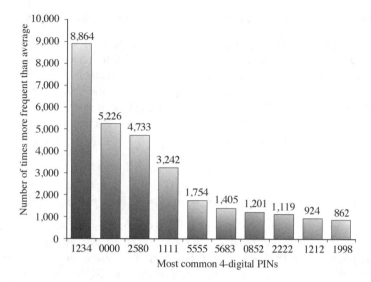

Figure 7.21   The figure shows the top 10 iPhone PINs: (1234, 0000, 2580, 1111, 5555, 5683, 0852, 2222, 1212, and 1998), out of 204,508 recorded PINs. Keep in mind that out of 204,508 PINs, a 4-digit PIN can only have a frequency of 20 if all PINs are distributed uniformly.

What is Joe's PIN?

Joe uses a PIN to access his PayPal account from his phone. But he does not want to have to remember another number, and he does not want to reuse his banking PIN. So he uses PayPal's new "password to PIN" feature so that he only has to remember his password. Joe's password is "Blu2thrules." Look at the screen-shot below and let us know what PIN he should enter.

Joe's password is "Blu2thrules." A PIN is a four digit number, such as "1234". What is Joe's PIN? Please provide any comments you may have below, we appreciate your input!

Figure 7.22   The figure shows what subjects on Amazon Mechanical Turk are asked. Out of the 200 subjects who took the test, 68% responded with the expected answer, "2582" and another 22% with an answer ("Blu2") that indicates that they misunderstood the question but would have passed the authentication.

7.3.6.1 A qualitative study to understand how well people derive PINs

A qualitative study was performed using 25 subjects. Sixteen of the subjects entered the expected PIN with no hesitation. Four of these cited similar user experiences for dialing phone numbers or for entering last names using the number pad. The remainder offered no particular explanation of why they knew what to do. Another six subjects (all of them men in the technology sector) took more than a minute to determine what to do, but then, correctly entered the PIN. Several of them argued that it would have been difficult to succeed if they had used a special character in the first four of the password. Three of the subjects failed initially. All of them understood the process when given an explanation corresponding to what was later added under the help button.

7.3.6.2 A quantitative study aims to understand how well people derive PINs

In another user experiment using 100 subjects, out of the 100 responses, 68 were correct ("2582"), 22 were wrong but simple misunderstanding of the question ("Blu2"). Those who responded "Blu2" were asked in a follow-up interaction what the PIN would be if they could only use digits, and all responded correctly. This amounts a total of 90% of who would have successfully entered the correct PIN. Of the remaining responses, one was a likely typo ("2182"); two were "1322" (the numerical string in the user name); two suggested that the subjects thought only letters mattered ("Blut"). Three believed "JoeS" (parts of the user name) was the correct response, and one cannot be explained. It is not clear what portion of these 10% of clearly unsuccessful logins would have occurred in a more realistic setting in which the users were more motivated to log in.

7.4   VISUAL PREFERENCE AUTHENTICATION

Yuan Niu, Markus Jakobsson, Gustav Rydstedt, and Dahn Tamir

Abstract. The issue of password reset is an old and expensive problem. Now mostly automated, password reset often relies on the usage of so-called "Security Questions" that rely on *what-you-know* for authentication. However, the answers to these questions are sometimes easily found or guessed. We describe an alternative password reset scheme, using visual passwords, that uses preferences expressed by classifying images in various categories under "Like" or "Dislike" for each user. Visual preference-based authentication can be a stand-alone dedicated server or a cloud service used by service providers.

7.4.1   Password Resets

Where there are passwords, there will be the need for password resets as human memory inevitably fails. Before automated password reset systems were in place, a forgetful user could call the tech support to set a new password. Each of these calls cost an estimated 22 dollars each [281]. Besides the cost of the call, the time wasted in waiting for the password reset could be potentially costly to an organization.

Now, self-service password reset systems are the norm for many online service providers, including email hosts and banks. The problem of password reset, along with the security issues associated with it, was famously brought to America's attention during the 2008 election when Vice Presidential candidate Sarah Palin's Yahoo! account was compromised.

7.4.2 Security Questions Aren't so Secure

As Section 4.7 has already outlined, the current prevalent system of password reset based is often based on security questions that test a user's knowledge, after which a one-time use link to reset the password is sent to a preset email account. These questions range from "Mother's Maiden Name" to "Frequent Flyer Account Number." The intent of the questions, such as naming a favorite teacher from elementary school or a childhood pet, are to ask for details that only the owner of the account should know.

Unfortunately, the nature of questions make them vulnerable to social engineering or statistical guessing. As Schneier points out [423], the fallback mechanism, in this case a series of questions that leads to a new password, should be more secure than the primary method of authentication—the original password. It should not be easier to reset a password than to guess the original password, but anecdotal evidence and academic research shows that, unfortunately, security questions can make it quite easy for an attacker to guess and subsequently reset his victim's password.

Griffith and Jakobsson showed that knowing as little as age, name, and place of birth can lead to discovery of a victim's mother's maiden name—a commonly asked security question [225]. This information is available in public databases.

Now, in the age of Facebook and social networks [394], there is even more information for an attacker to use. While a person might not post passwords online for all to see, she may have no such qualms about posting details of his life on blogs, Facebook, Twitter, and so on. The information, which is readily available for all to see, allow attackers to make educated guesses about their victims' lives.

According to a study of security questions from four email providers by Schechter, Brush, and Egelman, an acquaintance or family member who wishes to gain unauthorized access can guess the correct answer to security questions 17% of the time, while 13% of all answers could be guessed by simply using the most common answer for a particular question [416].

Furthermore, there remains the problem of what happens when a user forgets the answer to her own secret question, something that happens 20% of the time, as these researchers learned. In this case, the fallback mechanism has failed and the user must rely on the service provider to regain access her account or else lose access completely. Facebook [184], for example, does not allow security questions to be reset. Once forgotten, the user must resort to identifying photos of friends within her social network. For some online services, however, answers to password reset questions are the only "private" account information the service provider stores.

7.4.3 What is Visual Preference-Based Authentication

One alternative to traditional memory-based security questions is a system of visual preferences. A preference-based authentication scheme called Blue Moon Authentication, as described by Jakobsson et al. [281], provides users with a high entropy, low failure prone way of resetting their passwords by describing what they *like* or *dislike* (Figure 7.23). What we prefer is extremely personal and sometimes even illogical, and these preferences are mostly stable over time. By the time we reach adulthood, we have well defined opinions on food, politics, hobbies, music, and many other topics.

Figure 7.23   The visual Blue Moon Authentication system. Users choose some number of images they like and an equal number that they dislike to set up a password and authenticate by selecting either all "Likes" or all "Dislikes." Later, when they need to authenticate, they must correctly classify their choices by choosing all their "Likes" or all "Dislikes." As long as users select images honestly according to their real interests, there is little new information for them to memorize.

In the age of the smartphone, the use of touch screens and images in such an authentication system speeds up the interaction. Although we describe usage in the context of password reset, visual preferences can also be used as the primary method of authentication as well.

Visual preference-based authentication (VPA) is particularly useful for accessibility because of the flexibility of the media allowed. Users are increasingly reliant on smartphones, and password entry on these devices is a notoriously annoying task. For blind users, touch screen devices are particularly frustrating. Using VPA, however, they can choose to use the audio option, for example, "Do you like skating?" and answer by providing voice feedback, that is "Yes" or "No" to classify their preferences.

7.4.3.1   Use case: visual Blue Moon Authentication

Visual Blue Moon Authentication uses a display/classification scheme. During setup, images across various categories are shown and the user chooses a set of images classified as "Likes" and a set classified as "Dislikes." The number of images selected may vary according to the security needs of the site deploying Blue Moon. Though we describe a scheme with images, other types of media, such as sound or video, can also be used.

One significant advantage of using preferences to create a visual password is that there's very little information for the user to memorize. When she chooses the images in the setup, she does not need to memorize anything new. The image selection is there to put a bound on the number of "tests" the authentication service needs her to pass, as she will undoubtedly have an opinion about most, if not every image.

Figure 7.24 During the authentication process, the user must choose images corresponding to things she likes. All images are from the user's previously expressed likes and dislikes. This is an easy task for the user because she knows her own interests and preferences already.

In the verification stage, both sets of "Likes" and "Dislikes" are displayed and the user must correctly choose a number of images from one of the two sets (Figure 7.24). For example, if 12 likes and 12 dislikes had been chosen during setup, the user will see all 24 images and will be asked to select all the images she likes. To successfully authentication, she must correctly select a subset of the 12 images she had previously classified as "Likes." The number of images in this subset depends on the security needs of the service provider.

In both phases, the display order of images is randomized so that an attacker cannot derive the password by simply observing the position of the tapping, or looking for fingerprints on a touchscreen.

7.4.4 Evaluating Visual Preference-Based Authentication

To determine the effectiveness of this authentication scheme, there were several factors to consider.

- **False positive rates** estimates how well the system does under attack. That is, how often could an adversary successfully authenticate when he should be locked out? A system with low false positive rates might have very stringent policies to determine what a successful authentication means.
- **False negative rates** tell us how often the account owner is locked out when she should be granted access. False negative rates are affected by both how stringent the security requirements are and by user memory. For any system, when there are high false negative rates, the usability of that system suffers.

- **Entropy** can be thought of as a measure of uncertainty. It quantifies the minimum number of bits needed to encode a message. In the case of passwords, the number of bits estimates how good many tries it would take for an attacker to successfully brute-force the password. An 8-*bit* password made up of characters selected with uniform randomness, for instance, would take $2^8 = 256$ tries at most.

    To calculate the number of bits in a password, we look to the number of characters that could be used in forming that password. On a standard American keyboard, we have 52 letters (taking into account capitalization), 10 digits, and 33 symbols, including white space. This gives us a total of 95 possibilities for each character in the password. The number of bits needed to encode each character is $\log_2(95) = 6.6$ bits. An 8 character password would have an entropy of $8 \times 6.6 = 52.8$ bits.

    The higher the entropy, the better, theoretically, the security. In the context of visual preferences, the entropy we are interested are that of the images presented for the user to select.

- **Mutual information** tells us whether two images are likely to be chosen together, in the same way that the letters "Q" and "U" often go together in words. The measurement of mutual information reveals how much information two items share. Images with low pairwise mutual information will make it harder for an adversary to successfully guess sequences of images that may be part of a visual password.

The ideal authentication system would have very low false positive and false negative rates and high entropy. These three factors can be balanced out so that users are not overly frustrated with the authentication process. For example, standards for high entropy passwords often make it difficult for users to remember their own passwords [497], so they resort to practices such as saving the passwords on a browser or reusing passwords. In this example, by reducing the false negative rate, users may inadvertently make it easier for attackers to achieve a high false positive rate—particularly in the case of lost smartphones.

7.4.4.1   Amazon Mechanical Turk

In our experiments, we relied on Amazon Mechanical Turk (MTurk) for recruitment. Amazon Mechanical Turk is set up so that participating users take one of two roles: a *requester* or a *worker*. Requesters may set up "Human Intelligence Tasks" (HITs) with corresponding rewards (usually less than $1 and the desired number of workers. Workers then choose which HITs they wish to solve. requesters have the option of denying payment or giving a bonus based on worker performance. Additionally, requesters can specify how many times each worker may solve a HIT. Tasks are often simple and take a few seconds to a few minutes to complete. Longer tasks usually have larger rewards.

MTurk has recently become a popular tool for experiments in HCI and computer security [269]. MTurk is well suited for computer security experiments in which the participants should not be *primed*. Priming a user means that the user knows before entering the study what the study is for. It has been shown that users who are aware of the study's intent, for example, to password entry habits, perform differently from those users who have no idea what the experiment is really trying to determine [419].

7.4.5   Case Study: Visual Blue Moon Authentication

We conducted two studies using Amazon Mechanical Turk to evaluate the Blue Moon technology and a large image set containing 311 images spanning six categories (sports, hobbies, interests, food, places, music).

The experiment was carried out in three stages using several hundred recruited users.

Stage I Each user was asked to go through both setup and authentication once. Those who successfully chose more than 8 out of 12 "Like" images correctly were invited to join the next stage. Information regarding image entropy was gained from this stage.

  Here, the authentication stage was used to weed out cheaters who clicked arbitrarily.

Stage II We waited 1 week so that workers' short-term memories faded, and then asked each worker to authenticate. This stage allowed us to estimate the false negative rates.

Stage III At the end of Stage II, each user who successfully authenticated was invited to create a second profile. The purpose of this exercise was to determine how likely one person is to setup two disparate profiles for two different websites.

It is unlikely that today's online users will only have one account to authenticate. The practice of choosing the same credentials across multiple sites is frowned upon because if even one of those accounts is compromised, the adversary suddenly has access to every account that uses those credentials. Therefore, it is important to determine whether users can setup multiple profiles that are sufficiently disparate. Visual preferences is a system that makes it possible for users to create entirely different visual passwords for every site by taking advantage of users' predetermined biases.

7.4.5.1 Timing

On average, users required 27.3 s to read the instructions and start the task of setting up a visual password. The average time to make a classification was 6.4 and 5.9 s for likes and dislikes. The total setup time was 169.4 s on average for 12 likes and 12 dislikes. The time to make classifications did not change much as users approached the end of the selection process, which suggests that they did not run out of suitable images to choose from.

  Turning to authentication, the average and the median time was 39.33 and 31.14 s for $12 + 12$ images.

7.4.5.2 Entropy

In order to prevent attackers from guessing which images their victims chose, it is important to choose high entropy images—that is, images that are neither highly disliked nor liked by a significant number of users. Baseball, for instance, is likely to be a low entropy image because of its universal popularity in the United States. If an adversary knows his victim is a male living in New York, for instance, he can guess that baseball is a "Like." Image sets that work well in one country may not work well in others. For example, durian may evoke strong feelings from users in southeast Asia, but many Americans would not even know what it was.

  The average entropy per image was 0.806 bits, and median was 0.89 bits. We identified a number of images with entropy below 0.5 bits. These included "piano" (0, liked by most users); "accordion" (0.34, disliked by most users); "Texas," (0, disliked by most users.) In deployment settings, these images would be removed because they are easy to guess by adversaries. Images like "almonds," "chess," "knitting," and "newspapers" would be kept because users overall did not greatly like or dislike them. The ideal image, with an entropy of 1, would have been chosen just as many times for "Like" as for "Dislike."

  The *mutual information* between images was also considered. This is a measurement of the shared information between images. In other words, how likely is an accordion fan likely to pick Paris as well? In that case, there was a shared information of 0.04 bits. Over all images in the set, mutual information ranged between 0.01 and 0.12 bits for all pairs, meaning that there was little correlation between images. Therefore, an adversary who only knows that his victim enjoys eating fish cannot easily guess the victim is a also a chess champion.

For readers who wish to know in detail how the entropy was computed, we describe the methodology below.

For each image i, its Shannon entropy, e_i, was computed based on the frequency of its appearance as "Like" (p_i) and "Dislike" ($1 - p_i$):

$$e_i = (p_i * \log_2(p_i)) + ((1 - p_i) * \log_2(1 - p_i)) \tag{7.1}$$

The mutual information $I(X, Y)$ is calculated for two images, X (probability p_x of being picked), and Y (probability p_y of being picked):

$$p(x, y) = p_x * p_y \tag{7.2}$$
$$p(1 - x, 1 - y) = (1 - p_x) * (1 - p_y) \tag{7.3}$$
$$H(X) = -1(p_x * \log_2(p_x) + (1 - p_x) * \log_2(1 - p_x)) \tag{7.4}$$
$$= -(p_x * \log_2(p_x)) - ((1 - p_x) * \log_2(1 - p_x)) \tag{7.5}$$
$$H(Y) = -1(p_y * \log_2(p_y) + (1 - p_y) * \log_2(1 - p_y)) \tag{7.6}$$
$$= -(p_y * \log_2(p_y)) - ((1 - p_y) * \log_2(1 - p_y)) \tag{7.7}$$
$$H(X, Y) = -1 * (p(x, y) * \log_2(p(x, y))) \tag{7.8}$$
$$+ p(1 - x, 1 - y) * \log_2(p(1 - x, 1 - y))) \tag{7.9}$$
$$I(X; Y) = H(X) + H(Y) - H(X, Y) \tag{7.10}$$

The security associated with n images in the authentication phase can be estimated as $n\overline{E} - (n - 1)\overline{I}$, where $\overline{E}$ is the average entropy and $\overline{I}$ is the average mutual information. Plugging in $\overline{E} = 0.797$ and $\overline{I} = 0.105$, and $n = 24$, yields an estimate of 16.54 bits of security. This is a slight overestimate, since an adversary can easily discover that 12 images out of 24 must be selected as "like." Moreover, this does not take into consideration that a real system would require only a threshold of the results to be correct, and may allow users to retry a small number of times.

The entropy estimate is a meaningful starting point to understand the security of our chosen authentication scheme, and to determine if it is tolerable. Currently, the common tolerance for false positives for typical e-commerce applications (such as online auction payments) is approximately 1%. With over 16-bits of entropy for each password, the false positive rate should be well below 1% in the system of visual preferences.

7.4.5.3 Estimating false positives

False positives represent the chance that an adversary can successfully guess a user's visual password. If we have an adversary who guesses randomly "Like" or "Dislike" for each image, then the false positive rate is simply $\frac{1}{2^k}$, where k is the number of images selected during authentication. In other words, he has a 50–50 shot at guessing whether each image is liked or disliked, so for image sets of 24 total likes and dislikes, he has a $\frac{1}{16777216}$ chance of guessing correctly.

The first estimate above assumes an adversary who guesses at random with no other knowledge about the system, but realistically, the adversary may be more powerful. He could, for example, know that for a user there must be exactly 12 likes and 12 dislikes, and that to pass the authentication, only 8 choices are needed. Furthermore, he could know the correlation between choices and make a more informed guess.

Let's consider our slightly more advanced adversarial model in which the attacker "Like" or "Dislike" for each images and knows the necessary threshold for successful authentication. If k images are needed out of n for successful authentication, then there are $(n/2)/\binom{n}{k}$ possible successful combinations. That means, with 24 images and 8 needed for success, he has a $(24/2)/\binom{24}{8} = \frac{12}{735471} + \frac{1}{16777216} = 0.0016\%$ chance of success. These estimates indicate that visual preferences will have a very low false positive rate.

7.4.5.4 False negatives

False negatives represent the instances when a user does not successfully authenticate. Choosing the "success threshold" properly can lower the false negative rate. For instance, when users were required to be completely correct in their classifications of 24 images, only 38.3% succeeded, giving a false negative rate of over 60%. When the threshold was lowered from 12 to 10, however, there was a dramatic decrease in the false negative rate to only 6.2%, meaning that after 1 week, 93.8% of users still remembered the vast majority of their choices. The 1 week waiting period was needed so that the choices users made were no longer in their short-term memories. When the requirement was further lowered to 8 out of 12, the false negative rate is only 2.5%, but that is not significantly lower than the results from 10 out of 12, so in practice, choosing 10 as the threshold may be the better choice.

The false negative rates, in real-world deployment, may be lower. Our subjects, at the time of setup, were not briefed as to why they were choosing these images, and were not told that they would be contacted again to authenticate. Their only motivation to remember their image selection was an extra $0.15. Such an incentive is not enough for some MTurk users. One user, for instance, failed because his roommate took the test for him.

Real-world users, however, would know why they are choosing these images and would have greater motivation to choose according to their real biases if access to accounts depended on image selection and recall.

7.4.5.5 Multiple profiles

In Stage III of our experiment, users had, on average, 8.8 overlapping images for the first set and 4.3 for the second out of 24 images selected. This suggests that even if two different sites use the same set of images, it is highly unlikely that profiles created for those sites would strongly overlap. It is further advantageous that a user may create multiple profiles, in contrast to biometric systems in which only one profile would be possible.

7.4.5.6 Secure credential storage

On an actual VPA server, credentials are representations of the "Likes" and "Dislikes." For faster lookups, we can store, for each account, only the all-correct and almost-right choices. For example, if images are represented as 1, 2, 3, 4, 5, 6, 7, 8 for "Likes" and a, b, c, d, e, f, g, h for "Dislikes," and the accepted authentication answer is 1, 2, 3, 4, 5, 6, 7, 8 then we need only store 1, 2, 3, 4, 5, 6, 7, 8. In instances where the threshold is lower, for instance, 6 out of 8 correct, then we can store all $\binom{8}{6}$ nearly correct combinations with the images sorted in lexicographical order. Here, we would use two salts—one for the all correct entry, and another for all the almost-right entries.

Note that the policy of limiting the number of tries for authentication still applies here. An attacker will not be able to guess as many times as he wishes.

7.4.5.7 *Salts and hashes*

Salts are random values attached to passwords. They are used to make brute-forcing hashes much more difficult. Passwords are rarely (and should never) be stored in the clear in a database. Simply hashing them, however, is not sufficient because an attacker who manages to gain access to the file can simply guess all possible passwords until the hash matches and precompute these combinations in a lookup table. Salts make it much more computationally difficult by adding n extra bits. Using a salt also disguises the fact that two users may have the same password, or one user has the same password across multiple accounts.

For example, in the case of 7 out of 8 for images (a, b, c, d, e, f, g, h) we might store

Hash(salt1, "a,b,c,d,e,f,g,h"), salt1 – all correct
Hash(salt2, "a,b,c,d,e,f,g"), salt2 – almost right, last one wrong
Hash(salt2, "a,b,c,d,e,f,h"), salt2
Hash(salt2, "a,b,c,d,e,g,h"), salt2
...
Hash(salt2, "b,c,d,e,f,g,h"), salt2
etc.

When the user selects "1,2,3,4,5,6,7,e" during the authentication phase, we first compare the hash of this selection, using *salt*1, to the all correct hash. If that does not match, we remove one entry at a time and compare its hash, using *salt*2, to those of the "almost right" entries until we find a match or reach the end of our stored entries.

7.4.6 Conclusion

Password reset has come a long way from the early days of manual resets by a system administrator to the current standardized security questions. However, with the availability of public records and social networking profiles, answers to these questions are often easy to guess, putting valuable accounts at risk.

Using an authentication service that takes advantage of preferences creates secrets based on long lived personal knowledge and are not as easily guessed or forgotten. The corpus of images or media files can be constantly updated based on the observed entropies. By using Amazon Mechanical Turk to first test image entropy, strong and weak images were weeded out. At the same time, the testing of visual preferences on users demonstrated that visual preference-based authentication can be performed in a timely manner and that over time, users were able to recall their choices.

7.5 THE DEADLY SINS OF SECURITY USER INTERFACES

Nathan Good

Abstract. Consumer-facing security software solutions range from virus scanners and firewalls to access control mechanisms. Security software in some form is a "must have" for consumer PCs and a secure

Internet, but is universally unloved by consumers. In almost all cases, these solutions rely on user feedback and input in order to be configured properly, and must communicate the state of the system effectively to the end users in order for them to make the most appropriate choices. Four design practices have led to a large amount of consumer confusion, frustration, and potentially insecure systems. In this section, we argue that these have been ineffective, and may actually promote insecure systems and behaviors by end users. The four design practices are described below, as well as ways to address the most common issues.

7.5.1 Security Applications with Frustrating User Interfaces

Any PC user is all too familiar with the dreaded "popup" security message. It usually comes up during the worst possible time, interrupting an important email or breaking ones concentration when typing a document, asking for confirmation on some completely unrelated security task or upgrade confirmation. Angst with dreaded popups is so prevalent that it has made its way into popular culture. Apple made a commercial that mocked the verbose security warnings in Windows 7 as part of their popular "I'm a Mac" campaign. In it, an individual dressed as a secret agent repeatedly translates the "Mac's" questions into complicated security speech and asks the poor "PC" character to "cancel or allow" before proceeding. An exasperated "PC" character details this as the new enhanced "security" of Windows 7 and goes on to explain that he could completely disable the warnings, but then he wouldn't have any security at all. In a rather telling final moment, the agent says to the exasperated PC character, "You are coming to a sad realization, Cancel or Allow."

While the Apple commercials were exaggerated for comic effect, they do a good job of relating the frustration users have with common security user interfaces. An unfortunate part of computer security is that it is perceived as something that stops you from getting your work done and gets in the way of fun things you would like to do. The Apple example above clearly shows the tradeoff to users in stark terms: either enjoy your work or turn off all security. Cancel or Allow. Security practitioners and designers have known about this inherent tradeoff between security and usability for as long as there have been security needs. It is not a new concept, yet it is has been an incredibly difficult one for security practitioners to address.

Security practitioners are tasked with the difficult job of ensuring that an organization runs smoothly, and at the same time is protected from outside threats. Security practitioners in the consumer space are faced with an arguably more difficult task of ensuring security for end users for the multitude of idiosyncratic needs and choices that the Internet's users make on a daily basis. Users want to quickly visit sites, access and purchase content, sign up for an ever-growing number of web services and have all this done securely and without being bothered or inconvenienced. Bad actors in the system know this and actively work to exploit end user ignorance and ambivalence. Both security practitioners and end users would most likely agree that in an ideal world, security is something that the end user would never have to address. It would all work in the background in this highly idealized world. To many security practitioners, the ideal world would look much like a padded playpen with no sharp edges and a set of completely safe preapproved toys to play with. The oblivious consumer could wander around and explore the online world in complete ignorance while enjoying the security provided by the world's top professionals working tirelessly in the background for their protection.

Sadly, we are not in that world, and will not be for the near future. The world of tradeoffs will continue to exist for some time. In some cases, consumers demand choices that security practitioners balk at, and at the same time these consumers are unwilling to learn the security basics that are important to making informed security decisions. This disconnect leads to a feeling among security professionals as "users being the enemy" of security. At a high level these security professionals are correct. Configuration errors, non-adherence to procedure and human error account for the majority of security concerns. Matt Bishop, a security professor at UC Davis said that 90% of all security problems are configuration issues [117].

Further evidence coming from studies has shown that people using the internet are impulsive. Websites measure the time an end user spends on the page in tenths of seconds. Many users in the United States won't scroll results of search pages. If it is not in the top visible 10 results, it is very likely it will never be seen. Web designers have drastically retooled websites to cater to users' limited attention. Consumers want to do everything right away, and certainly don't want to go through the trouble of reading or clicking through extra screens. In the world outside of security, the consumers have already chosen what they are willing to interact with, and businesses have responded.

The Google home page is a famous example of the simplicity that users expect, with the one search box on its home page. Web 2.0 properties such as Groupon.com start off with one search box and one place to put an email address. Grooveshark.com and Pandora.com let users play music immediately once they get on the site, without having to log in, create an account or think much besides what kind of music they would like to hear. Websites realize that if they have content that people want, they need to get out of the way and give it to people as quickly as possible.

With such an amount of effort being applied to attract and maintain users' limited attention for things that they *actually* like to do, what chance does a security practitioner have for designing a good experience for a consumer that has no interest in performing that task at all?

The simple answer is to do nothing in terms of design and resign to the fact that consumers will always dislike any security-related interruptions in place. The next step is to apply the bare minimum amount of resources to design, such as putting all the info into a popup window, and hoping for the best.

In fact, the most common bare minimum implementation for notice and choice for security user interfaces have consisted of the "popup" message. Popups messages appear frequently in the security world, and are frequently misused by using them too frequently or filling them with irrelevant or confusing information.

The misuse of the popup has caused it to be the most despised method for informing end users, and arguably the most ignored. For the security community, this is very problematic. The need for security choices is only going to increase, as everyday consumers put more of their personal lives and valuable information online. The future will become more difficult for security practitioners, as consumers rely more heavily on mobile devices as more and more information gets stored in cloud services. To make matters worse, consumers also demand highly social applications and want to easily share information with web services, each other and the whole world instantaneously. What happens if the most commonly used method of communicating choices to end users may be ineffective?

Highly publicized events and proposed legislation have forced the security community to think of how security could better address the complicated needs of the consumer. Academics, policy makers, and industry are increasingly turning their attention to issues around consumer's online security. Anne Adams and Angela Sasse were one of the first to sound the call with their seminal paper that "users are not the enemy," and that such a mindset actually promotes insecurity [83] as did Ka-Ping Yee with his guidelines for Usable Security [500]. A dedicated group of multidisciplinary individuals in the academic[1], commercial and legal[2] worlds now recognize the importance of working together to address these questions, and are committed to finding solutions for this difficult task.

---

[1] http://cups.cs.cmu.edu/soups.
[2] http://docs.law.gwu.edu/facweb/dsolove/PLSC/.

7.5.2   The Four Sins of Security Application User Interfaces

Security practitioners are open to the concepts of making security easier for end users and are in many cases the biggest proponents of ease of use. However, in practice it has been very difficult to implement a good security experience. A seminal work on usable security by Alma Whitten, "Why Johnny can't encrypt," described the difficulty in getting users to reliably encrypt email [487]. To this day, email encryption is still not widely adopted. Security practitioners generally require very specific types of information from end users in order for the systems to run properly and ensure security as well as act in accordance to the end users' specifications. They need to inform end users to about the consequences of their choices and make sure they understand the implications to security, and the implied tradeoffs. Security practitioners also need the user to articulate what they want to protect, whether it is access to resources and sites or specific content. UI practices such as popups, checkboxes, and notification, and so on. have been used frequently to facilitate these kinds of choices. Unfortunately, misuse of these practices often ends up being ineffective and creating the opposite of the desired effect. These practices are as follows:

1. **Popup assault**   The practice of providing cryptic choices in uninformative popup windows, sometimes repeatedly, and almost always uninvited. Examples include pop up firewall warnings, "are you sure you want to continue" warnings, and the large space of difficult to understand frequent security related popups.

2. **Security by verbosity**   The practice of trying to get the user to understand the implications of their actions or provide background knowledge through the sheer weight of large quantities of words. Examples include lengthy descriptions of certificate errors.

3. **Walls of checkboxes**   The practice of giving the user a wall of choices in checkbox form, with the hope that the permutations of the choices they end up making will be correct and secure. Examples include access control user interfaces and file sharing user interfaces.

4. **All or nothing switches**   The practice of providing a single button, choice or switch that serves as an on/off switch between total security and the complete lack thereof. Examples include interfaces such as firewall software that provide only a choice of security or insecurity.

We will now describe some of the biggest challenges with these security UI practices, and propose ways to think about designing new solutions to make consumers a part of the solution to better security practices.

7.5.3   Consumer Choice: A Security Bugbear

Why can't we get rid of the need for consumer feedback?   For the antispyware coalition formed by the Center of Democracy and Technology,[3] one of the most challenging questions for the industry leaders involved was answering the question, "what is spyware?"[4] It was a very difficult question, as labeling a program as "spyware" and thereby ordering the antispyware software to remove it could invite an unwanted lawsuit. Even using the word spyware was too loaded, and some companies coined the term "PUPs" short for "Potentially Unwanted Programs" or the term "PUA" short for "Potentially Unwanted Applications." This additional classification was needed to address programs

---

[3]http://www.antispywarecoalition.org/about/.

[4]A Bugbear is defined as an object or source of dread, a continuing source of irritation.

that may report usage information and/or provide popup ads in exchange for some free software. Despite PUAs not directly being a security issue, many users associated popups and slower machines with security problems, so the reputations of the security programs were at stake. Complaints from users about unwanted advertising popups abounded, and suddenly PUPs put the security world in the awkward position of deciding for a consumer whether the security program felt it was a fair trade that the consumer should be allowed to have a kitten themed screensaver in exchange for popup advertisements.

PUPs or PUAs are examples of the types of choices that a security company can't make by itself. Exact classifications for PUAs vary per company, but one category of PUAs consists of adware, applications that gather information about websites visited or provide popup ads, and so on. If a consumer decides that he is ok with popups, then he will download the kitten-themed screensaver. To make matters worse, if a consumer is prevented by the antispyware software from getting his kitten-themed screen savers, he may turn off his security temporarily just to get it. In the worst case and perhaps after repeated warnings, the consumer may choose to uninstall or disable the antivirus/antispyware program altogether or choose a competitor's product that is less intrusive.

The practice that many companies use to address PUAs is a popup. This notice, or series of notices, is intended to (1) alert the user and (2) give the user a choice to install it or not. In practice misuses, such as confusing terminology or lack of transparency in these notices, have created consumer confusion. Over time, overuse, and confusing security jargon have caused these warnings to be widely ignored by consumers. In many cases, users are so adept at "swatting away" popup notices that they hardly notice they are there [220]. Designers implicitly acknowledge this fact by including a "do not show this window again" checkbox for users to not see these messages. At this point, the program is back to making choices on the consumers behalf, continuing the cycle of disconnect and frustration. For two illustrations, see Figures 7.25 and 7.26.

PUAs and popup warnings are one example demonstrating how important security choices are and will continue to be. They are also an example of how frustrating this choice is for consumers and security professionals.

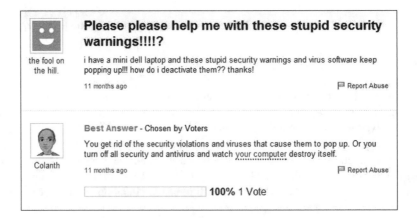

Figure 7.25   One of many examples of consumer frustration at frequent popup security warnings. Notice how the Best Answer chosen by other users in the forum is the tongue-in-cheek suggestion of removing all security.

Help with an annoying security warning that keeps popping up...?

Eddie P

It reads:

The current Web page is trying to open a site in your Trusted sites list. Do you want to allow this?

current site: http://yieldmanager.com
trusted site: res://ieframe.dll

It pops up rather frequently--it's annoying. Also, my internet explorer hasn't been working well recently. It frequently gets stuck on "Website found. Waiting for reply," and then it doesn't proceed.

Figure 7.26 An example of consumer frustration for cryptic and confusing text for security warnings that "block" their ability to browse the web. This user doesn't see the connection between his actions and the systems attempts to get him to understand the implications of having a third party open up a site in his trusted lists. Also note how the user correlates this attempt at protecting him with bad performance on his machine.

7.5.3.1 Popup assault—choice and informed consent for security actions

As described previously, misuse of popups is a common practice for security software. Examples of these types of misuse have been mentioned in passing above, but are described in detail below in the following scenario. The scenario below describes an example of two popup notices that require affirmative user action but are repetitive and confusing to end users.

> **The scenario** A user sees a free text editor that they would like to get on the web. The website says "100% Spyware Free." The user makes the choice to download it. Let the games begin!
>
> Unfortunately, though, this information isn't communicated to the user. The users have to make their decision based off of very technical jargon and obscure file locations. Undoubtedly, in the security analysis of SweetIM.B a decision to classify it as a PUA was made by the anti-virus program because it matched attributes or behaviors that made it potentially unwanted. Giving the user this information would be a great help to the user for making a decision that works for them.

There are several problems with the approaches shown in Figures 7.27 and 7.28 that demonstrate misuses of popup security warnings that are described in detail below:

1. **Crying wolf** Many security warnings appear so frequently that consumers become habituated to ignoring them. This warning uses a similar template and layout to a more serious virus warning. If the consumer gets in the habit of ignoring these warnings as a result of being frequently confronted with information he deems incomprehensible or irrelevant, then he may ignore a more serious warning down the line. Repeatedly ignoring false warnings causes users to let down their guard, and be more susceptible to real attacks.

2. **Unnecessary multiple warnings** The second popup warning offers very little benefit compared to the first. It could easily be combined into one warning. Security related interruptions should be respectful of users' time, and care should be taken in deciding how many screens are actually needed to answer the question.

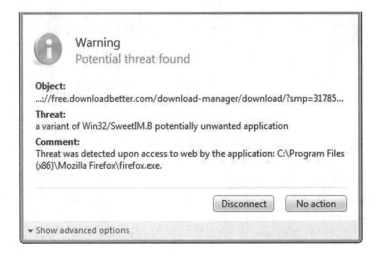

Figure 7.27 First popop. The security program does the right thing and detects that the application may indeed contain adware. In this example, a very oddly named program "SweetIM.B" is shown to be the threat. "SweetIM.B" it turns out is emoticons for and IM messenger and a toolbar. This information is potentially very valuable to the user. There is a good chance that seeing "100% Spyware Free" the consumer didn't know that the text editor they were downloading had ads or a toolbar in it.

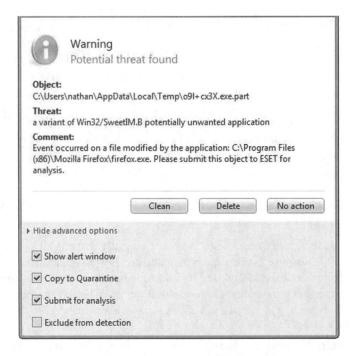

Figure 7.28 Second popup. Clicking "disconnect" brings up a second popup warning asking users what they want to do. It almost seems unnecessary additional step; at the previous popup, a user will decide if they want to install the program or not. There doesn't seem to be a distinction between "clean" or "delete," and the text description hasn't changed from the previous screen Figure 7.27.

3. **Lack of context**   The text lacks context. What is the connection to "SweetIM.B" and the text editor the user is downloading? What does all the text dedicated to long file and directory paths mean? How come these file-locations are incomplete or cutoff, and finally why does it say there is a something modified with Firefox, the web browser being used? End users need to be sure they know what the warning is reacting to so that they are certain they are making the right choices.

4. **Confusing terminology and jargon**   In Figures 7.27 and 7.28, the headings Object, Threat, and Comment are technical terms. The terminology does little to help the consumer answer questions such as "What will the program do?" and "Why should I care?" The buttons to continue are difficult to understand as well. "No action" sounds scary and "Disconnect" sounds worse. This is technical jargon talking.

5. **Lack of information for decision making**   The most serious issues shown in Figures 7.27 and 7.28 are that the users have very little information to help them make a decision. What is SweetIM.B? What does it do? Who makes it? Why should the user be worried? Advanced options are even less helpful to the end user, and include the dreaded "all or nothing" button to disable popups. By providing relevant information in context the program can assist the user to make the decision that is right for him.

If misuse of popups is so bad, then why are there still so many?   Is this just splitting hairs? Despite the fact that in practice some popups have been confusing, do they actually work in the security professionals favor if they scare users off from potentially insecure behavior? One could argue that the PUA scenario is perfectly designed for the ideal outcome: an intimidating technical form that scares away users from unwanted actions. Mission accomplished!

As attractive and clever as this argument sounds, there are several holes in it. The first is that confusion is rarely a good way to motivate a user to provide the right answers. The hope that users will repeatedly perform the action that is best for them, despite the technical jargon they don't understand is misguided and may not be the case. Will a confused user click on the desired button, or perform the desired action? A confused user isn't guaranteed to do the right thing.

Another issue is that the form may not actually be as intimidating as one thinks and in reality perceived much more as a nuisance. Through experience, users may not perceive any issue with previously downloaded programs and continue to install applications without really knowing the effects to their computers. Frequent confusing popups will be viewed as a nuisance, and eventually their computer may be full of adware. At that point, the users may blame their security software.

Finally a confused user may have unintended consequences. Even if users took the course of action of refusing all applications they had ever downloaded that were PUAs, what if they misunderstand what is happening, encounter an application they do want and completely disable security to get it? In this case, a simple PUA application can open up the avenue to more dangerous attacks.

The case of this backfiring is evident in firewall software. Many firewalls repeatedly provide popups asking users to allow or deny the use of the Internet. In many cases these repeated popups become so frequent and seemingly provide so little useful information to the end users disabled them altogether.

How to make it better   Just as the security designer needed information to make a choice about how best to defend the user, end users needs information and transparency for their choice as well. The problem is that end users are rarely security people, and the information they need has to be highly targeted to their context, perceptions and overall goals. In Figures 7.27 and 7.28 above, the end user purchased antiadware and firewall software to prevent both unwanted adware from being installed and unwanted software from accessing the Internet. The security application can fulfill this promise if the end user understands what the options are and why they are important. With this in place, an end user can tell the software when to work. The intention of the popups in the security world is to provide timely contextual information about the state of the program and a means of providing control over the programs' choices. The concept is based on sound principals, called "feedback and control" in the Human Computer Interaction literature. Bellotti and Sellen [111] suggested this notion of "feedback and control" as essential for security and privacy systems to maintain a level of transparency to users. Popups proliferate because they have been seen as a good, cheap and easy way to implement feedback and control.

The difficulty with providing popups for security choices, though, is that security is almost always a secondary task, and it is difficult to break a user's from their primary task once the user is engaged. It should only be done when something, really, really important needs to be told. Otherwise, for all the reasons discussed above, people will ignore the message, act on it incorrectly and the message will become meaningless. To further complicate matters, the tradeoffs in security that are obvious to the security practitioner are rarely made apparent to the end user, and the consequences of any security choices made at the moment when the popup message appears are difficult to communicate later. To avoid misusing popups and assaulting the user with them, here are three simple strategies to follow:

Provide information that helps the user's decision making process   In the PUA example shown in Figures 7.27 and 7.28 previously, what information is most relevant to consumers in order for them to make a decision of whether they want to install the text editor they downloaded or not? Table 7.4 shows information that the security program already knows and could provide the user to help make their decision easier.

Although the information in Table 7.4 may seem limited in scope and detail, it is immensely valuable to the consumer making a decision of whether to install the program or not. The program shouldn't keep this information to itself; it should share it with the end user.

When a security system requires a choice from a consumer, it helps consumers to have an understanding of the tradeoffs of their decision. While in all cases it may not be possible to articulate all the nuances of this tradeoff, effort should be made to decide what information the system has that can be given to the user to enhance their ability to make the most informed decisions.

Look for alternatives to just using popups   McAfee Site Advisor (see Figure 7.29) is a good example of an application that provides information to consumers before the decision to download has been made. What is very interesting about this approach is that it gives users a means of understanding tradeoffs while they are still cognitively in the state of deciding which program to download. The primary task the user is engaged in right now is selection and search, and site advisor provides information that is security related but directly relevant to the users primary task. The benefit of

Table 7.4   Information that the Security Program Knows for Figures 7.27 and 7.28

1. What is the user downloading?	Ans. A program from the website
2. Why did the security program flag it?	Ans. It has a toolbar and some popup ads
3. What choices does the user have?	
Install the program?	Don't install the program?
They will get a toolbar and may get some popup ads	They won't get the program from the website

This table describes the information the program knows that could be of benefit to the end user.

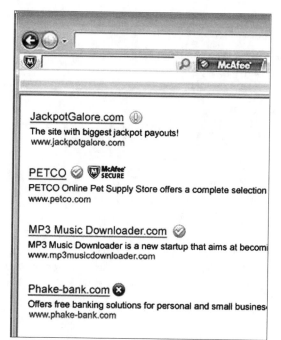

Figure 7.29 McAfee Site Advisor provides feedback about websites that potentially host spyware, viruses and adware and embeds this information directly in the users search results. This immediate feedback during the users' initial decision-making process that helps users make good choices before they start down the path of downloading and installing an application.

this approach is that the security program has a greater chance of informing the user when they are already spending time looking at the search results page trying to decide which links to click on.

Limit popup use Too much of a good thing is never good for anyone. Popups are the same. Limiting their use increases their value and lessens the impact of user fatigue. When designing popup notices, security practitioners should be aware of the limited user attention they have to work with. Being respectful of users' attention means being attentive to when is the most important times to get users' attention, as well as what information to ask.

7.5.4 Security by Verbosity

We have determined how popups for security applications can be better designed, and we have also discussed how the content of these popup notices can sometimes be very verbose and confusing to users. This next section focuses on attempts to push through security understanding by being overly verbose. Security can be complicated, and very nuanced. Sometimes security practitioners feel the need to communicate this through long prose in a popup window. Don't. There is very little chance users will read it (see Figures 7.30 and 7.31). Even if they do there is very little chance they will understand it and act on it in a way that is helpful to the system or the end users' goals. As for popups above, avoid using these. If they need to be used, layer text and put only the most important stuff up front, and structure choices in a meaningful way.

7.5.4.1 How to make it better

The key to making verbose warnings better is figuring out ways to remove the sources of verbosity. There are many ideas that HCI practitioners, marketers, advertisers as well as journalists have used to take apart

Security Warning

Certificate Warnings

An untrusted SSL certificate is installed on "strsmaltavum.strs.us" and secure communication cannot be guaranteed. Depending on your security policy, this issue might not represent a security concern. You may need to install a trusted SSL certificate on your server to prevent this warning from appearing.

Click Ignore to continue using the current SSL certificate.

| View Certificate | Ignore | Cancel |

☐ Install this certificate and do not display any security warnings for "strsmaltavum.strs.us".

Figure 7.30 A verbose description of a security warning that a system sends to the end user. Notice how quickly it can put a person to sleep. When a user looks at this warning, what they actually end up seeing is the warning in Figure 7.31.

paragraphs of text and focus on the main concepts. If the concept requires a paragraph or two to explain, then something has gone wrong. Rethink the information that is being described in paragraph form and tease out the main points and goals for the user interaction. If text is unavoidable, use less text and put the important items up front. Leverage the "inverted pyramid" concept created by journalists to describe what matters most.

7.5.5 Walls of Checkboxes

In many security applications, it is important for a user to indicate a set of choices. This is generally accomplished by the use of the checkbox. For example, in a file sharing application, a checkbox may be used to indicate directories to share, or indicating preference for access controls. It is never a pleasant moment for either the consumer or the security designer when a consumer is confronted with a wall of checkboxes. The security application anxiously hopes that whatever permutation arises from the multitude of possibilities is remotely in line with what the user expects and doesn't contradict itself in any way. The implications of the many choices can quickly get lost on the user, and subsequently cause the user to end up with a security configuration that is incomprehensible, leading in turn to unpredictable actions and unexpected results.

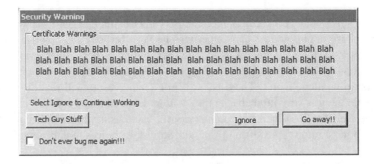

Security Warning

Certificate Warnings

Blah Blah Blah Blah Blah Blah Blah Blah Blah Blah Blah Blah Blah Blah Blah Blah Blah Blah Blah Blah Blah Blah Blah Blah Blah Blah Blah Blah Blah Blah Blah Blah Blah Blah Blah Blah Blah Blah Blah Blah Blah Blah Blah Blah Blah Blah Blah Blah

Select Ignore to Continue Working

| Tech Guy Stuff | Ignore | Go away!! |

☐ Don't ever bug me again!!!

Figure 7.31 Users interpretation of the warning above in Figure 7.30. Whatever meaning the text was hoping to provide was lost in its sheer volume and complexity. Unfortunately, the end user can't related to the text, and end up most likely canceling the form just to get their work done.

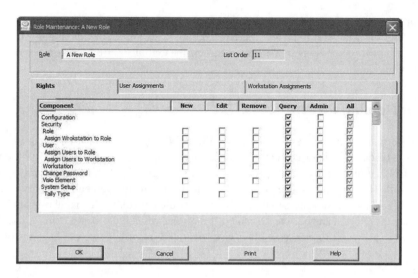

Figure 7.32   Interface for configuring roles provided for staff of Sequoia Voting Systems [129]. Using this interface, the staff creates a new role and assigns permissions and access controls. The large, intimidating wall of checkboxes continues down several screens and across three tabs. Given the scale of these settings, there are many opportunities for the user to choose incorrectly.

There are many examples of an exceeding plethora of choices resulting in confusion, frustration, and possibly, an insecure system. In the California Secretary of State Top-To-Bottom Review of California Voting Systems,[5] it was discovered that electoral staff were provided with over 615 checkboxes to configure a new user role for the system (see example in Figure 7.32). Similarly, a New York Times diagram of Facebook privacy settings[6] demonstrated that users had to configure over 50 settings consisting of 170 options.

7.5.5.1 *How to make it better*

The key to preventing walls of checkboxes is to not create them to begin with. When choices have expanded to a point where it is not humanly possible to keep track of them all, it is important to rethink the initial goals and reduce the space of options available to the user.

Ask questions such as "How important is it that users have access to that choice?" or "How likely is it that users will have to make that choice?" or "How can choices be grouped together or separated out?" Facebook improved its privacy selections by reducing the number of controls and reworking how it thought of privacy settings. In the case of the example shown in Figure 7.32, many of the options were meaningless, and the scope of them could have been greatly reduced in order to drastically reduce the selections that users would have to make.

Additionally, if choices are dependent on one other, complicated choice spaces can be more appropriately managed by grouping them according to their dependencies and similar items to benefit from "chunking"

---

[5]http://www.sos.ca.gov/voting-systems/oversight/ttbr/sequoia-doc-final.pdf.

[6]Facebook Privacy: A Bewildering Tangle of Options, The New York Times, March 12, 2010 http://www.nytimes.com/interactive/2010/05/12/business/facebook-privacy.html.

in memory. Other strategies involve creating a path of choices and showing only showing the most relevant choices depending on what path is taken. There are plenty of examples of this in daily life. If a customer chooses coffee, the next choice is sugar or cream. Breaking these choices up can make for easier understanding and simpler navigation.

7.5.6   All or Nothing Switch

We described user interfaces and elements of the user interface that contribute to user confusion for security user interfaces. The last user interface sin we will discuss is having the user make a stark choice between complete security and no security with no level in-between. Figure 7.33 shows an example of this with the Windows Firewall. The user can choose to have all security with the firewall enabled, or no security with the firewall turned off. There doesn't seem to be an obvious middle path that will enable users to have benefits of the firewall when they need it and be able to manage it for times when they do not. In many cases, this tradeoff almost comes as a last resort to please an otherwise frustrated user by giving the user a way to completely

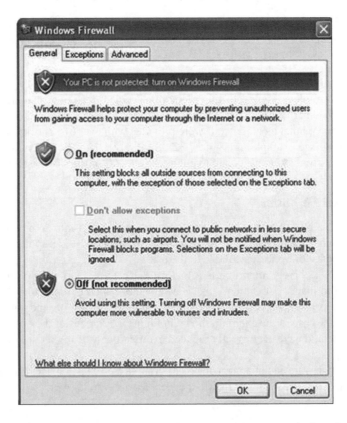

Figure 7.33   This Windows Firewall Warning consists of only two options. One is to turn on the firewall with all of its associated settings and limitations, or the other is to turn off the firewall and all protection. The user has no choice but to accept all the restrictions of the firewall including how it affects the users Internet experience, or choose not to have any security at all.

turn off the software. This tradeoff seems as a way of admitting that the communication between the user and the security software has failed, and the security software has given up trying to communicate anymore.

If the consumer has purchased the security software to protect them and the software does this well, only in the most extreme cases will the consumer need it to be completely turned off. Proper design is essential to ensure that this promise is kept. In many cases, the problem is that the culmination of repeated design errors such as those described previously (assaulting the user with popups, providing them inadequate control through walls of checkboxes and relying on verbose jargon), frequently cause the end user to demand a way to stop it all

Firewall software provides an example of this phenomenon. Firewalls are designed to protect users from malicious applications and attacks across the user's network connection. They work by stopping or preventing Internet connections for certain applications and ports that they deem as threats or which a user indicates are threats. Since some undesirable applications use the same ports and protocols as legitimate applications, a firewall needs to ask the user on occasion if the user would like to block or restrict Internet access for applications that the user has on their desktop. Creating good notifications for Firewalls are tricky because of the sheer number of times that applications and users access the Internet. A user can easily be overwhelmed by popup warnings.

For some firewall products, users reach their "popup limit" fairly quickly; users quickly become saturated with the number of popups that occur for the vast number of applications that connect to the internet. This is most apparent when a user first installs a firewall. It immediately pops up warnings for even the most common programs, such as Firefox, Internet Explorer, Microsoft Word, and so on. These constant warnings serve as a persistent interruption for the user. In the course of just doing the user performing their normal routines, the warnings become unbearable. In the case where a user can't manage the popups in a simple way, the user turns the firewall off entirely.

7.5.6.1 How to make it better

Symantec's Firewall is an example of a firewall product that gives users an interim choice between complete protection and not protection (see Figure 7.34). When users encounters a situation where they need to disable the firewall to perform some task, they are given a range of time durations they would like to turn it off for as opposed to turning it off entirely. Additionally, this approach does not require that a user needs to remember to go back and turn the firewall back on again. It automatically comes back online after a given amount of time. If the user needs more time, they can ask for it again, and with a longer duration if need be.

We should note that although this is not an ideal solution, as it leaves the end user without any firewall protection for a period of time during which the system could be compromised. However, it does serve as

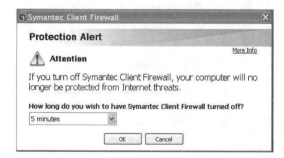

Figure 7.34 Symantec firewall that gives the user a choice to temporarily disable a firewall as opposed to disabling it entirely. Within the allocated time frame the firewall will come back without the users need to remember to turn it on again. While not a perfect solution (the user is without protection for an amount of time), it does serve as an example of ways that interim solutions to all or nothing choices can be explored.

an example of ways that interim solutions to all or nothing choices can be explored. The Symantec example illustrates one way that this problem can be addressed by given consumers relevant and helpful choices for "in-between" states that gives users flexibility while keeping the security software still alive and able to protect them. Giving users an option in addition to all security and no security is desirable. Ideally in future iterations, this current method could be improved on by preserving important security mechanisms.

Another approach of addressing issues of all-or-nothing security choices is to address some of the root causes that lead to an all-or-nothing decision to begin with. As discussed previously, all-or-nothing decisions are often the by-product of many poor design decisions that cause the user to want to turn off the security software. Addressing the poor designs that cause the user to want to turn the software off should help. A slightly more radical approach would be to challenge the systems underlying assumptions about when it needs user feedback, and attempt to redesign the interaction around ways that are more in-line with the way users work. For example, instead of assuming that a user needs an immediate warning regarding an application at that particular moment (if the system determines it is unlikely to be malicious), it could pool warnings and minor messages into a browsing interface for moments when a consumer was more likely to see them? It is still an open question of whether these kinds of interactions would be more helpful or not, but it is clear that with the stakes as high as they are for security, it is important to find a way for security to be much more usable.

7.5.7 Conclusion

They say the road to hell is paved with good intentions. The origins of the four sins of security user interfaces definitely speak to this point. While in many cases the desire to create user involvement in important security decisions is well intended, in practice, misuse of user interface practices has resulted in some security applications and interfaces actually making consumers less secure. With the challenges of mobile computing platforms, smaller screen real estate, cloud services, and even more active and visual content competing for a user's attention, good user interfaces and practices for usable security applications are incredibly important.

7.6 SPOOFKILLER—LET'S KISS SPOOFING GOODBYE!

Markus Jakobsson and William Leddy

Abstract. This section introduces the "SpoofKiller" approach to bypass a variety of attacks including the man-in-the-screen attack described earlier (see Section 3.3.5). The approach is not only a defense against man-in-the-screen, but should also thwart all webpage and application spoofing.

How can you kill spoofing? Assume that a user is tricked by the spoofing. If the actions he performs are the very same actions as would cause him to log in to a good website or app—if these actions somehow abort the bad website or app—then we would be done, right? (That probably made no sense to you, so please read it again.) Here is what it means: if the user's actions to log in are interpreted as "go ahead, log in" for a good site, but they mean "abort" for a bad site, then there is no point to spoof. If the would-be victim falls for the spoof, and tries to log in he will abort the site or app. That may sound like a pipe dream, but it can be done. We will explain how.

The key to the solution is to change how interrupts are interpreted by the machine, and then to train users to cause an interrupt as the first thing they do when they want to log in somewhere. Then, the machine can determine the context of the interrupt. Was it a certified site (i.e., a good site)? Then go ahead, continue with the logging in. Was it something else? Well ... then abort!

7.6.1 A Key to the Solution: Interrupts

The variety of malware and spoof attacks makes it possible for scammers to capture user information at many points between the user's keyboard and an Internet server. The users need a secure channel from end to end. With the SpoofKiller approach, the user triggers a secure interface that either confirms or terminates the interaction. Users initiate the secured interface with a hardware interrupt. For example, by pressing CTL-ALT-DEL on a PC or the Home or Power button on a mobile device, the user can trigger a low-level interrupt handler. This low-level handler can provide a better secured interface to allow users login or to confirm actions. The handler can confirm the authenticity of the site requesting user information and can bypass application level malware that might be on the user's system.

You are thinking: Wait a minute? Is this not the same as pressing CTRL-ALT-DEL on my PC to log in? Not quite. You do that, and then you see the login screen. What would happen if you were just shown the login screen? That's right you would probably type your user name and password that is what a phisher wants you to do. But that is not what we do. Think about it like this: When the user sees the login screen, then he has to press CTRL-ALT-DEL. And then he can enter his user name and password! Why does it matter? It matters a lot! This way, what would you do if you are shown the login interface? That's it: Press CTRL-ALT-DEL. That is the key to the solution: Train the user to cause an interrupt every time he wishes to log in. Then decide what to do when the interrupt is detected by the machine. This transfers the problem of distinguishing good from bad from the human to the machine. Machines are good at things like whitelists, certificates, and such things. Humans ... not so good.

And it works the same way on a handset, only that you do not press CTRL-ALT-DEL there, but the Home button, or the power button.

7.6.2 Why can the User Log in to Good Sites, but not Bad Ones?

While the user's behavior is easy to blame, it is unlikely to change until they are given a simple, clear, and consistent approach that lets them handle the variety of problems. The solution should be intuitive and must

- be fast and easy to use
- immediately terminate activity and connection to bad sites

The solution is to provide a secure interface that users can easily initiate when they need to enter personal information like passwords, account information, or credit card information. The users can trigger the secure interface through a hardware interrupt that cannot be caught or faked by application level software. The interrupt handler can check the validity of the website or app, through a certificate or whitelist, before the user enters his information. If the requesting webpage, application or mobile app is legitimate, then the user will be shown the screen to allow the user to enter their information. If it is a fraud attempt it should be terminated immediately. For example, if the user has a mobile phone they should initiate the secure interface by pressing the Home button or the power button if there is no Home button on the device. If the website is

Figure 7.35 The user is about to log in. The keyboard is not active until the user has pressed the Home button (or other similar hardware button). The button triggers a low-level interrupt. The interrupt handler enables the keyboard only if the site, application—or generally, the context—is whitelisted. See Figure 7.36 for what happens when a user accesses bad websites.

legitimate the user will simply transition to the page or app window to enter their credentials to authenticate as shown below in Figure 7.35. The identity of the requesting website should be shown near the data entry point so that the user knows who will be receiving his data.

But *if the website's identity cannot be confirmed by the Home interrupt handler, the app will be terminated* and the user will be returned to the home screen, as shown below in Figure 7.36. The user will never have the chance to give his information to the bogus website.

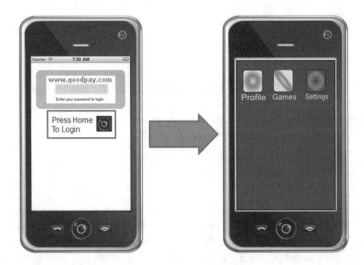

Figure 7.36 The user knows that she needs to press the Home or power button before she can enter her password. The button triggers a low-level interrupt. The interrupt handler determines that the requester is not valid (or does not conform to the logo or domain in the display) and terminates the application or webpage. This is what the user will see—the app gets terminated. See Figure 7.35 for valid website access.

The same interrupt action that allows a user to log in to a good website will terminate the activity on a bad website. This may initially seem like a contradiction, but the interrupt action just passes control to a more trusted software component that can determine if the action is safe.

If the user needs to terminate a good app or good website connection, the user can press the interrupt button twice or hold it longer. Alternatively, the interrupt handler could recognize when input is being requested and only present the secured interface when needed.

In the past, a fraudster could easily present a secure-looking interface for the user's information, but the user had no means to verify the authenticity or security of the interface. The user was left wondering whether the interface was secure and had to hope for the best. In the future, the user should be able to trigger the secured input interface through a low-level interrupt like the Home button on a mobile device or CTRL-ALT-DEL on a PC. If the user is in doubt about the security of an input interface, he can just push the Home button again.

The man-in-the-screen attack and various other attack attempts would be aborted by pushing the Home button when the user is asked for information. The handler would recognize that it was not a legitimate website. The SpoofKiller approach shifts safety decisions from the user to the handler.

The general adoption of this proposed approach across many applications and websites would condition users to push the Home button before entering personal information. Users should become suspicious of sites or applications that don't ask the user to press the Home button.

> The underlying principle of SpoofKiller is hard to understand at first. The idea is to train people to build a knee-jerk reaction that is triggered by login opportunities. Think of Pavlov's dog: The dog "learnt" to salivate when hearing a bell, after having been fed repeatedly after hearing a bell. We want to create the same reaction, but with Internet users replacing the dog, and with the generation of interrupts taking the role of the salivation.

But we must do this with abuse in mind. This is harder than you may expect. Assume that there were two stages:

1. The user sees a stimulus that he has been conditioned to associating with pressing the Home button. And then:
2. The users gets to the login screen, where the user enters his password.

That would *not* work. The user becomes conditioned to pressing home when he sees the screen of the first step above. But the second step does not cause it. The attacker could then send the user directly to the second step, and hope that the user would not press home, but simply enter his password. That would not be good.

Instead, assume we have this very similar flow:

1. The user sees a stimulus that he has been conditioned to associating with pressing the Home button. This screen looks *just* like the login screen.
2. The users gets to the login screen, where the user enters his password.

Now, the user becomes conditioned to press the Home button when he sees the login screen. An attacker cannot shortcut the process and hope to avoid that the intended victim does not cause an interrupt.

Figure 7.37 Legitimate legacy websites should warn users that they do not yet support the new approach. Users will need to use their judgment about trusting the website with their information. This is equivalent to the security that users have today. Over time websites that do not support SpoofKiller will look increasingly suspicious to users, so attackers will not want to display the "Don't Press" message.

7.6.3 What About Sites that are Good ... but not Certified Good?

During the transition to the new approach, legacy websites may need to explicitly tell users "Do Not press Home to login or you will abort" as shown in Figure 7.37. Users will then need to use their best judgment for these logins based on their expectations for each site during the transition to the new approach.

The exact trigger for the secured interface depends on the user's device:

- **iPhone** The "Home" button on iOS devices normally terminates the current App and returns the user to the main screen. Future versions of the iPhone may not have a Home button, but instead may use the Power button for the same functions.

- **Android** Android allows applications to capture the Home button and to replace the home page, but a handler could be inserted at the start of the event handling chain. By making the security event handler first in the chain, it would ensure that the correct behavior could not be masked.

This approach addresses spoofing of webpages and apps on both handhelds and traditional computers. The primary operating system used by end users employ low-level interrupts triggered by the user from their keyboard.

- **Windows PC** CTRL-ALT-DEL generates a hardware interrupt that normally displays the dialog to allow a user to "Lock Computer," "Log Off," "Shut down."

- **Mac** Command + Option + Escape brings up the Force Quit application to terminate applications.

To minimize the potential for key logging malware to intercept user information, this functionality should be added to the operating system for the device. Ideally, this should be in a hardware-based interrupt that is only catchable by the OS. The interrupt handler should interact directly with the keyboard rather than through an application stack that could allow keys to be intercepted.

7.6.4   SpoofKiller: Under the Hood

Let's talk about how to actually construct this!

7.6.4.1   *Component interaction*

Figure 7.38 shows the components of the entire system. A good user wants to access a good website but there are attack points throughout the system. Attackers can create phishing sites or man-in-the-middle (MITM) websites. They can also install components on the user system as applications or browser extensions. These attacks are difficult for the website and the user to detect.

When a user connects to a good website, the browser plugin will let the website know that the user's system can support a secure login through the browser string. When the user accesses the login page or other action requiring authentication, the page will tell the user to initiate the login with the interrupt action (like Home or CTRL-ALT-DEL).

The interrupt handler can confirm the identity of the requesting party by checking its certificate and matching the identity to the requesting URL. This confirmation could be managed through the exchange of certificates, through a whitelist of acceptable URLs or a combination of pluggable approaches.

The identity of the requestor is displayed in the secure screen area and the user is asked to provide account ID/password or other secure information. The interrupt handler could take direct control of the keyboard interaction so that application level malware cannot capture the keystrokes. By directly interacting with the keyboard, the application level malware is bypassed since keystroke logging malware inserts itself at the application level or in a browser plugin.

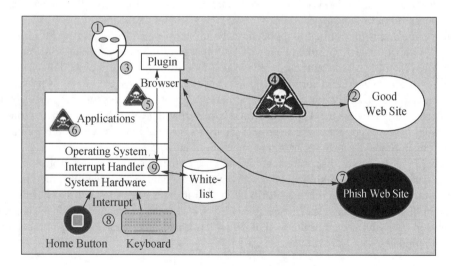

Figure 7.38   A user (1) accesses a good website (2) through his browser (3), but a malicious web server (4) could be in between just relaying requests. Alternatively there could be malware in the user's browser (5) or as an application (6) on the user's system that can capture user information. The user may also be tricked into accessing a phishing website (7). The user (1) can confirm that the request for the password is from a legitimate website by pressing the Home button or CTRL-ALT-DEL (9) that triggers a low-level interrupt. The interrupt handler (9) will confirm that the requesting site is legitimate or will terminate the connection to the site.

The interrupt handler sends user account information to the server through an SSL secured connection. The secure display area is closed and the user is returned to normal web browser interaction.

7.6.4.2 Malicious attempt interaction

If a phishing website requests the user to log in *without* first requesting the interrupt action, or tells the user not to trigger the interrupt action (see Figure 7.37), the user should be immediately suspicious. Users that have been conditioned to the new approach will press "Home" as a reflex just like they hit Enter to "Automatically" submit. These users will recognize the absence and be very cautious if they choose to proceed. User conditioning will require a combination of user education, clear identification of the secured interaction, and ubiquitous adoption of the approach across system vendors. The SSL lock for HTTPS access is a good example of security that has been broadly adopted by browser makers, is clearly marked and has some user awareness. Unfortunately, the awareness is not broad enough and users forget to look for it, but it is a start.

If a phishing website requests the user to initiate the interrupt action, the browser plugin and interrupt handler will detect a bad certificate. Any mismatch or suspicious URL can trigger a warning or more simply terminate the interaction. The user will be prevented from revealing their information to suspicious sites.

7.6.4.3 Addressing mobile malware apps

The rapid rise of mobile phone applications and the ability to make easy payments within the applications is a great convenience to users. The range of services and payment options should explode over the next few years but security concerns are likely to be ignored in favor of ease of use. This will make Mobile devices a new favorite target for attackers.

A primary concern is the vetting of applications before they are added to an App Store. Apps that are available through legitimate App Stores have typically had only minimal checking to determine that the application does not crash, all the buttons are connected, meets the look-and-feel guidelines of the OS, and meets the terms of use (avoids child pornography, does not break local laws, etc.) for the App Store. The App vetting does not extend to security of personal information of users, but users will have an expectation that they are protected since they got the App from a vendor they trust. The users have an expectation of security, but it is arguably not the App Store's job to protect the user's information once the App is purchased. There are no good tools to statically analyze the *future* behavior of an App.

Malware Apps can harvest user information and create invisible transactions from the user's phone once the user has connected their mobile phone to a payment account. Since the online merchants will want single-click experiences to get higher transaction completion rates, the Apps will likely link the phone's hardware ID to their online accounts. This makes it easy for malware to create additional transactions.

Here are some possible scenarios that will be difficult to detect among the growing number applications and application updates:

- The user makes a purchase through a legitimate looking App by selecting their favorite payment option and entering his information. The transaction completes successfully and the user gets what he expected. But, the App also records the user's information and sends it to an internet service that is collecting credentials. Later the user ends up with purchases he didn't expect. This attack does not require a corrupt company, just a corrupt underpaid programmer and 50 lines of code.

- A free fun game App is thoroughly vetted by the App Store team before it is offered to the public. The App contained no visible malicious code when first offered on the App Store, but once the App is installed and widely distributed, the fraudster modifies a small bit of content on a web server that the App regularly checks. This could be a single flag or something more complicated like a command buried in an image that the App downloads on start up. This flag or command triggers the hidden bad behavior that was previously unreachable and undetectable in the App. The fraudster can throttle the malicious behavior through the web server command so that it remains below a detection threshold for a very long time.

- In a free game App, the user is offered a *large pizza with one topping* for only $1 at any nearby location because they hit a new personal high score, but only if they buy immediately through the app. The user is given a choice of their favorite electronic payment options. The user quickly fills in their information and hits PAY. A few seconds later the App reports an error and says the transaction is cancelled. Instead of ordering a pizza, the app forward the information to a web server that collects credentials. A few weeks later the user's electronic payment account or credit card statement shows transactions that the user did not make.

- The line between App and web functionality is blurred by the web view controllers that allow a programmer to insert web interactive content into the application. The user believes that he is interacting locally with an App but he could really be entering information into a remote webpage. Malicious applications that use web content could occasionally request personal information from the users through the web control. Even good applications could be attacked by redirecting to different web content without ever touching the App itself.

The App Store vendors may themselves be questionable or corrupted. The current App Stores are run by well-known reliable trustworthy companies, but there is no reason to believe that there will not be other venues to purchase apps in the future. Independent App Stores with less web sophistication could be easily compromised to allow fraudsters to insert additional apps or substitute apps. Users that were previously inclined to install any executable on their system may be just as likely to install mobile Apps from unverifiable websites.

The proposed approach should provide additional protection against these likely scenarios. Before the user enters account information into their mobile app they should trigger a low-level interrupt by pushing the Home button on their device. Once the user has connected their mobile app to their web account, it may still be useful to require the interrupt action for confirmation of transactions. Additional user interaction may not be required but the hardware interrupt shows that a real person confirmed the action, not just malware on the device.

> The concept of SpoofKiller does not only apply to physical devices. A "Home button" can be added to the chrome of browsers, and users conditioned to pressing that to request action. As long as the button cannot be pressed by javaScript in a webpage, this provides protection against some attacks.

7.6.5   Say we Implement SpoofKiller—then What?

Since fraudsters have an ongoing opportunity to steal money they will not be completely deterred by this additional security. The fraudsters will continue to adjust their attacks over time.

Phishing sites can simply ignore the additional security in the hope that users will not notice. The phishing sites could attempt to provide a name and credentials for a name that sounds similar (www.pay_pal.com) to the legitimate websites. The plugin and interrupt handler would catch these suspicious names. A whitelist of legitimate supported names could be used as a filter. Man-in-the-middle servers would be caught by the same mechanisms that check the server name. Attackers would need to take over legitimate apps or websites for their phishing.

Man-in-the-screen and man-in-the-browser (MITB) and application level attacks should be largely addressed by the SpoofKiller approach since the important information bypasses these layers. This eliminates the chance for malicious middleware to capture or modify it. This includes display of information and keystroke interaction being handled directly by the interrupt handler without relying on potentially compromised middleware. This is true both for traditional PCs and mobile operating systems.

Malware writers would need to target the hardware interrupt handlers on the device to intercept or disable interactions with servers. Creating such malware requires a different class of technical skills than simple keystroke logging. The problem of tricking the user into installing such low-level malware is also more difficult. Ideally, the proposed low-level handler would be installed at the factory. It would be impossible later to install any handlers before it in the interrupt chain. This should make it much more difficult for an attacker to insert a bogus handler before the good handler to subvert the intended behavior.

7.7 DEVICE IDENTIFICATION AND INTELLIGENCE

Ori Eisen

Abstract. In this section we describe how to identify machines without having to rely on cookies.

As the proliferation of e-crime and fraud on the Internet continues, various solutions for the reduction of online anonymity have been devised. It has become apparent that merchants and financial institutions can no longer rely on matching the correct User Name and Password, PIN, CVV2, and other "shared secrets." User-held information—and user interaction in general—have been increasingly compromised by malware, phishing, data breaches and social engineering to the extent that all users and devices must be assumed to be suspect as a starting point.

To better understand the issues at hand for a risk practitioner, some background is necessary regarding a critical distinction between Internet communities:

- **Open communities** These are websites that do not, will not, and cannot control the hardware and software their users are using. Convenience is a market necessity for such communities, where easy access with minimum security is the recipe. Typical examples are email providers, social networks, banks, and e-commerce sites.

- **Closed communities** These are websites that do control the software and sometimes the hardware from which their user connect to them. Due to high-risk transactions and the nature of the business, these communities force their users to download "thick clients." Typical examples are gaming and gambling sites, employers, and some governmental agencies' restricted sites.

It is far more difficult to detect and prevent malicious activity in open communities than in closed communities, due to the lack of robust identifying information, and the myriad of combinations of devices and their software. Furthermore, the proliferation of new devices smartphones and tablets is extending the emphasis on nuance and attention to detail.

For example, when a new browser version is pushed to any OS, for example iPhone's iOS, there is always the chance of a change in behavior. Bugs or new software behaviors may cause the defense mechanisms set by the risk practitioner to suffer. The impact can result in an increase in "false positives" (good customers that are now suspected), as well as "false negatives" (rogue actors that are bypassing the controls). When Private Browsing was first introduced, users who wiped their cookies were challenged time and again during login, as their banks did not recognize them. This caused false positives and consumers calling the call-center to reset a password in cases they forgot the answers to their secret questions.

To solve these issues, different methods have been invented to attempt to identify the device the user is using. For closed communities, the job was fairly trivial; they could add code to their thick clients, as well as access data on the device that is only available to executables. In contrast, for open communities, where there is no client to download and only the browser is used—this task is far from trivial, as explained below.

7.7.1   1995–2001: The Early Years of Device Identification

As the capability to transact grew on the Internet, it was paralleled by the ability to commit crimes via these same emerging channels. Lacking any direct contact with the human behind the transaction, good or bad, some practitioners began looking to the device as the closest proxy.

One area practitioners began using was HTTP cookies. Cookies are text files stored on the browsing device, and were originally intended to keep relevant data on the user's device for use by the browser and the server. The potential value to risk practitioners was obvious, and cookies soon became a means of long-term identification of the device. However, cookies' value for tracking purposes was also obvious to fraudsters seeking to avoid being identified, who quickly learned how to steal and delete them. Fraudsters would have great benefit from stealing cookies of legitimate users, as they would gain easier access to their accounts. To do that, spoofed websites were setup that looked like real websites, such as online banking portals. In addition, emails were sent to unsuspecting users that led to these sites. Once on the site, the fraudsters would serve as an in-between, and were able to monitor what user name and passwords were used, and then would pose as the legitimate user on the real bank's website. This would result in getting a cookie on the fraudster's device, which then allowed to login. Alternatively, while cookies are domain specific, and will not serve themselves to a different domain they were set from – different tagging methods such as Flash Shared Objects (FSO/LSO) did. In this case, the crooks setup a website that looked like the bank (e.g., www.mybank2.com) and query the user's device to see if it has a Flash cookie from www.mybank.com (the real bank). Unfortunately, the victim's device would provide this information and let the crooks steal the cookie.

7.7.1.1   And then, browsers became "chatty"

Microsoft started its push to dominate the browser market at the end of 1995, beginning the "Browser Wars" between Microsoft and Netscape. This created a need for webmasters to know which browser was connecting to their website, because some code would not work or display content correctly on both types of browsers. From then on, browser needed to transmit their abilities to execute commands as well as basic information such as "I am a Microsoft IE 4.0" or "I am a Netscape 3.7 with build 12345." Therefore, browsers became chatty, and sent many more parameters over the wire than before.

This new data opened up opportunities for webmasters, who could design websites to accommodate the different behaviors of different browsers, as well as allow crooks and risk practitioners to glean more data about the device on the other end.

To communicate their browser's capabilities, software publishers began exposing Application Programming Interfaces (APIs) to identify the type and version of the browser. For example, HTTP User Agent headers came into use for "automated recognition [of the application] for the sake of tailoring responses to avoid particular [application] limitations," (RFC 1945 / HTTP 1.0 standards). In web traffic, User Agent headers typically identify the browser application type, operating system, software version, and vendor, but may provide many other pieces of information about the applications on the device.

Below are some sample strings gleaned from User Agent headers:

> Mozilla/4.0 (compatible; MSIE 6.0; Windows NT 5.0; .NET CLR 1.0.3705; .NET CLR 2.0.50727)
> This is a Microsoft Internet Explorer 6, on Windows XP

> Mozilla/5.0 (Macintosh; U; PPC Mac OS X Mach-O; en-US; rv:1.7.2) Gecko/20040804 Netscape/7.2
> This is a Netscape 7.2, on a Mac OS

> Mozilla/5.0 (Windows; U; Win98; en-US; rv:1.7.5) Gecko/20041107 Firefox/1.0
> This is a Firefox 1.0, on a Windows 98

Precocious risk practitioners began to realize (and others are still coming to realize) that this type of information about the browsing device can be useful to help identify it. These two approaches—using information or identifiers left on the device versus using information about the device itself—represent the major distinction in client device identification to this day, as discussed below.

7.7.2 2001–2008 Tagless Device Identification Begins

7.7.2.1 Not all device IDs are the same

The two type of device identification technologies are those that "tag" the device and those that are "tag-less," Tagging solutions, attempt to place a small file such as a cookie or FSO on the user's device, storing an identifier on the device itself. Tagless solutions attempt to read the characteristics and profile of the device without leaving any residue on it, and identify it with a composite of these characteristics.

Note that tags are generally "self-contained" in that a unique identifier is placed on the file, while tagless identification takes place through aggregation of many data points, ideally ones that have been thoroughly vetted for their stability over time, and ability to add differentiation. Examples of the methods / data sources appear below.

Tagging Solutions

- **Cookies** Small files that are capable of storing user preferences and unique ID
- **Flash Shared Objects** Small files, stored within the Flash sandbox, similar to cookies
- **Cache objects** Files or objects that are stored in the browser's cache

- **History**   A page the user navigated to and can help identify the user with a unique ID
- **HTML 5**   DOM storage

Tagless Solutions

- **HTTP headers**   Headers in the HTTP protocol that help identify the browser, like User Agent
- **JavaScript**   APIs for browser properties and other application or configuration information, originally designed for better navigation and usability
- **Plugins**   Additional components that a browser can install, such as Flash
- **TCP/IP**   Data from the TCP/IP transmission protocol, such as packet time signature

Tag-based solutions are attractive to practitioners because they are free to use, IT departments are already using them to identify users and their preferences, and they provide 100% unique identification (when the cookie remained on the device and is not stolen from a victim's device!).

Tagless solutions, on the other hand, allow practitioners to detect fraudulent behavior even if the attacker does not accept cookies or FSOs, and they are 100% ubiquitous across browsers and devices. However, in order to know what data different browsers can provide, extensive and continual research is needed to keep up with the changes.

7.7.2.2   Is IP address a device ID?

When a device is connected to a network, it is assign a somewhat unique IP address for that session. This leads many to believe that an IP address is a device identifier and can be easily substituted for most device IDs. However, this is often not the consistent identifier it is assumed to be. To borrow from another field:

> When the police are identifying criminals, they rely on more lasting features such as height, weight, hair color, eye color, and so on, rather than the clothes they were wearing or the bus they were riding. That is also why IP address is not a meaningful device identifier.

The same standard needs to be applied with devices. For example, a device could be using a public WiFi spot at an airport, and after the session is over an innocent user may use the same IP address. Moreover, in large organizations, Network Address Translation routing will cause many users to come from the same external IP address when they surf the Internet.

The inverse is true as well—the same criminal may easily use multiple IP addresses to subvert attempts to be identified. Without a more granular identifier (machine ID), the IP address alone may cause many false positives and false negatives.

7.7.2.3   Uses of device ID technologies

Online companies have been device identification and intelligence to solve or enhance a variety of business needs:

1. **Account opening and enrollment**   This use case involves the decision of whether a company will accept an application or enroll a user. Criminals may abuse this by misrepresenting who and where they are, and/or by opening many accounts.

The usual methods for detecting this are geolocation by IP address, and checking for velocities. Geolocation involves finding a person's location based on their IP address, and velocities are higher frequencies of occurrence than are allowed or probable for some specific data point—for example, the same email, IP, or physical address being used across many applications.

Unfortunately for the risk practitioner, both of these are easily avoided—criminals can route their IP connection through a proxy device, hiding the fact that they are operating out of a high-risk country or even making their IP-based geolocation match the enrollment information they entered. Velocities can be avoided by entering different information on each and by changing IP proxy with each enrollment or application attempt.

However, bringing in the user's device information can provide additional geolocation matching capabilities, based on factors other than IP address that the fraudster did not know to change. Additionally, velocities based on device identification have proven to be much more robust, in that covertly collected device configuration information is much less obvious and much more difficult to change than user-entered data. Where all other data looks different, the pattern of one device opening many accounts can still make a criminals fraud attempts obvious.

2. **Account authentication (risk-based authentication)**   This use case involves granting access to an online account. With a high rate of compromise for User IDs and passwords by phishing and malware, the need for additional factors in authentication has emerged, and is even required by regulation in some areas (e.g., required for banks by the Federal Financial Institutions Examination Council, FFIEC, a US government agency).

Verifying that a known or familiar device is returning to an account—especially if it has a history with the account or has been associated with "good" behaviors (e.g., bill payment)—allows for greater certainty that it is the legitimate user logging in. While cookies can be stolen to impersonate the real user and even the victims own IP address can be used as a proxy via malware, device identification is orders of magnitude harder to copy.

Additionally, the use of the device information allows for shades of gray matching, versus a binary match. Binary match has been a staple of information security from day one, yet, with consumer authentication and open communities the game changed.

Cookies and other tags are either there or not there, and they frequently are not available due to deletion by privacy-concerned individuals. Device identification, however, is not only impossible to delete, but it can be adjusted to allow for a closely matching device rather than only exact matches. If device identification looks at 100 factors and one of them changes, there may no longer be an exact match, but a match allowing for differences within a threshold (e.g., a 95% match to a previous device's profile) will still let the genuine user login and keep others out.

3. **Account takeover**   This use case arose as a result of phishing attacks and other means to steal credentials. The attackers could then log in into multiple accounts and either scrape screen information, or divert value from within the account.

When attackers compromise credentials and intend to sell them, they need to check periodically that the credentials are still valid to ensure they have not changed in the interim. This is usually done via scripts or bots—meaning one device is going into many accounts. Inversely, compromised credentials can be posted on a bulletin board or elsewhere online, and many devices access one account.

Practitioners using device identification can identify both of these attacks—when a rogue device logs into many accounts, or many devices logging into one account.

4. **Transactional fraud** E-commerce companies often lack the account context discussed. Many take orders from the general public rather than forcing a user to set up or come in through an account and risking losing business by inconveniencing the prospective buyer. This use case allows e-commerce companies to monitor many transactions emanating from one device. Alternatively, device data can help companies with compliance.

5. **Digital rights management (DRM)** This use case allows companies to monitor if there is abuse in an account. When a consumer pays for a subscription to digital content ranging from analysts' reports to online entertainment, and then willingly provides their credentials to friends and family they are violating their account terms and conditions. This form of abuse can be detected by monitoring how many unique and different devices use their set of credentials.

6. **Targeted marketing and advertising** This use case helps ad networks display a targeted ad to a user, based on their device characteristics and identification. Technological shifts and government regulations are redefining the landscape for online ads, and device identification is another tool for marketers to consider. Whereas to date mostly cookies and FSOs have been used to identify consumers, tagless methods are being considered at the time of printing as they are harder to undermine while providing more privacy by not being a one-to-one 100% match for a user device.

While this is not a complete list, it shows the versatility of uses and directionally alludes to additional uses in the future.

7.7.2.4 The game of tag

Practitioners need to balance the need for sales, good customer service and reduction of fraud. No one tool can provide a perfect solution, so it is important to know the pros and cons of the Client-less Device Identification (CDI) methods.

Tagged solutions—Pros

1. Tags 100% Unique as they are generated server-side by the site provider.

2. Free to use, relies on cookies and Flash as a platform for delivery (see notes about Flash under "Cons").

3. These are easily understood by technologists as binary identification—a tag either exists on the device and it is "known" within the domain that put it there, or it is not there.

4. May be in use already in the enterprise for marketing reasons.

5. Detects returning good customers.

Tagged solutions—Cons

1. 100% right or 100% wrong. When cookie legitimately represented, it indicates the true user coming back. However, when a cookie is stolen and represented, it will misidentify a crook as a legitimate user. Likewise, when crooks do not accept cookies, their return visits will not be recognized.

2. Use of VMWare renders all cookies placed on a device useless, when the virtual machine is rolled back.

3. Some devices (Mobile and game consoles) do not support Flash natively, or have limited cookie retention.

4. Antivirus and antimalware solutions routinely delete tracking cookies to protect user privacy.

5. Users who choose "Private Browsing" allow their browsers to erase their tags at the end of their session, rendering them useless across sessions.

Tagless solutions—Pros

1. 100% coverage—no device renders a null device print, including mobile, game consoles, and tablets.

2. Resilient to VMWare—while rolling back a VM to an earlier state clears all traces of tags, the same rolled back machine will generate the same device identification signals repeatedly (unless changed).

3. Disabling cookies and FSOs has no effect on tagless solutions because device data is still collected.

4. Tags are immune to antivirus software cleanups, as there is nothing to detect or delete.

5. Detects all levels of fraud modus operandi, from simple to sophisticated, including man-in-the-middle/man-in-the-browser.

Tagless solutions—Cons

1. Not 100% Unique as it is generated client-side and there can be "collisions" when unrelated devices coincidentally share identical device data.

2. Can morph as the user upgrades and downgrades the device; as versions of software change, the exact profile of the device will be altered.

3. Requires continuous R&D into new browsers and devices, and the signals they emit—devices and software can provide advanced capabilities or affect existing collection.

Based on these rules of thumb, most e-commerce and online banking websites consider the use of multiple layers of security, and avoid a single point of failure.

7.7.2.5 Tag or tagless: a practitioner's dilemma?

Apple published a study at an industry event (Merchant Risk Council Annual Conference, 2008), reporting their experience in comparing the effectiveness of the different methods device identification methods.

As the Apple Store's uses multiple layers of security, when the pilot was conducted, a few metrics were used to assess the value of adding tag and tagless device identification.

First, a practitioner should consider the "Total Fraud" covered by the new method. This shows how much of the total fraud events this single method would detect. For example, if there are 100 fraud cases in a period in total, and the technology identifies 20 of them, this would be 20%.

Second, another measure is how much fraud that would go undetected otherwise, the method will detect. Because the merchant would not detect it, and therefore not "block" the order, this measurement is the "Unblocked Fraud." For example, if there are 100 fraud cases in a period in total, and the merchant

Table 7.5 Result of Tag and Tagless Device ID Pilot

	PC Print	Cache ID	Cookie ID
% of total fraud covered	19.5%	0.14%	1.7%
% of unblocked fraud covered	30.4%	0.0%	0.2%
False positive rate	45.2%	62.5%	40.7%

caught 70 of them, then the maximum number the new method can detect is 30. If the new method detected 10 cases, which is 33% of the remaining 30 cases, the Unblocked Fraud rate would be 33%.

Lastly, a measurement of false positives needs to balance the effectiveness of any new method. If a tool detected 90% of all fraud events but flagged 90% of all orders, the false positive rate is high and undesirable. For example, if a method identified 20 events as suspected being fraud, and after review 10 of them are indeed fraud, the remainder 10 are false positives. This rate can be described as either a 2:1, or 50% false positive rate. The lower the false positive rate, the better the method.

The left most column of Table 7.5 shows the metrics for a tagless method while the other two are two forms of tagged methods.

David Moriarty, who runs Apple's business intelligence and fraud, provided this quote with the results of the pilot: "From that analysis [of the pilot], my conclusion is that tagging is useful for recognizing good guys, but not for stopping fraud. The good fraudsters defeat the tags. The ones that don't are easily caught through more basic tools (e.g., AVS, CVV2, velocities, etc.)."

7.7.3   2008—Present: Private Browsing and Beyond

7.7.3.1   *The effects of Private Browsing on device identification methods*

With the proliferation user tracking online, browser publishers offer tools to maintain anonymity with Private Browsing. For the most part, any tag placed on the browser/device during a Private Session is obliterated at session's end. This includes both HTTP cookies and FSO/LSO.

To demonstrate the effects of Private Browsing, consider the diagram below (Table 7.6). It shows the difference in data a browser sends before and after a Private Browsing session.

Table 7.6 Same Device Before and After Private Browsing

	Identifier	Return login data (post Private Browsing)	Login data	Match?	Result
Tagless	DeviceInsight	abcdefghijk	abcdefghijk	100%	DSP: 100%
	TDL Secs	−16	−16	100%	+0
	HTML 5 DOM	lmnop456	xyz123	Not equal	Not equal
Tagged	Cache	lmnop456	xyz123	Not equal	Not equal
	cookie	lmnop456	xyz123	Not equal	Not equal
	flash	lmnop456	xyz123	Not equal	Not equal
	history	lmnop456	xyz123	Not equal	Not equal

What we expect to see, is that when the device returns to the website, after it was wiped clean of any tags, the website will consider this user's device new, and therefore set new tags for it. However, any information that is tagless (is not stored in the device's storage and therefore wiped)—should remain the same.

This diagram shows the same device before and after a Private Session. Note that all the tagged methods show new values, as the old values were erased. On the other hand, the tagless method shows the same values as it is not relying on tags left on the device for future identification.

DSP stands for device similarity percentage , and is a measure of how similar is the device that logs in to the device on the account. In this case, the matching is perfect and the DSP is 100%. This also demonstrates that a Private Browsing session does not erase any of the data that composes this value. Nonetheless, this value is not permanent and will change as the user installs new applications, or upgrades/downgrades exiting applications.

Private Browsing and other market trends will prove to be challenging for those in charge of keeping websites safe and usable. Privacy advocates, government legislation as well as consumer demands will keep shaping the online technology landscape.

The EU is planning to make any tagging of a user by cookies an opt-in, starting May of 2011. This will reshape the ability for practitioners in both target marketing and security/fraud to identify their customers.

Users now have more control over what gets to be stored on their devices, and as a result drive websites to adopt new methods and strategies.

This chart shows the options users have in allowing third-party Flash content, as well as the total disk space they allow on their device. This shows that users have more power than ever to control what is stored and communicated from their browser, as well as the fraudsters (Figure 7.39).

Furthermore, with the introduction of Windows 7, users have more options to control what code executes on their machines. The diagram below shows an alert that popsup when Flash attempts to write a third-party FSO for the first time (Figure 7.40):

Note that the default selection highlighted is No, which will have users select it more often than not. Everything being equal, this gives the website a 50/50% chance that the user will comply with the request.

Changes like this will force practitioners to "think outside the box" when devising strategies and implementing methods in the future.

Figure 7.39   Adobe Flash 10.1 user settings.

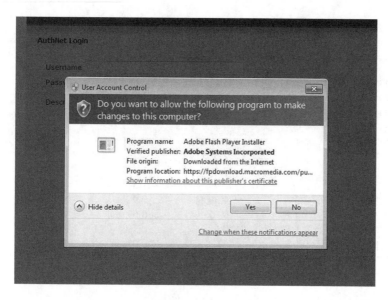

Figure 7.40   Windows 7 alert.

7.7.3.2   User experience decisions related to device ID

We have seen that different methods have different properties, including the false positives rates. This begs the question regarding the right balance between security and convenience. Consider a site that uses tags only for authenticating its users. If the cookie placed on the user remains, and the user returns—there will be no challenge and the user can login freely. However, if for any reason, the user does not present the expected cookie (deleted, not accepted in the first place, etc.), the site would most likely issue a challenge before the login is approved. The challenge can come in the form of OOB, which will send the user a one-time code via email, SMS, or phone call. However, this process introduces expense as well as user inconvenience.

In this scheme, there is no "gray area," as the method is binary and either matches 100% or it does not.

In recent years, a concept of risk-based authentication (RBA) has been gaining momentum, as this allows for "shades of gray" to be introduced. User experience can then be managed by "dialing-up" the matching threshold.

This chart shows that if there is no tolerance, and only 100% matching of a device would allow access, about 6–8% of accounts will be challenged over time. We can also note that from 99% match and below, not only the challenge rate drops in week 1, it also drops over time. This is a result of system learning and the fact that users usually have two to three primary devices they use (so they don't get challenged when one of their known devices return) (Table 7.7).

In the marketing and advertising space, where no account is created, the difference in efficacy is notable.

To measure the efficacy of cookies compared to the tagless options, some experiments are done side-by-side (Figure 7.41). Consider a website that sampled over 100MN user visits and then compared the results of cookies and tagless methods. In such experiments, the options are as follows:

1. Cookie and tagless are the same—the user is known to both.

Table 7.7   Challenge Rates at Different Matching Threshold Over Time

DDP	Week 1	Week 2	Week 4	Week 6	Week 8
100%	8.6%	7.6%	6.2%	7.7%	6.3%
99%	7.7%	6.4%	4.9%	4.6%	4.5&
98%	7.4%	6.0%	4.4%	3.9%	4.0%
95%	7.0%	5.5%	3.9%	3.4%	3.5%
90%	6.6%	4.9%	3.4%	2.9%	3.0%
85%	6.1%	4.4%	2.9%	2.5%	2.6%
80%	5.7%	4.0%	2.6%	2.2%	2.3%
75%	5.1%	3.5%	2.3%	1.8%	1.9%
70%	4.7%	3.1%	2.0%	1.5%	1.5%
60%	3.2%	2.0%	1.3%	0.9%	0.9%
50%	2.2%	1.4%	0.9%	0.6%	0.5%
25%	1.7%	1.1%	0.6%	0.5%	0.3%
15%	0.1%	0.1%	0.0%	0.0%	0.0%

2. Cookie and tagless are different—the user is new to both.

3. Cookie the same and tagless different—cookie recognized the user, but tagless did not (cookie is better).

4. Cookie is different and tagless is the same—cookie did not recognize the user, but tagless did (tagless is better). This chart shows that both cookies and tagless methods recognized 73% of the users with the same effectiveness. Ten percent both methods did not recognize, due to new users adding devices and other reasons. In 17% of cases, they differ, and in that segment cookies recognize 2% of users, and tagless 15%

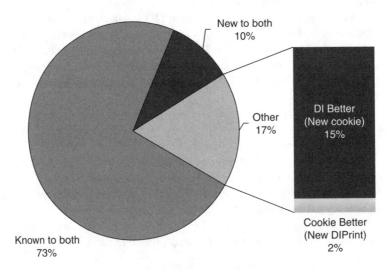

Figure 7.41   Comparison of cookies versus tagless device identification user recognition.

If history is any indication of the future, device identification will keep playing a role in online business decisions. The proliferation of devices will continue to drive innovation and research into how new parameters will be used. As the Internet evolves, the dominant market forces of convenience, security, and privacy will keep reshaping the landscape.

7.8 HOW CAN WE DETERMINE IF A DEVICE IS INFECTED OR NOT?

Aurélien Francillon, Markus Jakobsson, and Adrian Perrig

Abstract. We describe an alternative to the traditional antivirus paradigm—software-based attestation—and describe its benefits. Anti-virus relies on searching for known malicious code in memory while attestation verifies that the whole code in memory is in a predefined state. The difference is essentially black-listing versus white-listing: anti-virus searches for code that is on a black-list while attestation verifies that all code is on a white-list. While attestation can be performed by relying on dedicated hardware support (e.g., Trusted Platform Module (TPM)), that comes with distinct drawbacks, too. Systems that solely rely on software for attestation are called software-based attestation. Features of software-based attestation include low power consumption (making the method suitable for mobile devices and other power-constrained devices), and the possibility to make *guarantees* that a device is not infected, or otherwise corrupted.

7.8.1 Why Detection is Difficult

Traditional antivirus technology aims at blocking infection by identifying bad code before it is given control over a device. But this identification is based on comparison with known strains—whether in terms of code identity or behavior. Therefore, traditional antivirus technology is vulnerable to attacks by new malware that was previously unknown, also called *zero-day attack*.

With an increase of zero-day attacks and targeted malware, how can one then tell whether a device is infected or not? The problem is that the absence of matches with a blacklist still leaves the door open to the possibility of zero-day malware, rendering the device insecure. Verifying the security status is particularly important if the device is used for highly sensitive tasks—accessing a corporate network, performing a payment, casting a vote. We need to be as certain as we can that the device is not corrupted. Moreover, with an increasing population of mobile devices—whose limited power resources makes the use of traditional (and power intensive) antivirus techniques problematic—the problem is becoming increasingly urgent to address.

> We cannot simply query a device "are you infected?" That would be very much akin to asking a person "Are you a liar?" You always get the response "no, of course not!"—whether you ask a liar or a person who tells the truth. Same for the device: an infected device may be forced by malware to report that it was not infected.

For the same reason, a device cannot determine itself whether it has already been infected. Even if it *were* to detect an infection, the final result could be changed—by the malware—from "I *am* infected" to "I am *not* infected."

One possible answer to this dilemma is to use software-based attestation—a technique that determines that there is no other process running before performing a careful security assessment of the device. If we can be sure that only *our* routine is running, that it has not been manipulated, and that its execution cannot be interrupted by malware, then we can comfortably ask that routine to perform security-sensitive tasks, including reporting on its security status.

Security-sensitive tasks may include to copy the contents of the device to an external location, where they can be carefully scrutinized by a security vendor. Or they may be to allow the user to log in to perform a payment; cast a vote; or be given access to a local network. It may be to let the user access an encrypted memory area, where parts of the key is held by a security vendor—who will only release them after the device has passed the verification. And the device, of course, trusted as it is, will erase the keys after they have been used.

In all these settings, we assume the presence of a trusted verification device. As one cannot pull oneself up by one's own hair, we cannot bootstrap trust purely locally, but need to trust an external trusted entity to verify local operation. The security properties we discuss here are all with respect to the external trusted verifier. For the settings mentioned above, the verifier can be an additional external device that the user carries and that connects via USB to the device that is to be verified. For giving access to the local network, the verifier could be a network access router that inspects the device that is to be connected.

However, to obtain meaningful answers to verifier queries, the verifier needs to ensure that the device in question is not controlled by malware. To accomplish such secure verification, it is first necessary to set up an isolated environment that the external verifier can validate. Such an isolated environment can be set up by either providing guarantees for bootstrapping an isolated environment or by detection of malware interference. Second, once we have an isolated environment we can leverage it either by verifying the identity of code executing next or by enforcing a property on the code that executes next (e.g., erase all memory after the code terminates). Finally, we discuss how the isolated environment can launch another piece of code, possibly as part of an application and granting its untampered execution, essentially providing a software-based dynamic root of trust.

First things first, we discuss the most challenging aspect: how we can set up an isolated environment and ensure that it is not corrupted by malware in a way that can be validated by an external verifier?

7.8.2   Setting up an Isolated Environment

The objective in setting up an isolated environment is to be able to execute a piece of code that will be executed without being interrupted by any other—possibly malicious—code. This requires that the processor is exclusively made available to the attestation code, and that no mechanism can interrupt it (e.g., timer interrupts) or modify the state of the system during its execution (e.g., a device can modify a memory region using Direct Memory Access (DMA)). The goal of isolated execution thus is to prevent malicious code from tampering with the system while the attestation code is running.

Imagine that a memory checking routing is reading memory in sequence, if a malicious piece of code can be triggered by an interrupt, it could interrupt the routine and move the malicious code to avoid detection.

7.8.2.1   Enforcement and reporting

There are two different ways to achieve execution isolation: enforcement or reporting.

Enforcement provides the guarantee that the code cannot be interrupted or that the system state cannot be modified. Reporting is different, it does not prevent malicious modifications or tampering, but if it happens the verifier can detect it. Depending on the approach, the verifier can detect by observing a time delay or an incorrect checksum result.

Enforcement means that once the attestation routine starts it is impossible to be stopped by other software on the same system. This would require specific hardware support on a platform where peripheral devices, such as a network card or a Firewire device, can perform memory reads and writes with DMA on the main memory by completely bypassing the central processor. However, when no other device can access the main memory, enforcement can be achieved by ensuring and enabling external verification that interrupts are disabled.

> Enforcement is typically what is provided by hardware systems such as Intel TXT or AMD SVM. On the other hand, software-based attestation systems can only rely on already present functionalities to achieve reporting.

7.8.2.2 Achieving secure execution through ensuring code identity or enforcing properties

Once an isolated environment is established and validated by the verifier, how can we use it? How can malicious code be detected? There are two approaches that can be integrated into a software-based attestation scheme: ensuring code identity or enforcing properties. For ensuring code identity, the verifier essentially wants to ensure that only a specific piece of code can execute on the system, for example by specifying a cryptographic hash value of the code that is to be executed next. As the code executes within the validated isolated execution environment, the verifier obtains assurance that the desired code has started execution.

Alternatively, the verifier can use the isolated execution environment by loading a monitor code that enforces a security property on code that executes subsequently. For example, the monitor can enforce control-flow integrity on the code, which means that the actual control flow of the code follows intended code patterns (this is used to prevent control-flow-based attacks such as some forms of buffer overruns). In the research literature, this latter property is referred to as property-based attestation, semantic attestation, or active attestation.

Both approaches offer tradeoffs, but they are orthogonal and can be used in conjunction. Generally, validating code identity ensures that a specific piece of code executes, offering a high level of security but sacrificing flexibility with respect to code upgrades, different code versions, and so on. Analogously, enforcing code properties offers flexibility while sacrificing security. They can be combined by verifying code identity of a monitoring module as well as of a piece of code that executes under the auspices of that monitor.

> For example an embedded system will contain a given firmware image, the administrator that requests attestation will know exactly the firmware version expected on the device and all the code that should be present on it. Code attestation is then the process of verifying that the current code present on the device corresponds exactly to the original code.

7.8.2.3 Software-based dynamic root of trust

To achieve the isolated execution environment enabling secure code execution that an external verifier can validate, we can make use of techniques that are called software-based dynamic root of trust. Based on our discussion, this technique is based on detection, so that malware is not prevented from executing, but can be detected if it interferes with the desired code execution.

In a nutshell, this approach proceeds as follows. On the device, we initiate a self-checksumming function with the special property that any interference with its execution will result in a slow down of the execution of in an incorrect checksum. (A self-checksumming function is a sequence of operations that compute and return a checksum over their own code.) As part of the checksum function, an isolated execution environment is set up. In these schemes, the verifier needs to be familiar with the architecture and memory contents of the device, such that it can seed a fresh checksum computation with a random number (i.e., a nonce) and predict the exact computation time and checksum. As a consequence of these operations, the verifier is ensured of the correct establishment of a piece of code that will execute in an isolated execution environment, thus providing a software-based dynamic root of trust.

Establishing a software-based dynamic root of trust immediately opens up numerous challenges. For example, how can the verifier be assured that no malware can tamper with the code execution, that is, that the execution environment is truly isolated? One could attempt to turn off all interrupts and exception on the system and thus preventing malware from gaining control, but this immediately begs the question on how can an external verifier validate that interrupts and exceptions were indeed turned off? The short answer is that the architectural state of the system that describes interrupt handling is incorporated into the checksum—hence, any tampering with interrupts or exceptions will either result in an incorrect checksum or a delayed computation. The longer story is a bit more intricate and requires a more in-depth study of software-based attestation mechanisms.

7.8.3   What Could go Wrong?

As we have seen above, software-based attestation relies on the correctness and enforcement of several properties. There are a few strategies that can be used to hide the malicious code that would allow to prevent its detection.

7.8.3.1   What you execute is not what you see

Attestation inherently verifies the presence of the correct code but does not enforce that the code is executed correctly or that the attested code is flawless. The attested code can have flaws, like buffer overruns, that would allow a software attack to change the correct execution flow.

For example a malformed network packet can lead to a software fault that lead to an overwrite of a return address on the stack. This can be used by an attacker to execute already present, and attested, code on the device but in a way that would violate the security of the device.

Yet this class of vulnerabilities, called return to libc, is orthogonal to software attestation and can happen completely after attestation was performed. It therefore needs to be addressed but does not represent a direct attack of the software-based attestation scheme.

However, a related technique, called return-oriented programming, can be used to circumvent software-based attestation schemes themselves.

As an example, a program might be made of those three words:
bites, dog, man
and is normally "executed" in the following order :
dog bites man
but the sequence of the words is a dynamic property, an attacker could use the same words and execute them in a different order to obtain a different meaning:
man bites dog
this can be performed by controlling the execution of the chunks of code from the stack. A malicious action was possible while the "words" themselves were attested.

One idea is that, instead of abusing a software flow, the malicious code is present on the device before attestation and will erase and restore itself from the attested region of memory. This will allow to avoid detection, the malicious code is hiding itself in nonexecutable, and therefore not attested, memory.

While it is easy for code to erase itself, restoring it is more complex. One approach is to leverage return-oriented programming as follows: modify the stack before the attestation procedure is executed. Upon completion of the attestation procedure this pointer will modify the normal flow of execution, using the attested executable code in an unintended manner. This usage of return-oriented programming could allow to restore the malicious code after execution of the attestation routine.

To prevent such attacks there are several countermeasures: attesting all of memory, ensuring stack integrity before returning, or preventing return-oriented attacks altogether. Attesting to the entire memory is problematic as this would include dynamic memory (e.g., stack, heap, etc.) that can of course be included in the checksum, however, as we said above the content of such memory is difficult to predict which would complicate checksum verification for the verifier. Ensuring stack integrity is an option, but it needs to be possible to recreate a pristine stack or validate the existing stack. Preventing return-oriented programming is challenging, moreover while return-oriented programming usually relies on modifying return addresses on the stack it can be done by modifying function pointers as well.

7.8.3.2   Hiding in unused space

Programs usually do not use all available memory. If some memory is left unused malicious code could use that space to hide itself. However, attestation routines can of course attest to the entire memory, even unused spaces. Hiding in unused memory is therefore insufficient by itself and needs to be used together with weaknesses of the attestation algorithm.

A possible solution is to fill all empty memory with pseudo-random values, such that an attacker that uses those would have to overwrite it. Given that the overwritten pseudo-random values are not available on the device anymore, it would not be possible for attacker to compute the correct checksum.

7.8.3.3   Compressing original program

We have seen that if all available memory is either used or filled with randomness, the attacker cannot keep the original program, the randomness, and his malicious program on the device. Under some circumstances, there is still a possibility for an attacker to bypass this using compression. While the randomness cannot be compressed the original program can be. If the attacker replaces the original program with its compressed version he can then use the freed space to store the malicious code. Once this is set up, during an attestation request, the attacker has to decompress the original program on the flight to compute the checksum. This can be performed, even if memory is checksummed by accessing random memory locations, requiring that the malicious code embed the decompression as well as the attestation routine. There is a significant drawback to this approach, decompressing memory on the fly obviously requires more time than accessing it directly, so those attacks may significantly slow down responses. As a result, attestation protocols that rely on strict timing are not vulnerable to such attacks.

7.8.3.4 Proxy attacks

Since timing is used to ensure the absence of malware tampering with the software-based attestation function, we need to ensure that the checksum computation indeed happened on the correct device and the response indeed was sent by the correct device. Otherwise, a proxy attack is possible, where a faster helper device simulates the compromised device and computes the correct checksum sufficiently fast to fool the verifier.

This attack limits the use of software-based attestation to verify network-based devices. However, verification over networks is still feasible given additional methods to validate the origin of the attestation and ensuring the absence that the device could communicate with an external proxy or helper device.

7.8.4 Brief Comparison with TrustZone

TrustZone is a hardware feature of ARM processors, based on switching state between the "regular" applications and "trusted" applications. TrustZone requires certification of all secure code (Trustlets), which involves code review by a trusted party acting as a certification authority. Trustlets cannot currently be shared between vendors, but this may change onward as the lack of sharing increases the burden on software vendors.

While the scrutiny does not detect vulnerabilities (or intentional malware) with any certainty, it does of course add to the security by adding another layer of review. Therefore, TrustZone does not per se detect malware, but allows approved processes to run in a secure mode, while other processes runs in a normal mode. In contrast to solutions described above, TrustZone is a localized security measure: the device verifies what code it can and should run, and in what mode. If code is compromised, there is no external detection of this. Therefore, while methods for software-based attestation provide security assurances to external parties—such as financial service providers—TrustZone instead hardens the end points against compromise.

Another difference is the level of abstraction. Software-based attestation can be run as SaaS (Security as a Service), only requiring a party wishing to verify the state of a device to make a call to the appropriate routine. In contrast, TrustZone requires writing and certification of special code. However, on the flip side, TrustZone comes enabled with essentially every handset, while software-based attestation is in a more nascent state, as of the time of writing.

7.8.5 Summary

We have covered the high-level concepts of software-based attestation and software-based dynamic root of trust. The concept of isolated execution environment is important to ensure the untampered execution of a piece of code, unmolested by malware that may also be present on the system. Through the use of timing and specially crafted self-checksumming code that slows down when tampered, a function can be created that can provide these properties on hardware without support for these primitives.

However, software-based attestation needs to be used with caution as numerous attacks lurk to violate security. In many contexts, changing the hardware is not an option and software-based attestation may be one of the only approaches that is applicable to ensure the absence of malware.

FURTHER READING

For some more detail, we refer the interested reader to   [272,431]; for a deep-dive, also see [149,203,205,221,233,270,273,357,429,430,432,433,435,437,498].

Chapter **8**

The Future

Who *knows* what, exactly, the future holds? You do not, I do not either. And the guy who was hit by the truck *clearly* did not. But we can still make good predictions.

> I look in my refrigerator, and I think "I will soon need to buy more milk." How do I know? Do I know exactly how thirsty I will be tomorrow? Have I planned in detail what I will consume? Of course not, but I can think of my family's past milk consumption habits, see how much is left in the jug, and try to count how many people there are in my house. *We can do the same thing with security.*

- We can identify apparent market trends. For example, a whole lot of people are buying smart phones, but not everybody has one yet. (Therefore, we think, the number of smart phones may continue to grow.) We see faster connections and easier ways to pay and get paid. (Therefore, we think, there will be more services.)

- We can then look at changes in how people use these devices, and what the changes are in terms of user interfaces. For example, we may note that people get used to using handsets while doing other things (driving, listening to music, and having a conversation that does not require the device). What will future user interfaces look like? Will it be easy to detect deceit? Will it be easy to authenticate? How will people do it, and when?

- Then, think like the fraudster. What would you have done if you were a fraudster, whether in a today's reality or a likely reality of tomorrow? Then ask yourself "Why?" The answer is probably because you think this type of scam would expose you (the supposed criminal) to less risk, because it is easier, because the expected payoff is likely to be larger? If *you* think this, then why would not the real fraudsters, too? Which means that you are looking at a criminal opportunity—a trend waiting to happen!

This part of the book will briefly talk about trends—current trends, likely trends, and potentially imagined trends. We should worry about what these trends would mean to us, and we should be proactive about defending against the problems we imagine to become likely. We should be proactive. Only then will we actually protect the Internet—and everything it is related to—from becoming a casualty of its own dramatic success.

This is a short chapter. It begins with a vision of future user interfaces, and how these may affect us—and our security. I then turn to a brief note on how to *think* about the future in a way that allows us to support our predictions and identify our needs.

The Death of the Internet, First Edition. Edited by Markus Jakobsson.
© 2012 John Wiley & Sons, Inc. Published 2012 by John Wiley & Sons, Inc.

8.1 SECURITY NEEDS THE BEST USER EXPERIENCE

Hampus Jakobsson

8.1.1 How the User Won Over Features

We have already gone a long way. When human–computer interaction (HCI) and man–machine interfaces (MMI) were invented, it was mainly to make machines possible to interact with at all. Nobody would talk about user experiences of operating a nuclear power plant and few would mention "users" at all. Back then, in the mid-twentieth century, it was just to give machines buttons and gauges so that we could operate them. And the people who operated were educated how to use the machines and had plenty of time to study how the system worked. The operators of the power plant were probably specially trained and the designers probably knew as much about the power plant as they knew about cognitive science. Today, users seldom have training to use a specific gadget and as seldom want to read the manual.

Fast forward to today when all industries talk user experience (UX) and when interaction designers (IxD) have become the superstar engineers in the twentieth century. User interfaces (UI) have become so important that they are more worth than features. When the iPhone was introduced in 2007, it was inferior feature-wise, but the user interface was unsurpassed. Who would have thought that design would trump features? What once were technical terms like "HCI" and "MMI" have become "UX"—user experience— and as the term no longer contains the word computer or machine but instead talks about experience, it is evident that the focus has shifted.

> User interfaces have become more than just the superficial surface, just as industrial design is not just about beautiful material and stylish objects, but about how we use them and even more why we use them. We have come to realize that "good design" means "to be inviting to use for what it is intended for."

Still, getting a good design requires a lot of technical competence. All types of designers need this. Just like architects, who design buildings, have to understand material, construction, city planning, budgeting, and most of all *people*. And building a beautiful house that withstands the test of usage takes an orchestration of all of these competences. Look inside companies that create great products and you often find a symbiosis between designers and engineers. At least the design people do not report to the mechanical engineering department, who report to the engineering manager, who report to the CTO, but the design organization is on equal level with engineering within the organization chart.

8.1.2 So How Come the iPhone Became so Successful?

I would argue that most mobile manufacturers never thought the iPhone would catch on and be sold to anyone but the hard-core Apple fanboys. The phone was seen as a couple of years behind standard—battery life of a laptop, brittle as glass, a subpar camera, and really bad connectivity. The iPhone did not have 3G like most competitors but the older EDGE protocol, and it did not even have Wifi. In the minds of Nokia and other large OEMs, the iPhone was not competition; it was useless. But the strange thing is, as we know today, that Apple changed the whole mobile market and more or less is about to change computers as we know them. How come?

Apple's elegant design boils down to the power of the user—I think Steve Jobs in some sense is probably like most of the world's middle-aged men; when people come into his office and show him something he does not understand, he hates it and asks them to make it simpler and easier to use. Most companies that make devices or services do not have executives that can afford to be that brave. They are not supreme commanders, they have a board to report to and need a new product on the market that will improve the next quarter and be written about in the *Wall Street Journal*. So Apple's products are elegant because the person in charge thinks like his customers—the user and his experiences are the focus.

> And user interfaces are not just superficial. It is hard to value in money the difference between a good and a bad UI, but there are some data. Amazon increased their revenue by 45%, by $400 million in one quarter, by removing a button in their purchase flow. Did more people want to buy books because of the change? No—but it was a tad easier.

I think we should view users like 4-year-olds—impatient, cannot focus too long if it is not really interesting, and will not memorize things that would not be extremely useful. We cannot expect of people to memorize things, to work hard to use something they do not even know is good. Most of all not to take shortcuts.

The common problem is that most people who invent things or develop things know them, and if they do not, they can spend hours to learn. On the contrary, most normal people hate technology because it makes them feel stupid. So when a site generates a 10 character password with mixed numbers, letters, and infrequently used symbols, because it is the safest password possible, people write the password on a post-it and put it on their screen. The strange thing is that often the stronger the password is required to be, the less secure it will become. It is counterintuitive, but it is due to the fact that people do not want to memorize passwords and therefore take a shortcut, which is a lot less safe.

If a site would let you enter your own four-digit code, it will very likely be the same as your credit card PIN, but at least it will not be taped to the computer as you have a chance to remember it. What is safer? That depends on who will try to break in. If it is someone remote, a longer random password will take more time to find, but if it is a colleague or a finder of a lost laptop, the post-it will be easier to read. Most services that require complex passwords or force the user to change the password all the time will see that people forget their password more often. If the service resets passwords by sending reset links to the user's email, then the security is determined by the security of the user's email account.

8.1.3   A World of Information Anywhere

After the iPhone, user interfaces started to make quantum leaps. First of all, not only the focus but also the materials research bore fruit from the iPhone injection they got in 2007; for example, new types of touch screens emerged. At the same time, Amazon's Kindle proved that e-ink—screens that do not require any power when the image is static—could be produced at a price that spells "mass market." The first devices with autostereoscopic screens, flexible screens, and transparent screens are being built. Autostereoscopic screens are like today's 3D screens, with content looking three-dimensional if you wear special glasses, but *without* the need of glasses. Flexible screens will allow us to have a big screen that then folds nicely like a map into your pocket. And transparent screens allow for windows, windscreens, and other surfaces that need to be transparent to be able to superimpose information or change their opaqueness. For example, the windscreen of your car could show a cable in the sky that you should follow, instead of looking down at the GPS. Soon we would not be able to see what is digital and what not.

When communication hardware gets really cheap, we will see computing power in everyday objects. There are interesting devices on the market today that would not have been possible to perceive 10 years ago:

- **Fitbit**   The pedometer that senses exactly how you move, reporting to a computer that keeps your data stored on a server for your analysis.
- **Withings**   The scale that sends your data to a server and could tweet every time you weigh too much to give you more peer pressure to skip that Danish.
- **The Kindle**   The reading tablet that allows you to buy books when traveling in China behind the Great Firewall.

The first two are just beyond toys in a sense, but as a lot of innovation it starts with a smaller group and then grows mainstream to more common use cases. Few thought the pager was a good idea when it was introduced, but after proved and tested by doctors, more people wanted it, and then it gradually mutated and became the cell phone. The cell phone was first a niche, but today it is mainstream. We have to look at outliers when finding the future. The point is that we will be able to access and display information anywhere. And everyday objects could be connected to the Internet. You could dress your home with digital wallpaper and buy new patterns for the Caribbean party you are planning for the weekend on WallStore in a while. Desks can easily be screens—for you to put your notes on or pictures of your loved ones. We will wear sensors that help to predict seizures, tell you when you should eat or take insulin, or help you to improve your golf swing.

But it is not just about connected screens or projectors. These give us the material to see the information. There are interesting things happening in how we interact with devices—input technology. Let us look at how touch screen changed the way we talk to machines.

8.1.4   Midas' Touch Screens

Touch screens have been used for quite a while before the advent of the iPhone, but Apple changed us by adopting capacitive screens that allowed us to throw away the stylus, and instead to touch the information with our fingertips. Before touch screens, we interacted with *indirect* manipulations—when you steered your mouse to the YES button, you were channeling through the mouse instead of just touching the screen. Similarly, you clicked "up" on your mobile's four-directional arrow buttons to get further down in the email—you did not swipe the screen, but you let your brain control one object by interacting with another. It is much easier to learn to swipe the content than to touch a button next to it. Why? Because the real world works with *direct* manipulation, when you touch a book you can flip its pages by holding the book, and not by pressing buttons or pulling levers next to it.

So why did it take so long time for mobile phones to add direct manipulation? Because of the cost of hardware needed. As users will not tolerate any latency or lag, the performance need to be immediate. The system must be as responsive as real life. While picking up an object, you would be surprised if you need to wait a second—as if the object was stuck—and then start moving your hand, feeling all "laggy." (The only people used to this in real life are dog owners and parents of small children.)

Touch screens won over buttons as mobile phones got so many functions that you actually could not cram in more buttons. The Nokia N95 had more than 50 unique buttons on a device smaller than a regular deck of cards. So when we got too many functions, the user interface of phones had to become agnostic to its use.

Unfortunately, this has some drawbacks. Ask college students why they buy Blackberries. It is not just for the chat client (Blackberry Messenger), but also for the fact that you can type under the desk, in the pocket, or while biking (yes, people do, the author in particular). So with touch screens that are just one big surface with the user interface rendered dynamically to the context, we suddenly cannot feel what buttons we are touching. We cannot search the keyboard without looking at it, and we cannot develop a "motoric memory" for where the buttons are.

As the screen cannot know your intentions but get the input first when you touch it, we get new problems. Everything becomes an action. On a computer, a user can hover with the mouse over an icon and get more information, as the computer understands your intent. This problem is often called Midas Touch in interaction design language, as the user—like King Midas—cannot touch anything without affecting it (unfortunately, the analogy ends here, things do not turn into gold). The interaction on a computer between the user and the machine has three steps: no interaction, interest, and action. With a touch screen, there is suddenly just two: no action or action. So we lose a lot of fidelity and the computer loses the intent of the user.

8.1.5 New Input, New Opportunities

Things are however cooking. As this is written, there are a lot of things that have been in the lab for more than 10 years that probably will start to work is the coming 10 years—voice input, haptics (which means you could "feel" digital interfaces), and screens that can sense when you are close to them—so you can interact from a distance. Still, these technologies are not mature enough to feel perfectly realistic, but one day they will. Who would have thought a few years ago that for a couple of hundred dollars, one would be able to buy a game console that would interpret your gestures and body language in 2010? Microsoft showed with the XBOX360 Kinect system that the future was closer than we thought. And right now this is in games, but remember how the iPhone changed the way we interact and connect with the Internet. These new ways of interacting will soon have profound effects on everyday life.

8.1.6 Zero-Click and Real-Life User Interfaces

Now input technologies and presentation technologies are starting to blend, so it will be harder to spot the difference where the real life ends and the digital world starts. Mobile phones of today have massive processing power, abundant connectivity, and high-resolution cameras and other sensors all congregated in devices that you could hold in your hand. Suddenly we have high-fidelity input technologies, with great computing power and connectivity always with us. This open fields like visual augmented reality (AR).

Augmented reality means that you add a digital layer "on top of" reality—the most common use is to add information on the image that comes from your camera viewfinder. For example, you can point your mobile to a menu written in a foreign language. Then, the camera will "see" the text, the processor will recognize the characters, send it off for translation, and then add the translation to your language to the image of the menu. Suddenly the mobile phone removed 10 clicks of typing and translating to changing the user's "burden" to just glancing at the screen and looking at the "subtitled" and "augmented" information.

Previously, when the camera was attached to a computer, AR was not as interesting; but when you can hold the "computer" in your hand, the AR turns a mobile phone into a digital looking glass. Like in RoboCop or Terminator, we can look at the world around us and get a digital layer with information about what is around us. We can see where the closest public restroom is, or reviews and ratings on books overlaid on the covers. You can now—without reading all the miniscule text of a can of soup—find out that it contains something you are allergic to. Augmented reality gives us " zero-click user interfaces," where you can glance around you and see more than what the physical world can tell.

Naturally these new opportunities will also create new issues. Fraudsters will do their best to corrupt information and attempt to deceive users. Changes in the user interface will require us to rethink how to protect users.

8.1.7 Privacy and User Interfaces

The changes are not only on the surface, on how we interact with machines or each other, but also in what we talk about. It used to be that people told their most personal things only to close friends, but services like Facebook have changed the way we view private information. As a result of services like these, the question about your mother's maiden name or where you were born might not be such a secret thing anymore. We have gone from the fear of that big brother to a world where all "little brothers" see you. People expose things for people they trust or somehow think they know to the extent that private information is public. But the problem does not end here.

A lot of services of the future will want and need your personal details if they are to create the perfect experience. What is Amazon worth if it does not know what books you have bought or like? What is a site like PatientsLikeMe if you do not tell it what you suffer from, and maybe even how old you are, what you eat, and if any relatives suffer from similar illnesses?

8.1.8 It all Comes Together

Today, technology surrounds us, and we become more dependent on it. As a result of using technology more often, we remove a lot of barriers to usage. This means, for example, that people want the computer to autoinput passwords, addresses, and credit card details. To turn computers into the perfect servants, we must let them inside our minds. They should know what we want before we utter it.

Maintaining security and privacy in that context will pose new challenges. New services and user interfaces will pose both opportunities and complications. Most of all, those who create services and products need to remember that adding barriers in form of complex passwords or special security hardware commonly means that users will circumvent the security measures to simplify the usage. People do all kinds of "tricks"— forward mail from secure systems to private email accounts to access without VPN, reuse passwords, print secret documents to read on the plane, and write passwords on post-its.

> Frankly, we need to make security user friendly, as the easiest path wins. Barriers will be circumvented, so the secure way does not only need to be the best from security standpoint but also from the users' view point.

8.2 FRAUD AND THE FUTURE

Markus Jakobsson

What will happen next year? What will happen in 10 years, in *20*? We can all prophesize. Without the supporting logic for our predictions, however, prophesies are not very meaningful. Why should you trust *my* prediction if I cannot support it? So before discussing trends and predictions, we need to state our assumptions, explain the inferences, and describe how things relate to each other.

> The best way of predicting the future might be to think in terms of *technology, capabilities,* and *goals*. State your assumptions and explore the logical consequences.

Let us take a look at what I mean, and let us focus on the big picture.

On the technology side, I believe that we will see a greater adoption of ever-smaller consumer devices that do more and more. These devices are already phones, music players, and cameras, but they will soon also be collectors of health data, tools for marking up the world we see, and personal portals to the increasing amount of information we acquire. The media files you generate, your geolocations throughout the day, your preferences—online and offline. What you want to know about a situation, and what you do not want to know.

User interfaces are an important enabler of capabilities. The user interfaces of tomorrow will enable quick decisions, and users will become accustomed to *making* quick decisions. This, in turn, will make social engineering easier. All it will take is a short moment of weakness or confusion. We will always carry these devices with us, and we will see the world through them—marked up with the information we find valuable. Attackers will corrupt the markups to deceive us to see and do what they want us to.

Capabilities are also about access to information and resources. Information will be increasingly accessible—whether we are talking about information that society *wants* to be available and that which most people do not want. Examples of the former may be geolocation data and self-published data, such as social networking data. Examples of the latter might be leaked databases, stolen credentials, and harmful data derived from seemingly innocuous data. Any information that has ever been published—and its logical consequences—will be available at the tip of a finger.

Users will be able to *act* on this information and be *used to* doing it. Attackers will be able to spoof situations that require user action. Increased capabilities for users imply increased risks of social engineering, and increased capabilities for attackers will make it easier for them to deceive users. As attackers successfully deceive users, they gain access to resources—accounts, databases, knowledge, and so on.

Let us then consider *goals*. Throughout the book, we have argued that there are a tremendous number of ways in which fraudsters can deceive, steal, and monetize. To criminals, the cost of entry is *reduced* as crime flourishes. The more the criminals there are, the less likely it is for each particular criminal to be caught—given the constant resources for detection and prosecution. At the same time, the more the crime there is, the greater the burden is for the honest user. There is a tipping point at which he or she will become hesitant to engage.

This book has focused almost exclusively on fraud—goals that involve personal profit of attackers. The opportunity to commit fraud will lead to the criminal education of a large segment of competent people. Some of these will decide to take their skills elsewhere—beyond fraud. The natural use might be hacktivism for some. Others will be cyber warriors and cyber terrorists in a new era in which societies, countries, and organizations wage information war with each other. (This may sound like the plot of a cheap movie, and I wish I could believe that it would remain fiction. But I do not.)

These warriors and terrorists may use the tools that fraudsters use to corrupt data and seed uncertainty. They may use the tools to take over part of the infrastructure—air control, the power grid, traffic lights, law enforcement, and tax collection. They may attempt to influence politics. And they may use the tools simply to cause losses and inefficiencies—to hurt the economic backbones of the societies they attack.

Imagine a future in which our every move is monitored; where attacks are cleverly tailored to each victim; and where detecting and avoiding deceit becomes a daily activity. Imagine constant bombardment and fear.

How would we react? Most people would probably seek shelter by opting for restricted capabilities and technology that avoids attacks by clamping down on what it can be used for. We would witness the Internet replaced by closed networks, owned by countries and corporate conglomerates, running carefully screened applications owned by the same countries and conglomerates. We would witness the death of the Internet.

We would see the death of the Internet, and with it the freedom of expression, and the insanity and creativity we now associate with computing. How can we stop this? By stopping fraud. This, in turn, means that we have to make security easy and omnipresent. We must use the technology and capabilities to our advantage, and stay ahead of the attackers by anticipating and blocking their attacks. We must make crime risky by identifying and prosecuting criminals. This will require collaboration—between organizations and between governments.

But predicting the future is not everything. Let me end with a quote I love.

Predicting the future is much too easy, anyway. You look at the people around you, the street you stand on, the visible air you breathe, and predict more of the same. To hell with more. I want better.

—Ray Bradbury

If we want better, we need to start by understanding what does wrong, and why. I am hoping that this book will encourage you to be part of this movement.

When thinking about the future—and how to react to anticipated future needs—keep the following questions in mind: How can we put metrics in place to correctly identify likely trends? How can we translate such trends into needs? When do we have to abandon the existing paradigms, and when can we patch what we already have in place? What is really the problem, and *why* does it occur? (We often fool ourselves and think that the problem is different from what it *really* is, and this is one of the reasons we do not counter security threats proactively very well.) And finally, what resources need to be invested in making change? Be realistic; be humble.

References

1. 41st Parameter. http://www.the41.com/.

2. BlueCava. http://www.bluecava.com/.

3. Botnet caught red handed stealing from Google. http://www.theregister.co.uk/2009/10/09/bahama_botnet_steals_from_google.

4. Ettercap. http://ettercap.sourceforge.net.

5. Fine free file command. http://darwinsys.com/file/.

6. Getting around Internet Explorer MIME type mangling. http://weblog.philringnalda.com/2004/04/06/getting-around-ies-mime-type-mangling.

7. HotCRP conference management software. http://www.cs.ucla.edu/ kohler/hotcrp/.

8. How do you use your blackberry series: Password protection on your device. http://crackberry.com/how-do-you-use-your-blackberry-series-password-protection-your-device.

9. ICANN's response to information requested by the GNSO registration abuse policy working group. http://forum.icann.org/lists/gnso-rap-dt/pdfXeJsnntHgG.pdf.

10. Internet Explorer 8 Security Part V: comprehensive protection. http://blogs.msdn.com/ie/archive/2008/09/02/ie8-security-part-vi-beta-2-update.aspx.

11. Internet Explorer 8 Security Part V: comprehensive protection. http://blogs.msdn.com/ie/archive/2008/07/02/ie8-security-part-v-comprehensive-protection.aspx.

12. Internet Explorer facilitates XSS. http://www.splitbrain.org/blog/2007-02/12-internet_explorer_facilitates_cross_site_scripting.

13. List of countries by number of mobile phones in use. http://en.wikipedia.org/wiki/List_of_countries_by_number_of_mobile_phones_in_use.

14. MIME signatures used by content-sniffing algorithms. http://webblaze.cs.berkeley.edu/2009/content-sniffing/.

15. MSDN: MIME type detection in Internet Explorer. http://msdn.microsoft.com/en-us/library/ms775147.aspx.

16. Network stealth router-based botnet. http://dronebl.org/blog/8.

17. Parent guide to cyberbullying and cyberthreats. http://www.cyberbully.org/cyberbully/docs/cbctparents.pdf.

18. Portable Network Graphics specification, w3c/iso/iec version. http://www.libpng.org/pub/png/spec/iso/.

19. Race is on to 'Fingerprint' phones, PCs. http://online.wsj.com/article/SB10001424052748704679204575646704100959546.html.

20. Raising awareness about over-sharing. http://pleaserobme.com/.

21. Sites using mediawiki/en. http://www.mediawiki.org/wiki/Sites_using_MediaWiki/en.

22. Skyhook Wireless. http://www.skyhookwireless.com/.

23. SMF upload XSS vulnerability. http://seclists.org/fulldisclosure/2006/Dec/0079.html.

24. Suicide of Megan Meier. http://en.wikipedia.org/wiki/Suicide_of_Megan_Meier.

25. Understanding Health Information Privacy. http://www.hhs.gov/ocr/privacy/hipaa/understanding/index.html.

26. Wikipedia image use policy. http://en.wikipedia.org/wiki/Image_use_policy.

27. WineHQ. http://www.winehq.org/.

28. Cyberstalking: a new challenge for law enforcement and industry. http://www.justice.gov/criminal/cybercrime/cyberstalking.htm, 1999.

29. ICANN. Registrar Accreditation Agreement (2001). http://www.icann.org/en/registrars/ra-agreement-17may01.htm, 2001.

30. Organisation for Economic Co-operation and Development (OECD). Evolution in the management of country code top-level domain names. http://www.oecd.org/dataoecd/8/18/37730629.pdf, 2006.

31. Registerfly termination notice. http://www.icann.org/en/correspondence/jeffrey-to-medina-16mar07.pdf, March 2007.

32. International Telecommunication Union. *ITU Study on the Financial Aspects of Network Security: Malware and Spam*, 2008.

33. The VeriSign idefense malicious code operations team. iFrame attacks: an examination of the business of iFrame exploitation. VeriSign iDefense, March 2008.

34. ICANN. Contractual Compliance Semi-Annual Report. http://www.icann.org/en/compliance/reports/contractual-compliance-report-24dec09-en.pdf, December 2009.

35. ICANN. Registrar Accreditation Agreement (2009). http://www.icann.org/en/registrars/ra-agreement-21may09-en.htm, 2009.

36. State of spam report. http://eval.symantec.com/mktginfo/enterprise/other_resources/b-state_of_spam_report_07-2009.en-us.pdf, 2009.

37. WDPRS enhancements. http://www.icann.org/en/compliance/archive/update-wdprs-enhancements-09mar11-en.htm, March 2009.

38. Beta test on the IRTP audit plan was conducted in May 2010. http://www.icann.org/en/compliance/archive/compliance-newsletter-201010-en.htm, May 2010.

39. Certificate patrol, 2010. patrol.psyced.org/.

40. Consumer threat alerts, scareware makes cybercrooks hundreds of millions each year. http://blogs.mcafee.com/consumer/consumer-threat-alerts/scareware-makes-cybercrooks-hundreds-of-millions, October 2010.

41. Facebook fuelling divorce, research claims. http://www.telegraph.co.uk/technology/facebook/6857918/Facebook-fuelling-divorce-research-claims.html, 2010.

42. Half of employers 'reject potential worker after look at facebook page'. http://www.telegraph.co.uk/technology/facebook/6968320/Half-of-employers-reject-potential-worker-after-look-at-Facebook-page.html, 2010.

43. How many lines of code does it take to create the Android OS? http://www.gubatron.com/blog/2010/05/23/how-many-lines-of-code-does-it-take-to-create-the-android-os/, May 2010.

44. Kismet + fully functional monitor mode for the n900. http://david.gnedt.eu/blog/2010/05/11/kismet-fully-functional-monitor-mode-for-the-n900/, May 2010.

45. Linux kernel development: how fast it is going, who is doing it, what they are doing, and who is sponsoring it. http://www.linuxfoundation.org/docs/lf_linux_kernel_development_2010.pdf, December 2010.

46. Mobile telephone subscribers per 100 inhabitants, 1997–2007. http://www.itu.int/ITU-D/ict/statistics/material/graphs/Global_ICT_Dev_98-09.jpg, July 2010.

47. Monkeysphere, 2010. web.monkeysphere.info/.

48. ICANN. Notice of expiration of registrar accreditation agreement and non-renewal of accreditation. http://www.icann.org/en/correspondence/burnette-to-prakash-25jun10-en.pdf, June 2010.

49. Obtaining and using evidence from social networking sites. http://www.eff.org/files/filenode/social_network/20100303__crim_socialnetworking.pdf, 2010.

50. Panda Labs Annual Report 2010. www.pandasecurity.com, 2010.

51. UDel Models. http://www.udelmodels.eecis.udel.edu/, July 2010.

52. The VeriSign iDefense intelligence operations team, notable malware for 2010, April 2010.

53. Windows Root Certificate Program Members. http://support.microsoft.com/kb/931125, October 22, 2010.

54. HostExploit. http://hostexploit.com/downloads/view.download/4/14.html, last retrieved in June 2011.

55. ICANN GAC. http://gac.icann.org, last retrieved in June 2011.

56. ICANN. http://www.internic.org/alpha.html, last retrieved in June 2011.

57. ICANN. 5.3 Termination of agreement by ICANN. http://www.icann.org/en/registrars/ra-agreement-21may09-en.htm#5, last retrieved in June 2011.

58. OpenNIC. Access to domains not administered by ICANN. http://www.opennicproject.org/, last retrieved in June 2011.

59. ARPANET dialogues. http://www.arpanetdialogues.net/vol-i/4/, last retrieved in June 2011.

60. ICANN. ccTLD compliance program. http://www.icann.org/en/compliance/cctld-compliance.htm, last retrieved in June 2011.

61. ICANN. Core values. http://www.icann.org/en/general/bylaws.htm#I, last retrieved in June 2011.

62. DARPA, ARPA. http://www.darpa.mil/About/History/ARPA-DARPA_The_Name_Chronicles.aspx, last retrieved in June 2011.

63. Federal Register. Request for comments on the Internet Assigned Numbers Authority (IANA) functions. http://www.ntia.doc.gov/frnotices/2011/fr_ianafunctionsnoi_02252011.pdf, February 2011.

64. IronMountain. Frequently asked questions about the RDE program. http://www.ironmountain.com/resources/escrow/rde_faq.pdf, last retrieved in June 2011.

65. Internet Advertising Bureau. IAB Internet Advertising Revenue Report, 2010 Full Year Results. http://www.iab.net/media/file/IAB_Full_year_2010_0413_Final.pdf, 2011.

66. ICANN be independent. *The Economist*. http://www.economist.com/node/14517430?story_id=14517430, last retrieved in June 2011.

67. ICANN. Uniform domain-name dispute-resolution policy (UDRP). http://www.icann.org/en/udrp/udrp-policy-24oct99.htm, last retrieved in June 2011.

68. Increased number of malware assaults launched via social-networking websites. http://www.spamfighter.com/Increased-Number-of-Malware-Assaults-Launched-via-Social-Networking-Websites-15895-News.htm, 2011.

69. FoxNews. Iran's plan for 'Halal' Internet slammed by U.S.–Iranian group. http://www.foxnews.com/world/2011/04/26/irans-plan-halal-internet-repressive-iranian-group-says/?test=latestnews, April 2011.

70. Iron Mountain and escrow. http://www.tldmagazine.com/icann-considers-bringing-whois-escrow-in-house.html, last retrieved in June 2011.

71. Joint Project Agreement. http://www.ntia.doc.gov/ntiahome/domainname/agreements/jpa/icannjpa_09292006.htm, last retrieved in June 2011.

72. ICANN. Notice of breach of jobs registry agreement. http://icann.org/en/correspondence/burnette-to-johnson-fassett-27feb11-en.pdf, February 2011.

73. ICANN. Principles and guidelines for the delegation and administration of country code top level domains. http://gac.icann.org/system/files/ccTLD_Principles_0.pdf, last retrieved in June 2011.

74. ICANN. Registry information. http://www.icann.org/en/registries/, last retrieved in June 2011.

75. MaxMD. Secure communication for healthcare. http://www.max.md/, last retrieved in June 2011.

76. ICANN. Staff report to GNSO council: experiences with inter-registrar transfer policy. http://www.icann.org/en/transfers/transfer-report-14apr05.pdf, last retrieved in June 2011.

77. FS-ISAC. Threat viewpoint, advanced persistent threat. 2011.

78. ICANN. Transparency and accountability. http://www.icann.org/en/accountability/overview-en.htm, last retrieved in June 2011.

79. US Department of Commerce. Memorandum of Understanding. http://www.ntia.doc.gov/ntiahome/domainname/icann-memorandum.htm, last retrieved in June 2011.

80. ICANN. WHOIS Access Audit Report (Port 43). http://www.icann.org/en/compliance/archive/whois-access-audit-report-port43-06apr11-en.pdf, April 2011.

81. A. Acquisti and R. Gross. Imagined communities: awareness, information sharing, and privacy on the Facebook. Lecture Notes in Computer Science, Vol. 4258; Springer, Berlin 2006.

82. A. Acquisti and R. Gross. Predicting Social Security numbers from public data. *Proceedings of the National Academy of Sciences*, 106(27):10975, 2009.

83. A. Adams and M. A. Sasse. Users are not the enemy. *Communications of the ACM*, 42:40–46, 1999.

84. Adobe Systems. Cross-Domain Policy File specification. http://learn.adobe.com/wiki/download/attachments/64389123/CrossDomain_PolicyFile_Specification.pdf, August 2010.

85. Adometry. Adometry click fraud index. http://www.adometry.com/media/press/release.php?id=1, 2011.

86. D. Ahmad. Two years of broken crypto: Debian's dress rehearsal for a Global PKI compromise. *IEEE Security and Privacy*, 6:70–73, 2008.

87. M. Alicherry and A. D. Keromytis. Doublecheck: multi-path verification against man-in-the-middle attacks. *ISCC 2009: IEEE Symposium on Computers and Communications*, IEEE, Piscataway, NJ, 2009, pp. 557–563.

88. D. Amitay. Big brother removed from app store. http://amitay.us/, Jun 14, 2011.

89. Android Bug Report. Internet access without permission. http://code.google.com/p/android/issues/detail?id=8007.

90. M. Anka. SSL Blacklist 4.0. www.codefromthe70s.org/sslblacklist.aspx, January 31, 2010.

91. J. Arkko and P. Nikander. Weak authentication: how to authenticate unknown principals without trusted parties. In: B. Christianson, B. Crispo, J. A. Malcolm, and M. Roe, editors, *Security Protocols Workshop*, *Lecture Notes in Computer Science*, Vol. 2845, Springer, 2002, pp. 5–19.

92. F. Asgharpour and M. Jakobsson. Adaptive challenge questions algorithm in password reset/recovery. *First International Workshop on Security for Spontaneous Interaction*, September 2007.

93. F. Asgharpour, D. Liu, and L. J. Camp. Mental models of security risks. *Proceedings of the 11th International Conference on Financial Cryptography and 1st International Conference on Usable Security*, FC'07/USEC'07, Springer, Berlin, 2007, pp. 367–377.

94. R. Axelrod. The dissemination of culture: a model with local convergence and global polarization. *Journal of Conflict Resolution*, 41(2):203–226, 1997.

95. P. Bahl and V. N. Padmanabhan. RADAR: an in-building RF-based user location and tracking system. *IEEE INFOCOM*, Vol. 2, Citeseer, 2000, pp. 775–784.

96. P. Bahl, V. N. Padmanabhan, and A. Balachandran. Enhancements to the RADAR user location and tracking system, Technical Report MSR-TR-2000-12, Microsoft Research, 2000.

97. M. Baldwin. #Followfriday: The anatomy of a Twitter trend. http://mashable.com/2009/03/06/twitter-followfriday/, March 2006.

98. J. Baltazar, J. Costoya, and R. Flores. The heart of KOOBFACE: C&C and social network propagation. http://us.trendmicro.com/imperia/md/content/us/trendwatch/researchandanalysis/the_20heart_20of_20koobface_final_1_.pdf, 2009.

99. J. Baltazar, J. Costoya, and R. Flores. The real face of KOOBFACE: the largest web 2.0 botnet explained. Trend Micro Threat Research, 2009.

100. P. S. Bance. SSL: whom do you trust? www.minstrel.org.uk/papers/2005.04.20-ssl-trust.pdf. April 20, 2005.

101. G. Bard. Spelling-error tolerant, order-independent pass-phrases via the Damerau–Levenshtein string-edit distance metric. *Proceedings of the Fifth Australasian Information Security Workshop (Privacy Enhancing Technologies)* , Australian Computer Society, Inc., 2007.

102. A. Barrat, M. Barthelemy, and A. Vespignani. *Dynamical Processes on Complex Networks*. Cambridge University Press, 2008.

103. M. Barrett. Cybercrime: and what we will have to do if we want to get it under control. publius.cc/cybercrime_and_what_we_will_have_do_if_we_want_get_it_under_control.pdf, www.publius.cc, July, 2008.

104. A. Barth. HTTP State Management Mechanism. IETF Request for Comments, RFC6265. http://tools.ietf.org/html/rfc6265, . April 2011.

105. A. Barth. The web origin concept. IETF Internet-Draft (work in progress,). http://tools.ietf.org/html/draft-ietf-websec-origin, June 2011.

106. A. Barth, J. Caballero, and D. Song. Secure Content Sniffing for Web Browsers *or* How to Stop Papers from Reviewing Themselves. In *Proceedings of the 30th IEEE Symposium on Security & Privacy*, Oakland, CA, May 2009.

107. A. Barth, C. Jackson, and W. Li. Attacks on JavaScript Mashup Communication. *Proceedings of the Web 2.0 Security and Privacy*, Oakland, CA, May 2009.

108. J. Bartona, E. Speltena, P. Totterdella, L. Smith, and S. Folkarda. Is there an optimum number of night shifts? Relationship between sleep, health and well-being? *Work and Stress*, 9(2):109–123, 1995.

109. J. Bayuk, editor. Analyzing Malicious Software in Cyberforensics. *CyberForensics: Understanding Information Security Investigations*, chapter Springer, 2010.

110. M. Beck and E. Tews. Practical attacks against WEP and WPA. *Second ACM Conference on Wireless Network Security*, Zurich, Switzerland, March 16–18, 2009.

111. V. Bellotti and A. Sellen. Design for privacy in ubiquitous computing environments. *Proceedings of the Third Conference on European Conference on Computer-Supported Cooperative Work*, Kluwer Academic Publishers, Norwell, MA, 1993, pp. 77–92.

112. A. Benczur, C. Castillo, Z. Gyongyi, and J. Masanes. Overview of the ECML/PKDD discovery challenge 2010 on web quality. http://www.ecmlpkdd2010.org/indexd7fa.html, September 2010.

113. F. Benevenuto, G. Magno, T. Rodrigues, and V. Almeida. Detecting spammers on twitter. *CEAS 2010: Seventh Annual Collaboration, Electronic Messaging, Anti- Abuse and Spam Conference*, Redmond, WA, June 2010, pp. 1–9.

114. T. Berners-Lee, R. T. Fielding, and L. Masinter. Uniform Resource Identifier (URI): generic syntax. IETF Request for Comments, RFC3986. http://tools.ietf.org/html/rfc3986, January 2005.

115. S. Berry. One in five use birthday as PIN number. *Daily Telegraph*, October 27, 2010.

116. Y. Bhattacharjee. How a remote town in Romania has become cybercrime central. http://www.wired.com/magazine/2011/01/ff_hackerville_romania/, February 2011.

117. M. Bishop. Security: threats and solutions. Presentation to share 86.0, 1996.

118. J. Bollen, H. Mao, and X. Zeng. Twitter mood predicts the stock market. *Journal of Computational Science*, 2(1):1–8, 2011.

119. J. Bonneau. Measuring password re-use empirically. http://www.lightbluetouchpaper.org/2011/02/09/measuring-password-re-use-empirically/, 2011.

120. D. Boyd, S. Golder, and G. Lotan. Tweet, tweet, retweet: conversational aspects of retweeting on Twitter. *Proceedings of the 43rd Hawaii International Conference on System Sciences*, IEEE Computer Society 2010, pp. 1–10.

121. S. Brin and L. Page. The anatomy of a large-scale hypertextual web search engine. *Seventh International World-Wide Web Conference (WWW 1998)*, 1998.

122. G. Bruen. ccTLD research. http://www.knujon.com/ccTLD_Research_knujon_052109.pdf, September 2009.

123. G. Bruen. ICANN meeting transcript. http://brussels38.icann.org/meetings/brussels2010/transcript-atlarge-registrars-23jun10-en.pdf, June 2010.

124. G. Bruen. KnujOn Internet security audit. www.knujon.com/knujon_audit0610.pdf, June 2010.

125. G. Bruen. Policy failure enables mass malware. CircleID. http://www.circleid.com/posts/20100922_policy_failure_enables_mass_malware_part_i_rx_partners_vipmeds/, September 2010.

126. G. Bruen. Proxy-privacy use higher for illicit domains. CircleID. http://www.circleid.com/posts/20110310_proxy_privacy_user_higher_for_illicit_domains/, March 2010.

127. G. Bruen. Should a domain name registrar run from a PO Box? CircleID. http://www.circleid.com/posts/should_a_domain_name_registrar_run_from_a_po_box/, January 2010.

128. W. E. Burr, D. F. Dodson, R. A. Perlner, W. T. Polk, S. Gupta, E. A. Nabbus, C. M. Gutierrez, J. M. Turner, and A. Director. Draft i draft special publication 800-63-1 electronic authentication guideline, 2008.

129. A. Burstein and N. Good. Documentation review of the Sequoia voting system, July 2007.

130. E. Bursztein, R. Beauxis, H. Paskov, D. Perito, C. Fabry, and J. Mitchell. The failure of noise-based non-continuous audio captchas. *IEEE Symposium on Security and Privacy (SP)*, Berkeley, CA, May 2011, pp. 19–31.

131. E. Bursztein and S. Bethard. Decaptcha: breaking 75% of eBay audio CAPTCHAs. *Proceedings of the 3rd USENIX Conference on Offensive Technologies*, USENIX Association, 2009, p. 8.

132. E. Bursztein, S. Bethard, J. C. Mitchell, D. Jurafsky, and C. Fabry. How good are humans at solving CAPTCHAs? A large scale evaluation. *Security and Privacy*, 2010.

133. M. Bussiere and M. Fratzscher. Low probability, high impact: policy making and extreme events. *Journal of Policy Modeling*, 30(1):111–121, 2008.

134. E. Butler. Firesheep. http://codebutler.com/firesheep, October 2010.

135. J. Caballero, S. McCamant, A. Barth, and D. Song. Extracting models of security-sensitive operations using string-enhanced white-box exploration on binaries. Technical Report UCB/EECS-2009-36, EECS Department, University of California, Berkeley, March 2009.

136. C. Cadar, V. Ganesh, P. M. Pawlowski, D. L. Dill, and D. R. Engler. EXE: automatically generating inputs of death. *Proceedings of the ACM Conference on Computer and Communications Security*, Alexandria, VA, October 2006.

137. L. Carettoni, C. Merloni, and S. Zanero. Studying bluetooth malware propagation: the BlueBag project. *IEEE Security and Privacy*, 5(2):17–25, 2007.

138. C. Castellano, S. Fortunato, and V. Loreto. Statistical physics of social dynamics. *Reviews of Modern Physics*, 81(2):591–646, 2009.

139. C. Castillo, M. Mendoza, and B. Poblete. Information credibility on twitter. *WWW 2011*, January 2011, pp. 1–10.

140. C. Catizone. Letter to Sarah Akhtar Cooper, enom. National Association of Boards of Pharmacy. http://www.legitscript.com/download/NABP-Letter-to-eNom.pdf, December 2008.

141. M. Cha, H. Haddadi, F. Benevenuto, and K. P. Gummadi. Measuring user influence in Twitter: the million follower fallacy. *Proceedings of the International AAAI Conference on Weblogs and Social Media*, March 2010, pp. 1–8.

142. D. Chartier. Court awards Verizon $33 million in cybersquatting squabble. http://arstechnica.com/old/content/2008/12/court-awards-verizon-33-million-in-cybersquatting-squabble.ars, December 2008.

143. K. Chellapilla, K. Larson, P. Simard, and M. Czerwinski. Building segmentation based human-friendly human interaction proofs. *2nd International Workshop on Human Interaction Proofs*, Springer, 2005.

144. K. Chellapilla, K. Larson, P. Simard, and M. Czerwinski. Computers beat humans at single character recognition in reading based Human Interaction Proofs (HIPs). CEAS, 2005.

145. K. Chellapilla and P. Y. Simard. Using machine learning to break visual HIPs. *Conference on Neural Information Processing Systems,* 2004.

146. K. Chellapilla and P. Y. Simard. Using machine learning to break visual Human Interaction Proofs (HIPs). *Advances in Neural Information Processing Systems*, 17:265–272, 2004.

147. E. Chien. Techniques of adware and spyware. *Proceedings of the Fifteenth Virus Bulletin Conference*, Dublin Ireland, Vol. 47, 2005.

148. E. Chin, A. P. Felt, K. Greenwood, and D. Wagner. Analyzing inter-application communication in Android. *MobiSys*, 2011.

149. Y.-G. Choi, J. Kang, and D. Nyang. Proactive code verification protocol in wireless sensor network. *ICCSA (2)*, 2007, pp.1085–1096.

150. R. Chow, M. Jakobsson, R. Masuoka, J. Molina, Y. Niu, E. Shi, and Z. Song. Authentication in the Clouds: a framework and its application to mobile users. *CCSW*, 2010.

151. S. Christey, B. Martin, M. Brown, A. Paller, and D. Kirby. 2010 CWE/SANS Top 25 most dangerous software errors. http://cwe.mitre.org/top25/, December 2010.

152. S. Christey and R. A. Martin. Vulnerability type distributions in CVE, http://cve.mitre.org/docs/vuln-trends/index.html, May 2007.

153. Z. Chu, S. Gianvecchio, H. Wang, and S. Jajodia. Who is tweeting on Twitter: human, bot, or cyborg? *ACSAC '10: Proceedings of the 26th Annual Computer Security Applications Conference*, December 2010, p. 21.

154. R. A. Clarke and R. Knake. Cyber war: the next threat to national security and what to do about it. HarperCollins, 2010.

155. M. Cloppert. Evolution of apt state of the art and intelligence-driven response. US Digital Forensic and Incident Response Summit 2010, SANS. http://computer-forensics.sans.org, 2010.

156. T. Close. Petname tool, 2005. www.waterken.com/user/PetnameTool/.

157. comScore, Inc. comScore Media Metrix Ranks Top 50 U.S. Web Properties for March 2011. http://www.comscore.net/content/download/8377/145071/file/comScore0Metrix April 2011.

158. M. Conover, J. Ratkiewicz, M. Francisco, B. Gonçalves, A. Flammini, and F. Menczer. Political polarization on Twitter. *Proceedings of the Fifth International AAAI Conference on Weblogs and Social Media*, 2011.

159. CircleID. G. Cook. Is China preparing to go its own way with its own Internet root? http://www.circleid.com/posts/813112_china_internet_root_ipv9/, January 2008.

160. CircleID. A. V. Couvering. Will blocking a TLD fracture the internet? http://www.circleid.com/posts/20110412_will_blocking_a_tld_fracture_the_internet/, April 2011.

161. J. Cowie. Egypt leaves the Internet. http://www.renesys.com/blog/2011/01/egypt-leaves-the-internet.shtml, January 2011.

162. L. F. Cranor. A framework for reasoning about the human in the loop. *Proceedings of the 1st Conference on Usability, Psychology, and Security*, USENIX Association, Berkeley, CA, 2008, pp. 1:1–1:15.

163. R. Cringely. Google, Facebook, privacy, and China. http://www.pcworld.com/article/187259/google_facebook_privacy_and_china.html, January 2010.

164. B. Crispo and M. Lomas. A certification scheme for electronic commerce. *Security Protocols International Workshop*, Springer, 1996.

165. A. Cser, J. Penn, P. Stamp, A. Herald, and A. Dill. Identity Management Market Forecast: 2007 to 2014: provisioning will extend its dominance of market revenues. www.forrester.com, February 6, 2008.

166. R. G. D'Andrade. *The Development of Cognitive Anthropology*, Cambridge University Press, 2005.

167. N. Daswani and M. Stoppelman. The anatomy of Clickbot.A. *USENIX Hotbots07*, 2007.

168. P. Davidson. Cyberspies have hacked into power grid, officials say. http://www.usatoday.com/money/industries/energy/2009-04-08-power-grid-hackers_N.htm, 2009.

169. R. Dawkins. *The Selfish Gene*, Oxford, 1976.

170. R. Dhamija, J. D. Tygar, and M. Hearst. Why phishing works. *CHI*, ACM Press, 2006.

171. T. Dierks and C. Allen. The TLS Protocol Version 1.0. RFC 2246 (Proposed Standard), January 1999. Obsoleted by RFC 4346, updated by RFCs 3546, 5746.

172. T. Dierks and E. Rescorla. The Transport Layer Security (TLS) Protocol Version 1.2. IETF Request for Comments, RFC5246. http://tools.ietf.org/html/rfc5246, August 2008.

173. P. Diwanji. Detecting suspicious account activity. The Official Gmail Blog. gmailblog.blogspot.com/2010/03/detecting-suspicious-account-activity.html, March 24, 2010.

174. J. Donath and D. Boyd. Public displays of connection. *BT Technology Journal*, 22:71–82, 2004.

175. K. Dorrain. National arbitration forum comments on Uniform Domain Name Dispute Resolution Policy (UDRP). https://community.icann.org/download/attachments/13863844/Forum+Suggestions+for+UDRP.pdf?version=1&modificationDate=1304698591000, February 2011.

176. T. d'Otreppe. Aircrack-ng. http://www.aircrack-ng.org/.

177. H. Ebbinghaus. *Memory: A Contribution to Experimental Psychology*, Columbia University, 1885.

178. B. Edelman. Large-scale intentional invalid WHOIS data. Berkman Center for Internet & Society at Harvard Law School. http://cyber.law.harvard.edu/archived_content/people/edelman/invalid-whois/, June 2002.

179. B. Eich. The Origin of Origin and the Same Origin Policy. Private communication, June 2011.

180. J. Elson, J. R. Douceur, J. Howell, and J. Saul. Asirra: a CAPTCHA that exploits interest-aligned manual image categorization. *Proceedings of the 14th ACM Conference on Computer and Communications Security*, Association for Computing Machinery, Inc., 2007.

181. C. Emerson. Wasting time in cyberspace: the UDRP's inefficient approach toward arbitrating Internet domain name disputes. University of Baltimore Law Review. https://litigation-essentials.lexisnexis.com/webcd/app?action=DocumentDisplay&crawlid=1&doctype=cite&docid=34+U.+Balt.+L.+Rev.+161&srctype=smi&srcid=3B15&key=c9512dfdc94285e023e6ed1934eb04d4, 2004.

182. K. Engert. Conspiracy: A Mozilla Firefox extension. kuix.de/conspiracy/, March 18, 2010.

183. J. M. Epstein and R. L. Axtell. *Growing Artificial Societies: Social Science from the Bottom Up*, MIT Press, 1996.

184. Facebook Help Center. Privacy settings and fundamentals. https://www.facebook.com/help/?faq=15685&ref_query=security.

185. A. P. Felt, K. Greenwood, and D. Wagner. The effectiveness of install-time permission systems for third-party applications. EECS Department, University of California at Berkeley, Berkeley, CA, Dec. 2010.

186. E. Felten. Web certification fail: bad assumptions lead to bad technology. *Freedom To Tinker*. www.freedom-to-tinker.com/blog/felten/web-certification-fail-bad-assumptions-lead-bad-technology, February 23, 2010.

187. N. Fielding and I. Cobain. Revealed: US spy operation that manipulates social media. http://www.guardian.co.uk/technology/2011/mar/17/us-spy-operation-social-networks, March 2011.

188. R. T. Fielding, J. Gettys, J. C. Mogul, H. F. Nielsen, L. Masinter, P. J. Leach, and T. Berners-Lee. Hypertext Transfer Protocol — HTTP/1.1. IETF Request for Comments, RFC2616. http://tools.ietf.org/html/rfc2616, June 1999.

189. Flickr Photo Sharing. http://flickr.com/.

190. S. Flinn and J. Lumsden. User perceptions of privacy and security on the web. *PST'05*, 2005, p. 1.

191. D. Florêncio and C. Herley. A large-scale study of web password habits. *Proceedings of the 16th International Conference on World Wide Web*, WWW '07, ACM, New York, NY, 2007, pp. 657–666.

192. D. A. F. Florêncio and C. Herley. A large-scale study of web password habits. *WWW'07*, 2007, 657–666.

193. T. Frankel. Accountability and oversight of the Internet Corporation for Assigned Names and Numbers (ICANN). http://www.tamarfrankel.com/support-files/markle-report.pdf, July 2002.

194. J. Franklin, V. Paxson, A. Perrig, and S. Savage. An inquiry into the nature and causes of the wealth of Internet miscreants. *Proceedings of the 14th ACM Conference on Computer and Communications Security*, 2007.

195. N. Freed and N. Borenstein. RFC 2045: Multipurpose Internet Mail Extensions (MIME) Part One: Format of Internet Message Bodies, November 1996.

196. N. Freed and N. Borenstein. RFC 2046: Multipurpose Internet Mail Extensions (MIME) Part Two: Media Types, November 1996.

197. M. Froomkin. Wrong turn in cyberspace: using ICANN to route around the APA and the constitution. http://osaka.law.miami.edu/froomkin/articles/icann.pdf, 2000.

198. M. Froomkin. The extent to which registries and registrars control ICANN. http://osaka.law.miami.edu/froomkin/articles/icann-antitrust.pdf, August 2003.

199. S. Galam. Modelling rumors: the no plane pentagon French hoax case. *Physica A*, 320:571, 2003.

200. M. P. Gallaher, A. N. Link, and B. R. Rowe. *Cyber Security, Economic Strategies and Public Policy Alternatives*. Edward Elgar, 2008.

201. M. Gandhi, M. Jakobsson, and J. Ratkiewicz. Badvertisements: stealthy click-fraud with unwitting accessories. *Journal of Digital Forensics Practice*, 1(2): 2006, 2006.

202. V. Ganesh and D. Dill. A decision procedure for bit-vectors and arrays. *Proceedings of the Computer Aided Verification Conference*, Berlin, Germany, August 2007.

203. J. A. Garay and L. Huelsbergen. Software integrity protection using timed executable agents. *ASIACCS '06: Proceedings of the 2006 ACM Symposium on Information, Computer and Communications Security*, ACM, New York, NY, 2006, pp. 189–200.

204. D. Gardner. The marriage killer: one in five American divorces now involve Facebook. http://www.dailymail.co.uk/news/article-1334482/The-marriage-killer-One-American-divorces-involve-Facebook.html, 2010.

205. R. Gardner, S. Garera, and A. D. Rubin. On the difficulty of validating voting machine software with software. *EVT'07: Proceedings of the USENIX Workshop on Accurate Electronic Voting Technology*, USENIX Association, Berkeley, CA, 2007 p. 11.

206. M. S. Gast. *802.11 Wireless Networks: The Definitive Guide*, O'Reilly Media, Inc., 2005.

207. S. Gaw and E. W. Felten. Password management strategies for online accounts. *Proceedings of the Second Symposium on Usable Privacy and Security*, SOUPS '06, ACM, New York, NY, 2006, pp. 44–55.

208. D. E. Geer and D. G. Conway. The owned price index. *IEEE Security & Privacy*, 7(1):86–87, 2009.

209. G.-G. Geng, X.-B. Jin, X.-C. Zhang, and D. Zhang. Evaluating web content quality via multi-scale features. *Proceedings of the ECML/PKDD 2010 Discovery Challenge*, SpringerLink, 2010.

210. Georgia Tech Information Security Center. Emerging cyber threats report for 2009, October 2008.

211. E. Gerck. Overview of certification systems: X.509, PKIX, CA, PGP and SKIP. *The Bell*, 1(3):8 2000.

212. J. Giles. Twitter tool roots out disguised mass postings. http://www.newscientist.com/article/dn19649-twitter-tool-roots-out-disguised-mass-postings.html, October 2010.

213. D. K. Gillmor. Technical architecture shapes social structure: an example from the real world. lair.fifthhorseman.net/dkg/tls-centralization/, February 21, 2007.

214. Gnucitzien. More advanced clickjacking: UI redress attacks. www.gnucitizen.org/blog/more-advanced-clickjacking-ui-redress-attacks/, 2008.

215. P. Godefroid, N. Klarlund, and K. Sen. DART: directed automated random testing. *Proceedings of the SIGPLAN Conference on Programming Language Design and Implementation*, Chicago, IL, June 2005.

216. P. Godefroid, M. Y. Levin, and D. Molnar. Automated whitebox fuzz testing. *Proceedings of the Annual Network and Distributed System Security Symposium*, San Diego, CA, February 2008.

217. P. Golle. Machine learning attacks against the ASIRRA CAPTCHA. *CCS'08*, ACM, New York, 2008.

218. B. Gonçalves and J. J. Ramasco. Human dynamics revealed through web analytics. *Physical Review E*, 78:026123, 2008.

219. B. Gonçalves and J. J. Ramasco. Towards the characterization of individual users through web analytics. *Complex Systems*, 5:2247–2254, 2009.

220. N. S. Good, J. Grossklags, D. K. Mulligan, and J. A. Konstan. Noticing notice: a large-scale experiment on the timing of software license agreements. *Proceedings of the SIGCHI Conference on Human Factors in Computing Systems*, CHI '07, ACM, New York, NY, 2007.

221. V. Gratzer and D. Naccache. Alien vs. quine. *IEEE Security and Privacy*, 5(2):26–31, 2007.

222. R. Greenstadt and J. Beal. Cognitive security for personal devices. AISec'08, ACM, New York, 2008.

223. C. Grier, K. Thomas, V. Paxson, and M. Zhang. @spam: The underground on 140 characters or less. *CCS '10*, ACM, New York, 2010, p. 27.

224. M. Griesinger. Lets finally end registrar secrecy in RAA. http://www.atlarge.icann.org/node/1987, November 2008.

225. V. Griffith and M. Jakobsson. Messin' with Texas: deriving mothers maiden names using public records. *Applied Cryptography and Network Security*, Springer, 2005.

226. I. Grigg. VeriSign's conflict of interest creates new threat. *Financial Cryptography*. financialcryptography.com/mt/archives/000206.html, September 1, 2004.

227. I. Grigg. PKI considered harmful. http://iang.org/ssl/pki_considered_harmful.html, October 14, 2008.

228. I. Grigg. Why the browsers must change their old SSL security (?) model. *Financial Cryptography*. financialcryptography.com/mt/archives/001232.html, March 24, 2010.

229. I. Grigg and A. Shostack. VeriSign and conflicts of interest. forum.icann.org/lists/net-rfp-verisign/msg00008.html, February 2, 2005.

230. E. Griswold. The right to be let alone. 55 NW.U.L. REV. 216, 1960.

231. J. Grossman. Clickjacking: web pages can see and hear you. http://jeremiahgrossman.blogspot.com/2008/10/clickjacking-web-pages-can-see-and-hear.html, October 2008.

232. Group-IB. "Russian" market of computer crimes in 2010: current state and trends. http://www.group-ib.ru/wp-content/uploads/2011/03/GIB-Issl-rynka_2010.pdf, last retrieved in March 2011.

233. L. Gu, X. Ding, R. H. Deng, B. Xie, and H. Mei. Remote attestation on program execution. *STC '08: Proceedings of the 3rd ACM Workshop on Scalable Trusted Computing*, ACM, New York, NY, 2008, pp. 11–20.

234. W. J. Haga and M. Zviran. Question-and-answer passwords: an empirical evaluation. *Information Systems*, 16(3):335–343, 1991.

235. M. Hall, E. Frank, G. Holmes, B. Pfahringer, P. Reutemann, and I. H. Witten. The WEKA data mining software: an update. *ACM SIGKDD Explorations* Newsletter, 11(1):10–18, 2009.

236. S. Hansell. How hackers snatch real-time security ID numbers. www.nytimes.com, August 20, 2009.

237. B. Hansen. ICANN sued by irate registerfly customer, as class action rumble begins. http://www.theregister.co.uk/2007/03/28/icann_lisbon_lawsuit_registerfly, March 2007.

238. R. Hansen. Clickjacking. ha.ckers.org/blog/[20080915/clickjacking].

239. S. Havlin. Phone infections. *Science*, 324(5930): 1023–1024, 2009.

240. J. M. Hayes. The problem with multiple roots in web browsers: certificate masquerading. *WETICE '98: Proceedings of the 7th Workshop on Enabling Technologies*, IEEE Computer Society, Washington, DC, 1998, pp. 306–313.

241. M. R. Henzinger, R. Motwani, and C. Silverstein. Challenges in web search engines. *SIGIR Forum*, 36:11–22, 2002.

242. C. Herley. So long, and no thanks for the externalities: the rational rejection of security advice by users. *NSPW '09: Proceedings of the 2009 Workshop on New Security Paradigms Workshop*, ACM, New York, 2009, pp. 133–144.

243. C. Herley, P. C. van Oorschot, and A. S. Patrick. Passwords: if we're so smart, why are we still using them? *Financial Cryptography*, 5628: 230–237, 2009.

244. A. Herzberg and A. Jbara. Security and identification indicators for browsers against spoofing and phishing attacks. *ACM Transactions on Internet Technology*, 8(4):1–36, 2008.

245. P. Heymann, G. Koutrika, and H. Garcia-Molina. Fighting spam on social web sites: a survey of approaches and future challenges. *IEEE Internet Computing*, 11(6):36–45, 2007.

246. S. Hinduja and J. Patchin. *Bullying Beyond the Schoolyard: Preventing and Responding to Cyberbullying*, Sage Publications, Thousand Oaks, CA, 2009.

247. J. Hodges, C. Jackson, and A. Barth. Strict Transport Security. lists.w3.org/Archives/Public/www-archive/2009Dec/att-0048/draft-hodges-strict-transport-sec-06.plain.html, December 18 2009.

248. J. Hodges, C. Jackson, and A. Barth. HTTP Strict Transport Security. http://tools.ietf.org/html/draft-ietf-websec-strict-transport-sec, August 2011.

249. C. Honeycutt and S. C. Herring. Beyond microblogging: conversation and collaboration via Twitter. *Proceedings of the 42nd Hawaii International Conference on System Sciences*, Indiana University, Bloomington, IN, 2008, pp. 1–10.

250. A. L. Hors, P. L. Hegaret, L. Wood, G. Nicol, J. Robie, M. Champion, and S. Byrne. Document Object Model (DOM) Level 3 Core Specification. http://www.w3.org/TR/2004/REC-DOM-Level-3-Core-20040407/, April 2004.

251. HRC. National coming out day, 2010.

252. J. Hruska. Report: Inside the Network Architecture of Spam and Malware. http://arstechnica.com/security/news/2008/09/network-architecture-of-malware.ars, September 2009.

253. L.-S. Huang and C. Jackson. Clickjacking attacks unresolved. mayscript blog, July 2011.

254. S.-Y. Huang, Y.-K. Lee, G. Bell, and Z.-h. Ou. A projection-based segmentation algorithm for breaking MSN and YAHOO CAPTCHAs. *Proceedings of the World Congress on Engineering*, Vol. 1. Citeseer, 2008.

255. G. V. Hulme. Malvertising continues to pound legitimate web sites. http://www.csoonline.com/article/675064/malvertising-continues-to-pound-legitimate-web-sites, 2011.

256. E. Ian Hickson. HTML 5 working draft. http://www.w3.org/TR/html5/.

257. ICANN. http://www.icann.org/en/compliance/reports/privacy-proxy-registration-services-study-14sep10-en.pdf, September 2010.

258. ICANN. Board minutes. http://www.icann.org/en/minutes/board-briefing-materials-2-05aug10-en.pdf, August 2010.

259. ICANN. Summary and analysis of first IIC comment period. http://www.icann.org/en/jpa/iic/first-comment-period-summary.htm#capture, last retrieved in June 2011.

260. F. M. Alexander. ccNSO response to NTIA Notice of Inquiry (NOI) on the IANA functions. Office of International Affairs, National Telecommunications and Information Administration U.S. Department of Commerce, Washington, DC, ccnso.icann.org/about/ccnso-response-ntia-noi-iana-29mar11-en.pdf, March 29, 2011.

261. IETF. IAB technical comment on the unique DNS root. http://tools.ietf.org/html/rfc2826, last retrieved in June 2011.

262. Imperva. Consumer password worst practices. http://www.imperva.com/docs/WP_Consumer_Password_Worst_Practices.pdf.

263. P. Ipeirotis. Uncovering an advertising fraud scheme or "The Internet is for porn". http://behind-the-enemy-lines.blogspot.com/2011/03/uncovering-advertising-fraud-scheme.html, 2011.

264. C. Jackson and A. Barth. ForceHTTPS: protecting high-security web sites from network attacks. *WWW '08: Proceeding of the 17th International Conference on World Wide Web*, ACM, New York, NY, 2008, pp. 525–534.

265. A. Jacobs. China requires censorship software on new PCS. *The New York Times*, June 8, 2009. www.nytimes.com/2009/06/09/world/asia/09china.html.

266. A. Jacobs and M. Helft. Google, citing attack, threatens to exit China. http://www.nytimes.com/2010/01/13/world/asia/13beijing.html, last retrieved in June 2011.

267. T. N. Jagatic, N. A. Johnson, M. Jakobsson, and F. Menczer. Social phishing. *Communications of the ACM*, 50(10):94–100, 2007.

268. M. Jakobsson. Modeling and preventing phishing attacks. *Proceedings of the 9th International Conference on Financial Cryptography and Data Security*, Springer, Berlin, 2005.

269. M. Jakobsson. Experimenting on Mechanical Turk: 5 how Tos. http://blogs.parc.com/blog/2009/07/experimenting-on-mechanical-turk-5-how-tos/, July 2009.

270. M. Jakobsson and K.-A. Johansson. Assured detection of malware with applications to mobile platforms. http://dimacs.rutgers.edu/TechnicalReports/abstracts/2010/2010-03.html, 2010.

271. M. Jakobsson and K.-A. Johansson. Retroactive detection of malware with applications to mobile platforms. *HotSec 2010*, USENIX, Washington, DC, August 2010.

272. M. Jakobsson and K.-A. Johansson. Practical and secure software-based attestation. *Workshop on LightSec*, Mountain View, CA, March 14–15, 2011.

273. M. Jakobsson and A. Juels. Server-side detection of malware infection. *New Security Paradigms Workshop (NSPW)*, ACM, Oxford, UK, 2009.

274. M. Jakobsson and W. Leddy. SpoofKiller. http://www.spoofkiller.com.

275. M. Jakobsson and D. Liu. Bootstrapping mobile PINs using passwords. W2SP, 2011.

276. M. Jakobsson and S. Myers. *Phishing and Countermeasures: Understanding the Increasing Problem of Electronic Identity Theft*, Wiley-Interscience, 2006.

277. M. Jakobsson and Z. Ramzan, editors. *Crimeware: Understanding New Attacks and Defenses*, Addison-Wesley Professional, 2008.

278. M. Jakobsson and Z. Ramzan. *Crimeware: Understanding New Attacks and Defenses*, Symantec Press/Addison Wesley, 2008.

279. M. Jakobsson and J. Ratkiewicz. Designing ethical phishing experiments: a study of (ROT13) rOnl query features. *WWW '06: Proceedings of the 15th International Conference on World Wide Web*, ACM, 2006, pp. 513–522.

280. M. Jakobsson, E. Shi, P. Golle, and R. Chow. Implicit authentication for mobile devices. *HotSec '09: Proceedings of the 4th USENIX Workshop on Hot Topics in Security*, USENIX Association, Berkeley, CA, 2009.

281. M. Jakobsson, E. Stolterman, S. Wetzel, and L. Yang. Love and authentication. *CHI '08: Proceeding of the Twenty-Sixth Annual SIGCHI Conference on Human Factors in Computing Systems*, ACM, New York, NY, 2008, 197–200.

282. B. J. Jansen. Click fraud. *Computer*, 40:85–86, 2007.

283. T. Jiang, H. J. Wang, and Y.-C. Hu. Preserving location privacy in wireless LANs. *Proceedings of the 5th International Conference on Mobile Systems, Applications and Services*, ACM, 2007, p. 257.

284. B. Johnson. Internet companies face up to malvertising threat. http://www.guardian.co.uk/technology/2009/sep/25/malvertising, 2009.

285. P. N. Johnson-Laird. Mental models in cognitive science. *Cognitive Science*, 4:71–115, 1980.

286. P. N. Johnson-Laird, V. Girotto, and P. Legrenzi. Mental models: a gentle guide for outsiders. Web article, April 1998. (Mostly concentrates on the problems that humans are susceptible to when they reason as they don't use conventional logic, but rather mental models.)

287. A. N. Joinson. Looking at, looking up or keeping up with people?: motives and use of facebook. *CHI '08: Proceedings of the Twenty-Sixth Annual SIGCHI*

Conference on Human Factors in Computing Systems, ACM, New York, NY, 2008, pp. 1027–1036.

288. M. Just and D. Aspinall. Personal choice and challenge questions: a security and usability assessment. *Proceedings of the 5th Symposium on Usable Privacy and Security*, ACM, 2009, pp. 1–11.

289. D. Kaminsky. Email conversation with author, February 28, 2010.

290. D. Kaminsky, M. L. Patterson, and L. Sassaman. PKI Layer Cake: new collision attacks against the Global X.509 infrastructure. In: R. Sion, editor, *Financial Cryptography and Data Security*, Springer, 2010, pp. 289–303.

291. C. Kanalley. Egypt's Internet shut down, according to reports. http://www.huffingtonpost.com/2011/01/27/egypt-internet-goes-down-_n_815156.html, January 2011.

292. V. Kandylas and A. Dasdan. The utility of tweeted URLs for web search. *Proceedings of the 19th International Conference on World Wide Web (WWW)*, ACM, New York, 2010, p. 1127.

293. C.-M. Karat, C. Halverson, D. Horn, and J. Karat. Patterns of entry and correction in large vocabulary continuous speech recognition systems. *CHI '99: Proceedings of the SIGCHI Conference on Human Factors in Computing Systems*, ACM, New York, NY, 1999, pp. 568–575.

294. C. Karlof, J. D. Tygar, and D. Wagner. Conditioned-safe ceremonies and a user study of an application to web authentication. *SOUPS '09*, ACM, New York, 2009.

295. A. K. Karlson, B. R. Meyers, A. Jacobs, P. Johns, and S. K. Kane. Working overtime: patterns of smartphone and PC usage in the day of an Information Worker. *Pervasive Computing*, Springer, pp. 398–405.

296. D. Kellogg. iPhone vs. Android. *Nielsen Wire*, June 2010.

297. W. Kempton. Two theories of home heat control. *Cognitive Science*, 10(1):75–90, 1986.

298. J. Kim. Realistic mobility modeling and simulation for mobile wireless network in urban environments. Thesis, Faculty of the University of Delaware, 2005.

299. J. Kim, V. Sridhara, and S. Bohacek. Realistic mobility simulation of urban mesh networks. *Ad Hoc Networks*, 7(2):411–430, 2009.

300. H. Kneber. GoDaddy sites hacked. http://blog.sucuri.net/2010/09/godaddy-sites-hacked-myblindstudioinfoonline-com-and-hilary-kneber.html, September 2010.

301. S. Koffman. USSS malware update for FS/ISAC, March 2011.

302. G. Koutrika, F. A. Effendi, Z. Gyöngyi, P. Heymann, and H. Garcia-Molina. Combating spam in tagging systems. *AIRWeb '07: Proceedings of the 3rd International Workshop on Adversarial Information Retrieval on the Web*, ACM, New York, NY, 2007, pp, 57–64.

303. B. Krause, C. Schmitz, A. Hotho, and G. Stumme. The anti-social tagger: detecting spam in social bookmarking systems. *Proceedings of the Fourth International Workshop on Adversarial Information Retrieval on the Web*, ACM, New York, 2008.

304. L. I. Krauss and A. MacGahar. *Computer Fraud and Countermeasures*, Prentice Hall 1979.

305. B. Krebs. EstDomains: a sordid history and a storied CEO. http://voices.washingtonpost.com/securityfix/2008/09/estdomains_a_sordid_history_an.html, September 2008.

306. B. Krebs. 'Stuxnet' worm far more sophisticated than previously thought. http://krebsonsecurity.com/2010/09/stuxnet-worm-far-more-sophisticated-than-previously-thought/, September 2010.

307. B. Krebs. White house calls meeting on rogue online pharmacies. http://krebsonsecurity.com/2010/08/white-house-calls-meeting-on-rogue-online-pharmacies/, August 2010.

308. B. Krishnamurthy, D. Malandrino, and C. E. Wills. Measuring privacy loss and the impact of privacy protection in Web browsing, ACM Press, 2007.

309. B. Krishnamurthy and C. E. Wills. Characterizing privacy in online social networks. *WOSN '08: Proceedings of the First Workshop on Online Social Networks*, ACM, New York, NY, 2008, pp. 37–42.

310. P.-O. Kristensson and S. Zhai. Relaxing stylus typing precision by geometric pattern matching. *IUI '05: Proceedings of the 10th International Conference on Intelligent User Interfaces*, ACM, New York, NY, 2005, pp. 151–158.

311. D. M. Kristol. HTTP Cookies: standards, privacy, and politics. *ACM Transactions on Internet Technology*, 1:151–198, 2001.

312. C. Kuo, S. Romanosky, and L. F. Cranor. Human selection of mnemonic phrase-based passwords. *SOUPS '06: Proceedings of the Second Symposium on Usable Privacy and Security*, ACM, New York, NY 2006, pp. 67–78.

313. P. Laborge. XSS worm hits myspace.com. http://www.securityfocus.com/brief/18, 2005.

314. A. Langley. Opportunistic encryption everywhere. W2SP, 2009.

315. A. Langley. Http strict transport security. https://sites.google.com/a/chromium.org/dev/sts.

316. C. Larsen. Exploiting trust in advertising networks. http://rocket.bluecoat.com/blog/exploiting-trust-advertising-networks, 2010.

317. E. Lawrence. IE8 Security Part VI: Beta 2 Update. http://blogs.msdn.com/ie/archive/2008/09/02/ie8-security-part-vi-beta-2-update.aspx, September 2008.

318. E. Lawrence. IE8 Security Part VII: clickjacking defenses. http://blogs.msdn.com/ie/archive/2009/01/27/ie8-security-part-vii-clickjacking-defenses.aspx, January 2009.

319. E. Lawrence. Combating clickjacking with X-Frame-Options. http://blogs.msdn.com/b/ieinternals/archive/2010/03/30/combating-clickjacking-with-x-frame-options.aspx, March 2010.

320. S. Lawson. ICANN assigns its last IPv4 addresses. http://www.computerworld.com/s/article/9207961/Update_ICANN_assigns_its_last_IPv4_addresses, February 2011.

321. K. Lee, B. D. Eoff, and J. Caverlee. Seven months with the devils: a long-term study of content polluters on twitter. 5th International AAI Conference on Weblogs and Social Media (ICWSM), Barcelona, July 2011.

322. S. Lee and S. Zhai. The performance of touch screen soft buttons. *CHI '09: Proceedings of the 27th International Conference on Human Factors in Computing Systems*, ACM, New York, NY, 2009, pp. 309–318.

323. J. Leskovec, L. A. Adamic, and B. A. Huberman. Dynamics of viral marketing. *ACM Transactions on the Web*, 1(1):5, 2006.

324. J. Leskovec, L. Backstrom, and J. Kleinberg. Meme-tracking and the dynamics of the news cycle. *Proceedings of the 15th ACM SIGKDD International Conference on Knowledge Discovery and Data Mining (KDD)*, ACM, New York, 2009, pp. 497–506.

325. J. Levine. ICANN blows $4.6 million in stock market. http://www.circleid.com/posts/20090203_icann_blows_46_million_stock_market, February 2009.

326. E. Lex, I. Khan, H. Bischof, and M. Granitzer. Assessing the quality of web content. *Proceedings of the ECML/PKDD 2010 Discovery Challenge*, SpringerLink, 2010.

327. M. T. Louw, P. Bisht, and V. Venkatakrishnan. Analysis of hypertext isolation techniques for XSS prevention. *The Web 2.0 Security and Privacy Conference*, IEEE, 2008.

328. J. T. Ma. *Learning to Detect Malicious URLs*. PhD thesis, University of California San Diego, 2011.

329. I. S. MacKenzie and W. Soukoreff. Text entry for mobile computing: models and methods, theory and practice. *Human—Computer Interaction*, 17: 147–198, 2002.

330. M. Mahemoff. Explaining the "don't click" clickjacking Tweetbomb. Mahemoff's blog, February 2009.

331. G. Maone. NoScript. http://noscript.net/.

332. G. Maone. ABE: application boundaries enforcer. http://noscript.net/abe/, 2009.

333. G. Maone. ABE: for web authors. http://noscript.net/abe/web-authors.html, 2009.

334. B. Markines, C. Cattuto, and F. Menczer. Social spam detection. *Proceedings of the 5th International Workshop on Adversarial Information Retrieval on the Web (AIRWeb)*, ACM, 2009.

335. B. Markines, C. Cattuto, F. Menczer, D. Benz, A. Hotho, and G. Stumme. Evaluating similarity measures for emergent semantics of social tagging. *Proceedings of the WWW 2009*, ACM, 2009, pp. 641–650.

336. B. Markines, L. Stoilova, and F. Menczer. Bookmark hierarchies and collaborative recommendation. *Proceedings of the 21st National Conference on Artificial Intelligence (AAAI-06)*, AAAI Press, 2006, pp. 1375–1380.

337. J. Markoff. Surveillance of Skype messages found in China. *The New York Times*, October 1, 2008. www.nytimes.com/2008/10/02/technology/internet/02skype.html.

338. M. Marlinspike. More tricks for defeating SSL in practice. www.blackhat.com/presentations/bh-usa-09/MARLINSPIKE/BHUSA09-Marlinspike-DefeatSSL-SLIDES.pdf, 2009.

339. M. Marlinspike. SSLSNIFF. www.thoughtcrime. org/software/sslsniff/, July 3, 2009.

340. M. Marlinspike. SSLSTRIP. www.thoughtcrime.org/software/sslstrip/, December 18, 2009.

341. R. Mayer, J. Davis, and D. Schoorman. An integrative model of organizational trust. *The Academy of Management Review*, 20(3):709–734, 1995.

342. K. McCarthy. WHOIS in charge? ICANN't tell. http://www.theregister.co.uk/2010/02/17/domain_name_problems/, February 2010.

343. K. McCarthy. 77% of domain registrations stuffed with rubbish. http://www.theregister.co.uk/2010/02/17/domain_name_problems/, last retrieved in June 2011.

344. D. McConnell. Report: Chinese company 'hijacked' U.S. web traffic. http://articles.cnn.com/2010-11-17/us/websites.chinese.servers_1_web-traffic-china-telecom-security-review-commission?_s=PM:US, November 2010.

345. D. McCullagh. Court to FBI: no spying on in-car computers. *CNET News*, November 19, 2003. news.cnet.com/2100-1029_3-5109435.html.

346. D. McCullagh. Porn-friendly .xxx domains are a go. http://news.cnet.com/8301-31921_3-20044839-281.html, March 2011.

347. S. P. McGurk. Securing critical infrastructure in the age of Stuxnet. CSO Data Protection, November 2010.

348. D. L. Medin, N. O. Ross, S. Atran, D. Cox, J. Coley, J. B. Proffitt, and S. Blok. Folkbiology of freshwater fish. *Cognition*, 99(3):237–273, 2006.

349. P. Mell, K. Kent, and J. Nusbaum. Guide to malware incident prevention and handling. NIST SP 800-83, National Institute of Standards and Technology, 2005.

350. J. Menn. Fatal system error: the hunt for the new crime lords who are bringing down the Internet. Perseus Books Group, 2010.

351. Microsoft. Event 1046: cross-site scripting filter. http://msdn.microsoft.com/en-us/library/dd565647%28VS.85%29.aspx.

352. Microsoft. Mitigating cross-site scripting with HTTP-only cookies. http://msdn.microsoft.com/en-us/library/ms533046%28VS.85%29.aspx.

353. C. C. Miller. Seeking to weed out drivel, Google adjusts search engine. http://www.nytimes.com/2011/02/26/technology/internet/26google.html, February 2011.

354. R. Mitchell. Registrars under fire in domain disputes. http://news.idg.no/cw/art.cfm?id=16E03559-1A64-6A71-CE7DC113A7D13775, June 2009.

355. T. M. Mitchell. *Machine Learning*, McGraw Hill, 1997.

356. A. Modine. Verizon awarded $33.15m against cyber-squatter. http://www.theregister.co.uk/2008/12/26/verizon_awarded_33mil_against_onlinenic/, December 2008.

357. F. Monrose, P. Wycko, and A. D. Rubin. Distributed execution with remote audit. *Proceedings of the 1999 ISOC Network and Distributed System Security Symposium*, Internet Society, 1999, pp. 103–113.

358. K. Moore. RFC 2047: Multipurpose Internet Mail Extensions (MIME) Part Three: message header extensions for non-ASCII text, November 1996.

359. M. Motoyama, K. Levchenko, C. Kanich, D. McCoy, G. Voelker, and S. Savage. Re: CAPTCHAs–Understanding CAPTCHA-solving services in an economic context. *Proceedings of the 19th USENIX Conference on Security*, USENIX Association, 2010, p. 28.

360. B. Mungamuru, S. Weis, and H. Garcia-Molina. Should ad networks bother fighting click fraud? (Yes, they should.). Technical Report 2008-24, Stanford InfoLab, July 2008.

361. K. Murhpy. ICANN will not attend white house drugs meeting. http://domainincite.com/icann-will-not-attend-white-house-drugs-meeting, September 2010.

362. K. Murphy. ICANN hires weight loss guru as vice president. http://domainincite.com/icann-hires-weight-loss-guru-as-vice-president, March 2011.

363. K. Murphy. Laos to reclaim .la from Los Angeles? http://domainincite.com/laos-to-reclaim-la-from-los-angeles/, April 2011.

364. E. Mustafaraj and P. Metaxas. From obscurity to prominence in minutes: political speech and real-time search. *Proceedings of the WebSci10: Extending*

the Frontiers of Society On-Line, Raleigh, NC, April 26–27, 2010.

365. M. Namestnikova. Russia took the lead as the most popular source of spam having distributed. http://www.securelist.com/en/analysis/204792148/Spam_report_October_2010, October 2010.

366. M. Naor. Verification of a human in the loop or identification via the turing test. http://www.wisdom.weizmann.ac.il/naor/PAPERS/human.ps, 1997.

367. A. Naylor. Visiting onlinenic's non-office. http://dotsnews.com/domain-name-news/184, December 2008.

368. J. Nazario. 2008 h2 fast flux data. http://forum.icann.org/lists/gnso-ff-pdp-may08/msg00847.html, January 2009.

369. Netscape. Persistent client state: HTTP cookies. http://web.archive.org/web/20020803110822/http://wp.netscape.com/newsref/std/cookie_spec.html, September 1994.

370. Netscape Communications Corporation and Sun Microsystems, Inc. Netscape and Sun announce JavaScript. http://web.archive.org/web/20070916144913/http://wp.netscape.com/newsref/pr/newsrelease67.html, December 1995.

371. Neustar. Neustar DNS. http://www.dnsadvantage.com, last retrieved in June 2011.

372. E. Nigg. Email conversation with author, March 27, 2010.

373. J. Nightingale. SSL question corner. meandering wildly (blog). blog.johnath.com/2008/08/05/ssl-question-corner/, August 5, 2008.

374. V. Nikulin. Web-mining with wilcoxon-based feature selection, ensembling and multiple binary classifiers. Proceedings of the ECML/PKDD 2010 Discovery Challenge, SpringerLink, 2010.

375. NIST Special Publication 800-90. Recommendation for Random Number Generation Using Deterministic Random Bit Generators, National Institute of Standards and Technology, 2006.

376. Y. Niu, F. Hsu, and H. Chen. iPhish: Phishing vulnerabilities on consumer electronics. UPSEC '08, USENIX Association, Berkeley, CA, 2008.

377. Y. Niu, E. Shi, R. Chow, P. Golle, and M. Jakobsson. One experience collecting sensitive mobile data. USER Workshop of SOUPS, Redmond, WA, July 14–16, 2010.

378. Christian Coalition of America. Donate your status voter guide. http://www.cc.org/dyscampaign/donate_your_status_voter_guides, 2010.

379. L. O'Gorman, A. Bagga, and J. Bentley. Call center customer verification by query-directed passwords. 8th International Conference on Financial Cryptography, Springer, 2004.

380. OWASP. The open web application security project. https://www.owasp.org/.

381. A. Ozment, S. E. Schechter, and R. Dhamija. Web sites should not need to rely on users to secure communications. W3C Workshop on Transparency and Usability of Web Authentication, March 2006. http://www.eecs.harvard.edu/stuart/papers/w3c06.pdf.

382. Packet Forensics. Export and re-export requirements. www.packetforensics.com/export.safe, 2009.

383. Packet Forensics. Marketing materials for 5-series products. http://files.cloudprivacy.net/packet-forensics-materials.pdf, 2009.

384. P. Ipeirotis. Uncovering an advertising fraud scheme. Or "the Internet is for porn". http://behind-the-enemy-lines.blogspot.com/2011/03/uncovering-advertising-fraud-scheme.html, March 2011.

385. L. Parfeni. Domain name registration slows down. http://news.softpedia.com/news/Domain-Name-Registration-Slows-Down-122419.shtml, September 2009.

386. PayPal X Developer Network. The application showcase directory. https://www.x.com/community/ppx/showcase/ap_directory.

387. E. Pilkington. Blackmail claim stirs fears over facebook. http://www.guardian.co.uk/business/2007/jul/16/usnews.news, 2007.

388. M. Prandini, M. Ramilli, W. Cerroni, and F. Callegati. Splitting the HTTPS stream to attack secure web connections. IEEE Security & Privacy, 8(6):80–84, 2010.

389. K. Prettyman. Egypt's social media revolution. http://www.deseretnews.com/article/700109077/Egypts-social-media-revolution.html, February 2011.

390. L. Privat. Nielsen: US smartphone penetration to be over 50% in 2011. March 2010.

391. N. Provos, P. Mavrommatis, M. Rajab, and F. Monrose. All your iFrames point to us. Proceedings of the

17th Conference on Security Symposium, USENIX Association, 2008, pp. 1–15.

392. R. Quigley. Libyan turmoil could be trouble for bit.ly, .ly domains. http://www.geekosystem.com/libya-bitly-ly-domains, February 2011.

393. E. L. Quinn. Privacy and the new energy infrastructure. http://ssrn.com/abstract=1370731, February 2009.

394. A. Rabkin. Personal knowledge questions for fallback authentication: security questions in the era of facebook. *SOUPS '08: Proceedings of the 4th Symposium on Usable Privacy and Security*, ACM, New York, NY, 2008, pp. 13–23.

395. D. Raggett, A. L. Hors, and I. Jacobs. HTML 4.01 specification. http://www.w3.org/TR/1999/REC-html401-19991224, December 1999.

396. A. Rapoport. Spread of information through a population with socio-structural bias: I. Assumption of transitivity. *Bulletin of Mathematical Biology*, 15(4):523–533, 1953.

397. S. Rasmussen and D. Schoen. *Mad as Hell: How the Tea Party Movement Is Fundamentally Remaking Our Two-Party System*, HarperCollins, 2010.

398. J. Ratkiewicz, M. Conover, M. Meiss, B. Gonçalves, A. Flammini, and F. Menczer. Detecting and tracking political abuse in social media. *Proceedings of the 5th International Conference on Weblogs and Social Media (ICWSM)*, Barcelona, July 2011.

399. J. Ratkiewicz, M. Conover, M. Meiss, B. Gonçalves, A. Flammini, and F. Menczer. Detecting and tracking political abuse in social media. *Proceedings of the Fifth International AAAI Conference on Weblogs and Social Media*, AAAI, 2011.

400. J. Ratkiewicz, M. Conover, M. Meiss, B. Gonçalves, S. Patil, A. Flammini, and F. Menczer. Truthy: mapping the spread of AstroTurf in microblog streams. *Proceedings of the 20th International World Wide Web Conference (WWW)*, 2011.

401. M. Ray and S. Dispensa. Renegotiating TLS. extendedsubset.com/wp-uploads/2009/11/renegotiating_tls_20091104_pub.zip, November 4, 2009.

402. C. Reis, A. Barth, and C. Pizano. Browser security: lessons from Google Chrome. *ACM Queue*, 2009, pp. 1–8. http://www.adambarth.com/papers/2009/reis-barth-pizano.pdf.

403. C. Reis, S. D. Gribble, T. Kohno, and N. C. Weaver. Detecting in-flight page changes with Web tripwires. *NSDI '08: Proceedings of the 5th Symposium on Networked Systems Design and Implementation*, USENIX Association, Berkely, CA, 2008.

404. E. Rescorla. *SSL and TLS: Designing and Building Secure Systems*,. Addison-Wesley, 2000.

405. T. M. T. Research. A cybercrime hub. http://us.trendmicro.com/imperia/md/content/us/trendwatch/researchandanalysis/a_cybercrime_hub.pdf, 2009.

406. J. Resig. Clickjacking iPhone attack. ejohn.org/blog/clickjacking-iphone-attack, 2008.

407. E. M. Rogers. *Diffusion of Innovations*, 3rd edition, Free Press, 1983.

408. M. Roloff. *Interpersonal Communication: The Social Exchange Approach*, Sage, Beverly Hills, CA, 1981.

409. M. Rosenbach. US maintains Internet control. http://www.spiegel.de/international/spiegel/0,1518,385178,00.html, November 2005.

410. L. Rosencrance. Task force report looks at accuracy of WHOIS data. http://www.itworldcanada.com/news/task-force-report-looks-at-accuracy-of-whois-data/126810, December 2002.

411. C. Roussos. VeriSign anti-trust lawsuit paves way for more suits if there are no vertical integration exceptions. http://www.circleid.com/posts/verisign_anti_trust_lawsuit_paves_way_for_more_if_no_vertical_integration/, July 2010.

412. RSA Security. RSA identity verification. http://www.rsa.com/node.aspx?id=3347, 2008.

413. D. M. Russell, M. J. Stefik, P. Pirolli, and S. K. Card. The cost structure of sensemaking. *CHI '93: Proceedings of the INTERACT '93 and CHI '93 Conference on Human Factors in Computing Systems*, ACM, New York, NY, 1993, pp. 269–276.

414. G. Rydstedt, E. Bursztein, D. Boneh, and C. Jackson. Busting frame busting: a study of clickjacking vulnerabilities at popular sites. *IEEE Oakland Web 2.0 Security and Privacy (W2SP'10)* seclab.stanford.edu/websec/framebusting, 2010.

415. G. Rydstedt, B. Gourdin, E. Bursztein, and D. Boneh. Framing attacks on smart phones and dumb routers: tap-jacking and geo-localization attacks. *Proceed-*

ings of the USENIX Workshop on Offensive Technology, W2SP, 2010.

416. S. Schechter, A. J. B. Brush, and S. Egelman. It's no secret: measuring the security and reliability of authentication via 'secret' questions. *Proceedings of the 2009 IEEE Symposium on Security and Privacy*, IEEE Computer Society, 2009, pp. 375–390.

417. G. Sauer, J. Holman, J. Lazar, H. Hochheiser, and J. Feng. Accessible privacy and security: a universally usable human-interaction proof tool. *Universal Access in the Information Society*, 9(3):1–10, 2010.

418. S. Schechter, C. Herley, and M. Mitzenmacher. Popularity is everything: a new approach to protecting passwords from statistical-guessing attacks. *Proceedings of the 5th USENIX Workshop on Hot Topics in Security (Hotsec '10)*, USENIX, 2010.

419. S. E. Schechter, R. Dhamija, A. Ozment, and I. Fischer. The emperor's new security indicators. *SP '07: Proceedings of the 2007 IEEE Symposium on Security and Privacy*, IEEE Computer Society, Washington, DC, 2007. pp. 51–65.

420. R. Schifanella, A. Barrat, C. Cattuto, B. Markines, and F. Menczer. Folks in folksonomies: social link prediction from shared metadata. *Proceedings of the 3rd ACM International Conference on Web Search and Data Mining (WSDM)*, ACM, 2010, pp. 271—280.

421. S. Schillace. Default https access for Gmail. gmailblog.blogspot.com/2010/01/default-https-access-for-gmail.html, January 12, 2010.

422. B. Schneier. Myspace passwords aren't so dumb. http://www.wired.com/politics/security/commentary/securitymatters/2006/12/72300, December 2006.

423. B. Schneier. The curse of the secret question. http://www.schneier.com/blog/archives/2005/02/the_curse_of_th.html, February 2005.

424. M. Schultz. Handy light: tethering App camouflaged as Flashlight. http://appshopper.com/blog/2010/07/20/handy-light-tethering-app-camouflaged-as-flashlight/.

425. D. Segal. A rave, a pan, or just a fake? http://www.nytimes.com/2011/05/22/your-money/22haggler.html, May 2011.

426. L. Seltzer. Will ICANN reform? http://mobile.eweek.com/c/a/Security/Will-ICANN-Reform/, March 2007.

427. L. Seltzer. ICANN plans for disaster: a registry failure. http://mobile.eweek.com/c/a/Security/ICANN-Plans-For-Disaster-A-Registry-Failure/, August 2008.

428. W. Semich. .NU domain privacy policy restricts personal info in WHOIS database. http://www.nunames.nu/Press/privacypolicy.cfm, October 1999.

429. A. Seshadri, M. Luk, and A. Perrig. SAKE: software attestation for key establishment in sensor networks. *Ad Hoc Networks*, 9(6): 372–385, 2011.

430. A. Seshadri, M. Luk, A. Perrig, L. van Doorn, and P. Khosla. SCUBA: secure code update by attestation in sensor networks. *WiSe '06: Proceedings of the 5th ACM Workshop on Wireless Security*, ACM, New York, NY, 2006, pp. 85–94.

431. A. Seshadri, M. Luk, E. Shi, A. Perrig, L. van Doorn, and P. Khosla. Pioneer: verifying code integrity and enforcing untampered code execution on legacy systems. *SOSP '05: Proceedings of the Twentieth ACM Symposium on Operating Systems Principles*, ACM Press, New York, NY, 2005, pp. 1–16.

432. A. Seshadri, A. Perrig, L. V. Doorn, and P. Khosla. SWATT: SoftWare-based ATTestation for embedded devices. *Proceedings of the IEEE Symposium on Security and Privacy*, IEEE Conference Publications, 2004.

433. A. Seshadri, A. Perrig, L. van Doorn, and P. Khosla. Using SWATT for verifying embedded systems in cars. *2004 Embedded Security in Cars Workshop (Escar 2004)*, 2004.

434. A. Shamir. Cryptography: state of the science. *ACM A. M. Turing Award Lecture*, June 8, 2003. awards.acm.org/images/awards/140/vstream/2002/S/s-pp/shamir_1files_files/800x600/Slide8.html.

435. M. Shaneck, K. Mahadevan, V. Kher, and Y. Kim. Remote software-based attestation for wireless sensors. *ESAS*, 2005, pp. 27–41.

436. G. Shaw. Spyware & Adware: the risks facing businesses. *Network Security*, 2003(9):12–14, 2003.

437. E. Shi, A. Perrig, and L. V. Doorn. Bind: a fine-grained attestation service for secure distributed systems. *SP '05: Proceedings of the 2005 IEEE Symposium on Security and Privacy*, IEEE Computer Society, Washington, DC, 2005, pp. 154–168.

438. R. Singel. PGP creator defends Hushmail. www.wired.com/threatlevel/2007/11/pgp-creator-def, November 19, 2007.

439. R. Singel. Law enforcement appliance subverts SSL. www.wired.com/threatlevel/2010/03/packet-forensics/, March 24, 2010.

440. K. Singh, S. Sangal, N. Jain, P. Traynor, and W. Lee. Evaluating bluetooth as a medium for botnet command and control. *DIMVA '10: Proceedings of the 7th International Conference on Detection of Intrusions and Malware, and Vulnerability Assessment*, Springer, 2010, pp. 61–80.

441. N. Smith. Small Romanian town gets rich through eBay scams. http://www.foxnews.com/story/0,2933,328878,00.html, February 6, 2008.

442. D. Smythe. ICANN's wonderful WDPRS system does not work! http://gnso.icann.org/mailing-lists/archives/ga-200709/msg02683.html, March 2009.

443. Social Security Administration. Identity theft and your Social Security Number. SSA Publication No. 05-10064. http://www.socialsecurity.gov/pubs/10064.html, October 2007.

444. C. Soghoian. Caught in the cloud: privacy, encryption, and government back doors in the Web 2.0 era. *Journal on Telecommunications and High Technology Law*,

445. A. Sokolov, T. Urvoy, L. Denoyer, and O. Ricard. Madspam consortium at the ECML/PKDD discovery challenge 2010. *Proceedings of the ECML/PKDD 2010 Discovery Challenge*, SpringerLink, 2010.

446. Z. Song, J. Molina, S. Lee, H. Lee, S. Kotani, and R. Masuoka. Trustcube: an infrastructure that builds trust in client. *Future of Trust in Computing*, Vieweg and Teubner, 2009.

447. A. Sotirov and M. Zusman. Breaking the security myths of extended validation SSL certificates. www.blackhat.com/presentations/bh-usa-09/SOTIROV/BHUSA09-Sotirov-AttackExtSSL-SLIDES.pdf, 2009.

448. SPAMfighter. Malvertising attacks on Facebook farm town players. http://www.spamfighter.com/News-14247-Malvertising-Attacks-on-Facebook-Farm-Town-Players.htm, 2010.

449. A. Spong. Report: Wifi is a must for smartphones. *Phone Magazine*, April 2009.

450. S. Srikwan and M. Jakobsson. Using cartoons to teach Internet security. *Cryptologia*, 32:137–154, 2008.

451. F. Stajano and R. J. Anderson. The resurrecting duckling: security issues for ad-hoc wireless networks. *Proceedings of the 7th International Workshop on Security Protocols*, Springer, London, 2000, pp. 172–194.

452. A. Stamos, D. Thiel, and J. Osborne. Living in the RIA world: blurring the line between web and desktop security. https://www.isecpartners.com/files/RIA_World_BH_2008.pdf, 2008.

453. B. Sterne. Content Security Policy. https://dvcs.w3.org/hg/content-security-policy/raw-file/tip/csp-specification.dev.html, March 2011.

454. M. Stevens, A. Sotirov, J. Appelbaum, A. Lenstra, D. Molnar, D. A. Osvik, and B. Weger. Short chosen-prefix collisions for MD5 and the creation of a rogue CA certificate. *Proceedings of the 29th Annual International Cryptology Conference on Advances in Cryptology*, Springer, Berlin, 2009, pp. 55–69.

455. L. Stoilova, T. Holloway, B. Markines, A. G. Maguitman, and F. Menczer. Givealink: mining a semantic network of bookmarks for web search and recommendation. *Proceedings of the KDD Workshop on Link Discovery: Issues, Approaches and Applications (LinkKDD)*, ACM, 2005.

456. C. Stoll. *The Cuckoo's Egg: Tracking a Spy Through the Maze of Computer Espionage*, Pocket Books, 2000.

457. P. Stone. Next generation clickjacking. BlackHat Europe, 2010.

458. Stopmalvertising. Sponsored malvertisement for Adobe Flash Player. http://stopmalvertising.com/malvertisements/sponsored-malvertisement-for-adobe-flash-player.html, 2010.

459. D. Storm. Army of fake social media friends to promote propaganda. http://blogs.computerworld.com/17852/army_of_fake_social_media_friends_to_promote_propaganda, February 2011.

460. J. Sunshine, S. Egelman, H. Almuhimedi, N. Atri, and L. F. Cranor. Crying wolf: An empirical study of SSL warning effectiveness. *SSYM '09: Proceedings of the 18th Conference on USENIX Security Symposium*, USENIX Association, Berkeley, CA, 2009.

461. The H Security. Heise SSL Guardian: protection against unsafe SSL certificates. www.h-online.com/security/features/Heise-SSL-Guardian-746213.html. July 4, 2008.

462. The Internet Engineering Task Force (IETF). Request for comments (RFC). www.ietf.org/rfc.html, last retrieved in June 2011.

463. The United States Department of Commerce and the Internet Corporate for Assigned Names and Numbers. Affirmation of commitments. http://www.icann.org/en/documents/affirmation-of-commitments-30sep09-en.htm, last retrieved in June 2011.

464. THINQ. ICANN boss: DNS can fail at any time. http://www.thinq.co.uk/2010/3/11/icann-boss-dns-could-fail-at-any-time/, March 2010.

465. C. L. Toma. Affirming the self through online profiles: beneficial effects of social networking sites. *CHI '10: Proceedings of the 28th International Conference on Human Factors in Computing Systems*, ACM, New York, 2010, pp. 1749–1752.

466. J. Topf. HTML Form Protocol Attack. http://www.remote.org/jochen/sec/hfpa/hfpa.pdf, August 2001.

467. P. Traynor, K. Butler, W. Enck, P. McDaniel, and K. Borders. Malnets: large-scale malicious networks via compromised wireless access points. *Security and Communication Networks*, 3(2–3):102–113, 2010.

468. P. Traynor, M. Lin, M. Ongtang, V. Rao, T. Jaeger, P. McDaniel, and T. La Porta. On cellular botnets: measuring the impact of malicious devices on a cellular network core. *Proceedings of the 16th ACM Conference on Computer and Communications Security*, ACM, 2009, pp. 223–234.

469. A. Tsow, M. Jakobsson, L. Yang, and S. Wetzel. Warkitting: the drive-by subversion of wireless home routers. *Journal of Digital Forensics Practice*, 1(3):179–192, 2006.

470. A. Tumasjan, T. O. Sprenger, P. G. Sandner, and I. M. Welpe. Predicting elections with Twitter: what 140 characters reveal about political sentiment. *Fourth International AAAI Conference on Weblogs and Social Media*, AAAI, 2010, p. 178.

471. A. Tuzhilin. The laneÕs gifts v. Google report.

472. J. Uhrig, C. Bann, P. Williams, and W. D. Evans. Social networking websites as a platform for disseminating social marketing interventions: an exploratory pilot study. *Social Marketing Quarterly*, 16(1):2–20, 2010.

473. I. van Beijnum. Everything you need to know about IPv6. http://arstechnica.com/hardware/news/2007/03/IPv6.ars, March 2007.

474. A. van Kesteren. Cross-origin resource sharing (CORS). http://www.w3.org/TR/2010/WD-cors-20100727/, July 2010.

475. A. van Kesteren. XMLHttpRequest. http://www.w3.org/TR/2010/CR-XMLHttpRequest-20100803/, August 2010.

476. L. von Ahn, B. Maurer, C. McMillen, D. Abraham, and M. Blum. recaptcha: Human-based character recognition via web security measures. *Science Magazine*, 321(5895): 1465–1468, 2008.

477. N. Vratonjic, J. Freudiger, and J.-P. Hubaux. Integrity of the web content: the case of online advertising. *USENIX CollSec'10*, Washington DC, August 2010.

478. N. Vratonjic, M. Raya, J.-P. Hubaux, and D. C. Parkes. Security games in online advertising: can ads help secure the web? *WEIS 2010*, 2010.

479. A. H. Wang. Don't follow me: spam detection in Twitter. *Proceedings of the International Conference on Security and Cryptography (SECRYPT)*, April 2010, pp. 1–10.

480. K. Wang, C. Thrasher, E. Viegas, X. Li, and B. Hsu. An overview of Microsoft web N-gram corpus and applications. *HLT '10: Proceedings of the NAACL HLT 2010 Demonstration Session*, Association for Computational Linguistics, Morristown, NJ, 2010, pp. 45–48.

481. R. Wash. Folk models of home computer security. *SOUPS '10: Proceedings of the Sixth Symposium on Usable Privacy and Security*, ACM, New York, NY, 2010, pp. 11:1–11:16.

482. D. J. Watts and P. S. Dodds. Influentials, networks, and public opinion formation. *Journal of Consumer Research*, 34:441, 2007.

483. S. Webb, J. Caverlee, and C. Pu. Social honeypots: making friends with a spammer near you.

484. The WebKit Open Source Project. http://webkit.org/.

485. D. Wendlandt, D. G. Andersen, and A. Perrig. Perspectives: improving SSH-style host authentication with multi-path probing. *ATC '08: USENIX 2008 Annual Technical Conference*, USENIX Association, Berkeley, CA, 2008.

486. D. Wendlandt, D. G. Andersen, and A. Perrig. Perspectives: improving SSH-style host authentication

with multi-path probing. *ATC '08: USENIX 2008 Annual Technical Conference on Annual Technical Conference*, USENIX Association, Berkeley, CA, 2008, pp. 321–334.

487. A. Whitten and D. Tygar. Why Johnny can't encrypt: a usability evaluation of PGP 5.0. *Proceedings of the 8th Conference on USENIX Security Symposium*, Vol. 8, USENIX Association Berkeley, CA, 1999, p. 14.

488. J. Wiens. A tipping point for the trusted platform module?, www.informationweek.com, June, 2008.

489. Wikipedia. Cepstrum. http://en.wikipedia.org/wiki/Cepstrum.

490. Wikipedia. Fourier transform. http://en.wikipedia.org/wiki/Fourier_transform.

491. Wikipedia. Likejacking, 2011. en.wikipedia.org/wiki/Likejacking.

492. Wikipedia. Adobe Acrobat. https://secure.wikimedia.org/wikipedia/en/wiki/Adobe_acrobat.

493. Wikipedia. Adobe Flash Player. https://secure.wikimedia.org/wikipedia/en/wiki/Adobe_Flash_Player.

494. N. Wingfield and B. Worthen. Microsoft battles cyber criminals. http://online.wsj.com/article/SB10001424052748704240004575086523786147014.html, last retrieved in June 2011.

495. N. Wong. Judge tells DOJ "No" on search queries. googleblog.blogspot.com/2006/03/judge-tells-doj-no-on-search-queries.htmll. March 17, 2006.

496. J. Yan and A. El Ahmad. A low-cost attack on a Microsoft CAPTCHA. *Proceedings of the 15th ACM Conference on Computer and Communications Security*, ACM, 2008, pp. 543–554.

497. J. J. Yan, A. F. Blackwell, and R. J. Anderson. Password memorability and security: empirical results. *IEEE Security & Privacy*, 2:25–31, 2004.

498. Y. Yang, X. Wang, S. Zhu, and G. Cao. Distributed software-based attestation for node compromise detection in sensor networks. *SRDS '07: Proceedings of the 26th IEEE International Symposium on Reliable Distributed Systems*, IEEE Computer Society, Washington, DC, 2007, pp. 219–230.

499. S. Yardi, D. Romero, G. Schoenebeck, and D. Boyd. Detecting spam in a twitter network. *First Monday*, 15(1):1–14, 2010.

500. K.-P. Yee. User interaction design for secure systems. *ICICS '02: Proceedings of the 4th International Conference on Information and Communications Security*, Springer, London, 2002, pp. 278–290.

501. S. Yilek, E. Rescorla, H. Shacham, B. Enright, and S. Savage. When private keys are public: results from the 2008 Debian OpenSSL vulnerability. *Proceedings of the 9th ACM SIGCOMM Conference on Internet Measurement Conference*, ACM, New York, NY, 2009, pp. 15–27.

502. D. Younger. ICANN's WDPRS has crashed. http://does-not-exist.org/mail-archives/ga/msg01132.html, February 2008.

503. D. Younger. $0.18 per transaction for registrars. http://forum.icann.org/lists/joint-wg-snapshot/docOO92aQOTZh.doc, last retrieved in June 2011.

504. M. Zalewski. *Browser Security Handbook: Part 2. Same-Origin Policy for DOM Access*. http://code.google.com/p/browsersec/wiki/Part2#Same-origin_policy, 2009.

505. K. Zetter. Palin e-mail hacker says it was easy. http://www.wired.com/threatlevel/2008/09/palin-e-mail-ha/, September 18 2008.

506. C. Zhang, C. Huang, K. Ross, D. Maltz, and J. Li. Inflight modifications of content: who are the culprits? *Workshop of Large-Scale Exploits and Emerging Threats LEET 11*, Boston, April 2011.

Index